CAMBRIDGE STUDIES IN MUSIC

GENERAL EDITORS: JOHN STEVENS AND PETER LE HURAY

The Beneventan Chant

From the High Middle Ages the dominance of Gregorian chant has obscured the fact that musical practice in early medieval Europe was far richer than has hitherto been recognised. Despite its historical importance, the "Gregorian" is not the most consistent and probably not the oldest form of Christian chant. The recovery and study of regional musical dialects having a common ancestry in the Christian church and Western musical tradition are reshaping our view of the early history of Christian liturgical music.

Thomas Kelly's major study of the Beneventan chant reinstates one of the oldest surviving bodies of Western music: the Latin church music of southern Italy as it existed before the spread of Gregorian chant. Dating from the seventh and eighth centuries it was largely forgotten after the Carolingian desire for political and liturgical uniformity imposed "Gregorian" chant throughout the realm. But a few later scribes, starting apparently in the tenth century, preserved a part of this regional heritage in writing. This book reassembles and describes the surviving repertory. The book is thus of great importance, not only in providing a new orientation on the early history of Western music, but in presenting the musical repertory as an historical artefact with considerable significance for the history of Italy, particularly that of the Lombards and the duchy of Benevento.

The book includes a systematic presentation of all the surviving materials, and much of the original music is reproduced in facsimile.

CAMBRIDGE STUDIES IN MUSIC

GENERAL EDITORS: JOHN STEVENS AND PETER LE HURAY

Volumes in the series include:

THE BENEVENTAN CHANT

THOMAS FORREST KELLY

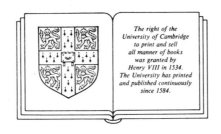

The right of the
University of Cambridge
to print and sell
all manner of books
was granted by
Henry VIII in 1534.
The University has printed
and published continuously
since 1584.

CAMBRIDGE UNIVERSITY PRESS

CAMBRIDGE

NEW YORK   PORT CHESTER

MELBOURNE   SYDNEY

Published by the Press Syndicate of the University of Cambridge
The Pitt Building, Trumpington Street, Cambridge CB2 IRP
40 West 20th Street, New York, NY 10011, USA
10 Stamford Road, Oakleigh, Melbourne 3166, Australia

First published 1989

Printed in Great Britain at
the University Press, Cambridge

British Library cataloguing in publication data
Kelly, Thomas Forrest
The Beneventan chant. – (Cambridge studies
in music).
1. Chants in Latin. Beneventan chants
I. Title
783.5

Library of Congress cataloguing in publication data
Kelly, Thomas Forrest.
The Beneventan chant / Thomas Forrest Kelly.
p.   cm. – (Cambridge studies in music)
Bibliography.
Includes indexes.
ISBN 0–521–34310–0
1. Chants (Plain, Gregorian, etc.) – History and criticism.
2. Catholic Church – Beneventan rite. I. Title. II. Series.
ML3082.K34 1989
783.5–dc19   88–27436   CIP

ISBN 0 521 34310 0

ME

To Peggy

CONTENTS

PLATES

PREFACE

On December 23, 1908, readers in Benevento of the diocesan newspaper *La settimana* were treated to an extensive account of the liturgical manuscripts of the cathedral library by Dom Raphaël Andoyer, a monk of Ligu99é, who had been summoned by Archbishop Benedetto Bonazzi to carry out this task. This was the first serious attention these manuscripts had received since the early eighteenth-century interests of Cardinal Pietro Francesco Orsini, archbishop of Benevento and later Pope Benedict XIII, who caused the handwritten tables, now bound with the liturgical manuscripts of Benevento, to be prepared.

Andoyer was aware of the importance of these manuscripts on this first visit, but he was not quite on the right track as regards a part of their unusual contents. In his remarks on a gradual that can be identified as the present manuscript 40, he says that "one notes many pieces that are outside the Roman liturgy of that time: they are probably remains of the Ambrosian liturgy, which was in use in this region before the Roman, and it is natural that it should not have disappeared completely when the Roman usage was introduced."

But Andoyer soon gave the matter more serious thought, and it is to his series of articles on "L'ancienne liturgie de bénévent" published before and after the First World War that we owe the first serious study of the Beneventan chant as a repertory distinct both from the Roman and from the Ambrosian. Andoyer's effort, perceptive as it was (he had shortly before given the first serious attention to what we now call the Old Roman chant), was marred both by his inclusiveness – he considered many more pieces than probably ought to be admitted to the Beneventan canon – and by his lack of attention to certain details of text and transmission.

Fifty years ago, Dom René-Jean Hesbert, monk of Solesmes, produced the only comprehensive studies to date of the Beneventan chant; in a series of articles in *Ephemerides liturgicae* (again interrupted by war), and in his introduction to the fourteenth volume of *Paléographie musicale*, Hesbert exhaustively studied the Holy Week rites of Benevento. Though his work is the basis of all subsequent efforts in this field, it remains sadly incomplete. In his last article Hesbert bids what sounds like a reluctant farewell to the pages of *Ephemerides*, promising to complete his study of the rest of the repertory in a separate monograph: a pledge he was, alas, not able to keep.

Since Hesbert's studies there has been much interest in such regional or local repertories as the Old Roman, the Mozarabic, and the Ambrosian chant, as important specimens of musical

style, and as keys to understanding the early history of Western chant. The Beneventan chant
has languished, however, until quite recently. Despite its importance for the history of Western
chant, there are few studies on the Beneventan chant beyond the brief notices by Karl-Heinz
Schlager in *The New Grove*, Bonifazio Baroffio in the Supplement to *Die Musik in Geschichte und
Gegenwart*, and in *Geschichte der katholischen Kirchenmusik*, although John Boe, Terence Bailey,
and Michel Huglo have all recently contributed significant studies or summaries.

I have thus made it my task to attempt this preliminary study in the hope that by making the
Beneventan chant accessible it may be studied further and understood better. This work would
be almost impossible if it did not stand on the shoulders of two giants (the old metaphor is a
good one): the work of Dom Hesbert on the liturgical side, and that of Elias Avery Loew,
whose classic book on *The Beneventan Script* (TBS) contains a handlist of manuscripts in
Beneventan writing. (Brought up to date in a second edition by Virginia Brown, this list, to
which many scholars have already contributed still more new items, is indispensable to anyone
working with Beneventan manuscripts.) My own census has turned up eighty-six manuscripts
which preserve some evidence of Beneventan chant. This is perhaps a surprisingly large number
for a repertory that is generally thought to have perished leaving only scant traces, but in fact,
such a survey has not been undertaken previously. What is more, the presence of Beneventan
chant has in many cases simply escaped detection: what survives is usually only a piece or two,
generally duplicating music already known elsewhere. So the increased number of sources does
not really increase the size of the surviving repertory, though it is a strong witness to the
chant's wide dissemination.

Earlier versions of parts of this book have appeared in *Early Music History*, *The Journal of Musicology*, and *Journal of the Royal Musical Association*.

My thanks are due to many people who have contributed in one way or another to the
making of this book. Dom Jean Claire of Solesmes suggested this study, and has encouraged it
at every step. For much help and advice I am grateful to Herbert Bloch, Mario Boscia, Virginia
Brown, Gugliemo Cavallo, Thomas Connolly, Elio Galasso, the late Jacques Hourlier, Michel
Huglo, Carmelo Lepore, Francis Newton, Agostino Ziino; special thanks for supplying photographs to Johann Drumbl, Gottfried Glassner, Richard Gyug, and Meinrad Wölfle.

The authorities of many libraries have generously made their holdings available for con-
sultation. Of particular importance is the Biblioteca capitolare of Benevento, whose late librarian, Monsignor Angelo Ferrara, first introduced me to the manuscripts, and whose successor,
Monsignor Laureato Maio, has been kind and generous in all things. The rich library of Montecassino was made available by Don Faustino Avagliano, and that of the Vatican by its Prefect,
Leonard Boyle.

A number of colleagues and friends generously agreed to read portions of this book in
manuscript; to them, for their patience and kindness as well as for many valuable discussions
and suggestions, go my sincere thanks: Bonifazio Baroffio OSB, John Boe, Kenneth Levy, Jean
Mallet OSB, Alejandro Planchart, Vera von Falkenhausen.

Dom André Thibaut, OSB, co-author with Jean Mallet of the catalogue of manuscripts in
Beneventan script of the library of Benevento, has combined a knowledge of the manuscripts

with rare photographic skill. He accompanied me, with unfailing good humor, on a number of interesting, but time consuming, trips to photograph manuscripts; most of the photographs in this book are his, and I am not the only scholar who owes him a great debt.

My first attempt to talk about this repertory took place ten years ago in an undergraduate seminar at Wellesley College. The participants, whose interest in the repertory was surely more a credit to their intellectual curiosity than to their teacher's skill, taught me much: in particular, Sarah McManaway first analyzed the arrangement of the Beneventan Alleluia verses.

I gratefully acknowledge the support of Wellesley College, the National Endowment for the Humanities, the American Academy in Rome, and the American Council of Learned Societies.

ABBREVIATIONS

The following abbreviations are used throughout the text. Full bibliographical details can be found under the abbreviation in the Bibliography. An author and short title system is also used throughout and full references can be found in the Bibliography.

AA SS	*Acta sanctorum*	Erchempert	"Erchemperti historia langobardorum beneventanorum"
Aggiornamento	*L'Art dans l'Italie méridionale. Aggiornamento dell'opera di Emile Bertaux, ed. Adriano Prandi*	Gamber, CLLA	Klaus Gamber. *Codices liturgici latini antiquiores*
AH	*Analecta hymnica medii aevi*	GRom	*Graduale Sacrosanctae Romanae Ecclesiae*
AMed	*Antiphonale missarum juxta ritum Sanctae Ecclesiae Mediolanensis*	IP	*Regesta pontificum romanorum. Italia pontificia*
AMon	*Antiphonale monasticum pro diurnis horis*	JAMS	*Journal of the American Musicological Society*
BHL	*Bibliotheca hagiographica latina*	LVesp	*Liber vesperalis iuxta ritum Sanctae Ecclesiae Mediolanensis*
Bloch, MMA	Herbert Bloch, *Monte Cassino in the Middle Ages*	MGH	*Monumenta germaniae historica*
CAO	*Corpus antiphonalium officii*	MMMA	*Monumenta monodica medii aevi. Band II: Die Gesänge des altrömischen Graduale Vat. lat. 5319*
Chron. mon. cas.	*Chronica monasterii Casinensis*		
Chron. salern.	*Chronicon Salernitanum*		
Chron. vult.	*Chronicon vulturnese*	The New Grove	*The New Grove Dictionary of Music and Musicians*
Cod. dipl. cav.	*Codex diplomaticus cavensis*		
DACL	*Dictionnaire d'archéologie chrétienne et de liturgie*	Paul, HL	"Pauli historia langobardorum"
EL	*Ephemerides liturgicae*		

PG	*Patrologiae cursus completus. Series graeca*	*Les Sources*	*Le Graduel romain. Édition critique par les moines de Solesmes.* Vol 2: *Les Sources*
PL	*Patrologiae cursus completus. Series latina*	TBS	Elias Avery Loew, *The Beneventan Script*
PM	*Paléographie musicale*		
SE	*Sacris erudiri*	*Vulgata*	*Biblia sacra iuxta Vulgatam versionem*
Sextuplex	*Antiphonale missarum sextuplex*		

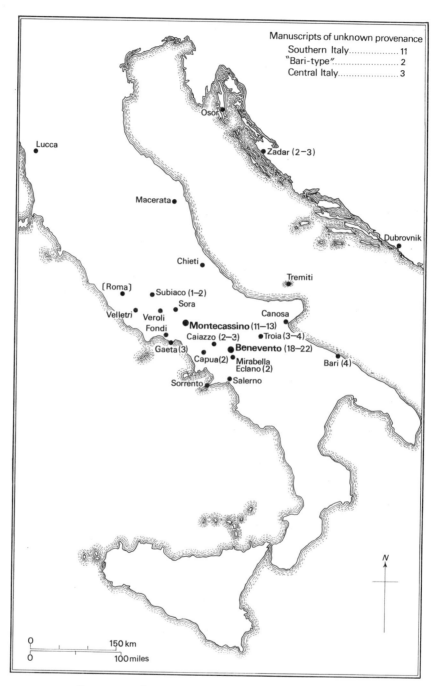

Provenance of manuscripts containing Beneventan chant

Numbers in parentheses indicate the number of sources which originate in a given place; where two figures are given, the first is the number of manuscripts securely attributable, while the second includes those whose provenance is less certain. Further information on the manuscripts is in Appendix 3.

INTRODUCTION

From the High Middle Ages onward, the supremacy of "Gregorian" chant was bolstered by the regular assertion that this music resulted from the creative and coordinating gifts of St Gregory the Great (d. 604). For a long time it was convenient to piety, politics, and scholarship, to disregard the somewhat embarrassing anomalies presented by certain repertories, or fragments of repertories, of Western chant which did not fit with the accepted Gregorian tradition: textual, liturgical, and musical remnants which cast serious doubt on the received tradition of Gregorian pre-eminence. Whatever the origin of Gregorian chant, it is clear that the Carolingian desire for liturgical and political uniformity imposed "Gregorian" chant throughout the realm. And with this tide of uniformity was swept away much music that, as it is gradually recovered and studied, gives a far richer picture of musical practice in early medieval Europe than was formerly known.

The very existence of this array of musical languages challenges us to study the scope and variety of the heritage of Western music. Comparative study of the various dialects of chant which have a common ancestry in the Christian church and in Western musical tradition can be of wide significance in reconstructing the origins and history of each member of the group: a group in which Gregorian chant, despite its historical importance and its particular beauties, is neither the most consistent, nor probably the oldest.

These regional musical dialects are an important part of the puzzle of the early history of Christian chant, which is nowadays engaging the attention of many scholars. They demonstrate their antiquity through textual, liturgical, and musical archaisms; they are the remnants of music preserved for a long time in oral transmission before being written down; and they can give us a view of what music was like when they were at their creative height. Despite the relatively late date of the musical sources, and the concomitant musical developments or corruption they may present, these local or regional chants give us a powerful tool for looking backward in time from the earliest written documents of Western music.

This book is about one such regional chant: that of southern Italy before the spread of Gregorian chant, preserved in manuscripts from the Lombard duchy of Benevento, founded in 568. Despite close contacts with Rome and Byzantium, and despite conquest by Charlemagne in 787, the region ruled from Benevento retained a measure of independence throughout the

Middle Ages; it developed a characteristic regional script that was brought to perfection at Montecassino in the eleventh century; and it developed a cultural and musical tradition largely independent of the rest of Europe.

This Beneventan repertory lies at the threshold of Western musical history. It documents a practice far earlier than the date of the surviving manuscripts, for the visible history of the Beneventan chant takes place almost entirely within the first half of the eleventh century. The music was not written down earlier than Gregorian chant; in fact, with rare exceptions, the repertory as we have it comes entirely from books of Gregorian chant in which Beneventan music is either supplementary or disguised among the very chants whose imposition caused its suppresion. Some eighty-six manuscripts preserve remnants of the Beneventan chant. They give evidence of the music's diffusion through the region, originating from Benevento, Montecassino, Bari, and as far north as Subiaco and Lucca. But most of these sources preserve only a fragment, a few pieces, usually connected with the special rites of Holy Week.

The manuscripts that preserve the Beneventan chant are like pearls: they are precious, of course, but also their composition is a series of superimposed layers of musical style and histori-cal influence. To peel back these layers is no easy matter, but they are important in understand-ing the context of the Beneventan chant as it survives.

Chief among the sources are the five graduals that survive in the Biblioteca capitolare of Benevento. These are now numbered 34, 35, 38, 39, and 40 (the previous numbering, which prefixed a Roman numeral, has been omitted in the new catalogue: Mallet, *Les Manuscrits*). Of these, two (Benevento 38 and Benevento 40) are the principal sources of Beneventan chant. But they, like their shelfmates, reveal many more layers of musical development; we can identify very roughly five.

(1) At the center – the seed of the pearl, to continue the analogy – is the common foundation of Western liturgy, elements shared alike by the many musical and liturgical areas of the West. This is a substratum difficult to detect and almost impossible to define, but the common language of liturgical shape, of musical form, of widely used texts, as well as the early history of Christianity in the West, make it clear that such a foundation is the basis of the other layers.

(2) Next comes the music of the Beneventan chant, originating in the seventh and eighth centuries – the principal subject of this book. Overlaid on this is another early layer – (3) Gregorian chant – a repertory which arrived in southern Italy, in a fully developed form, during the course of the eighth century. To it, the local musicians and liturgists added (4) a substantial body of music in Gregorian style, composed for local needs and used only in the area. This "Romano-Beneventan" chant fills gaps in the received Gregorian tradition (many of which are discussed in the next chapter), and provides music for feasts of purely local importance. The creative spirit of the tenth, eleventh, and twelfth centuries, however, turned from liturgical chant, by now essentially fixed, to the creation of (5) a rich body of tropes and sequences. Some of these are borrowed, but many are local products, witnesses to a thriving musical culture. It is worth noting that there is very little effort to preserve the Beneventan chant itself by disguising Beneventan pieces as tropes, although Alejandro Planchart, in "New wine in old bottles" (here, as elsewhere, short titles are expanded in the Bibliography), has suggested that Beneventan modes of procedure may have survived in some local tropes. And Beneventan chants

do not themselves bear tropes. The corpus of tropes in the Beneventan region is presently being edited by John Boe and Alejandro Planchart.

All of these layers, then, are present in the graduals of Benevento, and in many other regional manuscripts. They are presented together, so that, for example, the mass of the Holy Twelve Brothers of Benevento in manuscript Benevento 40 includes old Gregorian elements, local Romano-Beneventan pieces, a selection of tropes, and a second mass in Beneventan chant. The material is rich, and the Beneventan chant is only one of many elements preserved together; each layer deserves a complete study of its own. This volume seeks only to identify and discuss one of these elements, but its survival in a larger context should always be borne in mind.

Many historical factors affected the fortunes of the Beneventan chant: the history of the Lombards and of Benevento as the southern center of Lombard tradition; the Carolingian empire and its attempts at uniformity; the growing influence of the Roman church and the papacy in the south; the increasing importance of Montecassino; and, ultimately, the papal reform movement of the eleventh century and the advent of the Normans, which together put an end to Beneventan chant.

The Beneventan chant is linked closely with the fortunes of the Lombards, who made in southern Italy a political and cultural sphere of influence that lasted until the eleventh century. The history of the Lombards is mirrored in music: for there is another ancient chant connected with the Lombards (equally distinct from the Gregorian), the so-called Ambrosian chant of Milan – from the region, that is, of the Lombard kingdom of Pavia, whose kings, in principle, also ruled Benevento until the eighth century. Despite their many differences, the Beneventan and Ambrosian chants have so many characteristics in common as to suggest that the Lombard areas, north and south, once shared a similar liturgy and music, whose separate development produced the related repertories of Milan and Benevento. The Beneventan scribes were aware, in a way, of this link, for when they labeled their local music they invariably called it "Ambrosian."

It is in this "Lombard" aspect of the Beneventan liturgy that we can see its connection with politics; its preservation, over several centuries, as an artistic patrimony; and its ultimate suppression, in a much weakened Benevento peopled still with proud Lombard nobles, under the joint forces of Norman invasion and papal reform.

What is Beneventan chant like? How do we recognize it as a separate repertory? This book, of course, is a long answer to the question. But more briefly, for an observer familiar with the Gregorian repertory, a Beneventan chant is most readily recognized either by liturgical or musical anomalies.

The Beneventan liturgy almost never uses the same text in the same liturgical function as the Gregorian. Thus an unusual text (particularly a non-biblical one) in a south Italian manuscript, or a familiar text in the wrong place, immediately arouses interest in the hunter of Beneventana.

And there are other instant clues: any music in Beneventan writing which is labeled "Ambrosian" is Beneventan: this is its only local name; when it is distinguished from Gregorian chant it is always called Ambrosian. Beneventan chant uses an *ingressa*, not an introit; almost all the Alleluia verses have the same melody.

Musically, the Beneventan chant jumps to the eye of the practiced Gregorianist. This is not to say that it is paleographically different; it survives in the hands of the same scribes who wrote the first surviving Gregorian chant in the region. But the music itself has its own style, its own methods of procedure, its own turns of phrase, that set it apart from other chant dialects. It has a very standardized group of cadences written and used with extreme regularity; a limited stock of frequently-used melodic turns of phrase; and a tendency, in many cases, to form longer pieces from several repetitions of a single phrase. And, unlike the Gregorian repertory, these cadences, formulae, and repeated elements are not separated by liturgical category or by mode (a fact that would not be evident, of course, from looking at a single piece), so that their number is smaller, and their occurrences proportionately more frequent. The Beneventan chant, regardless of its liturgical category, proceeds at a uniform, rather elaborate pace, with much stepwise motion and relatively few dramatic melodic contours.

It is in this simplicity and regularity that the repertory has much of its value for us. An undifferentiated modality, a very limited number of musical formulae, an archaic liturgical usage, and a small number of pieces surviving: these make of the Beneventan chant an important specimen of a repertory in transition towards the "modern" features of more developed chant repertories. But there is much charm in its simplicity, much to observe about its arrangement of very limited materials, and much to learn from its position as a cultural artifact.

In *The Beneventan Chant* I propose to study this repertory in its liturgical, musical, and historical context, and to provide a badly needed research and reference tool. I shall be publishing, in the series *Paléographie musicale* (PM XXI), a volume of facsimiles of all the music of the Beneventan repertory. The combination of that volume with this study will make this liturgy and its music available for the first time in its entirety.

This book is not intended to be the final word on the Beneventan chant: if anything, it is an introductory word, an exploratory sounding, accompanied by materials that may serve as the basis for further much-needed research.

There are many important subjects that must be passed over in such an undertaking. Detailed paleographical matters are not treated here, nor is there space for a substantial study of the Beneventan musical notation as it varies over time and from manuscript to manuscript; though much could be said, and much remains to be done, there are the classic works of Lowe and Hesbert to which the paleographer can refer.

The musical examples presented here are transcribed, usually from notation without lines or clefs, as carefully as possible, but the use of a "modern" notation always omits much of interest in the original.

The examples are presented as stemless note-heads, grouped under slurs to show how they are joined into longer neumes. Clefs in brackets indicate that the manuscript itself has no clefs and that the pitch here is conjectural, but the Beneventan repertory, as we shall see in Chapter 5, is so uniform and so unified in its non-modal melodic ranges that there can be little doubt about the intervallic relationships implied by these clefs. The custos (a small check-mark [√] at the end of a line designating the height of the first note of the next line) is reported in transcriptions from clefless manuscripts because of its importance in deciphering pitch.

Certain special notations are indicated by symbols: liquescent notes are indicated by [x] and the quilisma by [w]. The symbol [ʌ] indicates lengthened notes, produced by the presence of an oriscus, a pressus configuration (where two neumes are joined at the unison), or an unusually extended note-form; in performance this is roughly equivalent to a note of double length. The sign [↔] is used for the top note of the climacus and other descending neumes when its initial note takes a form similar to this. This sign may or may not indicate a long note; just possibly it represents the "normal" form of the climacus (other forms are limited to situations in which the initial note of the neume is higher, lower, or at the unison relative to the preceding note). But certain situations (as well as its shape) suggest that it may represent a long note (compare the readings for the third syllable of *vesperum* in plate 4), and I preserve the readings in the transcriptions.

A solution to such problems of musical translation would be to reproduce alongside each transcription a facsimile of its original notation; an elegant version of such transcriptions from Beneventan manuscripts is forthcoming in Boe and Planchart, *Beneventanum troporum corpus*. Here, however, so many of the examples show musical relationships by aligning several parallel staves that the addition of facsimile notation would hopelessly obscure the point being made. This book contains a substantial number of plates, however, and I have included as many as possible which present music transcribed in the examples. Facsimiles of all the Beneventan music discussed here will appear shortly in a volume of *Paléographie musicale*.

The verbal texts of the musical examples have been normalized in some details of punctuation, spelling, and capitalization; editions of all the texts are to be found in Appendix 2.

Southern Italy is an area where new sources may turn up from time to time; perhaps a complete Beneventan mass-book lies in a dusty cupboard or a little-visited archive. We continue the search, but we cannot await that lucky discovery before attempting an overview of the Beneventan chant: much material is already at hand and the subject is a significant one; this liturgy and its music have an important role to play in the developing picture of early chant history.

I

BENEVENTAN CHANT IN ITS
HISTORICAL CONTEXT

Introduction

Beneventan chant is essentially a Lombard phenomenon, linked closely with the fortunes of those invaders who made in southern Italy a political and cultural sphere of influence that lasted until the eleventh century. The central historical themes of the Lombard south are the strong desire for independence and the proud self-consciousness of the Lombards. Despite the occasional temporary need to acknowledge one ruler or another (the King at Pavia, the Frankish Emperor, the Byzantines), geographical isolation and Lombard pride produce a continuing Lombard self-sufficiency.[1]

The Beneventan liturgy survives incomplete, and its origins cannot be precisely fixed. It shares in the essential kinship of all Western liturgies, having a fundamental layer of fidelity to the structure of the Roman liturgy. But the Beneventan chant itself is more specifically related to that of the Ambrosian liturgy of the Lombard north – a relationship suggesting a common fund of materials, but also a long separation, resulting in independent development, organization, and systematization. The Beneventan scribes were aware of this link in a way, for when they labeled their local music they invariably called it "Ambrosian".[2]

The Beneventan script, too, links north and south, for the tradition of Beneventan writing, as Lowe puts it, is "nothing more than the continuation in southern Italy of the traditional Italian school".[3] Eighth-century manuscripts from northern and southern Italy can scarcely be distinguished on the basis of their script. It is the northern scripts that changed, under the

---

[1] In the historical matter that follows much is drawn from the chronicles of the periods involved: Paul the Deacon's *History of the Lombards* (Paul, HL); Erchempert, *Historia langobardorum beneventanorum*; *Chronicon salernitanum* (Chron. salern.); Leo of Ostia, Guido, and Peter the Deacon, *Chronicon monasterii casinensis* (Chron. mon. cas.); a debt is owed in addition to the following works, from which a much fuller account of the history of this period may be constructed: Hodgkin, *Italy and Her Invaders*; Hartmann, *Geschichte Italiens im Mittelalter*; Gay, *L'Italie méridionale*; von Falkenhausen, "I longobardi"; Wickham, *Early Medieval Italy*.

[2] See Chapter 5, pp. 181–3.

[3] TBS, I, 95.

influence of Caroline minuscule, while Beneventan writers preserved and developed traditional elements originally common to north and south.[4]

The eighth century for the Lombards of the south marks a political and cultural high point; Benevento becomes the capital of a principality upholding Lombard culture and values, and its princes succeed, as the Lombard kings of the north do not, in avoiding entanglements with Popes, Franks, and Byzantines. Chroniclers of later ages remember the days of Arichis II with pride and nostalgia. This is doubtless the high point of the Beneventan chant as well; the period in which perhaps the last of it was composed, and during which, owing both to the power and influence of the southern Lombard capital and to the close allegiance which the church owed to the state, the chant spread throughout the Lombard south.

In the ninth century begins a holding action, an entrenchment, increasingly tenacious as the chant is threatened. The gradual independence of the church from the princes, increasing ecclesiastical contact with Rome, and the growing importance of Montecassino as an ecclesiastical, but also a temporal, power, all contributed to the eventual domination of the Roman chant. The decline in importance of the city of Benevento during the ninth and tenth centuries seems only to have fired a proud conservatism in the once central capital, and contributed to the preservation of the chant, as an element of Lombard history, until its ultimate suppression, along with Lombard power itself, in the eleventh century.

The origins of Beneventan chant

If the Lombards of the eleventh century cultivated the Beneventan chant, their more savage sixth-century ancestors cleared a path for it by eradicating much of the extant ecclesiastical life of southern Italy. Previous waves of invaders had succeeded in leaving the area virtually devoid of any ecclesiastical organization; most of the dioceses were vacant, many churches abandoned and in ruins.[5] The Lombards contributed their share to the devastation, including the destruction of the abbey of Montecassino in 568 or 569, which was to remain uninhabited for more than a hundred years.[6]

The Lombards began their rule at Benevento in the latter part of the sixth century under Zotto, the first duke.[7] Zotto's successor, Arichis I,[8] continued an expansionist and anti-Byzantine policy that was noted with alarm by Pope Gregory the Great.[9] By the end of Arichis' reign (about 640) most of southern Italy was in Lombard hands.

[4] TBS, I, 95–6. A particular closeness to the school of Nonantola (itself a Lombard foundation) is discussed in Bischoff, *Paläographie*, p. 140 and note 113.

[5] Duchesne, "Les évêchés," esp. pp. 104–7; Bognetti, "La continuità," p. 419; Hirsch, *Il ducato*, pp. 28–9.

[6] Paul, HL, MGH SS Lang., p. 122; Chron. mon. cas., 1, 2, 4; *Gregorii magni dialogi*, pp. 107–8.

[7] Paul the Deacon, the great historian of the Lombards from their beginnings until the middle of the eighth century, is not clear about their arrival in the south; he indicates that Zotto ruled for twenty years (MGH SS Lang., p. 112). Since Zotto's successor, Arichis I, is named in a letter of Gregory the Great of 592 (MGH Epistolae, I, 145) we can place Zotto near the end of the century. On Zotto see Gasparri, *I duchi longobardi*, p. 86.

[8] He was named duke by the Lombard King Agilulf (591–615), according to Paul the Deacon (MGH SS Lang., p. 122). Von Falkenhausen, "I longobardi," pp. 252–3, notes that this is unlikely since the duke of Arichis' native Friuli was a staunch Byzantine ally; Arichis may not have been sent by Agilulf, but recognized by him in exchange for his pursuit of an anti-Byzantine policy.

[9] Hirsch, *Il ducato*, pp. 12–18.

Despite occasional cooperation with the popes,[10] the pagan or Arian Lombards of Benevento remained essentially enemies of Rome; and already they were relatively independent from the Lombard kings ruling from Pavia to whom they were in principle attached. The king had the right to name his own dukes, but his distance, and his lack of personal holdings in the south, made the relative independence of Benevento almost inevitable. The Beneventans try to name new dukes themselves; and these in turn repeatedly name their own successors.

In this fallow Italian soil the Beneventan chant grew from imported seed. There were, of course, liturgical practices in the region before the arrival of the Lombards, and they undoubtedly affected the formation of the Beneventan repertory, though we have only very sketchy information. Gamber has hypothesized that Paulinus of Nola (d. 431) is the author of an important core of the Gelasian sacramentary;[11] clearer still is the evidence of a sixth-century Campanian system of lections, which seem to have survived the Lombard invasion only in exported versions.[12]

But the Beneventan chant and its liturgy, as a mature repertory, cannot be much older than the mid-seventh century, to judge from what we know of Lombard religious history. The Lombards were pagans when they invaded Italy in 568; Gregory the Great describes their sacrificing to a goat's head,[13] and the life of St Barbatus, bishop of Benevento in the 670s, describes the Lombards of Benevento worshipping a simulacrum of a viper and swearing oaths as they galloped past a hide hung on a tree.[14]

The northern kings and their court became Christians; though Procopius records the Lombard king as Catholic in 548,[15] by 568 they had become Arians,[16] and king Authar (584–90) promulgated an anti-Catholic edict that was remarked by Gregory the Great.[17] But Catholicism was on the rise among the Lombards. Grimoald, the Beneventan duke who seized the Lombard crown for himself, married his son Romuald at Benevento to the Catholic Theoderada; and at his death (671) there seems to have been no Arian objection to the return to the throne of the Catholic Pertarit. The course of the seventh century saw Arian kings in the Lombard north in the first part of the century, Catholics thereafter.[18]

---

[10] Gregory the Great treats amicably with Arichis in 599 in order to ensure the shipment of timbers to repair the roofs of St Peter's and St Paul's in Rome (Paul, HL, MGH SS Lang., pp. 122–3; MGH Epistolae, II, no. IX, 126, pp. 126–7); Honorius I (625–8) negotiates with the Arian duke Arichis ("Arogi") for the return of a monk: MGH Epistolae, III, p. 696.

[11] See Gamber, "Das kampanische Messbuch."

[12] The epistles survive in the Codex Fuldensis written about 546 for bishop Victor of Capua and carried to England by Hadrian, abbot of the monastery of St Niridan near Naples and later Archbishop of Canterbury (Fulda, Landesbibliothek MS Bonifatius I: Gamber, CLLA, no. 404); the gospel list was also brought to England, surviving as pericopes marked in eighth-century manuscripts, including the Lindisfarne Gospels (London, British Library, MS Cotton Nero D. IV), the "Codex Regius" (BL, MS Royal I B VII), and the Evangeliary of Bishop Burchard of Würzburg (Würzburg, Universitätsbibliothek MS M. p. th. f. 68); on these manuscripts see Gamber, CLLA, nos. 405–7. These Campanian Gospels, along with the epistles just mentioned, are studied in Gamber, "Die kampanische Lektionsordnung."

[13] *Gregorii magni dialogi*, p. 199.

[14] See the life in MGH SS Lang. at pp. 557, 561–2.

[15] Procopius, *History of the Wars*, VI.xiv.9 (III, 404–5).

[16] Alboin converted to Arianism about 565, hoping to get the support of the Arian Goths in north Italy; Bognetti, *L'età longobarda*, II, 45–9, 80.

[17] MGH Epistolae, I, p. 23.

[18] This can only be assessed roughly. After Authar, Agilulf (590–616) may have been an Arian; Arioald (626–36) and Rothar (636–52) certainly were; and Grimoald (662–71) may also have been Arian. The successors to Grimoald were all Catholics.

In the south, the diocese of Benevento, devastated like so many others by the Lombards,[19] was only reactivated in the course of the seventh century as the Lombards were converted to Catholicism. According to the life of St Barbatus, duke Romuald (661–71?) was one among many of the Beneventan Lombards to revert to pagan practices,[20] only returning to the Catholic fold through the connivance of his pious wife Theoderada with the saintly bishop.[21]

We cannot tell whether Catholic-Arian difficulties affected the Beneventan chant. There are no evidently Arian sentiments in the surviving chant texts, but the frequent presence of the creed in the Beneventan mass is probably a reminder of a heritage in which orthodoxy could not be taken for granted.[22] The Beneventan masses which include the creed hence also represent Catholic music among the Lombards; as such, they are unlikely to date from a time far in advance of the regular acceptance of Catholicism, at least among the Lombard kings and aristocracy.[23]

Thus we cannot push Beneventan chant, as a self-conscious repertory, much earlier than the mid-seventh century. This is not to say, of course, that liturgy and music were absent in southern Italy, or among the Lombards, before that time. Worshippers have prayed and sung from earliest times; and the evidence of Roman, or pan-Italian, elements in the Beneventan liturgy makes clear its connection with the longest traditions of Christian worship. But the Beneventan chant itself, though drawn in part from a fund of literary and musical materials brought south by the Lombards, developed its character only on southern soil. As a body of music it arose along with the area and the people it served – the Lombard Catholics of the south.

The age of Arichis II

Political and cultural divisions between north and south were a constant feature of Lombard relations. Romuald II of Benevento along with the duke of Spoleto had treated with Pope Gregory II (728–29) against the king of the Lombards,[24] and at Romuald's death the Beneventans selected their own duke, the gastald Adelais; but King Liutprand (712–44) intervened and imposed a non-native ruler, his nephew Gregory (739–40). Upon Gregory's death, however, the Beneventans again asserted their right to choose a local ruler, and again Liutprand intervened (742), removing Godescalc and installing Gisulf II, the grandson of Romuald, whom he had previously removed as a hostage to Pavia in order to install Gregory. Liutprand, in asserting his royal authority in a Benevento which preferred to name its own rulers, nevertheless found

Bognetti (*L'età longobarda*, 11, 42–57, 303–474) presents an extensive discussion of the importance of religion in the northern Lombard kingdom, contrasting a progressive Catholic party with a traditionalist Arian group of nationalist and warlike tendency. But see Wickham, *Early Medieval Italy*, 34–6; see also Cecchelli, "L'Arianesimo."

[19] See above, note 5.

[20] Duchesne, "Les évêchés", p. 106 sees the image of the viper as symbolic of Lombard Arianism.

[21] MGH SS Lang., pp. 561–3. Theoderada was the founder of St Peter's *extra muros* at Benevento.

[22] As Berno of Reichenau reports, Pope Benedict VIII explained to the Emperor Henry II that the creed is not needed in orthodox Rome, but where heresy abounds: "magis his necessarium esse illud symbolum saepius cantando frequentare, qui aliquando ulla haeresi potuerunt maculari"; PL, 142, col. 1061.

[23] For further discussion of the creed see Chapter 3, pp. 92–3.

[24] Duchesne, *Le Liber pontificalis*, 1, 407.

himself acknowledging the hereditary rights of the local dynasty when he recognized Gisulf.

Though Gisulf was faithful to Liutprand, the king's death (744) brought a new dynasty to the throne of Pavia, dissolving the personal and family loyalties at Benevento over which Liutprand had labored. King Ratchis considered Benevento to be foreign and enemy territory: among his laws is one forbidding any of his subjects to send unauthorized missions to "Roma, Ravenna, Spoleti, Benevento, Francia, Baioaria, Alamannia, Ritias aut in Avaria."[25]

This growing north-south division was irrevocably fixed by the fall of Pavia to Charlemagne in 774, and the establishment of an independent principality centered at Benevento under Arichis II (758–87).

The accession to power at Pavia of the last Lombard king, Desiderius (757), broke the bonds: the dukes of Spoleto and Benevento approached the Pope to seek the protection of Pipin, undoubtedly to separate their cause from that of the king of the Lombards.[26] Desiderius made what was to be the last effort to unify the Lombards north and south; occupying Spoleto, he installed his son-in-law Arichis II as duke at Benevento.[27]

Thus in 774 when King Desiderius fell to the Franks and Charlemagne proclaimed himself king at Pavia, Arichis assumed for himself the leadership of the Lombard people. He took the title *princeps gentis Longobardorum*;[28] he began to wear a crown,[29] and had himself consecrated by his bishops; he created an elaborate court ceremonial based on Byzantine models; he adapted elaborate chancery usages; he struck coins with his name and title;[30] and promulgated his own laws.[31]

Arichis' reliance on Byzantine models for his newly-assumed dignity is partly an effort to balance the power of the Franks in the north. To this end he put himself in contact with the Byzantine empire, seeking their support against the Franks: he promised to support a Byzantine reconquest of the Lombard kingdom of Pavia; to recognize imperial authority; and to adopt Byzantine style in dress and tonsure.[32]

Contact with Byzantium was interrupted – but only briefly – by Charlemagne's expedition to Benevento (786–87). Partly at the urging of Pope Hadrian I, whose letters reveal a passionate desire to subdue the "nefandissimos Beneventanos . . . una cum infedelissimo Arigihs,"[33] the self-styled *Rex Francorum et Longobardorum* took Capua in 787; but Arichis, shut up in his newly fortified town of Salerno, was able to turn Charlemagne back from Benevento by offering his

[25] MGH Leges, IV, 190.

[26] MGH Epistolae, III, 506. In a letter of 758 Pope Paul I writes to Pipin that Desiderius has betrayed Benevento and Spoleto, and that their dukes sought Byzantine support (MGH Epistolae, III, pp. 514–17). See Gasparri, *I duchi longobardi*, pp. 96–8.

[27] On Arichis see Bertolini, "Arechi II"; Gasparri, *I duchi*, pp. 98–100.

[28] "Domnus Arichis dux et primus princeps constituitur in Beneventum" (Bertolini, "Gli Annales Beneventani," p. 111). The title of *princeps* was one normally reserved for the Byzantine emperor. See Garms-Cornides, "Die langobardische Fürstentitel," pp. 354–74 and Kaminsky, "Zum Sinngehalt."

[29] Chron. mon. cas., I, 9: "Hic Arichis . . . ab episcopis ungi se fecit, et coronam sibi imposuit, atque in suis cartis, scriptum in sacratissimo palatio, in finem scribi precepit." See Chron. salern., p. 11; Garms-Cornides, "Die langobardische Fürstentitel," pp. 358–9.

[30] Oddy, "Analysis," p. 101 and plate 8, nos. 436–42.

[31] See the *Capitula domni Aregis principis* in MGH Leges, IV, pp. 207–10.

[32] MGH Epistolae, III, 617.

[33] MGH Epistolae, III, 591. See Hirsch, "Papst Hadrian I"; Bertolini, "Carlomagno e Benevento."

second son as hostage, paying a tribute, and acknowledging the emperor's authority with a solemn oath.[34]

Before these Carolingian incursions, the Beneventan chant was already securely in place in Arichis' Lombard capital. The Beneventan mass of the Holy Twelve Brothers points clearly to the Benevento of the second half of the eighth century. These are martyrs whose relics were gathered by Arichis himself and interred by him in the ducal church of Santa Sofia in 760.[35] Such a mass would not have originated elsewhere and been adopted later at Santa Sofia, and since the cult of these saints did not exist at all until their remains were collected by Arichis, we can be certain that the mass was composed neither before 760, nor, probably, much later than that date. At that time what we call the Beneventan chant must have already been in use at Benevento, since the ingressa of the Holy Twelve Brothers is an adaptation of the ingressa of the Beneventan Easter mass.[36]

The extension of the cult of these martyrs – intended by Arichis as "patroni patriae"[37] – throughout the region is evidence not only of the use of the Beneventan chant, but more directly, of the importance of Benevento as the political and cultural focus of the region, at least in the eighth century.[38]

The Holy Twelve Brothers were an aspect of the princely aspirations of Arichis II, who sought in them and in other relics which he acquired to focus on Benevento and Santa Sofia the religious nationalism of the southern Lombards. Until this time the undisputed patron of the Lombards was St Michael,[39] for whom the surviving Beneventan mass was doubtless already in use. But his shrine was not at Benevento, and it was not always easy for the dukes of Benevento to retain control of it.[40] The sanctuary of St Michael on Monte Gargano was an important place of pilgrimage for the Lombards from at least the seventh century, for his apparition there is credited by a ninth-century Lombard writer (perhaps basing his account on earlier material)

[34] Bertolini, "Carlomagno e Benevento," pp. 633–4.

[35] See the metrical description in MGH SS Lang., pp. 574–6; on the date, see lines 74–8.

[36] At least the borrowing would appear to have been in this direction. The form of the Twelve Brothers ingressa is not so balanced as the Easter version, owing to its reversing the order of two internal phrases. See Chapter 5, p. III. And the Easter ingressa itself uses a text known elsewhere; it is found, in a slightly different version and without notation, in the vast collection of processional antiphons in the ninth-century antiphoner of Compiègne (*Sextuplex*, p. 223), and with a non-Beneventan melody in Vat. Reg. lat. 334 and Oxford, Bodleian, MS Douce 222; with three additional lines, it serves as a Kyrie-trope in Ben34 and Ben39 (see Appendices 1 and 2). The Easter text itself thus may have been adopted at Benevento from a very old layer of hymnody; it is scarcely likely that the poem known in the north was modeled on a Beneventan text for the Twelve Brothers.

[37] MGH SS Lang., p. 575, line 52.

[38] The Beneventan mass is found also at Montecassino in the palimpsest gradual MC 361; see Chapter 2, source 3. The feast itself is noted widely in south Italian calendars and martyrologies. Alfanus I, monk of Montecassino and later bishop of Salerno, is the author of a thousand-line "Metrum heroicum domni Alfani Salernitani arciepiscopi in honore sanctorum duodecim fratrum," edited from Cassinese manuscripts in Lentini, *I carmi*.

[39] See Erchempert in MGH SS Lang., p. 244: "Nam octavo Ydus Maias, quo beati Michahelis archangeli sollempnia nos sollempniter celebramus, quo etiam die priscis temporibus a Beneventanorum populis Neapolites fortiter caesos legimus. . ."

[40] Benevento was always careful to retain control of the diocese of Siponto in which the shrine of this important national patron was located. The ninth-century life of St Barbatus is careful to elaborate how Barbatus was instrumental in subjecting Siponto to Benevento (MGH SS Lang., pp. 560–1); and in the same period the Chronicle of San Vincenzo (Chron. vult., 1, 300) is aware that the Beneventan domination of Siponto is the result of an unauthorized usurpation. A much later forged bull of Pope Vitalian, contemporary with Barbatus, makes a further attempt to justify an irregularity (IP IX, pp. 51–2, no. 5); see Gay, *L'Italie méridionale*, pp. 197–200; von Rintelen, *Kultgeographische*, pp. 3–21, 42–52.

with a Lombard victory over the "still pagan" Neapolitans (*paganis adhuc ritibus oberrantes*).[41]

The anonymous author of the *Chronica sancti Benedicti casinensis* perhaps borrows the words of the Beneventan communion *Celestis militie princeps* in his description of the arrival of the Lombards and their debt to St Michael: "Post hoc [Longobardi] dominantes Italiam, Beneventum properantes introeunt ad habitandum. Horum autem *princeps militie celestis* exercitus Michahel extitit archangelus; Neapolites ad fidem Christi perducti."[42]

In 768, eight years after the translation of the Holy Twelve Brothers, Arichis II acquired another apt patron for the warrior Lombards: the relics of St Mercurius, one of the greatest military saints of Byzantium, were enshrined with great pomp in a special altar in Santa Sofia.[43] Mercurius was evidently intended by Arichis to be a patron of the court, of the church of Santa Sofia, of the city, and of the Lombard people.[44] His cult was strong through the Middle Ages, at least through the time of the suppression of the Beneventan chant; a relief over the doorway of Santa Sofia, probably of the twelfth century, includes Christ with the Virgin and Saint Mercurius with a kneeling figure who may be Arichis II.[45] When the Norman, Roger II, arrived at Benevento in 1139 in company with the Pope, he made a point of visiting Santa Sofia to pray at the shrine of St Mercurius.[46]

Curiously, though, there is no surviving Beneventan mass for Mercurius like that for the Holy Twelve Brothers, translated eight years earlier.[47] It may be that in these very few years between the two translations the Beneventan chant changed from a growing repertory to a closed one; that it became a Lombard heritage of the past rather than of the present.

The age of Arichis at Benevento is one of significant cultural richness, and it is of primary importance for the future of the principality. Hans Belting has shown that the court of Arichis possessed a court school, under the influential Paul the Deacon; there was elaborate court ceremonial along Byzantine lines; and there was notable artistic and literary activity.[48] Arichis' interest in the church is evident. He was considered by his contemporaries and by those who looked back on him with Lombard pride to be a religious man,[49] and there are legendary tales of his personal piety.[50] His personal fervor affected the religious life of the court, the city, and

---

[41] See the account of the apparition in MGH SS Lang., pp. 540–43. On Lombard pilgrims to St Michael's shrine in the seventh century and later, see von Falkenhausen, "I longobardi," p. 317.

[42] Italics mine. The text of the Beneventan communion is elsewhere known only in the Ambrosian chant of the Lombard north; see Appendix 2.

[43] Binon, *Essai*, pp. 43–53; Delahaye, "La translatio"; for the passion ascribed to Arichis see Giovardi, *Acta passionis*, pp. 9–31; on the translation to Benevento, BHL 5936 (MGH SS Lang., pp. 576–78), 5937 (Giovardi, *Acta passionis*, pp. 55–62). On the importance of Mercurius at Benevento in the eighth century, see Belting, "Studien," pp. 157–60.

[44] "Dominii eiusdem loci tutor et urbis" (MGH SS Lang., p. 578); "ad tutelam Longobardi populi procurandam obtinet [Mercurius] Samniae principatus" (Martène, *Veterum scriptorum*, VI, col. 756); "effectusque est patronus Beneventani populi" (Binon, *Essai*, p. 44, n. 4).

[45] On this relief, see De Vita, *Thesaurus*, II, 99 and 104–5 plus plate. On its date see Belting, "Studien," p. 176–7, n. 271. That the relief might include a representation of Arichis see Rotili, *Benevento romana*, pp. 189–90.

[46] Lehmann-Brockhaus, *Schriftquellen*, no. 2124 (I, p. 440); he also went to the cathedral to venerate the relics of St Bartholomew.

[47] On surviving liturgical material for Mercurius, see p. 72.

[48] "Studien zum beneventanischen Hof."

[49] "Pietatis cultor et index" (Paul the Deacon, *Die Gedichte*, ed. Neff, p. 16); "Catholicus princeps" (Neff, p. 16); "Dux per omnia catholicus" (Capitulary of Adelchis, MGH Leges, IV, 210); "piissimus princeps" (Chron. salern., p. 13); "vir christianissimus" (Erchempert, MGH SS Lang., p. 235).

[50] See Chron. salern., p. 20.

the realm. Indeed, Belting has seen him as the author of specific liturgical innovations.[51] And in his gathering of relics Arichis not only displays the military and national aspects of his new principality and its court, but also indicates the centrality of their repository, Santa Sofia.

Santa Sofia

Though the diocese of Benevento had been reactivated in the seventh century, the eighth-century bishops of Benevento were still under the close control of the court, often serving on diplomatic and political missions. Bishop David (781/2–96), who was empowered by Arichis II to negotiate with Charlemagne, had evidently received his training at the court school under Paul the Deacon; his epitaph for Arichis' son Romuald shows his personal attachment to the court.[52]

The center of the ecclesiastical life of Benevento under Arichis was the court church built by him – Santa Sofia.[53] Like many other monasteries and churches founded by Lombard nobles,[54] it was effectively a private church, exempt from episcopal authority.[55] Santa Sofia was intended by Arichis as a national Lombard shrine – "ecclesia sancte Sophie, quam a fundamentis edificavi pro redemptione anime mee seu pro salvatione gentis nostre et patrie"[56] – and it certainly served that purpose, at least for a time. Arichis enriched it with gifts and relics; he attached to it a convent of nuns;[57] he established a special group of clergy to assure the regular performance of the liturgy;[58] and he himself is reported to have prayed there regularly.[59]

[51] See Paul the Deacon, "Flaminibusque ipsis famina sancta dabat" in Neff, *Die Gedichte*, p. 146. Belting ("Studien," p. 160) sees this as an indication of liturgical innovations.

[52] On David, see Maio, "Davide Beneventano." The epitaph for Romuald is edited in Chron. salern., p. 26, and in MGH Poetae, I, 111–12. It is possible to detect an anti-Frankish sentiment in the contrast between *Gallorum ira* and the *placida mens* of Romuald.

  Bishop David gives us what may be our only contemporary acknowledgment of the difference between the local rite and that of Rome. In a sermon preached at the cathedral on the Marian feast of December 18 (also the anniversary of the cathedral's dedication) he notes that the feast being celebrated is not known in the Roman church ("cum intra sanctam roma-nam non colatur ecclesiam"), and goes on to give an explanation for anyone who may be a stranger to the city (*hospes, advena*).

  The sermon is found in Benevento 18 (tenth–eleventh century; see Mallet, *Les Manuscrits*, p. 237) and in Vat. lat. 4222 (eleventh century), from which it is edited in Barré, "La fête mariale," pp. 458–61. That Mary is patron of the cathedral at Benevento, and venerated there from well before the great extension of her cult in the later Middle Ages, is perhaps attested by the survival of her Beneventan mass now placed at the Assumption in Ben38 and Ben40, whose communion concludes "quorum [christianorum] patrona pia es et domina."

[53] The foundation of Santa Sofia is reported by Erchempert (MGH SS Lang., p. 236), repeated by a later source at Montecassino, and quoted by Leo in the Chronicle; see Kelly, "Montecassino," pp. 48–50; on the local awareness of the parallel with Justinian, see MGH SS Lang., pp. 575 (lines 70–2) and 576–7; the importance of Santa Sofia to the princely aspirations of Arichis is discussed in Belting, "Studien," pp. 182–8.

[54] Including Santa Sofia; St Peter's *extra muros*, founded at Benevento by Duke Romuald's consort Theoderada about 675; and San Vincenzo al Volturno, founded by three nobles of Benevento in the early eighth century.

[55] The founder's monastery or church was, like all Lombard property, repeatedly subdivided among his heirs. See Ruggiero, *Principi, nobiltà, e chiesa*, pp. 27–36. See also Feine, "Studien," esp. pp. 11–20.

[56] Poupardin, *Les Institutions*, p. 135.

[57] According to Chron. mon. cas., I, 9, his sister was the first abbess; for further on this convent see below, pp. 32–7.

[58] This is clear from his *capitula*, which distinguish between the clerics who *in palatio deserviunt* and those who *extra palatium deagunt*. The terms appear in a series of penalties against the killers of ecclesiastics – monks, presbyters, deacons, and finally these ecclesiastics. MGH Leges, IV, 208; see Poupardin, *Les Institutions*, p. 29 and nn. 3, 4, 5. On the question of the chapel of San Salvatore in Palatio, which has sometimes been identified with Santa Sofia, and may be the location of those who "in

The eighth-century building is still standing at Benevento; this in itself is remarkable given how little else survives from the period: of Arichis' palace essentially nothing remains, and the eighth-century cathedral is witnessed by only a few arches in the present crypt. Santa Sofia, like so many buildings of its era, is small, polygonal in plan, and its current restoration gives little idea of the splendor it must once have had, with its rich decoration and splendid altars of saints.[60]

Santa Sofia was an ecclesiastical center that affected the religious life of the area. The cult of the Holy Twelve Brothers spread through the region from there, and as late as the eleventh century it was recognized as having an individual chant tradition. In the margin of the gradual Benevento 34 (f. 94) is a small melodic correction to the Gregorian-Beneventan communion *Lutum fecit*: the correction is marked *in Sancta Sophia* (see Plate 2).

The liturgy of Santa Sofia had visible effects on other surviving manuscripts of Benevento,[61] and there is some evidence of a scriptorium at Santa Sofia.[62] A note in a twelfth-century hand in Vatican lat. 4955, f. 209v, describes the bibliophile activities of the monk Landolphus of Santa Sofia who collected many books and had others copied, among them "libros quoque diurni vel nocturni cantus."[63]

The manuscript Vatican Ottob. lat. 145 may have been written for the use of Santa Sofia, though it is modeled to some degree on sources from Montecassino.[64] It contains, among much else, six Beneventan antiphons for use in a *mandatum* ceremony; all six are used elsewhere as communions or offertories, and one (for St Benedict) is otherwise known only at Montecassino.

Beyond this single manuscript, however, it is impossible to determine which (if any) of the surviving sources of Beneventan chant may have originated at Santa Sofia. Indeed, the origins of the two principal sources of Beneventan chant, Benevento 38 (Ben38) and 40 (Ben40), are

palatio deserviunt," see Belting, "Studien," pp. 186–7; Rotili, *Benevento romana*, p. 187. This practice may be modeled on the special "palace clergy" of the northern Lombard king Liutprand (712–44); see Paul the Deacon's report in MGH SS Lang., p. 186.

[59] "Quoniam vicinum eius [i.e., to Santa Sofia] palatium erat, frequentem consuetudinem in oratione pernoctandi haberet. . ." (Chron. mon. cas., 1, 9). "Pervigil in lacrimis tempora noctis agens," writes Paul the Deacon in his epitaph for Arichis (Chron. salern., p. 24).

[60] On the building, see Meomartini, *I monumenti*, pp. 365–74; Belting, "Studien," pp. 175–93; Rotili, *Benevento romana*, pp. 184–201; Gaetana Intorcia in her edition of De Nicastro, *Benevento sacro*, pp. 327–43.

[61] The calendar of Santa Sofia affected the missal London, BL, Egerton MS 3511 (formerly Ben29) from the abbey of St Peter *intra muros* and to a lesser extent the martyrology Benevento 37, which was used at St Peter *intra muros* (Mallet, *Les Manuscrits*, p. 81, n. 6).

[62] See Mallet, *Les Manuscrits*, p. 82, n. 8; on books from Santa Sofia, see note 65 below.

[63] The passage is reproduced in TBS, I, 78.

[64] A monastic vow (f. 121) contains the Cassinese phrase "in hoc sancto monasterio ubi sacratissimum corpus eius [i.e., of St Benedict] humatum est," but saints named in litanies suggest Santa Sofia; the Holy Twelve Brothers are named individually (f. 111v, as in the Santa Sofia litanies of London, BL, Add. MS 23776, ff. 36, 39v, 45v and Naples VI E 43, f. 154v), as are Saints Graficus and Quineclus (f. 112; "3 non dec Nat. scorum grafici septimi et quinecli in sca sophia," according to the Santa Sofia martyrology London, BL, Add. 23776, f. 32, which also names the saints in the litanies just mentioned; see Bannister, *Monumenti*, no. 348; Boe, "A new source"). Benevento 37 also uses all these saints in a litany on f. 64 and in the martyrology as saints "in sancta sofia." All twelve brothers, Saints Graficus, Septimus, and Quineclus are named in a litany in the second (thirteenth-century) part of Naples, Bibl. naz. MS VI G 31; the first part is a handsome book of monastic materials from the late eleventh century: not unlike the material in Ottoboni 145. The manuscript once belonged to the Biblioteca Vallicelliana, a rich source of Beneventan liturgical material. See TBS, II, 102.

difficult to define; Ben40 may be from Santa Sofia, Ben38 from one of the convents of Benevento (see Appendix 3): but we cannot be certain. The same difficulty arises for many of the sources of Beneventan chant: they are clearly of the region, many probably from Benevento itself, but they do not permit further localization. Liturgical books clearly from Santa Sofia date only from the twelfth century and, like all books from that date onward, contain essentially Gregorian materials.[65]

The centrality of Santa Sofia in the chant can be inferred from its prominence in Lombard life of the eighth century and later, from its importance as a center of literary and cultural life, and, as we shall see, from its connection with Montecassino, another strong center of Beneventan chant.[66]

The spread of Beneventan chant

The Beneventan chant, like the script that records its texts, spread throughout the zone affected by Lombard political and cultural influence. The power and independence of the eighth-century Lombards and their involvement in ecclesiastical affairs account for the rapid dissemination of the chant. The Lombards were an independent breed; they effectively resisted, at least for a time, the potentially overpowering influences of the Popes, of the Franks, and of the Byzantines, mostly by a delicate balancing act which preserved their own identity. The letters of

[65] The surviving books include Naples VI E 43 and Vat. lat. 4928, both containing calendar, *ordo officii*, and further liturgical materials (the latter is a very handsome decorated manuscript); the splendid lectionary Veroli, Biblioteca Giovardiana I; the martyrology London, BL, Add. MS 23776; perhaps at least the second part (ff. 39–48) of Naples XVI A 19 (Chapter 2, source 70); Naples VI G 31 (see note 64); and perhaps the martyrology Benevento 37 – though it was used at St Peter's *intra muros* and may have been designed for the convent (see Appendix 3). Other manuscripts of Santa Sofia include the cartulary Vat. lat. 4939; Vat. lat. 4955 (Paralipomena, Hrabanus Maurus, Augustine, Jerome, etc.); the twelfth-century martyrology Vat. lat. 5949. Further material on all these can be found in TBS, II; see also Mallet, *Les Manuscrits*, pp. 71–2, n. 6 and p. 82, n. 8.

[66] That so few liturgical manuscripts survive from Santa Sofia before the twelfth century may be related to a similar phenomenon at Montecassino. Leo Marsicanus relates that before the time of Abbot Theobald (1022–35) Montecassino was poorly supplied with books ("Codices . . . quorum hic maxima paupertas usque ad id temporis erat": Chron. mon. cas., II, 53). Though Theobald added much to the monastic library (Chron. mon. cas., II, 53 names some 20 volumes), the contribution of Abbot Desiderius (1058–87) was by comparison enormous. The list in Chron. mon. cas. (III, 63) runs to some seventy books. And whereas Theobald is shown in miniature offering a book to St Benedict (in Montecassino MS 73, p. 4; facs. in Bloch, MMA, fig. 2; "Monte Cassino, Byzantium," p. 218), the similar scene in the beautiful Cassinese lectionary Vat. lat. 1202 (f. 2; facs. in Bloch, MMA, fig. 48; "Monte Cassino, Byzantium," plate 220) shows Desiderius offering not only churches, but a whole heap of books.

A new style of manuscript production at Montecassino, fitting the power and importance of the abbey, was a feature of the early twelfth century (see Bloch, MMA, I, 71–82; "Monte Cassino, Byzantium," pp. 201–7; of primary importance will be the forthcoming study by Francis Newton on the scriptorium under Abbots Desiderius and Oderisius), and it is not surprising that many liturgical books (and not just those containing Beneventan chant) should be replaced with more beautiful examples.

A similar replacement may have taken place at Santa Sofia in the twelfth century – a time of enrichment in which the beautiful cloister was added to the monastery by Abbot John IV (on the date of the cloister and the identification of John, see *Aggiornamento*, v, 661). The books from this period are of an elegance and beauty parallel to those of Desiderius. The Veroli lectionary (see Battelli, "Il lezionario"), like the Desiderian lectionary Vat. lat. 1202, is a splendid book containing only materials for the principal feasts of the church: in this case, St Mercurius, the Holy Twelve Brothers, and the Dedication. Likewise the compendium of liturgical materials in Vat. lat. 4928, generously proportioned and decorated with gold, and the richly illuminated cartulary Vat. lat. 4939, are books of a richness unknown at Benevento before this time. Further bibliography on all these books is found in the catalogue in TBS, II.

the eighth-century Popes Stephen II, Paul I, and Hadrian I make it clear that the southern Lombards are seen as a threat to the church and usurpers of the patrimony of St Peter.[67]

The Lombards for their part were proud of their independence. The success of Arichis II and his legates in dealing with Charlemagne was remembered with pleasure in the chronicles and laws of later generations;[68] the ninth-century Cassinese chronicler Erchempert is full of pride in his Lombard heritage, in his admiration for Arichis, and his hatred for the Franks.[69] There is also much evidence of Lombard resistance. Arichis' son Grimoald's reply to Frankish threats may not originally have been cast in the distich reported by Erchempert, but their sense is clear:

> I was born of both parents free and unfettered;
> I believe I shall always be free, God willing.[70]

The Lombard influence on the church, at least in the formative years of the southern Lombard hegemony, was considerable. The church was closely controlled by the early Lombard princes, and they in turn, along with many nobles, made widespread foundations of churches and monasteries.[71]

Their presence was strongly felt at Montecassino. The rebuilding of Montecassino begun under Petronax of Brescia (*c.* 718) owes much to the support of the Beneventan dukes Romuald II (706–30) and Gisulf II (742–51).[72] Gisulf's wife Scauniperga established, in a former pagan temple, the church of St Peter "in Civitate" (or "in monastero").[73] Abbot Gisulf (796–817), who was responsible for a significant building campaign at Montecassino that included the basilica and monastery of San Salvatore below the mountain, as well as much extensive work above, was of "the noble family of the dukes of Benevento,"[74] and therefore had presumably been close to the court of Arichis II and his successors.

The Beneventan chant, like the script that records its texts, spread throughout the zone affected by Lombard political and cultural influence. The fidelity of its transmission, and its presence over the widest Lombard sphere, indicate its dissemination at the height of Lombard influence. An early date is suggested also by the presence of the Beneventan mass of the Twelve

---

[67] See MGH Epistolae, III, 494ff.

[68] A statue of Arichis stood in Santa Sofia in the seventeenth century (see Ferrante, "Chiesa e chiostro," p. 83; Zazo, *Curiosità*, pp. 14–15); and memorial prayers were said for him as late as the eighteenth century (Borgia, *Memorie istoriche*, I, 236). See Rotili, *Benevento romana* pp. 189–90, nn. 491, 492.

[69] For an evaluation of Erchempert and a bibliography, see Citarella, *The Ninth-Century Treasure*, pp. 51–2, n. 56.

[70] "Liber et ingenuus sum natus utroque parente;/Semper ero liber, credo, tuente Deo." See MGH SS Lang., pp. 236–7.

[71] On Theoderada's foundation of St Peter's *extra muros* see Paul, HL in MGH SS Lang., p. 164. Arichis himself founded Santa Sofia; three nobles of Benevento founded San Vincenzo al Volturno (see the history attributed to Ambrose Autpert in MGH SS Lang., pp. 546–55; *Ambrosii Autperti opera*, III, 893–905 with commentary on pp. 875–6). Many other examples could be cited of Lombard princes and nobles establishing churches and monasteries; see, for example, Chron. mon. cas., I, 6. For donations by princes of Benevento to San Vincenzo, see Chron. vult., I, 133–9 (Gisulf I, 689–706), 163–6 (Gisulf II, 742–51), 154–5 (Arichis II), etc. See also Bertolini, "I duchi."

[72] For Gisulf's extensive donation of territory to Montecassino, see Chron. mon. cas., I, 5. See also Leccisotti, *Montecassino* (1983), 32; Falco, "Lineamenti," pp. 476–7.

[73] See Chron. mon. cas., I, 5, which reports information from the *Chronica sancti benedicti casinensis* (MGH SS Lang., p. 480). On the church of St Peter see Avagliano, "Monumenti del culto," p. 79. The church was the site of a reunion of the monks from above (on the mountain) and those below for the special ceremonies of Easter Tuesday, which included singing in Greek. See Chapter 5, pp. 204–5, and Citarella, *The Ninth-Century Treasure*, pp. 111–16.

[74] Chron. mon. cas., I, 17.

Brothers in the palimpsest Montecassino 361. Such a mass must have come early from Benevento: surely before the destruction of Montecassino in 883, which broke the old link with Santa Sofia (see below), and certainly not at the height of Montecassino's power in the tenth and eleventh centuries, when transmission of liturgical materials, tropes, and other matter, much more often moved in the other direction, from the monastery to the city.[75]

The precise extent of the Beneventan chant is difficult to assess. Unfortunately many sources are of unknown provenance, though they are "Beneventan" in the widest sense, but the survival of many Exultet rolls helps to clarify the geography. These decorated documents, used for the blessing of the candle at the Easter Vigil, have long been of great interest to historians of art.[76] They are exclusively a southern Italian phenomenon, and thus by their very existence witness the presence of the regional liturgy when they record the widely used Beneventan recitation-tone (often with a specifically "Beneventan" text).[77]

The extent of the Beneventan chant, so far as we can trace it, is shown on the map facing page I, which indicates all the places where documents containing elements of the Beneventan liturgy are thought to have originated. The picture, of course, is that of the period of written documents – that is to say, the eleventh century – but it matches what we expect from political and ecclesiastical history.

Benevento is the center for the chant; not only does the music survive largely in manuscripts from the city, but it survives longer there than elsewhere. The sources are centered, both by weight of numbers and by geographical orientation, along a Benevento-Montecassino axis, with a number of sources from nearby sites. However, they come also from Bari, from the Cassinese dependency in the Tremiti Islands, and from along the Dalmatian coast.

A sort of monastic conduit leads north through Subiaco and Lucca. Subiaco shows, in a thirteenth-century missal written at the abbey of Santa Scolastica (MS XVIII), the full Beneventan vespers of Good Friday (though without notation), and the Beneventan melody of the Exultet. The manuscript is written in northern script, but with Beneventan notation.

Beneventan notation is found often at Subiaco, both in fragments of manuscripts written with Beneventan script and notation[78] and in sources using ordinary minuscule, but whose musical notation is Beneventan.[79] At least one of these last was made for Subiaco (MS XXII), and thus it appears that there was at least one scribe writing Beneventan notation there. That elements of the Beneventan liturgy should survive into the thirteenth century is perhaps not so surprising, since Subiaco is the place of St Benedict's earliest monastic life, and the place from

[75] The later liturgical influence of Montecassino at Benevento can be seen, for example, in Vat. Ottob. lat. 145; in the *ordo officii* Ben66, which is derived from Montecassino practice but adapted for the use of St Peter's *intra muros*; in the trope repertory of Ben34 (awaiting further discussions in Boe and Planchart, *Beneventanum troporum corpus*, see Boe, "The 'lost' palimpsest Kyries," esp. pp. 6 and 10).

[76] The bibliography on south Italian Exultet rolls is vast. See the indications in Appendix 3 accompanying each relevant source.

[77] On this melody and its relation to other melodies in the repertory see Chapter 5. The Beneventan Exultet is the object of a substantial study in PM XIV, 375–417; its melody is analyzed in PM IV, 171–85. On texts of the Exultet see Pinell, "La benedicció."

[78] The fragment of a gradual – eleventh–twelfth century – that now serves as the opening flyleaves of MS XX; two fragments of an antiphoner – twelfth century? – in the folder labeled "Miscellanea" no. LX.

[79] These include fragments of three separate antiphoners in the Miscellanea; three bifolia from a late twelfth-century antiphoner bound into MS CCXLVI; and the musical notation of the twelfth-century breviary MS XXII.

which he journeyed to found Montecassino. Doubtless the Beneventan liturgical material, like its scribe, came north in a monastic connection with Montecassino.

The monastic missal Lucca 606 is a similar case from much farther north. The book is written in northern script and notation,[80] but attached to the main body of the missal is an appendix, written by the same text-scribe (ff. 150v–156v), which supplements the foregoing missal with certain special rites of Holy Week: rubrics, lessons, chants, etc., which are outside the normal scope of a missal. Much of the material in this supplement is from the Beneventan liturgy and the musical notation is Beneventan. This is by far our northernmost source of the Beneventan liturgy, but we can infer from the notation that the direction of travel was south to north. There is a further connection in Montecassino manuscript 175, whose Good Friday *ordo* matches Lucca's almost exactly.[81] Montecassino had a dependency (San Giorgio) in Lucca, though it can be dated only from the mid-eleventh century.[82]

GREGORIAN CHANT IN SOUTHERN ITALY

After the initial dissemination of the Beneventan chant, the coming of Gregorian chant to southern Italy is of central importance in the history of Beneventan chant, for by the end of the eleventh century the repertory now generally called Gregorian (in a form essentially identical with the tradition of the rest of Europe), was the only liturgical chant sung in the Latin church of southern Italy. The imperatives of unity and uniformity had so successfully had their way that the Beneventan chant was abandoned, despite evidently tenacious local efforts to the contrary.

But when did the Gregorian chant arrive in the south? Judging only from the age of the surviving documents it might have arrived with the millenium. The series of Gregorian graduals and missals[83] surviving from southern Italy begins with Benevento 33 (which has relatively little evidence of Beneventan chant at all)[84] and the now incomplete Vat. lat. 10673 (which has more Beneventan chant, mixed with the Gregorian rites for Holy Week), both dating from about the turn of the century.[85] They are documents whose purpose is to record Gregorian chant, not Beneventan – and surely a new and unfamiliar rite and its chant are more important to write down than better-known local music. It is only with the next generation of manuscripts, Benevento 38 and Benevento 40 (both probably from Benevento, as those just

---

[80] One piece, however, is in Beneventan notation: the Alleluia ℣ *Adorabo*, fo. 137.

[81] See Appendix 3, under Lucca 606.

[82] *Chron. mon. cas.*, II, 90. The missal Vat. lat. 4770 is another example of a manuscript written in ordinary minuscule in which survive a few elements of the Beneventan liturgy (lections and chant texts for Holy Week – see Chapter 2, table 1), though essentially without musical notation. The origin of this manuscript is so widely attributed (see Appendix 3) that it has not been included on the map.

[83] From the same period or slightly earlier may be the Beneventan homiliaries MSS 8, 10, 11, 13, based on liturgical gospel series; see the catalogue entries in Mallet, *Les Manuscrits*.

[84] Ben33 is thought by some to date from the end of the tenth century (thus in TBS, II, p. 21, PM XIV, p. 136, etc., Dom Hourlier was inclined to date it in the eleventh century: see PM XX, 17*–18*), but it is not demonstrably from Benevento, see Mallet, *Les Manuscrits*, pp. 76–7, n. 5 and p. 90.

[85] For other early notated sources see Chapter 2, n. 1.

mentioned probably are not), that scribes attempt to include at least a portion of the Beneventan liturgy in basically Gregorian graduals, using the same notation for both repertories.

Do these early sources represent the beginnings of music-manuscript writing in the area, and also the beginning of the usage of Gregorian chant? Is it written as soon as it arrives? It is clear from much other evidence that both the Gregorian chant and the Beneventan had been in use in the region for a long time before these sources were written.

The Gregorian chant used in southern Italy has elements of considerable antiquity; features that disappeared as early as the eighth century elsewhere. Unless we believe that such a version arrived in the south in the eleventh century, when these archaisms had been absent elsewhere for centuries, we must conclude that the Gregorian chant, or at least the liturgy it accompanied, was used in southern Italy for a long time before the creation of the eleventh-century manuscripts. This is not a book about the Gregorian chant of southern Italy – though such a study would be of real value – but we should briefly review the evidence, much of it first brought to light by Dom Hesbert, of archaisms in the Gregorian chant tradition of southern Italy.

Gregorian manuscripts of the Beneventan zone retain texts from the Roman psalter for the verses of introits. Though chants themselves regularly retain older textual readings reflecting the early date of their composition, psalm verses adapted to a reciting tone, such as the verses of introits and communions, are generally drawn from the current psalter. Thus the so-called "Gallican" psalter, St Jerome's second revision, which gradually gained a wide ascendancy in liturgical usage, beginning at the time of Charlemagne, replaced the older Roman psalter in introit verses and elsewhere, even where an older translation of the same text persisted in the chant pieces more closely bound to their texts.

The Gallican psalter gained a real ascendancy in the ninth century; Amalar quotes regularly from it. Italy, though slower to abandon the Roman psalter, gradually took up the Gallican version in the tenth and eleventh centuries. But the manuscripts of the Beneventan zone, faithful to Italian tradition, uniformly retain the Roman psalter; the received version of Gregorian chant in the Beneventan region was old enough not to have been affected by the later psalter versions of the ninth and tenth centuries.[86]

Many details are revealed by a study of the lectionary. The gospels for the Sundays after Pentecost in the Gregorian-Beneventan tradition match closely those of the lectionary of Würzburg,[87] whereas almost all other medieval traditions follow the order in the lectionary of Murbach.[88] But Würzburg, the oldest surviving Roman lectionary, represents the Roman liturgy of the mid-seventh century; its calendar is that of the early Gelasian sacramentary of the sixth–seventh century. Murbach, however, the ancestor of the universal medieval and modern tradition, has the calendar of the eighth-century Gelasian sacramentary, and re-

---

[86] See PM XIV, 145–51. For an introduction to the various versions of the psalter and their use as chant texts, see Dyer, "Latin psalters."

[87] Studied and edited in Morin, "Le plus ancien *comes*" (for the epistles) and Morin, "Liturgie et basiliques" (for the gospels); see also Frere, *Studies*, II, 74 and III, 27.

[88] Studied and edited in Wilmart, "Le *comes* de Murbach"; on the manuscript see Wilmart, "Nouvelles remarques."

presents a Frankish adaptation of the mid-eighth century uniting the Gelasian and Gregorian sacramentaries.[89]

Three Beneventan manuscripts (Vat. lat. 10673, Ben33, Ben34) have two graduals for the Saturday of the fourth week of Lent. The oldest lectionaries, including those of Würzburg and Murbach[90] show for this day a double reading from Isaiah providing occasion for two graduals. Of the early manuscripts surveyed in Hesbert's *Antiphonale missarum sextuplex*, only the eighth–ninth-century Rheinau antiphoner shows two graduals for this Saturday.[91] Apparently the Beneventan manuscripts preserve an early usage universally abandoned elsewhere by the early ninth century.[92]

Unique Beneventan treatment of days which were without a proper liturgy in early stages of the Roman calendar suggest that the received version of Gregorian chant was an early one. These lacunae are given unique local formularies which show an ongoing familiarity with the musical style of the Gregorian chant.

The mass for the seventh Sunday after Pentecost (introit *Omnes gentes*) is omitted in some Beneventan manuscripts.[93] Some early witnesses of the Roman tradition also lack this mass. It is omitted in the eighth-century Cantatorium of Monza; the eighth-ninth-century Mont-Blandin antiphoner includes it, but with the rubric "This week is not in the Roman antiphoners";[94] the manuscripts of the Old Roman tradition also omit this mass. It is absent also in the lists of chants in the Gregorian sacramentary Vat. Ottob. 313. But the mass is otherwise uniformly present in the Gregorian tradition, with the sole exception of a group of manuscripts with ties to southern Italy. The absence of this mass, evidently added to the Gregorian repertory in the eighth century, testifies to a particularly archaic aspect of the received tradition at Benevento.[95]

The second Sunday of Lent, originally without a liturgy of its own – it is absent in all the early antiphoners of the *Sextuplex*[96] – was later provided with various masses in different places; manuscripts from the Beneventan area[97] uniformly supply a mass in Gregorian style which is unique to the region. The received tradition, then, lacked music for this Sunday, which was provided on the spot. Some of these pieces are newly made in elegant Gregorian style, others are adapted from existing Gregorian melodies.[98]

The Saturday before Palm Sunday was also originally aliturgical,[99] and Beneventan manuscripts again supply the lack in local fashion with a unique mass in Gregorian style. Two of the pieces are "second-stage" adaptations, rather badly handled reworkings of pieces known only in

---

[89] PM XIV, 129–44.

[90] Morin, "Le plus ancien *comes*," p. 53; Wilmart, "Le *comes* de Murbach," p. 40.

[91] *Sextuplex*, p. 80.

[92] PM XIV, pp. 242–3.

[93] For a list of manuscripts which omit this mass see PM XIV, 127.

[94] ISTA EBDOMATA NON EST IN ANTEFONARIOS ROMANOS; *Sextuplex*, p. 180.

[95] For further details on this mass, see Hesbert, "La messe 'Omnes gentes';" PM XIV, 125–9; *Sextuplex*, p. LXXVII.

[96] *Sextuplex*, pp. 62–3.

[97] For a list see the table in PM XIV, 220–1.

[98] See PM XIV, pp. 234–7.

[99] SABBATO VACAT. QUANDO DOMNUS PAPA ELEMOSINAM DAT: see *Sextuplex*, pp. 86–7.

the Beneventan region. The introit *Domine exaudi* is adapted from the Beneventan-Gregorian introit for Lent II, the communion *Judica domine* from the regional melody for the communion *Videns dominus*.[100]

The originally aliturgical Saturday after Ash Wednesday[101] is absent also in the Beneventan gradual Vat. lat. 10673. Most Beneventan manuscripts borrow the mass for the preceding Thursday for this day; a few use that of Friday. But Benevento 38 and Benevento 35 assemble a special mass whose elements are mostly borrowed from elsewhere, but whose introit, *Converte nos deus*, seems to be a local product in Gregorian style.[102]

The Mont-Blandin gradual indicates a second offertory (ITEM OFF.) for Pentecost; this same offertory (*Factus est repente*) is found also in Beneventan manuscripts, although with a different verse. Generally, it is assigned to the Thursday after Pentecost, but in Baltimore Walters 6 (f. 152) it is the only offertory for Pentecost itself. Evidently the use of this offertory for Pentecost was losing favor in the north already by the time of the late-eighth-century Mont-Blandin manuscript (if it ever was in regular use), since it occurs in none of the other *Sextuplex* manuscripts. Its transmission to the Beneventan region may thus antedate the composition of the Mont-Blandin antiphoner.[103]

This last item merits special attention because of a highly important forthcoming study by Kenneth Levy which adds much to our knowledge of the transmission of Gregorian chant to southern Italy. Levy has discovered another northern witness of the Pentecost offertory *Factus* in Paris, Bibliothèque Nationale, MS lat. 9448, a gradual-troper from Prüm of about 1000. On the basis of this neumed version he is able to make a strong argument for the arrival of Gregorian chant in southern Italy about 800, in a fully neumed version. Basing his discussion on a rich and wide background of Carolingian source materials, he concludes that a neumed version of Gregorian chant must have existed in the later eighth century.[104]

This is entirely consonant with the evidence we have of the liturgical archaisms in the Beneventan south. Until Levy's study, however, there was no clear evidence that the Gregorian liturgy arrived at Benevento with neumes. The written nature of the melodic transmission, however, is consistent with the fact that the Beneventan-Gregorian manuscripts (though themselves of later date) preserve details of melodic style characteristic of the earliest surviving musical sources, resisting the changes that characterize later transmission elsewhere, either through provincial fidelity or simply by preserving a received written tradition.[105]

Evidently, then, the Gregorian chant did not arrive at Benevento at the end of the tenth century, for it would not have preserved the many archaic features we have seen: the early liturgical lacunae would have already been filled, and the Beneventan manuscripts for these feasts

---

[100] See PM XIV, 238–40; sources are listed there in the table on pp. 220–1.

[101] It is omitted without mention in the Sextuplex manuscripts: see *Sextuplex*, pp. 52–3.

[102] PM XIV, 241–2 and table, pp. 220–1.

[103] This offertory is the subject of an extensive study by Hesbert ("Un antique offertoire"), who however was not aware of the offertory's presence in Walters 6.

[104] Levy, "Charlemagne's Archetype." An important additional piece of evidence adduced by Levy is the absence of any vestiges of the Carolingian "Missa graeca," widely known in the north from the ninth century, but of which no trace survives in the Beneventan region. I am grateful to Professor Levy for letting me study his paper before its publication.

[105] A substantial study of melodic archaisms in Beneventan transmission of Gregorian chant is in PM XIV, 153–213.

would match versions found throughout Europe. But there are so many liturgical features that had disappeared elsewhere by the end of the eighth century and the early years of the ninth that a Gregorian liturgy including these features must already have been present before these changes took place elsewhere. The Gregorian chant must have been in place in southern Italy by the end of the eighth century.

The arrival of Gregorian chant in its surviving form dates from the time of the Carolingian incursions into southern Italy in the later eighth century. Exactly how this Gregorian influence came to southern Italy, how it was received, and how it gradually overshadowed the Beneventan chant, will probably never be fully explained. But, as a paradigm of Frankish influence on the church – perhaps, indeed, as a direct cause – we cannot overlook the career of the eminent Paul the Deacon.

Paul, the famous historian of the Lombards, an important poet and teacher, is also a significant figure in eighth-century liturgical matters. He is credited with assembling a liturgical homiliary,[106] and was connected with the mass-book that Charlemagne requested from Pope Hadrian I.[107] He is likely to have had further liturgical influence as well on the "Gelasian Sacramentary of the eighth century."[108]

After his years at the Lombard court of Pavia, Paul was a significant presence at the court of Benevento from 763 to 774; his *Historia Romana* was undertaken at the request of his pupil, Arichis' consort Adelperga (the daughter of King Desiderius), to whom he dedicated an elaborate acrostic verse.[109] His verses in praise of Arichis and the prince's epitaph indicate Paul's devotion to the court of Benevento and its ruling couple.[110]

After Pavia fell in 774, Paul became a monk of Montecassino, where he remained until his death in 799 (except for three years at the court of Charlemagne (782–5/6)). Thus, he was associated closely both with the Carolingian world and with the centers of primary importance to southern Italy in this period.[111]

We cannot be certain that Paul himself was the intermediary of the Roman rite in the south, but his career exemplifies the cultural currents which brought the Gregorian liturgy from the Carolingian north to the Lombard south. And when we consider the Lombard saints of Benevento we cannot fail to notice the coincidence: the Twelve Brothers in 760 have a Beneventan mass; St Mercurius, brought to Benevento in 768, has none[112] – the arrival of Paul the Deacon in 763 falls between the two.

When Paul moves to Montecassino, that great abbey begins its active role as the recognized fountainhead of Western monasticism, its practices are studied as models, and perhaps under his

---

[106] Leclercq, "Tables pour l'inventaire," pp. 205–14; Grégoire, *Les Homéliaires*, pp. 71–114.

[107] Gamber, "Heimat und Ausbildung," pp. 128–9.

[108] Gamber, "Heimat und Ausbildung," esp. pp. 109–12; an Italian translation is Gamber, "Il sacramentario di Paolo Diacono;" see also Mohlberg, "Note su alcuni sacramentarii," pp. 151–4.

[109] Edited in MGH SS Lang., pp. 13–14; and in Neff, *Die Gedichte*, pp. 9–10.

[110] Edited in Neff, *Die Gedichte*, pp. 15–18, 145–9.

[111] On Paul's activities at Benevento and Montecassino see Chron. mon. cas., I, 15; Chron. salern., pp. 10–13, 22, 24–5; Bloch, "Montecassino's teachers," pp. 567–72.

[112] On liturgical materials for St Mercurius, see Chapter 3, p. 72.

influence it begins a rapprochement with the liturgy of Rome. Beginning in the later eighth century a series of *ordines* and letters relate the practices of Montecassino.[113]

That Montecassino had long-standing ties with Rome cannot be doubted, but liturgical connections can be verified only from Carolingian times. In the period between the Lombard destruction of Montecassino in 568/9 and its refounding by Petronax of Brescia in 717/18 the monks are reported to have resided in Rome under the protection of the Pope; but in fact very little is known about this period of Cassinese history.[114]

Our knowledge of the history of Gregorian chant usage is not much clearer. No complete musical manuscripts from Montecassino survive from before the age of Abbot Desiderius in the later eleventh century.[115] Our earliest liturgical information is from letters and *ordines* of the later eighth century – from the time, that is, of Paul the Deacon. A letter of Abbot Theodemar to the Emperor Theoderic (778–97) repeatedly indicates Montecassino's fidelity to the Roman church.[116] The same fidelity to Rome is expressed in a letter of Theodemar to Charlemagne (though this document is thought by some to date only from the ninth century), and in some sources this letter is actually labeled as "dictated" (*dictata*) by Paul the Deacon.[117] The late eighth-century Montecassino *ordo officii* suggests that the abbey follows Roman practice,[118] and a version of its text from the ninth century is full of liturgical details which make this clear.[119]

These Montecassino documents are all written to provide outsiders with information about the practices of the abbey; they are for external use, and perhaps for that reason state the case for Roman fidelity as strongly as possible. That the Gregorian chant was used at Montecassino seems certain. What is equally clear, but not mentioned, is that the Beneventan chant was used there also; we shall see the evidence shortly.

Though Montecassino was aware of the importance of Charlemagne and his desire for litur-

[113] Many of these are gathered in Hallinger, *Corpus consuetudinum*, I, replacing in large part the edition of Albers, *Consuetudines monasticae*, III; the latter, however, includes some documents not in Hallinger.

[114] See Paul, HL in MGH SS Lang., pp. 122 and 178–9; Chron. mon. cas., I, 2, 4; *Gregorii magni dialogi*, pp. 106–8.

[115] For a chronological survey of the liturgical manuscripts preserved at Montecassino see Avagliano, "I codici liturgici." Of some 120 liturgical manuscripts now at Montecassino, no complete missal, antiphoner, or gradual survives from before the Desiderian period. There are sparse musical notations in such earlier manuscripts as Montecassino 230 and 446, and fragments of an eighth-century palimpsest uncial mass-book in MS 271 (see Dold, *Vom Sakramentar* and Chavasse, "Les fragments"). Surviving lectionaries, homiliaries, and sermons in Beneventan script are no older than the eleventh century. A mid-tenth century version of a Cassinese *ordo officii*, written in Capua, is preserved in MS 175 (edited in Hallinger: see below, p. 30). This is perhaps the earliest precise information on liturgical practice at Montecassino (excluding, of course, the Rule of St Benedict).

A convenient survey of liturgical manuscripts in the region is in Gamber, CLLA, pp. 238–58 (nos. 430–99); 465–7 (nos. 1170–9), 571 (no. 1593), 573–4 (no. 1599). From about the same early period (tenth–eleventh century) are several missals and fragments of missals, mostly without notation, see nos. 431–4.

[116] "Nec ambiguus Romanum apud Gallias morem tam per singulas ecclesias quamque et monasteria in officiis et lectionibus, sicut et nos facimus, teneri" (Hallinger, *Corpus consuetudinum*, I, p. 129); "Reliqua vero officia secundum morem Romanum explemus" (p. 130); ". . . explentes omnia ordine Romano" (p. 130); "Unde et nos . . . Romanam in legendis veteris ac novi testamenti per ordinem libris consuetudinem sequimur" (p. 132); etc.

[117] Hallinger, *Corpus consuetudinum*, I, 157; on date, attribution, and authenticity see pp. 152–4, the text is edited on pp. 157–75.

[118] The *ordo* is edited in Hallinger, *Corpus consuetudinum*, I, 105–23. An earlier *ordo* of the eighth century (edited in Hallinger, pp. 93–104) gives too little liturgical detail to be useful here.

[119] This second version is edited in Hallinger as text C, pp. 113–23. The second version does, however, name a Maundy Thursday antiphon (*Dum recubuisset Dominus Ihesus*) that survives only with a Beneventan melody and another (*Dominus Ihesus postquam cenabit*) that may have been sung to its Beneventan melody. See Hallinger, p. 117.

gical reform[120] and the adoption of Gregorian chant as a uniform standard, it was equally concerned, as we shall see, with preserving the Beneventan chant. The eleventh-century musical miscellany Montecassino 318 includes a unique poem chronicling the triumph of Gregorian over "Ambrosian" chant[121] by means of a musical ordeal. It describes Charlemagne's decree and its effects in Italy:

The eminent Karolus ordered all the holy churches everywhere to sing the Roman song; whereupon throughout Italy there arose much contention, and the status of the holy church was everywhere in mourning.[122]

The poem goes on to describe an ordeal in which two boys, one representing Gregorian and the other "Ambrosian" (for which we should read "Beneventan") chant, engaged in a singing duel; the youthful Ambrosian representative was so outsung that he collapsed.

A "sententia" which accompanies this poem is rather sympathetic to the threatened "Ambrosian" chant:

it is not to be understood in such a way that the Ambrosian chant is to be despised, but by God's favor, the Roman chant is to be preferred, for brevity and the disdain of the people.[123]

This poem itself may date from the eighth century; at least it relates an eighth-century problem at Montecassino. And at least one scholar, Ambrogio Amelli, who first noticed it, was inclined to attribute the poem itself to Paul the Deacon.

This musical conflict may have had political overtones. Conflicting Frankish and Lombard parties existed in ecclesiastical institutions: the great Ambrose Autpert, the Frankish abbot of San Vincenzo, was harassed by a pro-Lombard faction in his monastery.[124] Northern influence is to be seen also at Montecassino, Santa Sofia, and other monasteries, which accepted the patronage of Charlemagne and a long series of northern emperors, though we shall see that Lombard influence was strong there as well.

As a result of the Carolingian urge to uniformity, the Gregorian chant arrived in southern Italy probably in the later eighth century. But the Beneventan chant was tenaciously preserved by a few conservative scribes until the middle of the eleventh century when, as we shall see, it was definitively eradicated. How did the two chants co-exist from the eighth until the eleventh century? Were they used in different places? Was the region in which the Beneventan chant was

[120] On Carolingian liturgical reform, see Vogel, *La Réforme cultuelle*, "Les échanges", and "La réforme liturgique".
[121] Ambrosian is, of course, the regional name for the Beneventan chant. See Chapter 5, pp. 181–2.
[122] "Insignis Karolus romanum pangere carmen/ Omnibus ecclesiis iussit ubique sacris:/ Unde per italiam crevit contemptio multa,/ Et status ecclesie luxit ubique sacre." (MC 318, p. 244.) The *Versi Gregorii, Ambrosii, Karoli, Pauli de canto romano vel ambrosiano* were published in Amelli, "L'epigramma" (with a facsimile), and in Cattaneo, *Note storiche*, pp. 23–6. The translations here and below owe much to Francis Newton, who has discussed this poem with me and generously shared his preliminary translations. For further discussion of the poem, see Chapter 5, p. 182.
[123] "Non est ita intelligendum ut cantum ambrosianum abominandus sit; set annuente deo, romanus cantus est preferendus pro brevitate et fastidio plebis" (p. 245).
[124] Autpert was elected abbot of San Vincenzo by its Frankish party in 777, while the Lombard monks elected Potone. A nationalistic controversy ensued, and Autpert abandoned his office in 778. After being called to Rome, with others, by Hadrian I to clarify the matter of Potone's being accused of infidelity to Charlemagne, he died in 781. See MGH Epistolae, III, pp. 594–7; Del Treppo, "Longobardi"; Falco, "Lineamenti", esp. pp. 463–9.

used small, or the individual churches few? Were there churches with separate rites, like the Greek churches of medieval southern Italy? Or was the Beneventan liturgy never more than a fragment, used only for the few feasts for which music survives?

We cannot be certain: the existence of the Beneventan chant is precarious in our written documents. But the two were evidently used sometimes in the same place. The rubric in Vat. Ottob. 145 suggests a choice: "Likewise when we do not sing these antiphons according to the Roman rite, as they are written above, we sing them according the Ambrosian, in this manner."[125] And the scribe of Vat. lat. 10673 is probably not speaking of vanished rites when he uses a hortatory subjunctive for each: "The reading *Hec est hereditas* which is placed fifth according to the Roman rite is to be read here; according to the Ambrosian it is to be read after the blessing of the candle."[126] Both rites exist, evidently as separate complete liturgies which are known and practiced by the same scribe; there is no evidence of a distinct "Ambrosian" clergy, or of separate churches where only the local rite is practiced.[127] It is the attempt to amalgamate the two rites that produces our chief surviving sources of Beneventan chant, and it is that same attempt that eventually results in its capitulation.

THE DECLINE OF BENEVENTAN CHANT

The history of Beneventan chant after the eighth century is one of gradual decline in favor of the Gregorian chant. The course of the ninth and tenth centuries saw the weakening of the city of Benevento and a rise in the importance of the Roman church in Lombard lands. Both these facts contributed to a decrease in the use of Beneventan chant – and doubtless also engendered the tenacious conservatism which preserved at least a part of it into the eleventh century.

Benevento in the ninth and tenth centuries

The assassinations of the Beneventan princes Grimoald IV (817) and Sicard (839) led to a ten-year civil war which ended only in 849, with the intervention of Louis II (son of the Emperor Lothar), by a division of the duchy between Sicard's *thesaurius* Radelchis at Benevento and Sicard's brother Siconolf at Arichis II's fortified second capital of Salerno.[128] Political divisions, here and among the many nobles in the area of Capua, evidently did not result in a dilution of the Lombard consciousness. The rulers of Benevento and Salerno both used the title *Langobardorum gentis princeps*,[129] and Bishop Landolf of Capua proposed to Louis II that Capua be made an archbishopric of "all Benevento"; by this he presumably intended Capua

---

[125] Item quando non canimus ipse a[ntiphone] secundum romano, quo modo supra scripte sunt canimus secundum ambro[siano] hoc modo (f. 124). See Boe, "A new source".

[126] Lectio hec est hereditas que quinta est ordinata secundum romanum legatur hic: secundum ambrosianum legatur post benedictionem cerei (f. 34–34v).

[127] Though the church of Santa Sofia in Benevento seems to have a special place in the Beneventan rite. See pp. 13–15.

[128] See *Radelgisi et Siginulfi divisio ducatus Beneventani* in MGH Leges, IV, 221–5. Chron. salern., pp. 86–7; Cilento, *Le origini*, p. 86–97.

[129] Garms-Cornides, "Die langobardischen Fürstentitel", pp. 400–1.

to have ecclesiastical dominance over all Lombard territories of the south, however divided politically.[130]

In the civil war of succession both Siconolf and Radelchis had recourse to Arab mercenaries. But the Arabs were not to remain in the service of the Lombards; they ravaged and pillaged widely, and gained a strong base in Puglia, where they established an emirate at Bari.[131] Louis II's expedition succeeded in liberating Benevento from an Arab garrison and in ending the civil war, but not in removing the Arab threat. Prince Adelchis (853–78)[132] acknowledged the continuing devastation in the writing of his laws,[133] and a joint appeal from him, the Capuans, and the abbots of Montecassino and San Vincenzo, resulted in a new expedition from Louis II which dragged on from 866 until, finally, the capture of Bari in 871. However, when Louis tried to assert his authority at Benevento the ungrateful Adelchis, with a characteristic resentment of Frankish domination, took the Emperor prisoner at Benevento, releasing him after forty days only upon his promise not to take revenge on the Beneventans.[134]

Anti-Frankish sentiment among the Lombards was as strong in the ninth century as it had been in the eighth. Adelchis, in the prologue to his *capitula* (enacted *c.* 865–6), makes it clear that Charles, "King of the Franks" (*not* Emperor), was the usurper of the Lombard kingdom, and that the Catholic and magnificent Arichis governed with honor what remained of his people.[135] And the ninth-century "Chronicle of Salerno" proudly reports of Arichis' son Grimoald that "the powerful King of the Franks could not make him bow before him."[136]

Benevento in these years was also at odds with Pope John VIII (872–82), to whom Charles the Bald had conceded sovereignty over the Lombard states of the south,[137] and whose energetic policy against the infidel was matched by his zeal for imposing pontifical authority in the Lombard south.[138] It is no surprise that Adelchis, the enemy of Emperor and Pope alike, turned to the more distant (and less threatening) East, pledging in 873 the tribute which formerly had been owed (but not always paid) to the Franks.[139]

Inserting themselves into the void left by the departure of Louis II, the Byzantines gradually reconquered the Arab-held lands of southern Italy, though they did not prevent the Arab

---

[130] Erchempert: "Per idem tempus iam dictus cesar (Louis II) Landulfum in familiaritatem alliciens, tertium in regno suo constituit; qua elatione innexus, archiepiscopatum totius Beneventi omni aviditate, et ut Capua metropolis fieret, quaesivit" (MGH SS Lang., p. 248). Landolf, who ruled religious and secular life at Capua from 863 to 879, did not get his wish. Capua, like Benevento, was not to become an archbishopric until the middle of the next century.

[131] See Musca, *L'emirato di Bari*.

[132] The son of Radelchis, he succeeded his brother Radelgar (851–3).

[133] ". . . quos iam infestatio multarum gentium valde opprimit, quae nostros concives conterere et dissipare non desinunt, plurimas nostrorum villas oppidaque cremantes et disperdentes." MGH Leges, IV, 210.

[134] Erchempert, MGH SS Lang., p. 247.

[135] "Carolus Francorum rex . . . regnum Italiae gentemque Langobardorum suo imperio subdidit . . . ducatum tunc Beneventi gubernabat Arechis dux, per omnia catholicus atque magnificus; qui imitator existens maiorum, suae gentis reliquias rexit nobiliter et honorifice." MGH Leges, IV, 210.

[136] Chron. salern, p. 32; see also Gay, *L'Italie méridionale*, p. 106: "Il est remarquable de voir quelle force avait gardée, dans cette petite cour de Bénévent, l'orgueil national lombard, et combien les souvenirs de la fin du VIIIe siècle, du temps ou Didier et Arichis luttaient contre Charlemagne, étaient encore vivants."

[137] MGH Scriptores, III, 722.

[138] Gay, *L'Italie méridionale*, pp. 114–18.

[139] MGH Scriptores, I, 495–6.

destruction of the great Benedictine monasteries of San Vincenzo (881) and Montecassino (883). Their progress was not hindered by the outbreak of civil wars in Campania. With Benevento ruled by the young Ursus (891–2), a Byzantine army under the *strategos* Simbatikios occupied Benevento and Siponto, and formed the Byzantine province of *Longobardia*, ruled by a series of *strategoi* from the palace at Benevento.[140]

The Byzantine occupation of Benevento for three years was a time of imperial domination close at hand, and it was detested by the Beneventans.[141] But by 895, with the help of the Duke of Spoleto (who himself ruled Benevento until 897), the last of the Byzantine troops were forced from the Lombard capital.[142] Radelchis II returned to rule Benevento (897–900), and as his successor the Beneventans chose his brother-in-law Atenolf the Count of Capua (900–10). The duchies of Benevento and Capua remained united until 982, and Atenolf's descendants ruled at Benevento until the coming of the Normans in the eleventh century.

After the joint effort of Lombards and Byzantines definitively defeated the Arabs at the Garigliano in 915, the Lombard principalities enjoyed relative stability in the early decades of the tenth century, under the continual presence of the Byzantines, who held Puglia and ruled the theme of *Longobardia* from their administrative capital at Bari. Lombard princes acknowledged Byzantine sovereignty, and eastern influence in social and cultural matters seems to have been on the increase: the princes sought and received imperial titles;[143] many court documents are dated with the year of the reign of the eastern Emperor;[144] the monks of San Vincenzo and Montecassino, restored to their monasteries after the Arab destructions, received charters from the east;[145] and personal contacts were frequent.[146]

It is worth noting that, so far as we can tell, the Byzantines made no effort to impose Greek ecclesiastical constitutions and customs on the Western church;[147] the charters of Greek rulers to the monasteries of San Vincenzo and Montecassino include a formula forbidding the introduction of new customs.[148]

---

[140] Gay, *L'Italie méridionale*, pp. 144–5, 147–9; von Falkenhausen, *La dominazione*, pp. 31–41.

[141] "Illi [Greci] tamen valde etenim durum gerebant de moris Grecorum"; Chron. salern., p. 150. The most vivid denunciation of the Byzantines at Benevento is in the *Catalogus regum langobardorum* in MGH SS Lang., p. 496.

[142] MGH SS Lang., p. 496; Chron. salern., pp. 150–2; Gay, *L'Italie méridionale*, pp. 149–50; on the period see Bertolini, "Longobardi e bizantini."

[143] Guaimar I of Salerno, after a personal visit to Constantinople, in 887 was officially recognized by the Emperors Leo VI and Alexander; he was given the title of imperial *patrikios* (*Cod. dipl. cav.*, I, 139, 147, 159, etc.; von Falkenhausen, *La dominazione*, p. 23, and n. 32); Atenolf I of Capua-Benevento sent his son and co-regent Landolf I to Constantinople in 910 to propose joint efforts against the Arab base on the Garigliano; also, the title of *patrikios* was conferred on him and on his brother Atenolf II (the latter probably intended for Atenolf I, who died before Landolf's return); see Deér, "Zur Praxis," pp. 7–18; Garms-Cornides, "Die langobardischen Fürstentitel," pp. 406–11.

[144] Von Falkenhausen, *La dominazione*, p. 35, and n. 62.

[145] Chron. vult., II, 77–9; Trinchera, *Syllabus*, no. 2, p. 2.

[146] Von Falkenhausen, "I longobardi," p. 276, and *La dominazione*, pp. 35–6.

[147] The only evidence to the contrary is the effort of the *patrikios* Georgius, shortly after the conquest of Puglia, to have a Greek elected bishop at Taranto – an effort strongly opposed by Pope Stephen V: see MGH Epistolae, VII, 343–4, nos. 18–19; IP IX, pp. 435 and 437, nos. 5, 6.

[148] A document from the *patrikios* Georgius, written in 893 from the [ducal] palace of Benevento to the abbot of San Vincenzo and the provost of St Peter's, Benevento (a dependency of San Vincenzo), includes: "Et nullus homo presumat . . . quamlibet novam consuetudinem super eosdem monachos, et eorum monasteria, et in omnibus eorum pertinenciis inducere, aut facere. . ." (Chron. vult., II, 23). The same formula is used for Montecassino by the *strategos* Simbatikios in a document of the previous year (Trinchera, *Syllabus*, no. 3, pp. 2–3).

Thus Benevento was weakened and reduced by the partition of the duchy in 849, and by the loss of Puglia to Byzantium. After the union of Benevento with Capua the region was ruled mostly from Capua throughout the tenth century. Benevento, the ancient capital, became a provincial city of the second rank.[149]

The church at Benevento in the ninth and tenth centuries

As the political power of the capital waned that of the church increased. We can trace this in the relics of the local saints. Robbed from Naples about 831, the body of St Januarius, who was identified with a historical bishop of Benevento,[150] was brought to Benevento by Duke Sico.[151] His relics were interred first in the church of St Festus, and later transferred to the church of "Hierusalem," said to have been the seat of the early bishops of Benevento before the cathedral of St Mary.[152] Though patron of the ducal family,[153] he was a bishop, and connected more with the cathedral than with the court church of Santa Sofia. Liturgical material for St Januarius is not abundant, and none of the chant is in Beneventan style.[154]

A few years later in 838, the relics of the apostle St Bartholomew were brought to Benevento, and the feast of his translation entered the calendar the following year.[155] His remains, which were to rest at Benevento until 1000, were interred in a church adjoining the cathedral,[156] and Bartholomew became the chief saint of the city and a second patron of the cathedral.[157] A mass for St Bartholomew, in Gregorian style, is unique to Beneventan manuscripts,[158] but no Beneventan music survives.

The cult of St Barbatus, although he was a seventh-century bishop of Benevento, seems to have gathered strength only in the early ninth century.[159] He was not "invented," like the Twelve Brothers and Mercurius, nor stolen, like Sts Januarius and Bartholomew. He was a local saint who had long been venerated, but the resurgence of his cult in the ninth century was related in part to his being a bishop. The ninth-century *vita*, in addition to crediting him with turning back the Byzantines in 663, justifies an anomalous situation in the organization of the church – namely that the diocese of Siponto, which included the sanctuary of St Michael the Archangel on Monte Gargano, had long been subordinated to the diocese of Benevento without

---

[149] Von Falkenhausen ("I longobardi," p. 274), working from Poupardin, *Les Institutions*, notes that three-fourths of the official acts of the tenth-century Lombard court originate in Capua.

[150] "Nativitas sci Ianuarii Beneventane civitatis episcopi": in the Santa Sofia martyrology London, BL, Add. MS 23776, f. 25v.

[151] Chron. mon. cas., I, 20; Chron. salern., p. 58; see Sico's epitaph in MGH Poetae, II, 649–51; BHL 4115–19 (AA SS September VI, pp. 866–70), 4140 (AA SS September VI, pp. 888–90); for a general account of Januarius see Mallardo, "San Gennaro."

[152] AA SS September VI, p. 889.

[153] Januarius is cited as intercessor in a number of funeral inscriptions for members of the ducal family, see MGH Poetae, II, 658–60.

[154] See Chapter 3, pp. 72–3.

[155] The date is reported in many sources: see Bertolini, "Gli *Annales Beneventani*," p. 114. The date of Bartholomew's translation is, however, often given as 808: see PM XIV, pp. 450–1; and Baroffio, "Liturgie in beneventanischen Raum," p. 205.

[156] Meomartini, *I monumenti*, pp. 432–3, and plates LIX and LX; Zazo, "Benevento che fu"; and Intorcia in De Nicastro, *Benevento sacro*, pp. 267–76.

[157] Lehmann-Brockhaus, *Schriftquellen*, nos. 2120 and 2124; Belting, "Studien," pp. 162–4.

[158] Ben38, f. 103; Ben40, f. 83v; etc.

[159] At least his *vita* was composed then. On the dating of the life about 840 see A. Viscardi, *Storia*, pp. 385–7.

any papal ratification. The *vita*, by asserting that St Barbatus originated this arrangement, may have sought to justify a state of affairs that became increasingly awkward as the church of Benevento sought closer connections to Rome.[160]

The chronology of these ninth-century saints indicates a change of emphasis in the Beneventan church, a transition from the centrality of the court church of Santa Sofia to the cathedral, with its closer ties to Rome, and hence a transition from a local "Lombard" orientation to a liturgy which seeks to be in uniformity with the church at large. The Holy Twelve Brothers are martyrs found and translated by Arichis to the court church; St Mercurius is a Byzantine military saint likewise interred in Santa Sofia – these are the eighth-century patrons of the new Lombard principality. But the saints of the ninth century are different: they are connected with the cathedral and with the bishop. St Januarius is identified (wrongly) as an early bishop of the city, and is interred in the former cathedral; and St Bartholomew becomes the cathedral's second patron. This shift of emphasis, over less than a hundred years, from court-centered to church-centered cults is paralleled by the shift from composition in Beneventan style to Gregorian.[161]

The church of Benevento rose in power and independence from the court in the course of the ninth and tenth centuries.[162] As early as the time of Bishop Ursus (consecrated in 833) there was a school of grammar at the cathedral led by the bishop,[163] and a few years later comes a famous reference to the thirty-two *philosophi* of Benevento.[164] At the end of the century it was Bishop Petrus of Benevento who led the principality during a vacancy of the throne.[165] In the course of the tenth century a significant chancery existed at the cathedral,[166] and episcopal documents begin to use the Lombard epithet "in sacratissimo episcopio" for the episcopal residence.[167]

The summit of this growth is reached in 969, when Benevento is raised to a metropolitan archbishopric by Pope John XIII.[168] This event was not without its political motivation: it strengthened the church against Byzantine incursions in Puglia and served to further the purposes of Prince Paldolf of Capua-Benevento. As the center of power had by now passed from Benevento to Capua, it is not surprising that the first archbishopric in southern Italy (966 or 967) was that of Paldolf's capital Capua, nor that the first archbishop was the prince's brother.[169]

---

[160] MGH SS Lang., p. 560; see also Klewitz, "Zur Geschichte," pp. 5–6. The concern at Benevento in the early ninth century that the diocese of Benevento had usurped power over Siponto without papal ratification is reported in Chron. vult., I, 300.

[161] On the shift from court to cathedral, see Belting, "Studien," pp. 156–164.

[162] On the history of the Beneventan church see Bonnard, "Bénévent" and Klewitz, "Zur Geschichte," pp. 4–16.

[163] Lentini, "La grammatica," pp. 233–4; Morelli, "I trattati," pp. 287–91; Cavallo, "La trasmissione," pp. 367–9. On intellectual life at Benevento in the period see Belting, "Studien," pp. 167–8.

[164] Chron. salern., p. 134. See Lentini, as above, 218–19.

[165] See Chron. salern., p. 163; Gay, *L'Italie méridionale*, p. 149; Zazo, "Un vescovo."

[166] See Bartoloni, "Note di diplomatica," pp. 425–49.

[167] See the charter of Bishop Johannes (Bertolini, "I documenti," no. 27) in Ughelli, *Italia sacra*, X, cols. 506–7; and that of Bishop Landolf (Bertolini, no. 28), Ughelli, X, col. 507.

[168] IP IX, pp. 54–5, no. 15; Ughelli, *Italia sacra*, VIII, cols. 61–3; Klewitz, "Zur Geschichte", p. 8.

[169] Gay, *L'Italie méridionale*, p. 299. As Gay puts it, "ainsi Paldolf cherche à faire du clergé lombard l'auxiliaire de sa politique, tout en accordant a l'amour-propre des Bénéventains, jaloux de Capoue, une habile satisfaction" (p. 312); see also pp. 353–8.

These developments, related as they are to politics, show the cathedral's growing independence from the power of the princes at Benevento and its increased connection with Rome. That such developments may have had an effect on the use of Beneventan chant can be surmised. From shortly after this period come the earliest manuscripts which preserve the chant itself, and in them the local music is secondary to the Gregorian chant of the Roman church.

However, there were also entire books of Beneventan chant. The palimpsests at the Vatican, the Vallicelliana, and Montecassino, and the "ingressarium" of Abbot Theobald (see below), all show that separate books of Beneventan chant were made in the earlier years of the eleventh century. For whom were they intended? Did Santa Sofia use the Beneventan chant while the cathedral used Gregorian? Did Theobald imagine that the older chant might be preserved at San Liberatore, though it was too risky for use at the mother house? Were the duplicate masses in Benevento 38 and Benevento 40 intended for use in a separate place, a "Beneventan chapel," after the standard Roman mass was sung? We cannot be sure; we can only chronicle the existence of the two repertories simultaneously in the early documents, and try to understand them as elements of changing cultural patterns.

The suppression of Beneventan chant: Montecassino and Santa Sofia

The written history of the Beneventan chant is the history of its decline and suppression: palimpsests or fragments are our only evidence of the existence of complete books, and the surviving material decreases in quantity with the progress of time and proportionally with the distance of the sources from Benevento. This gradual disappearance is detailed in the examination of sources in Chapter 2. Here we shall consider the eradication of the Beneventan chant in the context of eleventh-century events by considering the relationship between what seem to be the two poles of the chant at the time: Montecassino and Santa Sofia.

Our musical sources make it clear that Beneventan chant was used at Montecassino:

1 A tenth-century *ordo qualiter agatur in parasceben* from Montecassino manuscript 175, pp. 587–8, describes a mixed Beneventan-Gregorian Good Friday rite, including the Latin versions of the three adoration antiphons used regularly at Benevento, and two Beneventan antiphons for vespers. These directions match very closely the rubrics of Lucca 606.[170]

2 An "Ambrosian" communion for St Benedict survives in a fragment in the Montecassino Compactiones XXII (see Appendix 3).

3 There are six Beneventan antiphons in Ottoboni 145, a book perhaps relating Montecassino to Santa Sofia (see Appendix 3).

4 Montecassino 361 preserves parts of a whole book of Beneventan chant, probably designed for use at Montecassino itself. The present manuscript is in the hand of Peter the Deacon, who was appointed librarian of Montecassino in 1131 or 1132.[171] In his untrained ordinary minuscule

---

[170] See Chapter 2, p. 44; and Appendix 3, under Lucca 606. The *ordo* is edited in *Bibliotheca casinensis*, 4:33–4; the material from Lucca 606 is presented in facsimile in PM XIV, plates XLI–XLIII.

[171] See Meyvaert, "The autographs," pp. 129 and 134, n. 1.

– unusual for Montecassino at the time[172] – Peter the Deacon copied works of classical authors, to which he added a series of his own works.[173]

The manuscript is important as the unique source of certain classical texts, as a fascinating paleographical document, and as the autograph of a complex personality whose fantasies and falsifications sought to increase the growing power and renown of his abbey.[174] But our interest here is not so much in Peter the Deacon's writings themselves as in what they cover, for in making this book the Cassinese librarian preserved pages of a discarded volume of music for the Beneventan liturgy (see Appendix 3). The presence of the feast of the Holy Twelve Brothers in this Cassinese manuscript makes a connection with Benevento, since these are the saints whose relics were interred in Santa Sofia.

5 The abbey of Santa Maria de Mare in the Tremiti Islands (22 kilometers north of the Gargano peninsula) was, as we shall see, a daughter house of Montecassino. Its thirteenth-century cartulary is now Vatican MS Vat. lat. 10657.[175] Four bifolia of the present manuscript are recycled leaves from an eleventh-century Beneventan gradual.

6 What may be a further volume of Beneventan chant (though it may also be among the manuscripts that survive) was commissioned by the monk Theobald, who became abbot of Montecassino in 1022. For much of his life Theobald was associated with the Cassinese dependency of San Liberatore at the foot of Mount Maiella in his native Abruzzi. When he was appointed to San Liberatore as provost (*praepositus*) about 1007, Theobald found it poor and dark, the buildings in bad repair.[176] He set about making improvements and furnishing the church with books, ornaments, and vestments. In his partly autograph *Commemoratorium*,[177] begun in 1019 and continued in subsequent years, Theobald details the objects that have been provided at his behest for San Liberatore.[178]

From the *Commemoratorium*, a rich source of detailed information, I want to draw attention to just three words from a tiny entry at the end of a "codicil" added to the original document after Theobald's election as abbot in 1022. The complete entry, added in a contemporaneous hand, is at the extreme bottom right of the document, and reads: "Et unum antifonarium de nocte qui dedit Iohannes diaconus et monachus, et unum ingressarium"[179] (see plate 3).

---

[172] Virginia Brown, in her *Hand List of Beneventan MSS* (volume 2 of TBS), says that this writing "is by a Beneventan scribe trying to write ordinary minuscule" (p. 84).

[173] For a full list of the contents see Inguanez, *Codicum Casinensium*, II, pars II, pp. 208–12. The volume in its present form represents only about a third of Peter's original manuscript, the structure of which has been largely reconstructed in Bloch, "Der Autor," pp. 105–27.

[174] On the subject of Peter the Deacon and his falsifications see Bloch, "Der Autor," pp. 61–6; Meyvaert, "The autographs"; Caspar, *Petrus Diaconus*, esp. pp. 19–21; and the Introduction to Rodgers, *Petri Diaconi Ortus*.

[175] See Chapter 2, source 2.

[176] See Carusi, "Intorno al *Commemoratorium*," p. 182.

[177] The document is Montecassino, Archivio della Badia, Aula II, capsula CI, fasc. I, no. I. It will receive a new number when it is catalogued by Don Faustino Avagliano for Leccisotti, *I regesti*. A complete facsimile and transcription are provided in Carusi, "Intorno al *Commemoratorium*."

[178] These aspects of Theobald's life are described in Chron. mon. cas., II, 12, 42, 52, 56–8. See also Bloch, "Monte Cassino's teachers," pp. 577–8; and Gay, *L'Italie méridionale*, pp. 423–25, 438–41.

[179] The order of these lines is not entirely clear. It appears, from the ink of the lowest line, which is now darker than those above it, and from the capital D aligned not only with the lines above but also with a line to the left, that the bottom line, "Duo pluviali . . .," comes first, moving up to "& unum antifonarium . . .," with, last of all, the words "& unum ingressarium" squeezed between the two lines. See Carusi, "Intorno", p. 187.

These last three words are intriguing. In a document full of references to books by type –
ymnuarium, antiphonarium, psalterium, passionarium, etc. – it would seem that an "ingressarium" is a book, and that it is the book that contains ingressae.[180] Now the ingressa is the
entrance chant of the Beneventan mass, so an ingressarium might be like a graduale: a book of
ingressae and other pieces necessary for the principal liturgy of the day. Models for such a book
have just been reviewed: the palimpsest pages of Montecassino 361, or the more complete
fragments from Vat. lat. 10657.[181] It is not impossible that one of these is the very book
ordered by Abbot Theobald.[182]

Whatever the exact nature of Theobald's volume, it seems that the future abbot of Montecassino caused a book of Beneventan chant to be copied for San Liberatore in the early years
of the eleventh century, and the music used at a dependent abbey was surely not unfamiliar at
the mother house.

Montecassino is evidently an important center of Beneventan chant, at least in the period
of music writing. Also, there is naturally a continuing relationship between Benevento and
Montecassino: as between the capital of a powerful duchy and the neighboring monastic
foundation whose influence led it to play an ever larger role in the politics of southern Italy in
these same years.[183]

We have seen the importance of the Lombards in the early history of Montecassino, and the
constant cultural, political, and ecclesiastical exchanges between Montecassino and Benevento in
this period: Paul the Deacon, the great eighth-century Lombard historian was a teacher at the
court of Benevento before entering Montecassino; St Peter in Civitate which was founded by
the wife of Duke Gisulf; the late-eighth-century Abbot Gisulf who was of noble Beneventan
birth; the Cassinese monk Erchempert, whose history of the Lombard reveals a fierce pride in
his people. To these we can add John of Benevento, abbot of Montecassino and friend of
Theobald; and the great Abbot Desiderius, a native of Benevento and monk of Santa Sofia.

But one ecclesiastical connection is perhaps most useful for tracing the Beneventan chant:
surviving chronicles and other historical documents show an important ongoing relationship
between Montecassino and the monastery of Santa Sofia.

To the church of Santa Sofia, Arichis II attached a convent of nuns, and it is this community
which forms a principal link with Montecassino. But there are two versions of this relationship.
Montecassino argues that Santa Sofia was, from its founding, subject to Cassinese authority;
while the surviving Beneventan materials argue for the independence of the local monastery.

[180] The term is also used in Milan, but Ambrosian books, to my knowledge, are rarely called ingressaria, and never before the
fifteenth century. See Huglo, Agustoni, Cardine, and Moneta Caglio, *Fonti e paleografia*, p. 72, no. 125. On the possibility that
this may be a book of Ambrosian chant, see Chapter 5, pp. 182–3.

[181] Or, just possibly, an ingressarium might be just what it says: a book of ingressae. We have a model for that also, in the palimpsest pages of Rome, Vallicelliana C 9 which include a substantial series of ingressae, presented without their masses.

[182] For the survival of books prepared under Theobald's direction see Bloch, "Monte Cassino's Teachers," pp. 577–8; TBS, I, 50;
and Lowe, *Scriptura beneventana*, plates 56–62.

[183] Discussions of the history of Montecassino during this period may be found in TBS, pp. 1–21; Bloch, MMA; Bloch, "Monte
Cassino, Byzantium"; and Caspar, *Petrus Diaconus*. The standard work is Gattola, *Historia*, with his *Ad historiam*. There is also
a history by Tosti, *Storia della badia*. The earlier history of the abbey is studied in Falco, "Lineamenti" and in Citarella,
The Ninth-Century Treasure.

Among the first to refer to Santa Sofia is the Cassinese monk Erchempert, whose *Historia longobardorum beneventanorum* was written about 890 while the monks of Montecassino were in exile in Capua:

And within the walls of Benevento Arichis founded a most sumptuous and seemly temple to God, which he called by the Greek name Hagian Sophian, that is, Holy Wisdom; and, establishing a convent of nuns supplied with very ample estates and various resources, he placed it to remain forever under the authority of blessed Benedict.[184]

When, around 1100, Leo Marsicanus came to quote this passage in his Chronicle of Montecassino,[185] he was careful to change what might have referred only to the rule of St Benedict and not to this foundation: he specified the dependency of the new nunnery by adding the words "in monte Casino":

Of this Arichis, master Erchempertus refers thus, in the history of the Lombard people, which he composed after Paul the Deacon . . . Within the walls of Benevento he founded a most sumptuous and seemly temple to God, which he called by the Greek name ΑΓΗΑΝ ΣΩΦΗΑΝ, that is, Holy Wisdom. And enriched with very ample estates and various resources, and establishing a convent of nuns, he conveyed it to continue forever under the authority of blessed Benedict *in Montecassino*.[186]

Santa Sofia is also mentioned by Leo in an earlier passage, in which the chronicler seems aware of a controversial point:

This same Gisulf began to build the church of Santa Sofia in Benevento. When, prevented by death, he was not able to complete it, Arichis, who succeeded him, wonderfully brought it to completion, and there establishing a convent of nuns, conceded it to the monastery of St Benedict, as we shall show in what follows.[187]

Leo goes on to assert that Charlemagne confirmed to Montecassino the possession of Santa Sofia in 787.[188] A copy of such a charter exists, but the original never did. Peter the Deacon, whose handwriting covers the Beneventan gradual of Montecassino 361, wrote a twelfth-

[184] "[Arichis] Infra Beneventi autem moeniam templum Domino opulentissimum ac decentissimum condidit, quod Greco vocabulo Agian Sophian, id est sanctam sapientiam, nominavit; dotatumque amplissimis prediis et variis opibus sanctimoniale coenobium statuens, idque sub iure beati Benedicti in perpetuum reddidit permanendum." MGH SS Lang., p. 236.

[185] The passage is quoted, in fact, through an intermediary – an addition to the *Chronica sancti Benedicti Casinensis* in Montecassino MS 363, printed in MGH SS Lang., p. 488.

[186] Italics mine. "De isto Arichis, ita refert domnus Herchempertus, in historia quam de Langobardorum gente post Paulum diaconum composuit. . . . Hic intra męnia Beneventi templum Domino opulentissimum ac decentissimum condidit, quod Greco vocabulo ΑΓΗΑΝ ΣΩΦΗΑΝ, idest sanctam sapientiam nominavit. Ditatumque amplissimis prediis, et variis opibus, ac sanctimonialium cęnobium statuens, id sub iure beati Benedicti in monte Casino tradidit inperpetuum permansuram." Chron. mon. cas., I, 9. Quoted here is the version of Munich, Bayerische Staatsbibliothek, MS Clm. 4623 (Hoffmann's MS A), a manuscript prepared under the supervision of Leo and preserving the earliest version of the chronicle. A marginal addition in this manuscript, inserted after the word *statuens*, reads: "germanamque suam ibidem abbatissam efficiens, cum omnibus omnino pertinentiis et possessionibus eius."

[187] "Iste Gisulfus cepit ędificare ecclesiam sanctę Sophię in Benevento. Quam cum morte preventus explere non posset, Arichis qui ei successit mirifice illam perfecit, ibique sanctimonialium cęnobium statuens, monasterio sancti Benedicti hic in Casino concessit, sicut in sequentibus ostendemus." Chron. mon. cas., I, 6; the last four words are added above the line in Leo's first version (Hoffmann's MS A). The founding of Santa Sofia by Gisulf, and its completion by Arichis, are chronicled also in the *Annales Beneventani*, edited in Bertolini, "Gli *Annales Beneventani*," pp. 110 and 111. Belting argues that the church was built entirely by Arichis; see "Studien," pp. 180–2.

[188] Chron. mon. cas., I, 12.

century continuation of Leo's Chronicle and, as a sort of companion volume, he assembled copies of charters relating to the possessions of Montecassino. This volume, the so-called Register of Peter the Deacon, is still at Montecassino,[189] and it contains many documents mentioned in the Chronicle. But a great many of these are pure fabrication, probably by Peter himself, to justify and glorify the house of St Benedict in the unfortunate cases where no real charters happened to exist. The charter of Charlemagne mentioned in the Chronicle is just such a fabrication.[190] Peter also includes copies of Papal privileges from Nicholas I in about 860, confirming Santa Sofia as a possession of Montecassino (probably spurious),[191] from John VIII in 882 (possibly genuine),[192] and others.[193]

Why is the Chronicle so argumentative on this point? It seems clear that Arichis' original convent at Santa Sofia was indeed placed under the authority of Montecassino. We know that, in the ninth century, the convent at Santa Sofia was governed by provosts (*praepositi*) appointed by Montecassino; both the Chronicle and documents from Santa Sofia itself give us the names of some of them.[194] Abbots Bassacius (837–56) and Bertarius (856–63) of Montecassino built an oratory to St Benedict in Santa Sofia which was finished in 868.[195]

But the later ninth century brought invaders to both monasteries. Montecassino was sacked and destroyed by the Arabs in 883,[196] and the monks lived in exile in Teano and Capua until 949. During the subsequent Byzantine reconquest of the area, Benevento was besieged and occupied for three years (891–4).

A clear rupture between the two monasteries comes in the mid-tenth century. For one thing, the nuns of Santa Sofia are somehow replaced by monks. Rodelgarda, abbess in 938,[197] had by 953 been replaced by Abbot Leo;[198] we hear no more of provosts from Montecassino after a certain Iohannes in 945.[199]

The middle of the tenth century is evidently critical in the history of this relationship. From 943 an original document records the confirmation, by Princes Landolf I, Atenolf III, and Landolf III, of the possession of Santa Sofia to Abbot Balduin of Montecassino.[200] But at

---

[189] Regesto 3, see TBS, II, 94.

[190] MGH Diplomata, I, no. 158, pp. 213–16. On the falsifications in this diploma see Caspar, "Echte und gefälschte." See also Hoffmann, "Chronik und Urkunde," p. 105, no. 108, and p. 174.

[191] IP VIII, p. 125, no. 33. An eleventh-century copy of such a document is in the Archive of Montecassino (Aula III, capsula VII, no. 6); see Leccisotti, *I regesti*, I, pp. 223–4.

[192] IP VIII, p. 126, no. 37.

[193] For the series of privileges naming Santa Sofia in the register of Peter the Deacon see Bloch, MMA, I, 252–6.

[194] A document of 923 (Benevento, Archivio Storico Provinciale, Fondo Santa Sofia VIII.33) mentions "Antipertus presbiter et prepositus monasterii aecclesiae vocabulo Sanctae Sophiae (see Galasso, "Caratteri paleografici," p. 308); Chron. mon. cas., I, 39 names Pergolfus and Criscius. An early twelfth-century hand, now very faint, has added the names of several abbesses, abbots, and *praepositi* to the *annales* in Vat. lat. MS 4939. Among these are "Criscius prepositus erat" (868) and "Hoc tempore erat Criscius prepositus" (878), both on f. 11; "Iohannes prepositus" (945), f. 11v. See Bertolini, "Gli *Annales Beneventani*," pp. 116, 117, 121.

[195] MGH SS Lang., p. 471.

[196] Chron. mon. cas., I, 44.

[197] Rodelgarda is mentioned in documents of 923 (see Bertolini, "I documenti," p. 36, no. 139) and in the *Annales beneventani* for the year 938 (Vat. lat. 4939, f. 11v; Bertolini, "Gli *Annales Beneventani*," p. 121).

[198] "Leo abbas" is added to that year in Vat. lat. 4939, f. 12; see Bertolini, "Gli *Annales Beneventani*," p. 122.

[199] See note 194.

[200] Leccisotti, *Abbazia*, II, 70, no. 31; printed in Gattola, *Historia*, pp. 52–3.

almost the same moment the Beneventan monastery seizes the opportunity to assert its independence. Another original document of 945 gives specific details of a legal proceeding between the two abbots in the presence of Prince Landolf of Benevento. Each abbot was surrounded by his lawyers, and each presented in evidence as many charters, privileges, and other documents as he could assemble. After viewing stacks of conflicting evidence and examining the abbots, the judges noted that Montecassino's documents did not specifically name Santa Sofia, but merely reaffirmed, as so often such documents do, the monastery's rights to all its traditional possessions. They were aware of the historical authority of Montecassino at Santa Sofia through its provosts, but they declared that, since this power had not been exercised for forty years (that is, since shortly after the sack of Montecassino), it had effectively lapsed. And so, in the end, Magelpotus, abbot of Montecassino, was required to relinquish all control of Santa Sofia to Ursus, presumably its first abbot.[201]

The outcome of this case was surely inevitable in the circumstances. It was tried in the palace at Benevento before the prince, and it is hard to imagine that the adjoining court church and its monastery would be handed over to outside authority.

But the dispute was far from ended; both monasteries continued to accumulate documents – documents that reflect contemporary politics as much as they prove ecclesiastical possession.

Santa Sofia sought and received charters from the series of Holy Roman Emperors who made it their business to assert their authority in southern Italy.[202] With Montecassino under the influence of the Byzantine empire through the princes of Capua,[203] these imperial charters are perhaps more an assertion of imperial supremacy than an affirmation of ecclesiastical equity. In any case they are general confirmations of rights and possessions, with no specific reference to Montecassino.

But Montecassino was far from acquiescing to Santa Sofia's independence. Accepting, for their part, the protection of the Byzantine empire, the monks of Montecassino had obtained in June, 892, a privilege from Simbatikios, the imperial *protospatarius*, confirming their domains, including Santa Sofia, in Benevento.[204]

Montecassino went farther: it claims to have had the support of the Pope after the setback at the Benevento trial of 945, but while it is true that Pope Agapitus II helped the monks of Montecassino to regain possessions lost after the destruction of their abbey, it is equally true

---

[201] "Iudicabimus . . . ut amodo et deinceps perpetuis temporibus partem prephati cenovii sancte Sofie semper libera consistat cum suis pertinentiis et rebus hab omni condicione et subiectione atque dominatione a parte iamdicti monasterii sancti Benedicti. . ." The document is transcribed (with a facsimile as plates 5 and 6) in Galasso, "Caratteri paleografici," pp. 309–12; the passage quoted is on p. 311. This liberty was renewed later in the century by Abbot John III of Montecassino (998–1011) to Gregory of Santa Sofia. We know of Abbot John's renewal from the charters of Popes Benedict VIII in 1022 and Leo IX in 1052 (see notes 209 and 211 below).

[202] Abbot Azzo of Santa Sofia received charters confirming the abbey's independence from the Emperors Otto I in 972 (the original document, in the Archivio Storico Provinciale of Benevento, Fondo S. Sofia 11. 1 is reproduced and transcribed in Galasso, "Caratteri paleografici," plate 10, and pp. 314–16; from the copy in Vat. lat. 4939, f. 126v–128, it is printed in MGH Diplomata, I, no. 408, pp. 554–6) and Otto II in 981 (MGH Diplomata, II, no. 264, pp. 306–7). Otto III (999) confirmed the same privileges to Abbot Gregory (MGH Diplomata, II, no. 310, pp. 736–7).

[203] Bloch, MMA, I, 9–12 and "Monte Cassino, Byzantium," pp. 170–3.

[204] Chron. mon. cas., I, 49; Hoffmann, "Chronik und Urkunde," no. 136, p. 106. Edited in Leccisotti, *Le Colonie*, pp. 31–3; and in Trinchera, *Syllabus*, no. 3, pp. 2–3. See Gay, *L'Italie méridionale*, pp. 147–9.

that in her attempts to regain a lost "child," Montecassino was not above embroidering papal support by inventing documents from a friendly pontiff to establish her rights. As the Chronicle would have it, Abbot Balduin complained to the Pope that the monastery of Santa Sofia had been "violentia ab hac coenobio subtractum". The Chronicle further reports that in 946 (a year after the one-sided trial at Benevento) the Pope warned Atenolf, prince of Benevento-Capua, that he should not persist in keeping Santa Sofia;[205] a spurious document to this effect is recorded by Peter the Deacon.[206] And Atenolf's donation of Santa Sofia to Montecassino, recorded in Peter's *registrum*, is also spurious.[207]

The controversy intensified in the early eleventh century. In 1022 the Emperor Henry II invaded southern Italy to repulse the growing Byzantine influence, to which both Prince Pandolf of Capua and his brother Atenolf, abbot of Montecassino, had submitted.[208] Having re-established imperial authority at Benevento, both the Emperor and his ally Pope Benedict VIII provided diplomas of protection and independence to Abbot Gregory of Santa Sofia[209] – continuing Santa Sofia's collection of imperial diplomas, and surely displeasing the disloyal Atenolf of Montecassino.

From Benevento the Emperor proceeded by way of Capua to Montecassino. Abbot Atenolf had already fled the approaching imperial army of the Archbishop of Cologne and perished at sea. Henry pressured the monks into electing as abbot a suitable non-Capuan candidate, one of those who, many years before, had left the monastery rather than live under Abbot Manso of the house of Capua: Theobald, provost of San Liberatore.[210]

Thirty years later Santa Sofia's independence is confirmed by Pope Leo IX. A hostile Benevento had been excommunicated by Pope Clement II in 1051, but from fear of the Normans the Beneventans appealed to the Pope. Leo IX received the submission of the city, and confirmed by charter that Santa Sofia owed no allegiance except to the papacy, specifying that it should remain "liberum et immune ab omni subiectione ac iugo Casinensis monasterii."[211]

A year later (July 1053), the papal and imperial forces lost the crucial battle of Civitate to the Normans, effectively bringing the duchy of Benevento to an end after almost five centuries of Lombard rule.[212]

At the end of the century, reaching the apex of her power and influence, Montecassino continued her efforts, and continued to list Santa Sofia as a dependency,[213] but never regained

---

[205] Chron. mon. cas., I, 58.

[206] See IP VIII, pp. 128–9, no. 46; Hoffmann, "Chronik und Urkunde," no. II, p. 98, and, on its forgery, pp. 194–5; see also Böhmer, *Regesta II/5*, no. 203, p. 76.

[207] Hoffmann, "Chronik und Urkunde," no. 207, p. 114.

[208] Gay, *L'Italie méridionale*, pp. 417–19 and Chron. mon. cas., II, 38.

[209] Benedict VIII: Vat. lat. 4939, f. 139v; see IP IX, p. 82, no. 2. Henry II: Vat. lat. 4939, f. 132 and MGH Diplomata, III, no. 468, pp. 596–7; see Bertolini, "Gli *Annales Beneventani*," pp. 136–8.

[210] Gay, *L'Italie méridionale*, p. 424. Chron. mon. cas., II, 42; on Henry's intervention at Montecassino and Theobald's election, see Bloch, MMA, I, 15–17 and "Monte Cassino, Byzantium," pp. 173–5; Hirsch, *Jahrbücher*, pp. 198–210. Henry's charter to Montecassino is in MGH Diplomata, III, no. 474, pp. 603–4.

[211] Vat. lat. 4939, f. 141v; IP IX, p. 83, no. 5.

[212] Chron. mon. cas., II, 81–2, 84; Gay, *L'Italie méridionale*, pp. 477–90.

[213] The name Santa Sofia is inscribed on the bronze doors of the basilica built by Desiderius. The panel naming Santa Sofia is the fourth from the bottom in the central column of the left door (after the restoration of 1951). On these doors see Bloch, MMA, I, 139–94; III, figs. 126–58 (the panel naming Santa Sofia is in figure 133); Bertaux, *L'Art*, pp. 163ff.

control of her erstwhile daughter house. The continuation of the controversy is fascinating in its detail,[214] but it goes far beyond the period of our discussion.

What does interest us is the recognition on both sides of some historical relationship between the two monasteries. The separation originated in the accidents of history, but its continuation reflects the political divisions which brought Montecassino increasingly into contact with the papacy, while Santa Sofia continued to represent Lombard independence, its symbolic importance increasing perhaps as the real significance of Benevento waned.

Santa Sofia is not the only monastery to dispute its independence with Montecassino in the eleventh century. There is a similar connection between Montecassino and the distant monastery of Santa Maria in the Tremiti Islands, the source of one of our palimpsest Beneventan graduals. The story sounds familiar: Montecassino claimed Tremiti as a dependency, while the latter protests its long-standing independence.[215]

Leo Marsicanus in the Chronicle makes a case for the possession of Tremiti when he writes of "The cloister of Tremiti, which a great many papal privileges show to have belonged to us from earliest times,"[216] and notes that Paul the Deacon, who had been a court teacher at Pavia and at Benevento before entering Montecassino, had been exiled to Tremiti by the Lombard king Desiderius.[217]

But Montecassino's position in this case seems to be a weak one: the earliest genuine papal document asserting Cassinese authority at Tremiti is one from Urban II, as late as 1097.[218] The abbey of Santa Maria, however, procured its own charters in the eleventh century (which are copied into the very cartulary which obliterates our Beneventan chant) affirming the monastery's liberty.[219]

We cannot be sure whether Tremiti originated as a cell of Montecassino. But in the eleventh century we know of significant exchanges of personnel between the two monasteries, despite their disagreement. One eminent visitor was Frederick of Lorraine, papal chancellor, envoy to

---

[214] Leo Marsicanus, the great Cassinese chronicler who regarded Santa Sofia as "violenter a dicione huius loci subducta" (Chron. mon. cas., IV, 48), was himself involved in seeking justice in 1078 from Pope Gregory VII (Chron. mon. cas., III, 42; IP VIII, p. 147, no. 112; Gregory VII himself confirmed Santa Sofia's independence in 1084 [Vat. lat. 4939, ff. 142v–145; IP IX, p. 85, no. 12]) and wrote a history of the case ("Breviatio de monasterio sanctae Sophiae in Beneventum et iudicium papae Urbani ex eo") which is preserved in the *Registrum* of Peter the Deacon (Hoffmann, "Chronik und Urkunde," no. 37, pp. 100; ed. Gattola, *Historia*, pp. 54–6). Repeated appeals from Montecassino to Pope Urban II (detailed by Leo in his *breviatio*: see Chron. mon. cas., IV, 7) and to Pope Pascal II in 1113 (Chron. mon. cas., IV, 48) and 1116 (Chron. mon. cas., IV, 60), failed to resolve the dispute. For a summary of the documentation relating Santa Sofia to Montecassino see Bloch, MMA, I, 264–72.

[215] On relations of Montecassino with Tremiti, see Leccisotti, "Le relazioni," pp. 203–15 and Gay, "Le monastère de Trémiti": on confusion between Santa Maria and Sancti Jacobi see Leccisotti, "Le relazioni," p. 207 and Caspar, *Petrus Diaconus*, pp. 11–14.

[216] "Tremitensis cenobii, quod nobis antiquitus pertinuisse Romanorum quoque pontificum privilegia pleraque testantur," Chron. mon. cas., III, 25.

[217] Chron. mon. cas., I, 15.

[218] IP VIII, p. 154, no. 141. See Caspar, *Petrus Diaconus*, p. 13 and Leccisotti, "Le relazioni," pp. 206–7.

[219] Tremiti was taken under imperial protection by Conrad II in 1038 (MGH Diplomata, V, no. 272, p. 377 and Petrucci, *Codice diplomatico*, II, pp. 68–70, no. 20); the privilege was renewed by Henry III in 1054 (MGH Diplomata, V, no. 323, p. 441; Petrucci, *Codice diplomatico*, II, pp. 163–6, no. 52). Pope Leo IX in 1053 likewise confirms the monastery's independence: IP IX, pp. 181–2, no. 1 and Petrucci, *Codice diplomatico*, II, pp. 156–8, no. 49.

Constantinople, future abbot of Montecassino and later Pope Stephen IX.[220] Frederick's successor as abbot of Montecassino, the great Desiderius, traveled to Tremiti in the early years of his monastic life. Originally a monk of Santa Sofia in Benevento, Desiderius remained at Tremiti for a substantial time, departing only when he was invited to share in the monastery's administrative duties.[221]

In the later eleventh century, at about the time that Montecassino was making her strongest efforts to regain Santa Sofia, this conflict too came to a crisis, and it was Desiderius who, with toilsome and repeated efforts, brought the dispute to a conclusion in which Tremiti ultimately gained its autonomy.[222]

These two eleventh-century conflicts, in which Montecassino attempted to control Santa Sofia and Tremiti, are characteristic of a period of great expansion in all areas of Cassinese life. But they also link three localities which used books of Beneventan chant – and the central link is Montecassino.

Montecassino evidently used the Beneventan chant in the eleventh century and communicated it to daughter houses, judging from the sources: the ingressarium of Theobald for San Liberatore, the palimpsest Beneventan gradual at Tremiti, and the manuscript used by Peter the Deacon to make Montecassino 361. Such documents come from the earliest layer of sources – for surely a whole manuscript of this chant precedes sources like Benevento 38 and 40, where Beneventan chant is supplementary to Gregorian.

But these three early sources, important as they are, were short-lived: they are all palimpsests – pages newly written in the eleventh century, but already useless in the twelfth, except as parchment.

In discussing sources of Beneventan chant, we inevitably deal with the eleventh century, the period in which this music is first written, and also that in which it is suppressed. The final victory of the Gregorian chant came only in the second half of the eleventh century, and in the case of Montecassino we can isolate a specific moment of crisis.

---

[220] Chron. mon. cas., II, 86; see note 228.

[221] Chron. mon. cas., III, 6.

[222] In his capacity as apostolic vicar for all of southern Italy under Nicholas II, Desiderius was ultimately charged by Alexander II in 1071 (IP IX, p. 183, no. 5) to proceed to the reform of the monastery at Tremiti. He deposed Abbot Adam and appointed the Cassinese monk Trasmundus; the monks revolted against this outsider, and were repressed with ruthless violence. Desiderius was forced to recall and depose his appointee. For some time relations were suspended between Desiderius and Ferro, whom Trasmundus had left in charge at Tremiti. Finally, an appeal by Desiderius to the Norman, Robert Guiscard, resulted in a military occupation that sent Ferro away and turned the monastery over to Desiderius. Guiscard was willing to accept the fealty of the monks, but would not guarantee their independence from Montecassino; to rule Tremiti he appointed first three monks of Montecassino, later replaced by a single overseer. This last also rebelled against Desiderius, and he too was ultimately deposed and returned to his abbot. An attempt to make Tremiti subject to the abbot of Terra Maggiora (Torremaggiore) failed at the latter's death. The ultimate solution, approved by Pope Gregory VII (who recognised Desiderius as "tutor et defensor" of Tremiti [IP IX, pp. 183–4, no. 6]), was to entrust the government of Tremiti to Ferro, who in turn would be responsible to Desiderius, but only during his lifetime, afterwards reporting to the Pope (see Chron. mon. cas., III, 25; Gay, "Le monastère de Trémiti," pp. 387–97; Petrucci, *Codice diplomatico*, I, pp. XI–XLIX; and Picasso, "Montecassino," pp. 45–8).

Thus Montecassino ultimately failed to gain control of Tremiti. Indeed, in 1081 (or 1082: see Petrucci, *Codice diplomatico*, II, p. 251), Desiderius himself relinquished all authority over Tremiti, giving full liberty to the monastery and to its abbot, Ungrellus. The document detailing this event is copied onto folio 9 of Vat. lat. 10657, the cartulary made in part from a Beneventan gradual. The document is printed in Petrucci, *Codice diplomatico*, II, pp. 250–3; from MS Naples XIV A 30 it is printed in Gay, "Le monastère," pp. 406–7; see also Leccisotti, "Le relazioni," p. 206.

In 1058 Pope Stephen IX visited Montecassino and strictly forbade the singing of "Ambrosianus cantus."[223] "Ambrosian," however, is the local name for the local chant. Beneventan chant is only labeled when it is found alongside Gregorian chant, and then it is always called "Ambrosian."[224] Possibly this represents a mistaken belief that it is identical with the Ambrosian chant of Milan, but the appeal to St Ambrose is also a means of legitimizing an endangered local repertory. It recognizes a Lombard heritage from the north, and it provides the authenticity and authority that the local music needed to compete for a place among the chants attributed to St Gregory the Great. What Pope Stephen forbids is the singing of the local Ambrosian chant: the music we now call Beneventan.

And when the Pope forbids Ambrosian chant he speaks from experience. Pope Stephen IX was Frederick of Lorraine, a northerner educated at Liège, and chancellor to Pope Leo IX, the first great representative of papal reform. Leo, detained for almost a year in Benevento after his defeat by the Normans, sent Frederick as one of the famous legation to Byzantium that produced the great schism of 1054. In 1055, fleeing the wrath of the Emperor Henry III, Frederick took refuge at Montecassino. He subsequently retired to Tremiti, probably seeking greater security from imperial prosecution.[225] He remained only a short time, but perhaps long enough to hear the singing of some "Ambrosianus cantus."

After the death in 1055 of Montecassino's first German abbot, Richerius of Niederaltaich,[226] the election of one of the oldest monks was overturned by Leo IX's legate, Cardinal Humbert, who oversaw the election as abbot of Frederick, his fellow ambassador to Constantinople.[227] Only a few weeks later Frederick himself was elected Pope, taking the name of Stephen IX.[228]

It is this German, Pope Stephen IX, the second northerner among the abbots of Montecassino, who forbade the singing of "Ambrosianus cantus" at Montecassino in 1058. Frederick had opportunities to hear the "Ambrosianus cantus" as it was sung at Montecassino, at Benevento, and indeed at Tremiti. Raised and trained in the north, an ecclesiastical reformer like his master Leo IX, and now Pope, it is easy to imagine how unsuitable, even barbaric, he found the singing of this local chant to be. And, from the point of view of an abbot of Montecassino, forbidding the chant at the mother house ought to silence the daughters as well.

Frederick's successor as abbot was his personal friend, and the future Pope Victor III, the great Desiderius (1058–87). For students of art and architecture, for paleographers and historians, the age of Desiderius marks the summit of Montecassino's fame and power, and her greatest artistic, literary, and cultural flowering. It is this same Desiderius who presided over the suppression of the Beneventan chant, for as Frederick's designated successor at Montecassino in 1058 he was responsible for enforcing the papal decree.

---

[223] "Tunc etiam et Ambrosianum cantum in ecclesia ista cantari penitus interdixit": Chron. mon. cas., II, 94.

[224] See Chapter 5, pp. 181–2.

[225] Chron. mon. cas., II, 86; Leccisotti, "Le relazioni," p. 204.

[226] Richerius was appointed by the Emperor Conrad II, at the request of the community, to re-establish imperial protection from Pandolf of Capua, who, supported by the Byzantine empire, had imprisoned Theobald and imposed his own servant as abbot of Montecassino. See Chron. mon. cas., II, 56–65; Amatus, *Storia de' Normanni*, II, 61–2; Desiderius, "Dialogi," I, 9; Bloch, MMA, I, 30–2 and "Monte Cassino, Byzantium," pp. 187–8.

[227] The dramatic story of this election is told in Chron. mon. cas., II, 88–92.

[228] Fuller discussions of Frederick's career and the events leading to his election as abbot and Pope can be found in Bloch, MMA, I, 30–40 and "Monte Cassino, Byzantium," pp. 189–93; Gay, *L'Italie méridionale*, pp. 509–11.

Desiderius, like Frederick of Lorraine, links Montecassino, Benevento, and Tremiti. Born at Benevento of noble parents, at an early age he became a monk of Santa Sofia, and traveled to Tremiti as a youth,[229] before entering Montecassino, like his friend Frederick, in 1055. We can imagine that Desiderius might have been less inclined to thoroughness than his northern predecessor in suppressing the local chant; it may in fact have been as familiar to him as Gregorian chant. Desiderius was, after all, a child of the region, and he may well have had the opportunity to hear and sing the Beneventan chant as a young monk of Santa Sofia, in his early travels to Tremiti, and indeed in his early years at Montecassino. Whatever his personal inclinations, however, by the height of Desiderius' abbacy the Beneventan chant had disappeared from Montecassino.

And so the Beneventan manuscripts of Montecassino became obsolete. Montecassino 361, the relatively new ingressarium of Abbot Theobald, and perhaps other manuscripts were no longer tolerated. Their best use was to serve as raw material for more modern matters. An occasional piece might be saved – a favorite communion for the founder, or a few votive antiphons. Many new liturgical books were made, and the old swept away: the Desiderian reform was so successful that no complete gradual or antiphoner survives from pre-Desiderian Montecassino.

Only the accidental survival of fragments gives us a hint of what music may have been like at Montecassino before the tumultuous events of the eleventh century effected their changes. In fact, the written history of the Beneventan chant begins so shortly before its suppression that, were the history of events only slightly rearranged, we might not even have suspected its existence. But the evidence does survive, and we may be sure that Montecassino sang this chant, and that as her influence increased she played an important role both in its dissemination and, later, in its suppression.

The Beneventan chant survived, in fragmented fashion, for a few years longer at Benevento, where (as we shall see in the next chapter) scribes, even in the twelfth century, sought to retain a few special elements for Holy Week, a few pieces disguised as antiphons.[230] But the gradual submission to the inevitable can be traced even at the former Lombard capital, and the chant of the Roman church eventually silences that of ancient proud Benevento.

---

[229] *Chron. mon. cas.*, III, 6.

[230] In a few sources Beneventan elements survive even later: the thirteenth-century missal Subiaco XVIII preserves Beneventan vespers for Good Friday and the Beneventan melody of the Exultet; Paris, Bibliotheque nationale, lat. 829, a fourteenth-century Capuan missal, retains elements of the Beneventan rite for Holy Saturday (see p. 90); Vatican MS Barb. lat. 697, a fourteenth-century ritual of Capua, retains the text of the scrutiny antiphon *Dum sanctificatus*; and a fifteenth-century missal of Salerno reportedly retains the Beneventan Exultet and its melody. See Appendix 3.

2

THE MANUSCRIPT SOURCES OF
BENEVENTAN CHANT

The manuscripts that preserve Beneventan chant are not many, and most of them are fragmentary, palimpsest, or record the survival of only a piece or two. Of formerly complete books of Beneventan chant, we have only partial remains. The sources, moreover, are not particularly early. The writing of Beneventan chant begins, so far as we know, only in the late tenth century, at about the same time as Gregorian chant.[1] Although our knowledge of the repertory must remain incomplete owing to the fragmentary nature of our sources, they can still tell us much about the survival of this chant, and of the manner in which it was eradicated, suppressed, and forgotten.

With this in mind the chapter that follows begins with a consideration of manuscript sources according to the place that the Beneventan chant occupies in the arrangement of the manuscript, for the scribe's understanding of this music tells us about its state of health and its possible corruption. Further information and full references for all these manuscripts are given in Appendix 3. Abbreviated forms of reference are used for manuscripts referred to both below and elsewhere.

MANUSCRIPTS CONTAINING BENEVENTAN CHANT

A first category consists of those manuscripts that, if only they were complete, would be our most reliable sources of Beneventan music; for although they are eleventh-century witnesses of a repertory undoubtedly much older, they nevertheless give evidence of integrity and completeness. They are books devoted exclusively to Beneventan chant, and hence do not face the problem of including forbidden music where it does not belong, with all the attendant conflicts and confusion. But these sources survive only because pieces of them were used to protect other more timely documents (no. 1 below), or as raw materials for the writing of more modern matters (nos. 2–4 below). The amount of music that can be recovered from these documents is

---

[1] What may be our earliest source, the Exultet of St Peter's *intra muros*, Benevento (Vat. lat. 9820), is palimpsest. Other early sources (the Bari benedictional, Ben33, Vat. lat. 10673), are generally thought to date from about the year 1000. Other early sources include the palimpsest Wolfenbüttel 112 and the peripheral Vat. lat. 4770. Early Gregorian noted missals include Baltimore, Walters 6; the fragments now in Zurich, Peterlingen, and Lucerne (Dold, "Umfangreiche" and Omlin, "Ein Messbuchfragment"); and those at the Vatican (Vat. lat. 10645, ff. 3–6). For surveys of early liturgical books in the region, see above, p. 18 and p. 23, note 115.

lamentably small. In the palimpsests we can only recognize pieces we know from mixed (and unerased) sources. But many rewritten pages, clearly Beneventan, but not quite decipherable, remain from a larger Beneventan repertory that has not come down to us.

1 (Ben35) Benevento, Biblioteca capitolare, MS 35, ff. 202–202v. A single page from an eleventh-century gradual of the Beneventan rite. It includes the end of a mass for Christmas (including parts of the ordinary) and the beginning of one for Saint Stephen, with no intervening Gregorian music.

2 Vatican MS Vat. lat. 10657. The thirteenth-century cartulary of the abbey of Santa Maria (Tremiti Islands); four bifolia, arranged in two fascicles, are re-used leaves of an eleventh-century Beneventan gradual, including music for Holy Week and for the masses of Peter and Paul and of John the Baptist.

3 Montecassino MS 361. The manuscript was written by Peter the Deacon, appointed librarian of Montecassino in 1131 or 1132. Many pages of an eleventh-century Beneventan gradual were re-used in its making. However, only a little Beneventan music can still be identified, including a Credo and propers for the Holy Twelve Brothers of Benevento, Sts Peter and Paul, and All Saints.

4 Rome, Biblioteca Vallicelliana, MS C 9. Many palimpsest pages from another eleventh-century Beneventan gradual are included in this twelfth-century manuscript. They include music for Holy Week and Easter, and a series of ingressae (apparently without their accompanying masses). Identified pieces are listed in Appendix 3.

5 Bari, Archivio del Duomo, benedictional roll. A decorated eleventh-century rotulus from Bari with benedictions of fire and water for use on Holy Saturday, including the related Beneventan antiphon *Omnes sitientes* and the tract *Sicut cervus*. Preserved because of its great beauty, this is the only surviving complete document that has no evidence of Gregorian chant.

6 Leningrad, Biblioteki Akademii Nauk SSSR, MS F. no. 200. This codex comprises an incomplete lectionary and a pontifical, both probably written in southern Italy near the beginning of the twelfth century but in early use in Dalmatia. Folios 78 and 83v, a bifolium, are from an earlier manuscript, apparently a missal, now palimpsest. Almost nothing of the lower script is readable, but the presence of mass prayers, together with a small portion of Beneventan music with text *alleluia alleluia*, suggests that the folio may once have been part of a Beneventan missal.

Gregorian manuscripts consciously transmitting Beneventan chant

The scribes of a few surviving Gregorian manuscripts make conscious efforts to retain, in separate units, smaller or larger portions of the local chant. These are our central sources, for they have not been erased or mutilated, nor has the chant itself become confused with, or assimilated to, the Gregorian chant which surrounds it here and ultimately supplants it. In these sources, groups of Beneventan pieces stand side-by-side with the Gregorian music for the same rite. Thus Benevento 38 and Benevento 40 provide a substantial series of whole masses for the annual cycle. These "doublet" masses follow their Gregorian counterparts in books that are essentially Gregorian graduals. The scribe's purpose in including these pieces remains unclear. Are they meant as alternatives, to be used in certain circumstances to replace the

Gregorian mass? Are they intended as second masses, to be performed on the same day, but in another place or at another time? Or do they have a purely antiquarian value, testifying to the tenacity of a local tradition, preserved by a scribe reluctant to abandon the last vestiges of an indigenous chant?

7 (Ben38) Benevento, Biblioteca capitolare, MS 38. A Gregorian gradual, with tropes, sequences, and Kyriale, temporal and sanctoral mixed, from the first half of the eleventh century. It begins incomplete with Septuagesima, and has lacunae, notably in Holy Week. The provenance of the manuscript is uncertain, though it is probably from Benevento.

This is one of two principal sources for the Beneventan repertory. It contains music preserved in three ways: (1) eight Beneventan "doublet" masses; (2) substantial survivals of Beneventan music in mixed Gregorian-Beneventan rites of Holy Week; (3) four Beneventan rogation antiphons within a basically Gregorian series. The Beneventan contents are listed in Appendix 1.

8 (Ben40) Benevento, Biblioteca capitolare, MS 40. A Gregorian gradual, with sequences and tropes, from the first half of the eleventh century, possibly from Santa Sofia. Incomplete at the beginning, and with several lacunae, the manuscript now begins with Monday in Holy Week. With Benevento 38 this is one of two principal sources of Beneventan music. It includes thirteen "doublet" masses, and mixed Beneventan-Gregorian rites for Holy Week. It does not, however, include any Beneventan rogation antiphons.

9 Vatican MS Ottob. lat. 145. A monastic manual in various formats. The manuscript is based on a Montecassino original but it was perhaps designed for Santa Sofia in Benevento. The *mandatum* ceremony includes (ff. 124–124v) six Beneventan antiphons (used elsewhere as communions or offertories), described as being "Ambrosian."

10 Montecassino Compactiones XXII. Folder XXII in the *compactiones* contains four leaves from a twelfth-century Gregorian gradual in Beneventan script and notation typical of Montecassino. The last leaf contains most of the pseudo-Gregorian mass *Vir dei Benedictus* for St Benedict. Following the Gregorian communion *Hodie dilectus* is the rubric *ali. cō. ambrō.*, followed by the Beneventan communion *Gloriosus confessor domini* (incomplete).

11 "Solesmes flyleaves": private collection, facsimiles at abbey of St Pierre, Solesmes. Four leaves from a Gregorian antiphoner, in eleventh-century Beneventan script and notation: inserted before the Gregorian office of St John the Baptist is a Beneventan vespers of St John the Baptist preceded by the rubric "viiij [ante] k[a]l[endas] iul[ii] vig[ilia]. s[ancti]. ioh[ann]is bap[tistae]. a[ntiphonae] ambro[sianae]. ad vesp[eras]."

12 Macerata, Biblioteca comunale, MS 1457.XII. A much mutilated folio from an eleventh-century Gregorian antiphoner. On the recto is a series of antiphons of lauds for the second Sunday of Lent, followed by the rubric *al [alia? aliae?] sec[undum] ambro[sianum]*, indicating the beginning of a section of Beneventan music. The verso, where these antiphons should follow, is now illegible, and apparently was blank.

Beneventan remains in Holy Week rites

Since Holy Week rites are unusually solemn, and since their ceremonies, so different from those of the ordinary round of mass and office, differ from place to place, the retention of the Beneventan Holy Week rites and music presents special problems and opportunities. Many scribes make an attempt to create a synthesis of Gregorian and Beneventan rites. The results are varied, complex, confused, and confusing, but from the variety of the sources we can sort out a substantial amount of Beneventan material, and gain a close view of the problems of preservation and suppression of the older chant. Dom Hesbert has considered these sources, and many of the problems of transmission, with magisterial authority both in *Paléographie Musicale*, XIV and in separate studies.[2] Thus, we shall not want to repeat his work, but only to point out some details of transmission which illustrate the problems facing the Beneventan scribes. In this category, as in others, sources already listed are repeated where they also transmit Beneventan music in this way. (The specific Beneventan music for Holy Week in these manuscripts is detailed in table 2.1 below.)

7 Ben38, see above.

8 Ben40, see above.

13 Vatican MS Vat. lat. 10673. An incomplete early eleventh-century gradual, from Septuagesima to Holy Saturday Exultet. The substantial Beneventan contents for Holy Week, including a complete *ordo* for Good Friday, are the subject of Hesbert's classic study in PM XIV.

14 Lucca, Biblioteca Capitolare, MS 606, ff. 150–156v. An integral part of this plenary missal is an appendix (ff. 150–156v), in ordinary minuscule with partially distematic Beneventan notation, containing music for special Holy Week rites. The appendix compiles additional materials for special functions, with rubrics appropriate for a monastic church. Much of the music is Beneventan. The arrangement for Good Friday matches closely an *ordo* found in Montecassino MS 175.

15 (Ben30) Benevento, Biblioteca capitolare, MS 30. An almost complete but only partly noted missal, probably from Benevento, of the thirteenth century. Only two Beneventan pieces are included: ℟ *Lavi pedes* for Good Friday and Alleluia *Resurrexit* in the Easter mass.

16 (Ben33) Benevento, Biblioteca capitolare, MS 33. An early eleventh-century plenary missal, in Beneventan script and notation, extending from the vigil of Christmas to 11 November. With Vat. lat. 10673 the oldest witness of Gregorian chant in southern Italy, and also possibly the oldest substantial example of Beneventan notation.

17 (Ben34) Benevento, Biblioteca capitolare, MS 34. A nearly complete twelfth-century gradual, with tropes, sequences, and Kyriale. Probably the latest of the five surviving graduals from Benevento; contains very little Beneventan chant.

18 (Ben35) Benevento, Biblioteca capitolare, MS 35. An early twelfth-century gradual with tropes, sequences, and Kyriale. Incomplete at the beginning (begins 1 January). A final flyleaf, from an earlier manuscript, is manuscript no. 1 above.

19 (Ben39) Benevento, Biblioteca capitolare, MS 39. Gradual with tropes and sequences, beginning with Monday of Passion Week, perhaps from one of the convents of St Peter in Benevento. In addition to materials for Holy Week the manuscript contains two adaptations of the Beneventan Alleluia *Resurrexit tamquam dormiens*, for St Peter and the Transfiguration.

20 Benevento fragments B. Three fragments from a leaf containing music for the end of

---

[2] Hesbert, "L'antiphonale" (3)–(6).

Good Friday and the beginning of Holy Saturday in eleventh-century Beneventan script and notation very similar to that of Benevento 40. In addition to portions of Gregorian canticles there are portions of the Beneventan Good Friday responsory *Tenebre* and the Holy Saturday antiphon *Ad vesperum*.

21 Farfa MS A F. 338 Musica XI, together with Trento, Museo Provinciale d'Arte, s.n. (formerly the property of Lawrence Feininger). Two mutilated eleventh-century Beneventan bifolia, originally the inner two of a quire, containing part of the ceremonies of Holy Saturday, beginning with the Exultet, for which there are two versions, the "Vulgate" text being accompanied by an unusually elaborate melody. The fragment concludes with the neumes of the Alleluia V *Laudate pueri*.

22 Vatican MS Vat. lat. 4770. A monastic missal in ordinary minuscule and middle Italian notation, tenth–eleventh century. Beneventan musical contents include pieces for the Good Friday adoration and chants for the Easter vigil mass, without notation.

23 Vatican MS Barberini lat. 560. Related to Vat. lat. 4770 by its script and its liturgy, but almost all the Holy Week rubrics have been erased and altered. A rubric for Good Friday, in a second hand over an erasure, indicates the Beneventan adoration antiphons. Original rubrics indicate the chanting of the canticles of Jonah and of the Three Children on Holy Saturday (see Chapter 4).

24 Vatican MS Ottob. lat. 576. A plenary missal, Beneventan script and notation of the twelfth century, perhaps from Montecassino. In addition to the Holy Saturday antiphon *Omnes sitientes* and the dismissal *Si quis catechuminus est*, the manuscript contains the Exultet with "Vulgate" text, but Beneventan melody, and notated Beneventan lection-tones for Holy Saturday.

25 Rome, Biblioteca Vallicelliana, MS C 32. A late eleventh-century monastic ritual in Beneventan script and notation. The ritual for Holy Saturday contains the antiphon *Omnes sitientes*, the dismissal of catechumens, heretics, pagans, etc., and the Exultet, with essentially a "Vulgate" text.

26 Baltimore, Walters Art Gallery, MS W 6. A missal of the eleventh century from Canosa (near Monte Gargano), including the Easter Alleluia *Resurrexit tamquam dormiens* and an adaptation of it (*Hodie natus est*) for Christmas.

27 Bologna, Biblioteca del Civico Museo Bibliografico Musicale G.B. Martini, Cod. 144 (Q 10), framm. 3. A fragmentary leaf from a late eleventh-century Beneventan antiphoner, including fragments of the Beneventan responsory *Lavi pedes*.

28 Wolfenbüttel, Herzog-August-Bibliothek, MS Gudianus graecus 112. A triple palimpsest whose two upper scripts are in Greek. Palimpsest folios from an eleventh-century Beneventan missal include traces of the Beneventan tract *Domine audivi*.

29 Subiaco, Biblioteca del Arcicenobio di Santa Scolastica, MS X VIII (19). A thirteenth-century missal in northern script, whose occasional notation is Beneventan. The entire Beneventan vespers of Good Friday appears without notation, and part of the Exultet ("Vulgate" text) has the Beneventan melody.

30 Oxford, Bodleian Library, MS Canonici liturg. 342. A Dalmatian noted missal of the

thirteenth century including an Exultet with a highly-elaborated melody that may be a version of the Beneventan melody (see PM XIV, 399–416); and the Good Friday antiphon *Crucem tuam.*

31 Macerata, Biblioteca comunale, MS 378. This twelfth-century pontifical from Benevento cues the Beneventan version of the canticle *Benedictus es, Domine* for Holy Saturday.

32 Vatican MS Urb. lat. 602. A troper of the eleventh–twelfth century, probably from Montecassino. The thirteenth-century hand that rewrote much of the manuscript included the Beneventan dismissal *Si quis cathecuminus est procedat.*

Rotuli and other manuscripts preserving the Beneventan melody of the "Exultet"

The "Praeconium paschale" sung at the blessing of the paschal candle in the Easter vigil produced in southern Italy a wealth of richly decorated manuscript rolls containing the Deacon's sung portion (beginning "Exultet iam angelica turba"). The Exultet itself, as used in the Beneventan liturgy, has a text (sometimes referred to as the "Vetus Itala" or the "Bari" text)[3] and melody substantially different from that found more widely in the Roman church (often called the "Vulgate" text). The Beneventan melody is clearly related to other recitation and lection tones of the Beneventan liturgy studied in Chapter 5. These rolls then, to the extent that they preserve a single portion of Beneventan ceremonial, are important witnesses to the geographical extent and the chronological persistence of at least one element of the former Beneventan liturgy. All these sources use the characteristic Beneventan melody; they are divided here according to their use of the Beneventan or Vulgate text.

Exultets with 'Beneventan' text

13 Vatican lat. 10673, see above. Only the opening of the Exultet survives, but it is surely Beneventan.

16 Ben33, see above.

21 Farfa AF. 338 Musica XI, see above.

33 Vatican MS Vat. lat. 9820. An almost entirely palimpsest late tenth-century Exultet roll from St Peter's *extra muros*, Benevento. In the twelfth century the original text was replaced by the "Vulgate" text with the Beneventan melody.

34 Manchester, Rylands Library, MS 2. A fragmentary roll of the early eleventh century.

35 Bari, Archivio del Duomo, Exultet Roll 1, written before 1056.

36 Bari, Archivio del Duomo, Exultet Roll 2. An eleventh-century roll, now overwritten with a thirteenth-century "Vulgate" text of the Exultet and the Roman melody.

37 Mirabella Eclano, Archivio della Chiesa Collegiata, Exultet roll 1, eleventh century.

38 Gaeta, Archivio del Duomo, Exultet roll 1. An eleventh-century roll now overwritten with the "Vulgate" text and fourteenth-century staff notation.

39 Vatican MS Vat. lat. 3784. This eleventh-century roll from Montecassino now contains

---

[3] The Beneventan text of the Exultet is edited in Bannister, "The *Vetus Itala*," pp. 48–51; PM XIV, 385–6; Cavallo, *Rotoli*, p. 26 (after PM XIV).

only the introduction up to the preface *Vere dignum*, using the Beneventan melody, to which has been attached a fourteenth-century Neapolitan "Vulgate" continuation.

40 Montecassino, Exultet Roll 1. An eleventh-century fragment of the Beneventan Exultet with notation.

41 Velletri, Museo capitolare, Exultet roll. A late eleventh-century fragmentary roll from Montecassino.

42 Troia, Archivio del Duomo, Exultet 1. A rotulus of the later eleventh century, doubtless from Troia.

43 Troia, Archivio del Duomo, Exultet 2. A twelfth-century rotulus, probably also from Troia.

44 [Salerno, Archivio Capitolare, missal (without number?) of 1431, containing an Exultet with Beneventan text and elaborated melody, according to Latil, "Un 'Exultet'."]

Exultets with Vulgate text

21 Farfa, A F. 338, see above.

24 Ottob. 576, see above.

25 Vall. C 32, see above.

29 Subiaco X V I I I, see above.

45 Avezzano, Curia Vescovile, Exultet roll. Mid-eleventh century, perhaps from Montecassino.

46 Capua, Biblioteca Arcivescovile, Exultet roll. An incomplete roll of the eleventh century, doubtless from Capua.

47 Gaeta, Archivio del Duomo, Exultet roll 2. An incomplete roll of the eleventh century, probably from Gaeta.

48 Pisa, Museo Nazionale di San Matteo, Exultet roll. This eleventh-century roll contains additions from the Beneventan text.

49 Mirabella Eclano, Archivio della Chiesa Collegiata, Exultet roll 2. An incomplete roll of the second half of the eleventh century, perhaps from Mirabella Eclano.

50 London, British Library, Additional MS 30337. Late eleventh century, from Montecassino.

51 Oxford, Bodleian Library, MS Canonici Bibl. Lat. 61. A late eleventh-century decorated gospel-lectionary from Zadar containing the Vulgate Exultet with a brief interpolation from the Beneventan text.

52 Vatican MS Barberini lat. 592. A fragmentary roll closely related to BL, Add. MS 30337. Later eleventh century, from Montecassino.

53 Vatican MS Borg. lat. 339. A Dalmatian gospel-book of 1082 whose Exultet contains an extended praise of the bees (ed. PM X I V, 383).

54 Gaeta, Archivio del Duomo, Exultet roll 3. Eleventh–twelfth century, modeled on Gaeta 2.

55 Paris, Bibliotheque nationale, MS n. a. lat. 710. St Peter's, Fondi, *c.* 1100; clearly related to Montecassino by its texts and its miniatures.

56 Montecassino, Archivio della Badia, Exultet Roll 2. This roll, made in Sorrento between 1106 and 1120, contains additions from the Beneventan text.

57 London, British Library, MS Egerton 3511 (formerly Benevento 29). This twelfth-century

missal from St Peter's *intra muros*, Benevento, contains the Vulgate Exultet with Beneventan text and melody, as well as notated lection-tones for the canticles of Jonah and Azarias.

58 Troia, Archivio del Duomo, Exultet 3. An Exultet of the twelfth century whose Beneventan melody has been erased and replaced with the "Roman" melody in Beneventan notation.

59 Rome, Biblioteca Casanatense, MS 724. A twelfth-century roll, now bound with two earlier rotuli from Benevento, a pontifical and a benedictional.

60 Vatican MS Vat. lat. 6082. This twelfth-century missal, from Montecassino or San Vincenzo, in addition to the Exultet (ff. 120v–122v), contains noted lessons from Jonah and Daniel for Holy Saturday using Beneventan recitation tones.

61 Bari, Archivio del Duomo, Exultet Roll 3. Late twelfth century; an earlier Greek text has been overwritten with the Exultet and a curiously elaborated version of the Beneventan melody.

62 New York, Pierpont Morgan Library, MS M. 379. An eleventh–twelfth century monastic missal, perhaps from Subiaco, in ordinary minuscule with very rare notation derived from Beneventan practice. The Exultet (Vulgate text) uses the Beneventan melody up to *Vere dignum*.

63 Rome, Biblioteca Vallicelliana, B 23. An early twelfth-century missal from the region of Macerata, in ordinary minuscule with occasional Beneventan notation. The Exultet (Vulgate text) has the Beneventan melody up to the preface, the Roman preface tone thereafter.

64 Rome, Biblioteca Vallicelliana, B 43. A twelfth-century sacramentary from central Italy in ordinary minuscule. The Exultet, in Beneventan neumes, uses the Vulgate text with the Beneventan melody.

65 Vatican MS Barb. lat. 603. A twelfth–thirteenth-century missal from Caiazzo. The Exultet begins and ends with a slightly elaborated Beneventan melody, but most of the portion after the preface uses the now standard preface tone.

Gregorian graduals and processionals preserving Beneventan antiphons

In these last two categories of manuscript sources the identity of the Beneventan chant has apparently been lost. Beneventan melodies are preserved in places where the liturgy is flexible, or where some local product needs to be supplied when the official, received Gregorian liturgy provides no formularies, for example, for the offices of local saints. In these cases, however, Beneventan antiphons are presented as though they were part of a unified fabric of Gregorian liturgy; the masqueraders have become accepted elements of the established local liturgy. And indeed they are sometimes musically related to the Gregorian liturgy, showing that assimilation takes its toll. The purity of the chant is sometimes diluted so that the dividing line between Gregorian and Beneventan becomes difficult to fix.

7 Ben38, see above.
8 Ben40, see above.
17 Ben34, see above.
18 Ben35, see above.
19 Ben39, see above.

66 Vatican MS Vat. lat. 10645, ff. 3–6. Fragments from an eleventh-century noted missal ("Bari-type") including the antiphon *Ipse super maria* for the vigil of Pentecost.

67 Bologna, Biblioteca universitaria, MS 2551. The final flyleaf, from an eleventh-century Beneventan gradual, contains a series of processional antiphons for the Purification, one of which (*Lumen ad revelationem*) is Beneventan.

68 Oxford, Bodleian Library, MS Canonici liturg. 277. A late eleventh-century book of hours from Zadar. An unlabeled votive office contains the texts (without notation) of two Beneventan antiphons used elsewhere for rogations: *Peccavimus* (f. 125) and *Gemitus noster* (f. 125v).

69 Vatican MS Reg. lat. 334. Folios 57–100, an incomplete eleventh-twelfth century processional from Sora, include a Beneventan responsory (*Ante sex dies*) and processional antiphons, as well as an antiphon in Gregorian style using a text related to the Beneventan Easter ingressa.

70 Naples, Biblioteca nazionale, MS XVI A 19, ff. 1–15, an incomplete twelfth-century processional from Benevento, includes three Beneventan antiphons: *In tribulationibus*, *Peccavimus*, and *Respice*.

71 Naples, Biblioteca nazionale, MS VI G 34. A late twelfth-century processional, perhaps from Troia, including a single Beneventan antiphon (*Peccavimus domine peccavimus*) and the responsory *Magnus es Domine*, whose Beneventan melody has been adapted with Gregorian cadences.

72 Vatican MS Barb. lat. 697. A fourteenth-century ritual of Capua, in Gothic script, which preserves the text of the scrutiny antiphon *Dum sanctificatus*, notated only in Ben38.

Gregorian antiphoners and breviaries preserving groups of antiphons or individual antiphons with Beneventan melodies

In these sources, mostly Gregorian office books, Beneventan melodies are presented as part of the normal round of music for the office. Often there are groups of Beneventan antiphons for local saints, like Saint Barbatus and the Holy Twelve Brothers. Elsewhere, only an occasional Beneventan melody is present in an otherwise Gregorian office. Except for the first two manuscripts, already listed above, the Beneventan melodies are not rubrically distinguished from their Gregorian neighbors. Specific Beneventan contents can be determined by reference to Appendix 1.

11 Solesmes flyleaves, see above.

12 Macerata 1457, see above.

73 (Ben19) Benevento, Biblioteca capitolare, MS 19. A twelfth-century combined breviary-missal for non-monastic use, *pars hiemalis*. A companion volume is Ben20 (no. 74).

74 (Ben20) Benevento, Biblioteca capitolare, MS 20. A twelfth-century companion volume to Ben19, *pars aestiva*.

75 (Ben21) Benevento, Biblioteca capitolare MS 21. An almost complete monastic antiphoner, twelfth–thirteenth century.

76 (Ben22) Benevento, Biblioteca capitolare, MS 22. A twelfth-century noted monastic breviary, *pars hiemalis*.

77 (Ben37) Benevento, Biblioteca capitolare, MS 37. A late eleventh-century monastic book containing a collection of responsories, hymns, litanies, martyrology-necrology, Rule of St Benedict, etc. Perhaps from Santa Sofia, certainly used at St Peter's *intra muros*, Benevento. It includes the responsory *Magnus es Domine*, a Beneventan melody adapted to Gregorian usage.

78 Melk, Stiftsbibliothek, MS 1012, ff. A–B; MS 1027, f. z. Three leaves from an eleventh-century Beneventan antiphoner containing the beginning of the office of the Holy Twelve Brothers.

79 Berkeley (California), Bancroft Library, MS ff 2MS A2M2 1000:6. A mutilated leaf from an eleventh-century Gregorian antiphoner, in which is included (as an antiphon) the Beneventan communion *Sancta Maria exora*.

80 Zadar (Zara), Ordinarijat Zadar, MS 38 (15/b). Of five bifolia from a late twelfth-century Gregorian antiphoner used as wallpaper in the choir-stalls, this one contains the Beneventan responsory *Ante sex dies pasche* in the fragmentary office for Palm Sunday.

81 Venice, Archivio di Stato, Atti diversi manoscritti b. 159 n. 28. Eleven unnumbered folios from a Gregorian antiphoner. At the end of the (unidentified) feast preceding St Eustasius (20 May) is an antiphon in Beneventan style beginning *Sancti enim ducati ad Diocletianum*.

82 Montecassino, Compactiones v. This folder contains, among other things, 113 folios from a large late eleventh-century noted monastic breviary; Beneventan antiphons are found in the offices of the Holy Twelve Brothers, Sts John and Paul, and St Vincent.

83 Montecassino, MS 542. A twelfth-century monastic antiphoner, Advent 4 through Maundy Thursday, containing the office of St Vincent with its antiphon *Insigne preconium*.

84 Vatican MS Vat. lat. 14733. Folios 11–12, two badly damaged leaves from an eleventh-century antiphoner, contain portions of two Beneventan antiphons of St Apollinaris.

85 Vatican MS Vat. lat. 14446. An incomplete thirteenth-century noted breviary (secular) from Caiazzo. Among the surviving materials are the office of St Barbatus and an incomplete office of St Benedict, both of which contain antiphons in Beneventan style.

86 Vatican MS Vat. lat. 10646. Folios 48–51, two bifolia from an eleventh–twelfth-century noted breviary, including the Beneventan antiphon *Dum famis inopia* (f. 51) for St Benedict.

INDIRECT EVIDENCE OF FURTHER SOURCES

We know that there existed more books of Beneventan chant than have survived. In one case, as we have seen, the monk Theobald of Montecassino caused a book of Beneventan chant to be written in the first half of the eleventh century. And the *ordo* for Good Friday in Montecassino 175 indicated the use of Beneventan chant at Montecassino far in advance of the surviving musical manuscripts.[4]

Evidence of further Beneventan books is found among the sources themselves, notably Ben38 and Ben40, for the scribes of both these manuscripts, in setting up a single book that would represent the Gregorian tradition while retaining something of the Beneventan, used sources which contained more Beneventan chant than they chose to preserve. Both scribes occasionally use textual and musical cues to refer the singer to another place. Such cues are normally used in

---

[4] On Theobald's manuscript see Chapter 1, pp. 31–2; on MC 175 see Appendix 3, under Lucca 606.

chant manuscripts to avoid writing the same piece twice in the same book, but both these scribes refer to pieces that, although they are not present in the surviving manuscripts, were surely found in their exemplars.

The scribe of Ben38 cues the following Beneventan pieces:

Function	Feast	Text	Other sources
Grad.	Andrew	*Constitues eos*	Ben40
Off.	John Bapt.	*Johannes est*	Solesmes (ant.)
Comm.	John Bapt.	*Inter natos*	Ben40 (comm.), Ottob. 145, Solesmes (ant.)
Comm.	Michael	*Multos infirmos*	Ben40
All.	P & Paul	*In omnem terram*	Ben40 (cued)
Off.	P & Paul	*Tu es pastor*	no
Comm.	P & Paul	*Petrus apostolus*	Ben40 (off.), Ottob. 145 (ant.)
Comm.	Assumption	*Sancta maria exora*	Ben40; Ottob. 145, Berkeley (ant.)

These pieces, though incomplete in Ben38, are not lost to us, owing to their use elsewhere as antiphons, or to their appearance in Ben40.[5] But the scribe of Ben38 must have used a Beneventan exemplar that contained these pieces. Many of them, because of the specific nature of their texts, could hardly be used for another feast. Exceptions are the gradual *Constitues* and the Alleluia *In omnem*, which might have been in the now missing earlier portion of the same manuscript, and the communion *Sancta Maria* might have served for an earlier Marian feast. The other four pieces, however, are unlikely to have appeared in two distinct Beneventan masses. Two of these pieces, moreover, are known to be used as antiphons in the office of St John the Baptist, and one is found elsewhere as a *mandatum* antiphon. Hence, if the scribe of Ben38 repeats the cues found in his model, we must conclude that his exemplar was a "totum," including music for both mass and office.[6]

The scribe of Ben40 cues the following Beneventan chants:

Function	Feast	Text	Other sources
Off.	MThursday	*Popule meus*	Ben38 (Palm Sunday)
Comm.	MThursday	*Quis te*	Ben38 (Palm Sunday)
All.	Lawrence	*Posuisti*	Ben35, Stephen
Off.	Holy Cross I	ADORAMUS	[antiphon?]
Comm.	Holy Cross I	CRUCEM TUAM	[antiphon?]
All.	Simon & Jude	IN OMNEM TERRAM	cued in Ben38
Off.	Simon & Jude	CONFORTATUS EST	no
Comm.	Simon & Jude	NOLITE TIMERE	no

[5] Except for the offertory *Tu es pastor* and the Alleluia verse *In omnem terram*, which is cued in both Ben38 and Ben40.
[6] On books of this kind, and their relation to the arrangement of Ambrosian books, see Chapter 5, p. 184.

Many cues in this manuscript, not listed here, work as such cues usually do, referring to the fully written-out version elsewhere in Ben40. The pieces for Maundy Thursday duplicate those used in Ben38 for Palm Sunday, and probably they too were contained in the original music, now lost, for that feast in Ben40. Likewise the Alleluia for St Lawrence, used in the Ben35 flyleaf (manuscript no. 1 above) for St Stephen, may have been in the lost portion of Ben40. The two pieces for the Holy Cross have incipits (without notation) that match texts of antiphons for the adoration of the cross on Good Friday, present earlier in the manuscript. These antiphons are in a simple style unlike that of most mass chants, but the relatively late date of the introduction of feasts of the Holy Cross[7] makes this sort of adaptation at least a possibility. The pieces for Saints Simon and Jude are found nowhere else. Their texts are not so unusual as to preclude their use with other feasts, such as an earlier feast of an Apostle, now lost. Hence, unlike the situation in Ben38, we cannot be certain that the abbreviations in Ben40 are the exemplar's and not those of the scribe himself, referring to portions of the same manuscript. But in either case we can be sure that the scribe's source contained more of the Beneventan repertory than now survives to us.

CONTRACTION OF THE REPERTORY: THE "PURE" BENEVENTAN BOOKS

In addition to the indirect evidence just cited, we have the sources in category 1 as evidence of the existence of complete books of Beneventan chant. We cannot, however, determine the make-up of a complete gradual (ingressarium?) or antiphoner, as no entire book survives. Indeed, in one of these sources we can already glimpse a contraction of the repertory. Manuscripts listed above as nos. 1, 2, and 3, though they are extremely fragmentary, give no evidence of being anything other than complete mass-books of the Beneventan repertory. But Vall. C 9 (no. 4) presents, on ff. 168v–169v, a series of ingressae without their accompanying masses. Two of these ingressae are accompanied by psalmodic endings, suggesting that their function here may not be that of a standard Beneventan entrance chant (which is without psalmody). Although this book did contain whole masses (the Easter offertory and communion are visible on f. 167), the series of ingressae suggests a re-ordering, a selection from the larger repertory, for some other purpose. A similar collection, for functions on the fringe of the liturgy, is the series of *mandatum* "antiphons" of Ottob. 145 (no. 9), a selection of pieces used elsewhere as communions.

BEN38 AND BEN40 COMPARED

The chief surviving sources of the Beneventan chant are already engaged in abbreviating the repertory. These are Ben38 and Ben40, each of which preserves Beneventan music in several ways: series of "doublet" masses, mixed Holy Week rites, and a few Beneventan antiphons among Gregorian processional chants. In the comparison of these two it is clear that, as compared to Ben40, Ben38 represents a more advanced state of abbreviation and suppression.

For one thing, Ben38 contains fewer Beneventan masses. Though the feasts are present, there

[7] See Chapter 3, pp. 86–8.

are no Beneventan formularies for St Lawrence, the Holy Twelve Brothers, Sts Simon and Jude, All Saints, or St Martin – for all of which Ben40 has doublet masses. Beneventan music for the Holy Cross is present in Ben38, but only as a single offertory included within the Gregorian mass.[8] (The combination of Beneventan with Gregorian, as we shall see in the rites of Holy Week, inevitably leads to the suppression of the former.) For Good Friday Ben38 omits the whole Beneventan rite except for vespers. And we can see the physical obliteration of the Beneventan repertory of Ben38. The doublet Beneventan mass of Pentecost is erased to give room for the Sequence *Sancte spiritus adsit*, and a portion of the Beneventan music for Holy Saturday has been erased and replaced with a litany.

The two central manuscripts can be compared also in their solutions to the problems of creating a mixture of Gregorian and Beneventan music for the rites of Holy Week. Here there seems to be no possibility of "doublets," or of writing out one rite followed by another; these are days of central solemnity, and the notion of duplicate, alternative, or successive ceremonies is out of the question. The rites of Holy Week have been studied in exhaustive detail by Hesbert,[9] and I do not wish to duplicate his masterful studies, but in the matter of manuscript transmission a few observations may illustrate some of the factors contributing to the eradication of the Beneventan repertory.

The scribe of Ben40 has, as a basic principle, the intention to separate the Beneventan chant by placing it after the Gregorian. When this is not entirely possible in Holy Week, he still makes the attempt. The somewhat more adventurous scribe of Ben38 tries to combine the two, with often unfortunate results.

For Palm Sunday, Ben40's solution is simple. A Beneventan mass follows the Gregorian version, and for the ceremony of the blessing of the palms, the Beneventan responsory *Ante sex dies pasche* is inserted between lessons as a gradual, in a ceremony that no doubt allows for some flexibility.[10] The processional music is in Gregorian style.[11]

For Maundy Thursday we cannot compare Ben38 and Ben40, for we have only the witness of Ben40, where we see the scribe pursuing his policy of separation: Gregorian mass followed by Beneventan mass, Gregorian antiphons for the *mandatum* followed by Beneventan music for the same ceremony. The whole is closed by the Gregorian verses *Ubi caritas*, placed at the end perhaps because of their length and their special character.

On Good Friday begin the problems. The Beneventan music for the Good Friday ceremonies is described for us by the scribe of Vat. lat. 10673, and preserved in its entirety only in Ben40. In Vat. lat. 10673, the scribe made an initial effort to combine Gregorian and Beneventan,[12] but in fact does not succeed either in combining the two rites, or in including all the Beneven-

---

[8] On feasts of the Holy Cross, see Chapter 3, pp. 86–8.

[9] PM XIV, 248–465, and Hesbert, "L'antiphonale" (3)–(6).

[10] Lucca 606 also includes *Ante sex dies* as a gradual; this manuscript, which has a supplement containing additional materials for Holy Week, does not contain a mass. The scribe of Vat. lat. 10673 also included *Ante sex dies*, but at the end of the processional pieces, rather like a doublet. Ben35 preserves *Ante sex dies* as the second in the series of (otherwise Gregorian) processional pieces; perhaps the scribe did not realize the origin of the piece.

[11] The antiphon *Viam justorum*, which Hesbert thinks is Beneventan, shares none of the melodic turns common to Beneventan pieces with this degree of melodic elaboration.

[12] See PM XIV, 291–4.

tan elements. As a result, he tries again by writing a long rubric describing the Beneventan rite alone ("Item qualiter peragatur officium sexta feria in parasceben secundum ambrosianum," ff. 33–4),[13] and the Beneventan music in Ben40 matches this specification.

Now Ben40 is not a book of ceremonies; it simply includes the music required, often without any explanatory rubric. The user must know the function and placement of the pieces. But whereas the scribe of Ben40 is compelled to combine the two rites, he still follows his principle of separating Beneventan groups, and as a result his three sequences of Beneventan pieces, included in the course of a longer Good Friday section, preserve the Beneventan music intact. Ben38, on the other hand, omits some of the Beneventan music; though its Good Friday section is truncated by a lacuna, we can see that the music for the Adoration is not included.[14]

Holy Saturday presents insuperable problems to both scribes. As Hesbert has pointed out in detail,[15] both scribes recorded an unusual tradition that called for tracts after each of twelve lessons (rather than the usual four canticles). The insertion of the four Beneventan tracts, then, provided special problems, as there were no available spaces without tracts. The scribe of Ben40 began with one plan and changed to another: the first Gregorian tract, *Domine audivi*, was replaced by its Beneventan counterpart; but, when the second Beneventan tract had found no match, and he had arrived at the place where the third tract, *Attende*, could replace its Gregorian counterpart, he reverted to his earlier system of doublets, and copied all three remaining Beneventan tracts after the Gregorian *Attende*.

Ben38's scribe planned doublets from the outset, using the first two Beneventan tracts as individual doublets, but the second, *Cantabo*, has no counterpart in the Gregorian tracts – the same problem that baffled Ben40. The scribe noticed, however, its textual similarity to the Gregorian *Vinea* (this is the second verse of the Beneventan tract), and began the Beneventan *Cantabo* at the place of the Gregorian counterpart. He quickly changed his mind – the scratched-out initial letter on f. 45 is all that remains of this intention – and wrote the Gregorian *Vinea*, using the Beneventan *Cantabo* after the cue for the Gregorian *Ad te levabo*. After this hesitation, and his unsatisfactory solution, he reverts to the safer procedure of preserving the other two tracts by writing them at the end of the series.

In both these manuscripts the scribes are making a first effort at combining two rites. Evidently they have at their disposal the unadulterated Beneventan liturgy, and they apparently have no model for how the two rites might work together. The nature of their confusing results suggests that their compilations would have only very limited liturgical value. It is difficult to imagine an actual Holy Saturday liturgy sung from these books. What they both show, however, is a desire to preserve a liturgy no longer in favor, or as much of it as can be managed, in a context where both cannot be maintained.

---

[13] Facsimile in PM XIV, plates 65–7; transcribed on pp. 294–5, and table, pp. 296–7.

[14] See the repertory table in Appendix I, and the table in PM XIV, 296–7. For details on the Good Friday rite in Ben38, see PM XIV, 290–305.

[15] PM XIV, 339–60; Hesbert, "L'antiphonale" (6), pp. 154–71, table, p. 166.

THE SURVIVAL OF BENEVENTAN MUSIC FOR HOLY WEEK IN
SELECTED MANUSCRIPTS

Most other manuscripts preserving Beneventan music for Holy Week represent a later stage in the disappearance of the Beneventan liturgy, for they include gradually less and less of a rite that is perhaps scarcely used and little favored. Table 2.1 illustrates some of the principles involved in the gradual disappearance of the Beneventan music for Holy Week.[16] These principles, which apply equally elsewhere in the repertory, may be summarized as follows:

1 Pieces connected with occasional ceremonies (processional, *mandatum*, vespers antiphons) are more easily maintained than the central liturgical items of the mass.
2 Bilingual pieces in Greek and Latin tend to drop out in two stages: first, by the elimination of the Greek version and second, by the disappearance of the Latin.
3 Beneventan texts closely matching a Gregorian counterpart disappear sooner than those with no Gregorian parallel, and the nearer at hand the Gregorian, the sooner the Beneventan doublet disappears.

For Maundy Thursday the Mass preserved in Ben40 (and probably also originally present in Ben38 and Vat. lat. 10673) drops out immediately. It is omitted in those sources that still preserve other Holy Week rites, even when they preserve *mandatum* antiphons for the same day, since the liturgical content of the *mandatum* is not fixed. But these antiphons gradually disappear also, in an order that illustrates the third principle above. The antiphon *Dominus hiesus postquam cenavit*, which is omitted in Ben33 and Lucca 606, has the same text as the communion of the Gregorian mass of Maundy Thursday; the presence of so similar a piece in such proximity is surely an incentive to omit the Beneventan version from a ceremony used on the same day. And the subsequent reduction from two Beneventan *mandatum* pieces (in Ben33 and Lucca 606) to one (in Ben30 and Ben39) is the result of a similar confrontation, for the Gregorian antiphon *In diebus illis*, also used for the *mandatum*, recounts the same story, and uses much of the same language, as the omitted Beneventan antiphon *Cum recubuisset*.[17] In our two youngest sources, then, the Beneventan Maundy Thursday rite is represented only by the responsory *Lavi pedes*, which duplicates no Gregorian material; in both Ben30 and Ben39 this piece is preserved at the end of the *mandatum* series, in accordance with the principle of doublets.

In the rites for Good Friday we can observe the gradual disappearance of the Greek-Latin antiphons. All four bilingual antiphons are found in Ben40, but in Vat. lat. 10673, the antiphon *Panta ta etni* is accompanied by a Latin cue only.[18] Ben33, Ben35, and the central Italian Vat. lat. 4770 have eliminated Greek versions altogether; Lucca 606 (related to the *ordo* of Montecassino 175) includes only Latin and gives only an incipit (*Omnes gentes*) for *Panta ta etni*; while the central Italian Vat. Barb. lat. 560, in which the original Good Friday rubrics have been obliterated, cues the three adoration antiphons in Latin only, and omits *Omnes gentes* altogether.

[16] The chant pieces, whose appearances are summarized here, can be studied in detail as to their placements and texts in Appendices 1 and 2.
[17] Textual and musical relationships between the Beneventan and the Roman liturgies are summarized in table 5.1, pp. 164–5.
[18] Note that Vat. lat. 10673 is the older manuscript, but here it may represent, not a later stage in the disappearance of the Beneventan chant, but the fact that *Omnes gentes* is used elsewhere in the Gregorian liturgy. See Appendix 2.

* cued only
L latin version only
abb abbreviated
pal palimpsest

Table 2.1 *Surviving Beneventan music for Holy Week*

	Ben40	Ben38	VatLat 10673	Ben33	Ben35	Lucca 606	VatLat 4770	Barb 560	Ben39	Ben30	Ben34	Farfa	Ottob 576	Vall c 32
Maundy Thursday														
Mass														
I. Postquam surrexit	4v													
G. Vadit propitiator	5													
O. Popule meus	5*													
C. Quis te supplantavit	5*													
Mandatum														
a. Cum recubuisset	6			66v*sn	62v	152v								
a. Dominus hiesus	6v				62v									
R. Lavi pedes	6v			66v*sn	63	153			21	71				
Good Friday														
a. Tristis est						155								
Adoration														
a. Proskynumen/Adoramus	10v		10v	68vL	65vL	155vL	91vLsn	51L*sn						
a. Ton stauron/Crucem	10v		10v	69L	65vL	156L	91vLsn	51L*sn						
a. Enumen se/Laudamus	11		11	69L	65vL	156L	91vLsn	51L*sn						
R. Amicus meus	11		11	69		156L								
Afternoon liturgy														
a. Panta ta/Omnes gentes	12v		12v	69vL	65vL*sn 156L*		91vLsn	91vLsn	23		119			
Tunc hi. . .Ben. es, domine	12v		12v	71abb					23					
R. Tenebre facte sunt	14		14	71v*sn										

Table 2.1 (cont.)

	Ben40	Ben38	VatLat 10673	Ben33	Ben35	Lucca 606	VatLat 4770	Barb 560	Ben39	Ben30	Ben34	Farfa	Ottob 576	Vall c 32
Vespers														
a. Heloy heloy	14v	43		72v*sn		156			25					
a. Cum accepisset	15	43v				156			25					
a. Inclinato capite	15	43v				156			25v					
a. Velum templi	15	43v				156			25v				166v	
Holy Saturday														
Vigil														
a. Ad vesperum	15v	43v	34	73	66v	156v			25v					
T. Domine audivi	15v	44												
T. Cantabo	17v	45												
T. Attende	18	46pal												
T. Sicut cervus	18	46v/pal	34v									Br		
a. Omnes sitientes	18v	46v/pal		78	67v				27			B	210	30
a. Doxa/Gloria	19	46v/pal										Bv		
Mass														
A. V Resurrexit V Laudate	19v	46v		79	68				27v	75v		Bv		
O. Omnes qui in Christo	19v	47		79v	68		113v							
C. Ymnum canite	20	47		79v	68		114							

Good Friday also witnesses the gradual elimination of the responsories *Amicus meus* and *Tenebre facte sunt*, each of which has counterparts in the Gregorian liturgy for Tenebrae.

Beneventan vespers for Good Friday is rather like a doublet: generally the whole office is either preserved or rejected, and it survives complete as late as the thirteenth century in Subiaco XVIII.

But there is a second tradition, beginning early, that gradually eliminates the central antiphons of vespers. The *ordo* for Good Friday found in Montecassino 175 (pp. 587–8)[19] duplicates almost exactly the provisions found also in Lucca 606, which is itself of later date. But MC 175 provides for all the psalms to be sung under the single antiphon *Eloy*, followed by the antiphon *Velum templi*, evidently for Magnificat. The same intermediate stage is shown in Benevento 23 (not shown in the table), a thirteenth-century breviary without notation, which uses the single antiphon *Heloy* for all the psalms, and *Velum templi* for the Magnificat.[20] This change of usage is reflected in Ben38, where a later hand has traced a red clef-line only in the currently used parts of the older vespers: only the antiphons *Heloy* and *Velum* are so marked, but not their verses, nor the other antiphons. The twelfth-century *ordo officii* of Benevento 66, derived from later Montecassino practice, retains *Velum templi* for Magnificat, but replaces *Heloy* with the antiphon *Considerabam*. This becomes the practice of a number of later sources, like Vat. Ottob. lat. 576, where only *Velum templi* survives from the Beneventan series, as a Magnificat antiphon in the context of a Gregorian vespers.[21]

In assembling music for Holy Saturday, the Beneventan tracts posed particular problems, as we have seen, for the scribes who preserved them, and they are the first to be eliminated. An exception is *Sicut cervus*, which functions in the Beneventan rite not as a tract among the series of vigil lessons, but as a part of the separate rites of baptism. Thus, it is preserved in the Bari benedictional, along with the processional antiphon *Omnes sitientes*, in a document concerned only with these ceremonies. The scribe of Vat. lat. 10673 preserves it also, but at a place, following the fifth lesson, that might make it seem an unnecessary Gregorian doublet. To explain that the lessons and the tract serve another function in the Beneventan rite, he adds a rubric: "Lectio Hec est hereditas que quinta est ordinata secundum romanum legatur hic. Secundum ambrosianum legatur post Benedictionem cerei" (ff. 34–34v). It is this special litur-

---

[19] Edited in *Bibliotheca casinensis*, IV, Florilegium, pp. 33–4.
[20] Ben23, despite its late date, undoubtedly represents an earlier practice than Ben66. The shift from the one to the other, with the consequent elimination of *Heloy*, can be seen in Ben25, a twelfth-century antiphoner without notation, which is, in all details except this one, a duplicate of Ben23, and might otherwise be thought to be its model.

The scribe of Ben25 copied *Considerabam* as the antiphon for none (as it is in Ben23), but before finishing its text he added a rubric indicating its use for vespers (the rubric is written to the *right*, and the text of the antiphon has had to be written so as to leave space for it; the rubric was not added later), he then switched to the practice of Ben66, continuing as though *Considerabam* were the antiphon for vespers psalms, and concluded with *Velum templi*. In the margin to the right of *Considerabam* a later hand has written the correction *Ihesus clamans*, to bring the manuscript into agreement with Ben66, which uses this antiphon for none, and thus inserting what appears to be the missing antiphon for none, if *Considerabam* is to be used for vespers.

The original scribe was undoubtedly copying a manuscript that followed the practice of Ben25, but he was more familiar with that of Ben66. Therefore, in copying *Considerabam* (which in his model was for none) he erroneously thought it was for vespers (as it is in Ben66) and labeled it so, thus skipping *Velum templi* in his model. It was not he who made the correction, for he would not have added the *Ihesus clamans* of Ben66, but would simply have looked back at his model (of which Ben23 is a more faithful copy) and seen that he had skipped *Heloy*.

[21] The antiphon *Heloy* also survives in some later antiphoners, often with a different melody: see Appendix I.

gical function that preserves these pieces, as well as the opening antiphon *Ad vesperum*, which has no counterpart in the Gregorian liturgy and which, consequently suffering no collision with another piece having the same function, survives in a number of manuscripts.

The progressive disappearance of the Beneventan Holy Week rite is thus the result of the decisions of a number of scribes; each one, having received a greater or lesser portion of Beneventan music, is faced with the question of preserving or eliminating music whose function may be doubtful and whose continued use may in fact be under attack. The simple solution is to omit the Beneventan – and we cannot tell how many Gregorian manuscripts may be purified copies of mixed exemplars. But for those scribes who made the effort to preserve at least a portion of the older rite, the principles used to determine what might best be preserved give us a picture of the ways in which solving the problem of liturgies in conflict results gradually in the elimination of the older.

TRANSMISSION OF THE EXULTET

The many decorated Exultet rolls from southern Italy chronicle the gradual disappearance, first of the Beneventan version of the text and, then, of its characteristic melody. The oldest versions of the Exultet in the region are all examples of the special Beneventan text, and they are among the very earliest musical documents of the area, including the late tenth-century roll from Benevento (Vat. lat. 9820). But as early as the middle of the eleventh century the Vulgate text begins to make headway. Those places that preserve several Exultet rolls give a particularly clear picture of the stages of eleventh-century change.

1 In all cities with multiple Exultet rolls (Bari, Gaeta, Troia, Mirabello Eclano) the oldest extant rotulus has the Beneventan text and melody. This is, of course, a reason for the existence of multiple rolls in these places, for the Beneventan text is soon replaced with the more widespread Vulgate.

2 At some point in the late eleventh or early twelfth century, each center creates a new Exultet roll using the Vulgate text (Gaeta 2, Mirabella 2, Bari 3, Troia 3: see the list of manuscripts above). A more drastic measure was taken with the Exultet of St Peter's *extra muros*, Benevento (Vat. lat. 9820), which in the twelfth century was erased and re-ordered to serve for the Vulgate text. Some other early Vulgate Exultets show a transitional stage by the retention of smaller or greater portions of the older Beneventan text (Pisa, Oxford Can. Bibl. lat. 61; Montecassino Exultet 2).

3 Sometimes a more elaborate version of the Beneventan melody is to be seen in successive Exultets. This does not necessarily accompany the change to Vulgate text: though Bari 3 is the city's first Vulgate and also has an elaborated melody, Troia 2 (twelfth century) retains the Beneventan text while adding an elaborated melody. A few other Vulgate sources also include such elaborated melodies (Berlin 920; Oxford, Can. lit. 342: see Chapter 4, note 25). A particularly interesting transitional document is the fragment surviving at Farfa and Trento, for this contains remnants of two versions of the Exultet in the same manuscript: the one Beneventan with the usual melody, and the other Vulgate with an elaborated melody.[22]

---

[22] Studied extensively in PM XIV, 390–9, with facsimiles as plates XXVI–XXVII.

4 At a later stage, an older roll is sometimes re-used to fill the need for a "Roman" melody and a Vulgate text. Thus two old rolls with Beneventan text were altered (Bari 2 in the thirteenth century and Gaeta 1 in the fourteenth) to preserve their illustrations while rejecting both their text and their melodies. Similarly, Troia 3, whose text was already the Vulgate, had its elaborated Beneventan melody altered in the fourteenth century. An even more brutal alternative was simply to chop off the parts of an old roll that did not correspond with the Vulgate text, and to append new text and music; this is the fate of the Montecassino roll Vat. lat. 3784. An intermediate stage in melodic change can be seen in the twelfth–thirteenth-century Vat. Barb. lat. 603, whose Vulgate Exultet, in a slightly later hand, begins and ends with the Beneventan melody, slightly elaborated, but most of the portion after the preface has the now usual preface tone, reciting apparently on c.

The history and relation of the Exultet rolls of southern Italy is worthy of a lengthy study of its own. We unfortunately do not have clear enough information to give details of this history either for Montecassino or Benevento, but it is no surprise that our earliest Beneventan text is from Benevento.[23] The relatively early (Avezzano roll) and repeated appearance of the Vulgate version in sources connected with Montecassino (Montecassino Exultet 1, Vat. lat. 3784, Vat. Barb. lat. 592, London, BL, Add. 30337, and Paris 710) is not inconsistent with the abbey's increasing contact with Rome and its widespread influence in the eleventh century.

PROCESSIONAL ANTIPHONS

A number of manuscripts contain one or more Beneventan processional antiphons for use in rogation processions during Lent, or for the greater litanies, occasionally for the Purification procession. The number of Beneventan pieces is small compared to the number of antiphons normally included in such groups, and they are not generally set apart either in a group or at the end of such a series. (Perhaps an exception is the pair of Beneventan Purification antiphons at the end of a group of four in Ben35 – each of them found alone in one other source.) Evidently such pieces were acceptable members of flexible parts of the liturgy. The repertories of rogation antiphons in southern Italy present many interesting questions, including, as they do, not only Beneventan music, but also a substantial amount of local music in a quasi-Gregorian style which sometimes verges on the bizarre. But the size of these repertories, and the many problems they pose that are not directly related to the study of the Beneventan chant, make it necessary to postpone a full-scale examination for a separate study. It should be sufficient to note here that the preservation of these few Beneventan pieces gives no evidence of their coming from a deep level of the repertory. Their texts match, in style and tone, those of other Rogation antiphons, and the pieces do not seem to be items from elsewhere in the liturgy (communions, for example) preserved where their non-Gregorian origin can go undetected.[24]

---

[23] Bannister ("The *Vetus Itala*," p. 44) reports the existence of the Beneventan Exultet in two fifteenth-century (!) missals of Salerno (see also Latil, "Un Exultet"), but the ongoing re-ordering of the cathedral museum of Salerno has made it impossible to verify this.

[24] An exception may be the processional antiphon *Congregamini*, whose fully developed style is related to that of Beneventan mass chants.

These pieces can be found at their place in the repertory list of Appendix 1, and their texts are edited in Appendix 2.

OFFICE MUSIC

The sources of Beneventan office music present special problems, and special opportunities. The surviving music consists almost entirely of antiphons,[25] either in series or occasionally as individual items in an otherwise Gregorian office. These are studied at greater length elsewhere.[26] In the context of the study of the sources, however, we can distinguish three types of transmission:

1 The filling in of the office of a local saint which the received Gregorian repertory lacks. Series of Beneventan antiphons for the Holy Twelve Brothers and for Saint Barbatus, saints of purely local veneration, are to be found in a number of manuscripts of the twelfth century and later. A similar, but more complex case, is that of the south Italian offices for Saint Apollinaris and for Saints Nazarius and Celsus, both feasts of saints particularly venerated in Milan; in these cases the south Italian sources provide non-Gregorian antiphons, but the music is a mixture of Ambrosian and Beneventan chant. For St Apollinaris the sources provide what is basically two separate series of antiphons, Ambrosian and Beneventan. For Sts Nazarius and Celsus Ben21 provides an Ambrosian series concluding with a final elaborate Beneventan antiphon for Magnificat and Benedictus, while Ben20 provides a shorter series, using many of the same texts, in Beneventan style.[27] The Ambrosian and Beneventan versions of the same text share a similar underlying melody. It would appear that there is a three-level importation here: firstly, Ambrosian melodies arrive with the cult of Ambrosian saints; secondly, they are reworked to echo the local Beneventan musical style; and thirdly, they are preserved as Gregorian antiphons where the received office music lacked formularies.

2 The preservation of older Beneventan mass chants as canticle antiphons. The Gregorian practice of adapting gospel-antiphons as communions is related to this phenomenon, but since the Beneventan communion texts are not taken from the gospels, it is difficult to establish a connection between an antiphon and a possible mass in which it might have served as communion. What seems clear, however, is that many pieces can survive as antiphons long after the mass to which they may also belong has been eliminated. At least one Beneventan communion (*Hos duodecim* for the Holy Twelve Brothers) is used as a Magnificat antiphon in a south Italian Gregorian antiphoner (Ben21, f. 236), and a number of other pieces in elaborated Beneventan style are found in similar places for other saints in Gregorian offices.[28] These pieces, in scope and style similar to the Beneventan communions and offertories preserved in Vat. Ottob. 145 as

---

[25] There is a Beneventan responsory for John the Baptist, and some responsory melodies found in south Italian antiphoners are unique to the area and may well bear some relation to older local music; but these latter do not give evidence of close kinship with the central layers of Beneventan chant, and they are best passed over in an initial study designed to focus attention on the older layers of the chant uncontaminated by long transmission in Gregorian sources.

[26] Chapters 3 (for the melodies), 4 (for the relation to Ambrosian chant), and in Kelly, "Non-Gregorian."

[27] The ordinal Ben66 shows a mixture of the two versions. For more detail, see Chapter 4, pp. 197–203, and Kelly, "Non-Gregorian."

[28] See Chapter 3.

mandatum antiphons, may be remnants of Beneventan mass formularies not surviving elsewhere.

3 The adjustment to Beneventan style of melodies which may be of later non-Beneventan origin. We have seen this process already in the office of St Apollinaris, and there are many antiphons in our sources for the office which bear traces of cadences and melodic details reminiscent of Beneventan chant, though their underlying melodies are in many cases those of Gregorian (or Ambrosian) chant. Such melodies are found in the offices of Sts Benedict, Scolastica, Vincent, John and Paul, Silvester, Germanus of Capua, and doubtless others as well.[29] To include these within the canon of Beneventan chant, however, is to mistake the echo for the long-departed singer, and although this music bears clear witness to the persistence of the Beneventan melodic style, and shows yet another way in which it was preserved, its hybrid nature makes it more a souvenir than a document.[30]

The manuscript sources of Beneventan chant make it clear that we must bear in mind the problem of preservation when attempting a study of this music, for in no case do we have the entire repertory in its pure form. The resistance of the local music before the advancing wave of Gregorian reform, and the valiant efforts of scribes, in several places and over several generations, to preserve the local rite, testify to the esteem in which it was held by at least some conservative elements. And the variety of means – all ultimately without success – which were discovered to preserve the Beneventan chant, can be a valuable model for the study and reconstruction of other vanished repertories.

---

[29] See below, pp. 69–70, 138–9.

[30] A curious case in reverse is the responsory *Magnus es domine* in Ben37, which preserves its (probably original) Beneventan melody, but adapts it by altering the cadences to Gregorian style.

3

THE BENEVENTAN LITURGY

It is ironic that the liturgy of Benevento is preserved for us largely in manuscripts of mixed Gregorian and Beneventan usage. Perhaps this might have pleased the scribes of these books, who labored to preserve a portion of the native rite. The results, however, must be viewed in the light of their intentions: what is preserved reflects, not the Beneventan liturgy in its full flowering, but in its last gasp – a liturgy under siege, now incomplete, and perhaps rearranged to fit within an Gregorian gradual.

Though there are remnants of several "pure" Beneventan music books, none of them is now more than a fragment, or a few notes or letters in an almost perished palimpsest. In them we can see only faint traces of the larger practice, a few refinements of our understanding of the liturgy and its music. Their chief witness is to the extent of this repertory's transmission during the very brief period between its having been written down and its extinction a few years later.

The wider aspects of the Beneventan liturgy – that is, beyond the musical pieces that survive – are closed to us. We have no lectionaries, sacramentaries, or other service books of the Beneventan rite which might give the basis for a comparison between Benevento and other Western liturgies. It is only from small bits of evidence, like the Good Friday *ordo* of Vat. lat. 10673, that we can be sure that the Beneventan rite was as independent liturgically as it was musically.

There are, however, many non-standard features in the Gregorian masses of Beneventan manuscripts. Lacking an old Beneventan lectionary or sacramentary, we cannot be certain that these are features of the older Beneventan liturgy, but their exceptional quality merits attention.[1] They include, for the lectionary: (1) lessons that vary from Roman practice, especially as regards the Lenten Sunday gospels, (2) the use of non-scriptural lessons at mass, and (3) the remnants of a system of three readings for the mass.

1 The gospels for the Sundays of Lent provide a series of pericopes from John that do not match the Roman gospel series.[2] These are found in Ben33 (though they have been corrected to

---

[1] An overview of the unique liturgical features of Beneventan and central Italian mass-books is provided by Gamber, "La liturgia."

[2] The unanimous surviving Roman practice uses these gospels elsewhere in Lent; the present system is already clearly in place in the Lectionary of Würzburg. See Hesbert, "Les dimanches." On the possible early use of these pericopes at Rome in connection with the Lenten scrutinies see Callewaert, "S. Grégoire."

agree with the Roman lectionary),[3] in the early eleventh-century homiliary Naples VI B 2 (also corrected), and in the Dalmatian missal Oxford, Bodl. Can. liturg. 342, though it lacks the evidence of the fifth Sunday;[4] Ben38 shows by the communion *Qui biberit* the gospel of the Samaritan woman for the second Sunday.[5] These are essentially the same pericopes as those used at Milan. In the Ambrosian rite, Sundays in Lent are named for their gospels: "De Samaritana" (Lent II), "De Abraham" (III), "De Caeco" (IV), "De Lazaro" (V),[6] and the same names are used for Lenten weeks in south Italian liturgical books.[7]

2 The use of a reading from hagiographical literature is occasionally found in the mass. Benevento 33 provides, for the feasts of St Martin and St Nazarius, a lesson from the life of the saint, and the same usage for St Martin is found in the palimpsest of Wolfenbüttel 112; this is a practice to be found also in the Milanese liturgy.[8]

3 A number of Beneventan sources provide three readings at mass. Benevento 33 follows, for the Sundays after Pentecost, a system of three lessons like that used in Milan: Old Testament, epistle, gospel.[9] Traces of this system of three lections can also be found in other Beneventan and central Italian books.[10] Michel Huglo has shown that in at least some cases the additional lesson, taken from a pre-Vulgate translation, is duplicated elsewhere in a Vulgate version,[11] suggesting that these readings, and the wider practice they represent, are remnants of the older regional rite.

Unusual elements of the sacramentary may be remnants of the older rite: (4) a large number of proper prefaces, (5) a prayer *post evangelium*, and (6) the final prayer *super populum*.

4 Beneventan manuscripts preserve an unusual number of proper prefaces. Those for Sundays in Lent in Ben33 are identical with ones used at Milan,[12] and Klaus Gamber, in fact, has

---

[3] Complete facsimile in PM XX; see Rehle, "Missale beneventanum", pp. 343 (no. 44), 344 (nos. 51, 58), 346 (no. 65), 348 (no. 72).

[4] See Hesbert, "Les dimanches," p. 211. Another Dalmatian book, the Zara Gospel-book, Berlin, Staatsbibliothek Preussischer Kulturbesitz, MS Theol. Lat. Quart. 278, gives these four pericopes special treatment (they are the only Lenten weekday gospels retained, and they are performed in an elaborate manner); they are evidently the remainder of the older tradition in which they held a higher place. See Hesbert, "L'évangéliaire," pp. 202–3.

[5] See Hesbert, "Les dimanches," pp. 205–6; PM XIV, 227–8, and table, pp. 220–1. On the survival of this arrangement in the homiliaries of Benevento see Mallet, *Les Manuscrits*, pp. 58–60.

[6] For the Milanese gospels and the names of the Sundays from a ninth-century Ambrosian sacramentary, see Paredi, *Sacramentarium*, pp. 100, 109–10, 119–20, 129–30, 137–9.

[7] Ben33, f. 50v: "require retro in dominica de Abraam"; f. 51v: "require in dominica de Abraam"; Vat. lat. 10645 (fragments from a Beneventan plenary missal, studied in Dold, "Fragmente"), f. 6v: "require retro in ebdomada de samaritana in feria iii" (facs. in PM XIV, plate VIII); Benevento 18 (homiliary, tenth–eleventh century), f. 58: "Dominica de Lazarum"; Naples VI B 2 (homiliary, early eleventh century): "Dominica iij de Abraham" (f. 137v), "Dominica iiij de ceco" (f. 169), "feria vi require in dominica de Abraham" (f. 196), "Dominica de Lazaro" (f. 200).

[8] See Gamber, "Väterlesungen," and Dold, "Untersuchungsergebnisse," pp. 238–9.

[9] Gamber, "Die Sonntagsmessen."

[10] In a missal fragment in Altamura for the Epiphany season (see Kelly, "Beneventan Fragments"), and in fragments of a missal now scattered in Zurich, Peterlingen, and Lucerne (see Dold, *Die Zürcher*, table, p. LII, and pp. 1, 4, 5–6, 10, 24, 29, 32; and Omlin, "Ein Messbuchfragment," p. 47); prophetic third readings for Christmas masses are found in the twelfth-century missals Vatican, Barberini lat. 603 (Caiazzo) and Barberini lat. 699 (Veroli), and in the thirteenth-century Dalmatian missal Oxford 342. A third reading is found for St Michael in Vat. lat. 6082 (see Dold, "Die vom Missale," p. 306).

[11] Huglo, "Fragments de Jérémie," pp. 83–4.

[12] See Moeller, *Corpus praefationum*, CLXI, pp. LXXXI–LXXXVIII; the shared prefaces for the Sundays in Lent are numbers 502, 627, 799, 920, and 1594 in Moeller's catalogue. Additional prefaces from Ben33, used also at Milan, include Moeller's numbers

suggested that the Milanese arrangement for these Sundays may have been borrowed from Benevento.[13]

5 Beneventan and central Italian missals have an *oratio post evangelium* for many principal feasts.[14] Antoine Chavasse has suggested that this corresponds to the Ambrosian prayer *super sindonem* and was, at its origin, a prayer said by the celebrant, following a litany by the deacon, having its place after the gospel.[15]

6 The *oratio super populum* found at the end of Roman Lenten masses is found outside of Lent in the Swiss missal fragments and in the palimpsest missal of Vat. Ottob. lat. 576; it may have been a regular feature of the local liturgy.[16]

All these unusual features of the sacramentary (*post evangelium*, proper prefaces, *super populum*) are to be found also in the central Italian missal Vat. lat. 4770, whose Beneventan connections are numerous.[17]

THE BENEVENTAN CALENDAR

Three manuscripts provide almost all our information on the Beneventan mass. Ben40 and to a lesser extent Ben38 include Beneventan masses as doublets after the Gregorian masses for major feasts of the liturgical year. Since these two manuscripts, like many at Benevento, are incomplete at their beginning (Ben38 begins in pre-Lent, Ben40 in Holy Week), the final flyleaf of Ben35 – apparently a leaf from a pure Beneventan gradual – is our only clear witness to the Beneventan rite in the period before the end of Lent.

Some twenty masses – more or less complete – are preserved in Ben35, Ben38, and Ben40, for the major festivals of the year. They are detailed in Appendix 1, and are summarized in table 3.1. Most of the major feasts we should expect in a group this size are included here, along with some that are peculiarly regional (St Michael *in monte Gargano*, the Holy Twelve Brothers). The somewhat involved question of the feasts of the Holy Cross will be reconsidered later; they may be of relatively late institution.

What additional feasts of the Beneventan rite may be lacking in what survives from these three manuscripts?

In the proper of the time, there is a lacuna between the Christmas and Stephen masses in the Ben35 flyleaf and the beginning of the testimony of Ben38 and Ben40. Into this period fall

---

616 bis, 637, and 1051. On prefaces in the Swiss fragments from Zurich, Peterlingen, and Lucerne, see Dold, *Die Zürcher*, p. XLI; Omlin, "Ein Messbuchfragment," pp. 45, 49; see also Gamber, "Fragmente," p. 368.

[13] Gamber, "Die kampanische Lektionsordnung," pp. 344–5, and "Das kampanische Messbuch," pp. 31–42.

[14] Nine survive in the Swiss missal fragments: see Dold, *Die Zürcher*, pp. XLVI–XLV and 3, 9, 22, 26, 27, 30, 31. Ben33 preserves the *post evangelium* for Sundays after Pentecost: see Rehle, "Missale beneventanum," pp. 386, 388; this is also a feature of the central Italian missal Vat. lat. 4770: see Gamber, "Die mittelitalienisch," pp. 276–7; and a further example is a fragment of a Beneventan missal including a *post evangelium* for the Transfiguration: Macerata, Archivio di Stato, Tabulario diplomatico 491.

[15] "L'oraison super sindonem": see Gamber, *Missa romensis*, pp. 46–55. Opposing Chavasse's view is Martelli ("Un fenomeno," and especially "I formulari," pp. 570–1), who prefers, with Dold (*Die Zürcher*, pp. XXXI–XXXIII) to view the *post evangelium* as an influence of the Byzantine liturgy of St John Crisostom.

[16] Dold, *Die Zürcher*, pp. XLI and 23, 28, 29, 32; and Gamber, "Fragmente," pp. 368, 371.

[17] See Gamber, "Die mittelitalienisch," pp. 276–7.

Table 3.1 *Preserved Beneventan masses*

	Ben40	Ben38	Ben35
1 Christmas	///	///	202
2 St Stephen	///	///	202
/////	///	///	///
3 Palm Sunday	///	37v	///
4 Maundy Thursday	4v	///	///
5 [Good Friday liturgy]	10v	43	///
6 Holy Saturday	15v	43v	///
7 Easter	159v/27	52v	///
8 Invention of the Holy Cross	—	[79:Off]	///
9 St Michael (8 May)	61	83	///
10 Ascension	71	93	///
11 Pentecost	79v	99	///
12 St John the Baptist	89	110	///
13 Sts Peter and Paul	99	115v	///
14 St Lawrence	112v	—	///
15 Assumption	118	128	///
16 Holy Twelve Brothers	121v	—	///
17 Exaltation of the Holy Cross	124v	—	///
18 Sts Simon and Jude	128v	—	///
19 All Saints	133v	—	///
20 St Martin	138v	—	///
21 St Andrew	142	140	///

Epiphany and Lent, as well as the feasts of many saints. Possibly missing owing to lacunae are the following:

1 Advent. It seems unlikely that Advent masses should be part of this group, which consists of major feasts of the year. Ordinary Sundays of the year are not included after Pentecost (nor, probably, were they included after Epiphany), and there is no evidence that Advent is different. (However, the same cannot be said of Lent: see below.)

2 St John the Evangelist and the Holy Innocents. Where St Stephen is present in Western manuscripts we generally find the feasts for the two succeeding days as well. The palimpsest folio 37 of Rome, Vall. c 9 gives a tantalizing hint of the feast of St John, though its evidence is equivocal. A melismatic piece beginning on line 1 of this palimpsest folio has a text now practically illegible, but twice in its course the text includes the name of St John: *beatus iohannes* (line 1) and *iohannes* (line 2). No other text is readable, nor is there any indication of where this piece occurs in its mass. The text is not any of those known for the feast of St John the Baptist (whose ingressa appears on f. 169v of the same manuscript). A puzzling aspect of this piece, however, is that the other leaf of the same bifolium from the original manuscript (f. 32) contains music for Holy Saturday. This bifolium, now reversed to receive upper script, may have been the outside leaf of a gathering, with the present f. 37 preceding f. 32.[18] In such a fascicle there might possibly have been room for the feast of St John the Evangelist, the Holy Inno-

[18] See Kelly, "Palimpsest evidence," pp. 15–18.

cents, Epiphany, and masses of Lent and Holy Week, especially if there were an additional bifolium making the gathering into a quinternion.[19]

3 Epiphany. There can be no doubt that in a full series of Beneventan masses there would have been a formulary for the feast of the Epiphany, and there may be the remnants of such a mass. A palimpsest piece in Vall. c 9 (f. 20v) reveals fragments of text (*iordanis stupuit [co]lumba prote[statur]. . .filius [meus hic est. . .?]*) matching that of the Ambrosian *transitorium* for Epiphany.[20] The melody is clearly Beneventan.

4 Lent. Though we can detect hints of a distinct Lenten practice at Benevento in the Sunday gospels and the naming of Lenten weeks, almost nothing remains of its chant, except for the special rites of Holy Week.

Though Ben38 preserves much of Gregorian Lent, it does not include Beneventan doublet masses (though it has the Beneventan antiphon *Dum sanctificatus fuero* for Lenten scrutinies[21]). Ben40, which generally has more Beneventan music than Ben38, lacks all of Lent before Monday in Holy Week; we cannot tell whether it contained Beneventan masses for Lenten Sundays.

Probably, however, there were individual Lenten masses included in the compilation that has come down to us in fragmentary form in Vall. c 9. The bifolium ff. 24/29 contains several suggestive elements. On f. 24v, line 1, begins a Beneventan offertory (identified by its rubric) whose text includes the letters *quadra*[illegible] *dies*, perhaps a reference to the forty days of Lent. This is preceded (line 1) by the end of a melismatic piece – perhaps it is the only surviving evidence of a Lenten tract – whose text concludes with *libera nos*. On the recto of the other leaf of the bifolium (now f. 29), in addition to evidence of much Beneventan music, part of a rubric can be read: . . .*esima Ingsa*. This may mark the ingressa at the beginning of another Lenten mass. Though much music is visible on these pages, and occasional letters and syllables, we cannot reconstruct the entire text or melody of any of these pieces. This Lenten music – if that is what it is – must remain tantalizingly out of reach for the moment, until new techniques or old persistence can elicit more evidence from the palimpsest.

5 St Benedict. All three principal sources lack the portion of the manuscript where the feast of St Benedict would appear. But a single communion, presented like a Beneventan mass after the Gregorian propers, survives in Montecassino Compactiones xx11 labeled as "another, ambrosian, communion" (*alia cō. ambro.*). In another guise the same piece survives also in Vat. Ottob. 145 as one of several "antiphons" for a *mandatum* ceremony.[22] Given what we know of the place of Beneventan chant at Montecassino it would seem odd if there were not a Beneventan mass for the founder. That the whole mass does not survive owes partly to the incompleteness of the early Beneventan books, and partly to the zeal with which Beneventan chant was eradicated at Montecassino.[23]

---

[19] Other possible feasts naming *beatus iohannes* seem unlikely prospects for a collection of major feasts: beheading of St John the Baptist, 29 September; conception of St John the Baptist, 24 September; St John before the Latin gate, May 6; Sts John and Paul, June 26; deposition of blessed John archbishop of Constantinople, November 13. All these feasts are found in the eleventh-century calendar of Walters 6: see Rehle, *Missale beneventanum von Canosa*, pp. 31–47.

[20] See AMed 70–1.

[21] See PM x1v, 243–8.

[22] These pieces, as we shall see (p. 79, note 83), are also communions.

[23] We know, however, that Ben38, at least, contained the feast of St Benedict: the communion for St George, *Letabitur*, is marked *require in sancti Benedicti*. We cannot tell, however, whether there was a Beneventan doublet mass.

In addition to feasts occurring in the calendar between the end of the Ben35 flyleaf and the beginning of the evidence of Ben38 and Ben40, some additional dates for the Beneventan calendar may be the following:

6 St Paul. In the palimpsest Beneventan gradual MC 361 (p. 150), the communion of the Beneventan mass for St Peter (presumably the last item for the feast) is followed by a piece, a shred of whose text (and music) can be read: *te paul[e?] ap.*[24]

Ben38 and Ben40 both follow the practice, adopted at Rome in the course of the seventh century, of celebrating St Peter on June 29 and St Paul on June 30,[25] though their martyrdoms were originally celebrated together on June 29. The later practice of recombining their feasts on June 29, as the Roman church now does, prevailed in the eighth and ninth centuries under Frankish influence.[26] The Beneventan mass between the Gregorian masses for St Peter and St Paul celebrates both saints, at least in its offertory (*Petrus apostolus et Paulus doctor*) and communion (*Ut cognosceris*).[27] The fragmentary text in MC 361 might be an additional piece (a second communion is not rare in Beneventan masses) for the joint celebration, or it might be the beginning of a separate mass for St Paul. The latter seems less likely in view of the inclusion of St Paul in the earlier mass and because no Beneventan mass for St Paul survives in Ben38.[28]

The Beneventan rite varied from the received Roman practice by celebrating Saints Peter and Paul together, and they were never separated as they were in seventh-century Rome to permit separate stational celebrations. Since the Gregorian rite of eleventh-century Benevento preserves an older usage than that current elsewhere, the Beneventan practice must be older still (though by accident it matches the later usage).

7 One or more feasts of apostles. The scribes of Ben38 and Ben40 occasionally use cues to refer to the full version of a chant found elsewhere; in a few cases, these cues refer to pieces found nowhere in the surviving sources.[29] Among these are the Alleluia *In omnem terram [exivit sonus eorum?]*, cued in Ben38 and in Ben40 for Sts Simon and Jude; Ben40 cues two further pieces for Sts Simon and Jude (*Confortatus est [principatus eorum, et honorati sunt amici tui, Deus?]* and *Nolite timere [eos qui corpus occidunt?]*) which have not survived elsewhere. Undoubtedly these pieces were used for at least one other feast in the Beneventan rite, likely for apostles (*In omnem terram*) or martyrs (*Nolite timere*). To speculate as to their assignment (St Vincent? Philip and Jacob? John and Paul?) is to go beyond the evidence. Such pieces, of course, may have served more than one feast, as the beginning of a common of saints; we have already the example of the Alleluia *Posuisti*, used for both St Stephen and St Lawrence.

What may be a mass for the common of apostles survives in fragmentary form in Vall. C 9

[24] The visible music makes it clear that this is not the Gregorian Alleluia *Sancte Paule apostole.*

[25] See *Sextuplex*, pp. 137–9.

[26] See Chavasse, "Les fêtes."

[27] Ben38 uses *Petrus apostolus* as offertory, and has the communion *Tu es pastor*, whose incomplete text may or may not refer to St Paul.

[28] The feast of St Paul, as it is called in Ben38 and Ben40, follows the Beneventan mass of Sts Peter and Paul in both manuscripts, and in both it is a substantial feast, with tropes and sequences. There is a lacuna at the end of St Paul, after f. 99v, in Ben40; if a Beneventan mass followed the Gregorian (perhaps with an ingressa *Sancte Paule apostole*), it is now lost. There is no Beneventan mass of St Paul in Ben38, though St Peter, on the preceding day, has one; Ben38, however, lacks many Beneventan masses of saints which are present in Ben40.

[29] See Chapter 2, pp. 50–2.

(f. 173). This palimpsest page continues from f. 172v with the end of the ingressa *Prima predicationis* for St Andrew; next comes an offertory (rubric *of*), very difficult to read, which may well be the offertory *Salve crux* for St Andrew. Several lines lower on the page are the remnants of the ingressa *Michi autem nimis*, used in Ben40 for Sts Simon and Jude. After a gap of two lines is a piece in Beneventan musical style whose text can be reconstructed as: "[in omnem] ter[ram exi]vit sonus eorum et [in] fines orbis terre [ver]ba eorum." This piece (which is not the missing Alleluia *In omnem* cued for Sts Simon and Jude in Ben40) is followed in turn by a further indecipherable piece.

In view of the liturgical ordering of this fascicle,[30] whatever follows St Andrew is likely to be part of the common of saints. These two texts, frequently used for apostles,[31] may belong to a common of saints to which the cues in Ben38 and Ben40 refer.

8 There is indirect evidence for masses of other saints. A number of later Gregorian office books contain occasional pieces – often a single Magnificat antiphon – in developed Beneventan style, often for saints of local importance. In some cases at least, these pieces may be discarded elements from a Beneventan mass. The Beneventan repertory, like the Gregorian, furnishes several examples of pieces used both in the mass and the office: (1) the communion of the Holy Twelve Brothers is a Magnificat antiphon in Ben21; (2) the communion *Sancta Maria* survives as an antiphon in Berkeley 1000:6; (3) a number of Beneventan communions are grouped in Vat. Ottob. 145 as antiphons without psalmody; (4) the "Solesmes flyleaves" (no. 11 above), preserving Beneventan vespers of John the Baptist, include three antiphons used in Ben38 and Ben40 for the mass.[32]

The following offices have Beneventan music, and hence connect the saint with the Beneventan liturgy.[33]

a Sts John and Paul (26 June): *Mandaverunt iuliano*, the canticle antiphon in Ben21 and Montecassino Compactiones v, is in Beneventan style.

b St Sylvester (31 December): *Vir dei silvester* in Ben21 and Ben22 is the last antiphon in a series of otherwise Gregorian melodies. This feast is in the oldest witnesses of the Gregorian tradition, though the feast is not one of particular solemnity at Benevento.[34]

c St Vincent (6 June). The canticle antiphon *Insigne preconium* (Ben21: Magnificat; MC Compactiones v: Magnificat and Benedictus) includes a number of Beneventan musical traits, and has a text which is used also in the Ambrosian and Gregorian rites for a variety of martyrs;[35] the antiphon itself may be a reworking of imported material. The regional office of St Vincent[36] has melodies reminiscent in some ways of Beneventan chant, particularly in the use of characteristic cadences. We should not be surprised, of course, to find local music for the

---

[30] See Appendix 3 for contents of the palimpsest.

[31] See the index in *Sextuplex* for the use of the analogous texts *Nimis honorati* and *In omnem*.

[32] *Iohannes est nomen eius* (cued in Ben38 as an offertory); *Inter natos mulierum* (cued in Ben38 as a communion; offertory in Ben40) – this piece is also among the Beneventan antiphons in Vat. Ottob. 145; and *Zacharias pater* (used in Ben40 as communion).

[33] We must not be deterred by the fact that many of these antiphons are narrative, drawing their texts from the life of the saint; for, although such texts are rare in the Roman mass, they are not uncommon at Benevento. Consider such texts as *Tunc imperator Eraclius* and *Quid ad nos Egea* (see Appendix 2): both are communions.

[34] See *Sextuplex*, pp. LXXXIV–LXXXV.

[35] See Appendix 2.

[36] In Ben19 (f. 33ff.), Ben21 (f. 66ff.), Montecassino 542 (f. 86ff.), and MC Comp. v.

patron of San Vincenzo al Volturno, one of the great and powerful monasteries of the region, founded by nobles from Benevento. In fact, however, with these equivocal exceptions we have no evidence of the chant of San Vincenzo itself, nor of a Beneventan mass for its patron.[37]

d St Barbatus (19 February). The antiphoners of Benevento[38] present a series of antiphons in Beneventan style.[39] Some have texts drawn from the life of the saint, who was bishop of Benevento in the seventh century,[40] and whose cult seems to have been developed by the first half of the ninth century.[41] Ben38 and Ben40 now lack the portions that may have contained a Beneventan mass of St Barbatus.

e Sts Nazarius and Celsus (28 July). The antiphons in Ben21 for these Milanese saints match music in Ambrosian books, but the same antiphons have Beneventan melodies in Ben20.[42] Both series conclude, however, with the substantial Beneventan antiphon *Beatus Nazarius una cum Celso*, which may be the remnant of an earlier layer of local music.[43]

f St Apollinaris (23 July). The Beneventan antiphoners preserve a combination of Ambrosian and Beneventan music for the office of Apollinaris, bishop of Ravenna, who is highly venerated at Milan.[44]

g St Xistus (6 August). The final antiphon, *Usque in senectam*, in Ben20 and Ben21 is in Beneventan style, but its melody is closely related to an Ambrosian antiphon for the same feast (Oxford, Bodleian MS Lat. liturg. a. 4, f. 174). This feast is celebrated in the earliest Gregorian manuscripts, but this antiphon is found only in the south of Italy and at Milan.[45] It may, of course, have been borrowed from the Ambrosian liturgy, but, unlike the wholesale parallels in the offices of St Apollinaris and Sts Nazarius and Celsus, which may represent some portion of later borrowing, this single antiphon has a melody in Beneventan style that resembles, but is not identical with, its Ambrosian counterpart. That there is a close and ancient relationship between Milan and Benevento will become increasingly evident, and is discussed in more detail in Chapter 5. Most of the shared melodies descend from a common original that may well have originated in the Lombard kingdom of northern Italy. But the Beneventan forms are Beneventan, not Milanese, and that there is at least one Beneventan piece for the office of St Xistus suggests there may at one time have been more local music for his feast.

The evidence of Beneventan music for additional feasts increases the number of days for which we can suppose that the Beneventan rite provided liturgical formularies, probably including

---

[37] This is partly owing to the scarcity of manuscripts from the abbey. See Duval-Arnould, "Les manuscrits"; and TBS, I, 75–6.

[38] Ben21 and Ben22; in Ben20 St Barbatus is represented only by a *vita* divided for liturgical reading.

[39] To these, Ben21 adds a final antiphon *O quam pretiosis beneventus*, adapted to the melody of the Advent O-antiphons.

[40] The *vita* edited in MGH SS Lang., pp. 555–63, cannot have been composed before the ninth century, according to its editor (see MGH SS Lang., p. 555). See also Gay, *L'Italie méridionale*, pp. 197–8; and Viscardi, *Le origini*, pp. 385–7.

[41] Belting, "Studien," p. 161.

[42] See Chapter 5, pp. 39–41, and table 5.4.

[43] Though Nazarius does not appear in early Roman documents, his feast is an important one at Milan, and also appears regularly in Beneventan manuscripts. Indeed, there is a special alternative mass for him in Ben40 (ff. 102v–104), which includes the Ambrosian ingressa and the full texts and music of a Milanese *Gloria in excelsis*: see Kelly, "Beneventan and Milanese."

[44] See Chapter 5, pp. 197–9, and Kelly, "Non-Gregorian music."

[45] *Sextuplex*, p. CII; CAO 5283.

masses. This group is summarized in table 3.2; those feasts which have no surviving music for the mass are shown by further indentation. There are a few surprising omissions from this list: saints whose particular cult at Benevento would lead us to expect music for their feast days in the Beneventan liturgy, but for whom none survives.[46]

Table 3.2 *Beneventan feasts*

A Proper of the Time
    Christmas
       Epiphany?
    Lenten Sundays
       (Lenten weekdays?)
    Palm Sunday
    Maundy Thursday
    [Good Friday]
    Holy Saturday
    Easter
    Ascension
    Pentecost

B Proper of the Saints
    St Stephen (26 December)
       St John (27 December)
       Holy Innocents (28 December)
       St Sylvester (31 December)
       St Barbatus (19 February)
    St Benedict (21 March)
    Invention of the Holy Cross (3 May)
    St Michael (8 May)
       St Vincent (6 June)
    St John the Baptist (24 June)
       Sts John and Paul (26 June)
    Sts Peter and Paul (29 June)
    St Paul? (30 June)
       St Apollinaris (23 July)
       Sts Nazarius and Celsus (28 July)
    St Lawrence (9 August)
    Assumption (15 August)
    Holy Twelve Brothers (1 September)
    Exaltation of the Holy Cross (14 September)
    Sts Simon and Jude (28 October)
    All Saints (1 November)
    St Martin (11 November)
    St Andrew (30 November)

C Common of the Saints
    Apostles and/or Martyrs

---

[46] Omitted from the following list are two saints who ought not to go unmentioned despite the extremely scanty evidence of their cults.

St Helianus was one of a group of forty Byzantine martyrs, whose remains were brought to Benevento in 763, according to the *Translatio* in Benevento 4, printed in MGH SS Lang., pp. 581–2 (see Mallet, *Les Manuscrits*, p. 137). The place of the saint's interment is unclear ("honorifice situm est in basilica, quam ille [Count Gualtari?] antequam iret construxerat": MGH SS Lang., p. 582). See Belting, "Studien," p. 157.

A St Mercurius. In 768 Arichis II brought the relics of Saint Mercurius, one of the greatest military saints of Byzantium, to the church of Santa Sofia, to serve as patron of the church, the court, the city, and the Lombard people.[47] The early twelfth-century calendars of Santa Sofia (in Vat. lat. 4928 and Naples VI E 43) indicate five feast days: the dedication of the altar in Santa Sofia (18 August), the Translation (26 August), and the feast (*nativitas*) itself (25 November), with vigil and octave.[48] Surviving twelfth-century Beneventan lectionaries provide readings for the Translation and the feast of November 25.[49]

But the musical remains for this significant Beneventan feast are slight. There is no mass of St Mercurius in Ben38 or Ben40, Gregorian or Beneventan,[50] nor any office in Ben19 or Ben20.[51] Ben21 preserves a series of office pieces, including a set of unique antiphons in Gregorian style, but these appear, not at their place in the calendar, but at the end of the manuscript after the common of saints. These antiphons are all named in the extensive office of St Mercurius, with twelve responsories, indicated in the Santa Sofia ordinal Naples VI E 43, ff. 73v–74. There is no evidence of Beneventan music – or of any music whatever – before the twelfth century.

B Saint Januarius (18 September). Though venerated as an early bishop of Benevento after the theft of his relics from Naples about 830,[52] there is no mass for this saint in Ben38 or Ben40.[53] Ben20 and Ben21 have office music in Gregorian style which, though it is unique to Benevento, gives no evidence of the local chant dialect. The feast is named in the calendars and office music

The prophet Elijah, much venerated in the East, also has the remnants of a cult in the Beneventan zone. He is named in the calendar of Baltimore, Walters W 6 for 10 July: "assumptio sci helie precursoris dni" (Rehle, *Missale beneventanum von Canosa*, p. 39). The remnants of a mass for this feast in the fragmentary Vat. lat. 10645, f. 6v ("Missa in assumptione sci helie," facs. in Hesbert, "Les dimanches," after p. 200, and in PM XIV, plate VIII) includes a collect and a secret (incomplete), cues for the lessons, but no chants. A mass is provided also in the thirteenth-century Dalmatian missal Oxford, Bodleian Library, Canon. liturg. 342, ff. 88–9; all the chants are from the Gregorian common; the lessons match those of Vat. lat. 10645, and their collects agree, though the secrets do not. A gospel "In festivitate sancti Helie" (Luke 4:23–30) is in the Zadar Gospel-book Berlin, Staatsbibliothek, Theol. Lat. Quart. 278: see Hesbert, "L'évangéliaire," p. 193.

Such a distinctive feast in widely separated sources suggests a common note of antiquity, though there is no clear evidence of this feast's belonging to the Beneventan liturgy. Feasts of Elijah elsewhere in the West are almost unknown: there is a mass *in natale S. Helie* in Vat. lat. 4770, entirely different from this (Hesbert, "Les dimanches," p. 200), and one is found also in the masses of Mone (Mohlberg, *Missale Gallicanum vetus*, pp. 88–9).

[47] See Chapter I, p. 12.

[48] These, except for the vigil and octave of November 25, are included in the Santa Sofia martyrology London, BL, Add. MS 23776.

[49] Translation: Benevento I, see Mallet, *Les Manuscrits*, p. 115. November 25: Montecassino, Archivio privato MS I, see Mallet, *Les Manuscrits*, p. 252 (on the Beneventan origin of this manuscript, see Mallet, p. 31).

[50] A mass for November 25 assembled from the Gregorian common is found in London, BL, Egerton 2511 (f. 281v). Naples XVI A 19 (f. 44, probably from Santa Sofia, at least in this part) provides a mass using largely metrical texts adapted to Gregorian melodies: Int. *Gaudeamus*; Gr. (second mode) *Glorioso mercurio*; All. *Ortum in armenia* (based on *Justus ut palma*); Off. *Letare felix sampnium* (based on *Laetamini*); Co. *Missa sursum hostia* (based on *Quinque prudentes*). The manuscript also provides masses for the Translation (f. 43) and the Passion (f. 45) of the Holy Twelve Brothers; that these masses are not found in earlier sources, as well as the metrical texts for Mercurius, suggests that all three are twelfth-century creations.

[51] The feast of 25 November is missing from the beginning of Ben19, but no feast of August 18 or 26 was part of the sanctoral of Ben20.

[52] See Chapter I, p. 28.

[53] Ben40 has two masses, all of whose pieces are cued, between St Nicomedis (15 September) and Sts Cosmas and Damian (27 September), but their introits, *Ego autem sicut oliva* and *Os iusti*, along with the rest of the masses, suggest that they are designed for the vigil and feast of St Matthew.

listed in the *ordines* of the Santa Sofia manuscripts Vat. lat. 4928 and Naples VI E 43, and a *Passio* and *Translatio* are included in the monastic lectionary Benevento I.[54]

C Saint Bartholomew (17 June). After the translation of his relics to Benevento in 838, St Bartholomew became the chief saint of the city and a second patron of the cathedral. All the surviving local music is in Gregorian style. A mass for St Bartholomew, unique to Beneventan manuscripts, is found in many of the central sources of the region.[55] This mass (introit *Gaudeamus*, gradual *Exsultemus*, offertory *Digna promamus*, communion *Beatum canimus*) is a series of adaptations of unique texts to pre-existent Gregorian melodies.[56] Likewise there survives a unique series of pieces for the office in Gregorian style.[57]

From the chronology of the cult of these Beneventan saints, we developed in Chapter 1 a picture of the use and decline of Beneventan chant. We have seen that the absence of Beneventan music for ninth-century saints connected with the cathedral (Barbatus, Januarius, Bartholomew) may be associated with the increasing importance of the bishop (archbishop from 969), and the concurrent decline of Benevento as a center of political power. It is evident, for example, that the earliest local feast for which dating is certain, that of the Holy Twelve Brothers, was provided with Beneventan music which fortunately survives. Equally clearly, St Bartholomew was not provided with such a mass in 838. Instead, a new mass in Gregorian style was composed then or later. From this Hesbert concluded that Gregorian chant had so well supplanted the Beneventan by the early ninth century, that a mass for St Bartholomew could be composed in Gregorian style.[58]

But there are puzzling elements here. The cult of St Barbatus, though he was a seventh-century bishop, seems to have gathered strength only in the early ninth century; at a time when we expect Gregorian chant, there are clear remnants of Beneventan chant in the music for his office. Saint Mercurius, translated to Santa Sofia only a few years after the Holy Twelve Brothers, has no Beneventan music – the local office is in Gregorian style, much like the surviving music for St Januarius of some seventy years later.

Although we can imagine substantial changes in the liturgy of Santa Sofia between the eighth century and the comprehensive ordinals of the twelfth (Naples VI E 43 and Vat. lat. 4928, in which the Beneventan mass for the Twelve Brothers has disappeared), the original Beneventan chant was not entirely eradicated: the Beneventan antiphons for Barbatus and the Holy Twelve Brothers survive among those listed in the twelfth century, but there is no evidence that any of the many pieces cued for St Mercurius is in Beneventan style. It seems likely that, as early as 768, there were pressing reasons to avoid composition in Beneventan style.

THE BENEVENTAN MASS

Unlike the Gregorian *antiphonale missarum*, whose texts are almost entirely biblical, the

---

[54] Mallet, *Les Manuscrits*, p. 119.

[55] Ben38, f. 103; Ben40, f. 83v; Ben34, f. 226v, etc.

[56] See. PM XIV, 450–1.

[57] See CAO, II, 469.

[58] PM XIV, 449–51.

Beneventan liturgy includes many non-scriptural texts, and many others that rearrange biblical phrases and ideas. Such a preponderance of non-scriptural texts (almost half of the surviving Beneventan pieces) is reminiscent of the liturgy of Milan, which likewise allows a far greater variety of textual sources than does Rome. And such a usage, in both rites, inevitably recalls the liturgical poetry of the Byzantine rite.[59]

But, as regards the structure of the mass, the Beneventan arrangement is essentially that of the Roman mass. Differences of detail (an ingressa without psalmody, for example) must not blind us to the parallel structure of the two rites. As we shall see in Chapter 5, the Beneventan and Ambrosian rites share many texts and much music, but the essence of the mass at Benevento is far closer to Roman use than to the Milanese. It undoubtedly reflects a long liturgical practice in the region, though much affected by later developments and importations.

The normal complement of proper pieces for a Beneventan mass in the chief surviving documents (Ben35, f. 202; Ben38; and Ben40) is four: ingressa, Alleluia, offertory, communion; occasionally a gradual is provided as well, sometimes replacing the Alleluia. The Alleluia is omitted in Holy Week (and probably throughout Lent). A number of masses have two communions, and one has two offertories.

The preservation of Beneventan chant in books designed principally for Gregorian music can account for some of these similarities. Some of the anomalies of presentation suggest a rearrangement of an earlier ordering – a rearrangement prompted, no doubt, by an urge to present the Beneventan masses as alternatives, rather than as competitors, to the received Gregorian counterparts. A look at each of the components of the mass is a starting point before moving to a consideration of certain irregularities in particular masses and feasts, which give hints both of the chronology of the repertory and of its rearrangement.

Ingressa

As in the Ambrosian mass, the entrance chant of the Beneventan rite is called an ingressa, and like its Milanese counterpart, it is presented without accompanying psalmody.[60] The melodies are often elaborate, rather longer than would be convenient if repeated as antiphons. One ingressa, however, is followed by two verses: *Venite omnes* for the second mass of the Holy Cross (a mass in many ways unusual). The two verses are not from the psalter, and their melodies are not psalmodic recitation formulas (like the *versus ad repetendum* in the Beneventan Good Friday vespers); there is no indication of a reprise of the ingressa. Their presence, and their use, are puzzling.

In several cases the same melody serves for more than one ingressa; these represent, not the repeated formulaic patterns seen in many ingressae, but the adaptation of a new text to an earlier melody. They will be considered in the context of the later feasts.

---

[59] The relation of Benevento to Rome, Milan, and Byzantium is discussed in Chapter 5.

[60] A series of ingressae in Rome, Vall. C 9, on three consecutive pages (ff. 168v–169v) includes two (*Michi autem absit*, f. 168v, and an unidentified piece at the top of the same page) with psalmodic endings, but these pieces are arranged in a series separated from their masses, and are perhaps intended as processional or occasional pieces.

Gradual

Only six graduals, each with a single verse, survive in the three main sources. Two of them (*Scribite hunc* for St Stephen and *Vadit propitiator* for Maundy Thursday) include a cue at the end of the verse for a partial reprise, while the others indicate no such reprise, nor do they have texts which might suggest one.

Graduals were probably a regular part of the Beneventan mass, despite their rare appearance in the masses of Ben38 and Ben40. The palimpsest pages of a Beneventan mass-book in Vat. lat. 10657 indicate the presence of three graduals, each marked with the sign ℟ (*responsorium*). Two are for feasts whose masses have no gradual in Ben40,[61] the third is indicated on f. 101v, where only the very faint sign ℟ in the margin, followed by the sign *of* farther down the page, indicates the presence of a mass with a gradual.

Montecassino 361, which also preserves fragments of a Beneventan *antiphonale missarum* has rubrics (p. 144) indicating the gradual verse, the Alleluia with verse, and the offertory of an unidentified Beneventan mass. It is much to be regretted that for none of these graduals can we recover the text or music. We can only note their existence as an indication that, at least in these "pure" Beneventan books, a gradual is a regular feature of the mass.[62]

Only two of the surviving graduals have texts from the psalms; there is little reason to think that the Beneventan gradual represents a curtailed and stylized psalmody. They are apparently conceived in their present responsorial form.

To these known graduals for the mass we may add the *responsoria* that serve in the Beneventan Holy Week rites as quasi-graduals following lessons. These include *Ante sex dies* (at the blessing of palms on Palm Sunday), *Amicus meus* and *Tenebrae* for Good Friday. The latter two are named as *responsoria* in the Vatican Good Friday *ordo* (ff. 33 and 33v) – a term evidently used for the gradual as well, at least in MC 361 and Vat. lat. 10657, though Ben35, Ben38, and Ben40 uniformly indicate the gradual with the sign G̅ or G̅R̅.

In the mass books there are two responsories not connected with lessons (*Lavi pedes* for Maundy Thursday in Ben40 and *Precursor domini* for vespers of St John the Baptist in the Solesmes flyleaves). These two, and the three quasi-gradual responsories just mentioned, all indicate a partial repetition of the respond. That the respond is repeated sometimes in part, and sometimes not (presumably repeated entire?), is a puzzling inconsistency. We cannot explain it, but simply point it out as possible evidence of the impurity of the Beneventan transmission. Whether the *responsorium* and the gradual are interchangeable terms cannot be determined with certainty, since we know so little about office responsories in the Beneventan rite.[63]

---

[61] St John the Baptist (f. 103, the gradual follows the ingressa *Lumen quod*, and is followed by a piece marked as an offertory) and Sts Peter and Paul (f. 100v, following the ingressa *Petrus dormiebat*).

[62] The frequent omission of the gradual in Ben38 and Ben40 is probably not the result of a distinction between solo and choral music, since the Alleluia and its verse are a regular feature of these masses.

[63] It would be extremely useful to know whether the gradual of St John the Baptist in Vat. lat. 10657 is the same piece as the "responsorium ambrosianum" in the Solesmes flyleaves; the answer might establish the equivalence of gradual and responsory. Unfortunately it is impossible to see anything of the text or music of the piece in the Vatican manuscript.

Tract

There is little evidence that tracts are part of the Beneventan mass. This is owing, in part, to the absence of masses for Lent,[64] but the one surviving mass where we might expect a tract (Palm Sunday, in Ben38) has none. The only other Lenten mass, that of Maundy Thursday, has no tract at Benevento or in the Roman rite (though a *cantus* is used at Milan).[65]

There are four surviving Beneventan pieces called *tractus*: these are chants for Holy Saturday; three of them follow lessons, and the fourth (*Sicut cervus*) is used during the procession to the font.[66] Three of these tracts use the pre-Vulgate texts which are also used in the Roman Holy Saturday rite, but they are not identical with their Gregorian counterparts, for they use different amounts and selections of the original text, and their melodies are Beneventan. The fourth tract, *Domine audivi*, is a curious melange; the same scriptural passage is used in the Roman rite on Good Friday, but the Beneventan text is from the Vulgate – except the first verse (*Domine audivi auditum tuum*), which matches the older biblical version of the Gregorian tract, and which in fact also borrows from its music.[67]

The surviving Beneventan tracts, in short, are not a homogeneous group. They are affected, or at least one of them is, by Roman practice, and musically their styles vary. All four are based on the same core of melodic material, but two of them (*Attende celum* and *Sicut cervus*) consist of a series of psalmodic verses; while the two others appear to be responsorial, having an opening period with its own melody followed by a series of formulaic verses.

Alleluia

With the exception of St Stephen and Holy Saturday all the Alleluias in Beneventan masses use the same melody. They represent a stage of development preceding the great medieval flowering of individual melodies for the Alleluia. Other repertories also have a limited number of Alleluia melodies: essentially ten melodies at Milan,[68] and a similar paucity in the Old Roman rite. The Beneventan melodies lack the long melismas with repeated segments, and the musical repetitions from jubilus to verse, that characterize the later Gregorian Alleluia style.[69]

All masses outside Lent have Alleluias, except for that of St Martin.[70] Two verses are used

---

[64] The fragment *libera nos* in Vall. c 9, f. 24v, may be the remnant of a Lenten tract, see above, p. 67.

[65] The palimpsest Vall. c 9 (f. 19) has the tract *Domine audivi* placed after the Maundy Thursday ingressa *Postquam surrexit* and after an intervening space for a rubric and at least one chant piece (a gradual?). This tract, usually used for Holy Saturday, is repeated for that feast on f. 32v, where the end of its last verse precedes the Holy Saturday tract *Cantabo*.

[66] The complex mixture of Gregorian and Beneventan tracts for Holy Saturday, complicated by the fact that the Gregorian tradition at Benevento called for twelve tracts, has been studied in detail by Hesbert: see PM XIV, 339–75 and "L'antiphonale" (6), pp. 154–83.

[67] PM XIV, 361–5; this piece, as we have seen (above note 65) is used both for Maundy Thursday and Holy Saturday in Vall. c 9. For the musical relationship, see example 5.3.

[68] Bailey, *The Ambrosian Alleluias*, pp. 46–52 and 88–91.

[69] The melody and its settings are considered in detail in Chapter 4.

[70] Unfortunately, we cannot verify the presence of an Alleluia in the incomplete mass for Christmas in Ben35, which now begins with the end of the Credo.

more than once: *Posuisti* is for feasts of martyrs (St Stephen and St Lawrence)[71] and *In omnem terram* for apostles (Sts Simon and Jude and Sts Peter and Paul).[72]

Two Alleluias have a melody that is not the standard one: *Posuisti*, whose full melody is found only for St Stephen in the final flyleaf of Ben35, and *Resurrexit tamquam dormiens* for Holy Saturday.

Resurrexit is used in a variety of combinations. In several cases it includes a second verse *Laudate pueri*, and once (Farfa) the latter verse appears without *Resurrexit*. These are not, however, two verses set to the same melody (like the "standard" Beneventan Alleluia verses), but two verses with related melodies, attached to the same opening Alleluia.[73] Perhaps this combination represents an amalgam of originally separate functions: one Alleluia for Easter (whose text is shared with the Ambrosian liturgy) and one connected to the rites for the newly baptized (*Laudate pueri* – a text also used in the Roman rite in connection with the neophyte's rites of the Saturday *in albis*).[74] Despite its presence in early sources and its connection with the ancient rites of initiation, the melodies of this complex do not represent the purest strain of the Beneventan melodic tradition, and may represent a local composition or adaptation derived from elsewhere, or at least not unaffected by foreign musical styles. Sometimes, *Resurrexit* is found in the Gregorian Easter mass (Ben34, Ben30), and its melody serves for Alleluia verses of three other Gregorian masses.[75] This may be an attempt to retain older music by including it in the Gregorian repertory, but the fact that the "standard" Beneventan melody is not saved by this strategy (nor are other Beneventan mass melodies transferred to the Gregorian repertory) suggests that *Resurrexit* may have its origin outside the Beneventan liturgy.

Offertory

Though each surviving mass has an offertory,[76] there are only sixteen surviving pieces, since five masses cue the singer elsewhere at this point. Two masses refer to offertories used elsewhere,[77] one cues a piece used earlier as a communion,[78] and two give the incipits of pieces not

[71] The verse is cued in for Lawrence, Ben40, without notation; evidently at least one feast – possibly St Stephen – using this Alleluia appeared in the now missing earlier portion of this manuscript.
[72] This Alleluia is nowhere preserved complete. It is cued without notation in Ben40 (for Sts Simon and Jude) and cued also in Ben38 for Sts Peter and Paul, but this time with enough notation to make it clear that the standard melody is intended. The appearance in Ben38 is curious, for the feast already has a fully written-out Alleluia *Tu es petrus* – the same as that which appears in the corresponding Beneventan mass of Ben40; but the second Alleluia is not found in Ben40. A full version of *In omnem terram* must have appeared in the earlier, now missing, portions of each manuscript. See Chapter 2, pp. 50–2.
[73] In some versions (Ben38 and Ben40) the second verse is transposed with respect to the first, owing to different conclusions for the verse *Resurrexit*. See Chapter 4, pp. 122–4, and PM XIV, 442–3.
[74] See Levy, "The Italian Neophytes' chants," pp. 217–23.
[75] *Hodie natus est* (Christmas, Walters 6), *Hodie migravit*, and *Hodie transfiguratus* (for St Peter and the Transfiguration in Ben39).
[76] Baroffio ("Le origini," p. 46, n. 79), Bailey ("Ambrosian chant," p. 1), and Huglo ("L'ancien chant," p. 282) indicate that Benevento uses the term *offerenda*, but I have seen no evidence of it (the word is nowhere written out, so far as I know).
[77] *Popule meus*, the offertory for Palm Sunday in Ben38, is cued in Ben40 for Maundy Thursday. It may have served for the two feasts in both manuscripts, but each now contains only one of the feasts. *Paraclitus autem* is used in Ben38 both for Ascension and for Pentecost.
[78] *Ad honorem*, for the second mass of All Saints in Ben40, is used one folio earlier as a communion in the first mass: see on All Saints below.

otherwise known. These last are the offertory for Sts Simon and Jude (*Confortatus*), suggesting its use for one or more feasts of apostles, now lost, and the offertory *Adoramus* for the first feast of the Holy Cross in Ben40.[79]

Four offertories are used elsewhere as communions. Two offertories in Ben40 are cued as communions in Ben38: *Inter natos* for St John the Baptist (also found as an antiphon in the Solesmes flyleaves) and *Petrus apostolus* for Sts Peter and Paul; both are found also as *mandatum* antiphons in Ottob. 145. A third piece, *Ut cognosceret*, for Sts Peter and Paul, is an offertory in Vat. lat. 10657, but a communion in Ben40. *Ad honorem* serves each function in successive masses of the Holy Cross.

Two feasts have two offertories. For the Ascension, Ben40 adds to the offertory *Ascendit deus* a second offertory, *Paraclitus autem*, marked *ali*, which is cued later in the same manuscript as the offertory for Pentecost.

The offertories are generally the shortest pieces in the mass repertory, owing partly to their relatively simple melodies. Unlike their Gregorian counterparts, the Beneventan offertories have no verses. A single exception is *Adhesit anima mea* for St Lawrence (Ben40, f. 112v), which adds the verse *In craticula*, whose relatively simple melody is surprisingly lacking in characteristic Beneventan elements. The verse (and indeed the offertory itself) has parallels in the Roman and the Ambrosian liturgies considered in Chapter 5; it should probably not be assigned to the oldest levels of the Beneventan chant, owing to its musical anomalies and its liturgical uniqueness.

One offertory has a psalmodic ending (*euouae*) attached: *O quam pretiosum*, part of an unusual and especially festive mass for All Saints (which also includes three communions, all with psalmodic endings).

There is, in the Beneventan offertories, no evidence of the elaborate melodies, the extended melismas, or the subsequent verses that in the Gregorian rite are commonly seen as contributing to a picture of a change from congregational psalmody to soloistic, and hence elaborated, singing, with a consequent reduction of the number of verses.[80] There are no verses, and no psalmody, in the Beneventan offertory, if we discount the two anomalies listed above. Indeed, there is little evidence of the book of psalms; only one of the offertories, *Ascendit deus*, has a psalmodic text.[81] The offertory, in short, seems little different from the communion, or from the briefer ingressae; some offertories are actually used as antiphons. In the surviving Beneventan liturgy there is no evidence that the offertory ever was, or ever became, responsorial.

Communion

In addition to their great musical variety, communions are curious and flexible in a number of

[79] This last piece, which lacks musical notation, may be identical with the Good Friday antiphon for the adoration of the cross. The communion of this mass, also cued without notation, is *Crucem tuam*, recalling another of the adoration antiphons. On the masses for the Holy Cross, see below.

[80] Joseph Dyer, in "The Offertory chant," p. 30, rejects the commonly held view that the offertory was originally antiphonal. Reviewing liturgical and musical documentation, he concludes that "not a shred of evidence can be found to support the commonly held view that its mode of performance changed from antiphonal to responsorial." (The quotation is garbled in print, but the sense of his argument – and the author's personal assurance – make this version certainly correct).

[81] Although the text of *Adhesit anima mea* is drawn, in part, from Psalm 69, v. 2: see Appendix 2.

ways. Three are used for more than one mass[82] and several serve other functions in the liturgy. We have seen that three offertories serve also as communions, and nine communions are found elsewhere as antiphons[83] – a situation familiar from the Gregorian repertory.

Many of the communions are cued in the manuscripts. In some cases, as where the piece in question serves also as an offertory, or is used for two masses, it can be completed from elsewhere in the same book. Often the scribe cues a piece that may have been present in his exemplar, but is not retained in the book he is copying: sometimes it seems unlikely that the piece would have served for a different feast (*Multos infirmos curasti, Inter natos mulierum, Petrus apostolus*) and we must conclude that it was available from another liturgical category, such as an offertory or an antiphon. Because of this cuing, two communions are lost to us.[84]

Many feasts have two communions, where either the mass has two (St Michael, Ascension, both masses of All Saints, St Martin, and St Andrew), or two manuscripts assign different communions to the same feast (St John the Baptist and Sts Peter and Paul). Perhaps the Beneventan liturgy once regularly included two chants, corresponding to the Ambrosian *confractorium* and *transitorium*, for the fraction and the communion. The very flexibility of placement of the surviving communions may be a witness: of pieces not all in their original place; of a compression into a Rome-oriented communion rite, with a single chant; or of an earlier practice which included two separate chants. Arguing against this, however, is the flyleaf of Ben35, from a complete Beneventan gradual, which uses only one communion for Christmas. And the case would be stronger if, where there are two communions, the text of the second had the tone of many Ambrosian transitoria, centering on access to the altar for communion (*Accedite ad altare dei. . ., Venite, convertimini ad me. . ., Accedite et edite. . .*, etc.).

Four communions are followed by psalmodic endings.[85] Are these more antiphons, transferred to the mass without omitting the psalmody? Or was psalmody practiced with these, with many, or with all communions? We cannot be sure. The presence in several masses of more than one communion suggests that there may have been at least three ways of assuring enough music for the communion rite: the elaborate verses of the unusual Easter communion, the use of psalmody, or the performance of several pieces at this point. However, the fact that psalmody occurs only in masses with multiple communions leaves some occasions where none of these options seems possible, and provides a superabundance of material for others.

---

[82] *Quis te supplantavit*, for Palm Sunday in Ben38, is cued for Maundy Thursday in Ben40; *Pacem meam* is used for both Ascension and Pentecost in Ben40; *Gaudent in celis* is cued in Ben40 for both masses of All Saints.

[83] All six of the *mandatum* antiphons in Vat. Ottob. 145 are found also as communions (see Appendix 1); one of them (*Sancta Maria*) is found also in Berkeley ff 2MS A2M2 1000:3, a mutilated fragment of an eleventh-century antiphoner; in addition, the communion *Zacharias pater* (Ben40, f. 89v), with its extraordinarily long final melisma, is an antiphon in the Beneventan vespers of the Solesmes flyleaves; and the communion *Hos duodecim* is the Magnificat antiphon for vespers of the Holy Twelve Brothers in Ben21.

[84] *Nolite*, cued in Ben40 for Sts Simon and Jude, and *Omnes sancti*, cued in Ben40 as the second communion for the first mass of All Saints.

[85] Two of them, *Omnes sancti* and *Dum visitaret*, have euouae without notation. Three of the four are in the rather unusual first mass for All Saints, which also has a psalmodic ending for the offertory; the fourth is the first communion for St Andrew.

VARIATION IN LITURGICAL ASSIGNMENT

The preceding survey repeatedly shows elements of the Beneventan mass that are not stable: duplicate pieces for the same feast, chants with more than one function, differences in assignment among manuscripts, cues which suggest that a piece belongs in more than one liturgical category.

Leaving aside, for the moment, the rites of Holy Week, where the combination of Beneventan and Gregorian rites adds a further element of confusion, we list the areas in the "pure" Beneventan masses where there are conflicting assignments, or multiple pieces for a single function (table 3.3).[86]

Table 3.3 *Beneventan masses with conflicting ascriptions*

Pieces used in more than one mass are in italics.
Pieces used in more than one liturgical category are in small capitals.
* = cued
** = cued, but not found elsewhere in manuscript

Ben40	Ben38	Other sources
	Palm Sunday	
	I. Testificatur	
	G. Dum congregarentur	
	O. *Popule meus*	
	C. *Quis te supplantavit*	
Maundy Thursday		
I. Postquam surrexit		
G. Vadit propitiator		
O. *Popule meus**		
C. *Quis te supplantavit**		
St Michael		
I. Dum sacra misteria	I. Dum sacra misteria	
	A. In conspectu	
O. Milia milium	O. Milia milium	
C. CELESTIS MILICIE		Ant: Ottob. 145
C. Multos infirmos	C. Multos infirmos**	
Ascension		
I. Ecce sedet	I. Ecce sedet	
A. Dominus in celo	A. Dominus in celo	
O. Ascendit deus	O. Ascendit deus	
O. *Paraclitus autem*		
C. *Pacem meam*		
C. Psallite domino	C. Psallite domino	
Pentecost		
I. Factus est repente		
A. Spiritus domini		
O. *Paraclitus autem**		
C. *Pacem meam**		

[86] Omitted from this table are the masses for St Stephen and St Lawrence, which share the Alleluia *Posuisti*; each mass appears in only one source, and thus gives no evidence of instability except for this Alleluia, whose sharing, as though it were an element of the common of martyrs, causes no real surprise.

Table 3.3 (*cont.*)

Ben40	Ben38	Other sources
St John the Baptist		
I. Lumen quod animus	I. Lumen quod animus	
A. De ventre matris	A. De ventre matris	
O. INTER NATOS MULIERUM		Ant: Solesmes; Ottob. 145
		Comm: Ben38
	O. IOHANNES EST NOMEN**	Ant: Solesmes
C. ZACHARIAS PATER		Ant: Solesmes
	C. INTER NATOS MULIERUM**	Ant: Solesmes; Ottob. 145
Sts Peter and Paul		
I. Petrus dormiebat	I. Petrus dormiebat	
A. Tu es petrus		
	A. *In omnem terram***	
O. PETRUS APOSTOLUS		Comm: Ben38; Ant: Ottob. 145
	O. Tu es pastor**	
C. UT COGNOSCERET		Off: Vat. lat. 10657
	C. PETRUS APOSTOLUS**	Off: Ben40; Ant: Ottob. 145
Assumption		
I. Surge propera	I. Surge propera	
A. Specie tua	A. Specie tua	
O. Que est ista	O. Que est ista	
C. SANCTA MARIA EXORA	C. SANCTA MARIA EXORA**	Ant: Ottob. 145, Berkeley
Twelve Brother Martyrs		
I. Sancti videntes		
A. Germana fratrum		
O. Circuierunt		
C. HOS DUODECIM		Ant: Ben21
Holy Cross I		
I. Michi autem absit		
A. *Dicite in gentibus*		
O. ADORAMUS*		Good Friday antiphon?
C. CRUCEM TUAM*		Good Friday antiphon?
Holy Cross II		
I. Venite omnes		
A. *Dicite in gentibus**		
O. Miraculo de tam		
C. Tunc imperator		
Sts Simon and Jude		
I. Michi autem nimis		
A. *In omnem terram***		All: Ben38, Peter and Paul
O. Confortatus est**		
C. Nolite timere?**		
All Saints I		
I. Gaudeamus omnes		
A. *Justorum anime**		All: Ben40, All Saints II
O. O quam pretiosum		
C. *Gaudent in celis*		
C. Omnes sancti		
C. *AD HONOREM SANCTORUM*		Off: Ben40, All Saints II (?)

Table 3.3 (*cont.*)

Ben40	Ben38	Other sources
All Saints II		
I. Isti sunt sancti		
G. Anima nostra		
A. *Justorum anime*		All: Ben40, All Saints I
O. AD HONOREM (sn)*		Comm: Ben40, All Saints I (?)
C. *Gaudent in celis* (sn)*		Comm: Ben40, All Saints I
A. Hodie exultat		
St Martin		
I. Stolam iocunditatis		
G. Ecce magnum et verum		
O. Martinus abrahe sinu		
C. Dixerunt discipuli		
C. O QUANTUS LUCTUS		Ant: Ottob. 145
St Andrew		
I. Prima predicationis	I. Prima predicationis	
G. *Constitues eos*	G. *Constitues eos***	
A. Territus andreas	A. Territus andreas	
O. Salve crux		
C. Dum visitaret	C. Quid ad nos	
C. Quid ad nos	C. Dum visitaret	
St Benedict		
		GLORIOSUS CONFESSOR:
		Comm: MC Comp V
		Ant: Ottob. 145

Only two of the masses contained in both Ben38 and Ben40 agree in their contents exactly (Easter and the Assumption). Even at the core of the Beneventan repertory, the discrepancies are substantial. Not every mass has the same elements: graduals are often missing; there is no Alleluia for St Michael in Ben40, though one is present in Ben38; there is no offertory for St Andrew in Ben38, though there is one in Ben40.

Clearly a single sort of piece can reasonably serve many functions: communion, offertory, office antiphon. Four pieces are used in one place as offertory and in another as communion; eleven mass chants are also antiphons, of which seven are communions, two are offertories, and two have both functions. We have noted elsewhere that in the music for the office in Beneventan antiphoners are antiphons which may have served at one time in the Beneventan mass. To these we may add the offertory and communion for the first mass of the Holy Cross in Ben40. Cued without notation, these pieces have the same incipits (*Adoramus* and *Crucem tuam*) as two of the bilingual antiphons for the adoration of the cross on Good Friday in the Beneventan rite.[87]

Such pieces went freely from office to mass,[88] and from place to place within the mass. Indeed, in some cases the variation of liturgical placement between Ben38 and Ben40 is

---

[87] On these pieces, see Chapter 5, pp. 000–000; on the masses of the Holy Cross, see below, pp. 209–214.

[88] For a discussion of the cues that suggest that additional pieces may also have been used in the office, and the suggestion that some Beneventan manuscripts may have contained office and mass together, see Chapter 2, pp. 50–2.

astounding given their proximity of origin in time and place, and the fidelity with which they reproduce the same musical versions of these pieces. Notable examples are the masses for St John the Baptist and for Sts Peter and Paul. For the first of these, Ben38 and Ben40 between them provide two offertories and two communions, each of which is known also as an office antiphon. In addition, Vat. lat. 10657 provided a gradual for St John the Baptist which is not present in Ben38 or Ben40.[89] The same phenomenon is seen for Sts Peter and Paul. Here, however, only one of the offertory–communion complex also survives as an antiphon, doubtless because we have no Beneventan office for this feast. And one manuscript gives a proper Alleluia, the other an Alleluia from the common of apostles.

This flexibility in the assignment of pieces to a mass increases as the mass nears its end. Each Beneventan mass has its own ingressa, which never varies.[90] Graduals are rare in these manuscripts,[91] but they do not travel from mass to mass, or category to category. Alleluias are only slightly less regular: most use the same melody, only occasionally are they omitted (St Michael and St Martin in Ben40), and only once, for Peter and Paul, are there conflicting assignments.

It is with the offertory and communion that we arrive at the area of greatest flexibility. The evidence presented so far almost makes it appear that there is a sizable repertory of musical pieces from which to select offertories, communions, *mandatum* antiphons and office antiphons. There are no distinctions of genre, and a great many pieces are used in more than one such category; the presence of two or more communions for some masses may simply be another manifestation of this pool of chants. At the end of the mass are added additional pieces, generally labeled as communions (but not always, note the "antiphon" which concludes All Saints II), from the general repertoire of suitable pieces. The few communions with psalmodic endings attached might be the result of a too-hasty transfer of antiphons.

That this repertory of "general antiphons" was ever collected and preserved may be doubted; they probably always existed as they do now, in a variety of suitable places, but the preservation in a separate place of a series of ingressae (in Vall. c 9) may strengthen this notion of flexibility. For the ingressa is the chant which identifies the mass; it does not vary or travel among categories. Such a series of ingressae might be thought of as an abbreviated *antiphonale missarum*. It only needs the addition of an Alleluia sung to a formula perhaps too well known to be written down, and of a couple of "antiphons" from the general repertory for the offertory and the communion, to make a mass as complete as many of those in Ben38 and Ben40. And if we consider that the Alleluia and the gradual are soloist's chants, perhaps their omission is the more logical. Armed with the ingressae, and with access to the general repertory of antiphons, nothing more is needed for all the chants of the schola.

What we see in the surviving masses, then, is a compilation which somewhat misrepresents usage, a compilation designed to fit the format of a Gregorian gradual fixed in its details, with a single piece in each liturgical category for each mass. To write Beneventan masses in this way seems to fix them as well, but we can see from the differences between contemporaneous manuscripts that the Beneventan chant until that point had been little affected by the Carolin-

---

[89] The rubric ℟ is visible on f. 103v, following the ingressa *Lumen quod animus*; the text of the gradual is unfortunately illegible.
[90] Though some ingressae are modeled on others, see Chapter 4, p. 111–4.
[91] But not so rare in other sources, see p. 75.

gian urge to liturgical uniformity, or by the sort of standardization that affected the surviving traditions of the Gregorian and the Ambrosian chant.

TRANSFERRED PAIRS

Palm Sunday and Maundy Thursday share the same offertory and communion; and Pentecost has an offertory and communion used also for the Ascension. It almost seems that the pieces are transferred in pairs.

The Beneventan Maundy Thursday mass, as we have it, may be a later compilation for a day originally without its own liturgy. We know that in the Gregorian rite the mass for Maundy Thursday is assembled from pre-existent pieces, and hence is not original.[92] The Beneventan ingressa is related to texts in the Milanese and Gregorian rites, and its melody is similar to one from Milan. At Milan it is used for the Saturday *in albis*, and in Roman sources the text is used for two *mandatum* antiphons. The gradual *Vadit propitiator*, a translation from the Byzantine liturgy, is likewise a widely used text. In Milanese sources, and also in a number of manuscripts of the Roman liturgy, it is used generally for Good Friday or Holy Saturday, rarely for Maundy Thursday.[93]

Though these texts may be old, their placement in a Maundy Thursday mass at Benevento may be the result of borrowing from the existing liturgy to form a new mass. When the offertory and communion, used earlier for Palm Sunday, are added, the mass is complete.

But do these latter pieces, *Popule meus* and *Quis te supplantavit*, belong originally to Palm Sunday? Their texts might seem to anticipate events later in Holy Week. *Popule meus* is essentially the same text used in the Roman liturgy on Good Friday, and *Quis te supplantavit* is addressed to a Judas who has already effected his betrayal.

Evidently, the Beneventan mass of Palm Sunday emphasizes the contrast between the triumphal entry into Jerusalem, recalled by the procession (a Beneventan processional piece survives) and the ingressa, and the events to be commemorated in the ensuing days. The dividing point, if we can safely presume that Benevento follows other western liturgies, is the gospel reading of the passion; after this point the chant pieces reflect desperation and betrayal in contrast with the earlier hosannas.

Because these two movable texts refer to events yet to be commemorated in the course of Holy Week, Dom Hesbert argued that they must have originated at Maundy Thursday.[94] But in cases where a text is used in two places, it seems likeliest that the *more* suitable place is the second affectation; that is, a piece thought *unsuitable* would hardly be moved from a place where it fits well. More logical borrowings are those where the borrowed material fits as well, or even better, in its new place. Hence, for my part, I must conclude that the Maundy Thursday mass of Benevento, like that of Rome, consists of a series of pieces whose original affectation lay elsewhere.

As to the pieces shared by Ascension and Pentecost, the Pentecost offertory and communion

[92] See *Sextuplex*, p. LIX.
[93] See PM XIV, 278.
[94] Hesbert, "L'antiphonale" (3), pp. 189–90.

are cued in Ben40, since they were written earlier for Ascension, but these pieces are supernumerary in the Ascension mass, which already has a proper offertory and communion, with texts perfectly suited to the feast. The Ascension mass in Ben38 omits precisely the pieces shared with Pentecost, leaving one piece in each category, with no doublets.[95]

But why should pieces which fit Pentecost better be borrowed into the Ascension mass? They must have been associated first with the Ascension – or with both feasts together. For we know that originally these feasts were not distinguished. In early centuries, Pentecost was a long festal season in which the celebration of the Ascension was included; the development of the Ascension as a separate feast is a subsequent phenomenon.[96] It may be, then, that the Beneventan offertory and communion for Ascension are of somewhat later origin than those for Pentecost. They are the only texts in this mass that speak directly of the Ascension. The ingressa and Alleluia refer to heaven without mentioning the specific event; perhaps they were constructed for the Ascension, or perhaps they are transferred from some other feast.[97]

LATER FEASTS

Some of the preserved Beneventan masses represent later layers in the composition of the repertory.

All Saints

Ben40 provides two Beneventan masses which follow the Gregorian mass for All Saints. Though neither of them is labeled, their position and their contents make their purpose clear.

The feast of All Saints is not an early one, probably not adopted by the Roman church before the first half of the ninth century.[98] And there is no evidence that it was adopted earlier at Benevento. The texts for both these masses are generally found in other liturgies for feasts of martyrs, often adapted also for All Saints.[99]

These Beneventan masses are also compilations of pieces originally used for martyrs. What is not sure is whether these texts served, with Beneventan melodies, for feasts of martyrs before being adapted to All Saints, or whether borrowed texts were fitted with Beneventan music to serve the new feast. That not a single one of these pieces is found elsewhere in the surviving Beneventan liturgy is suggestive; probably these are newly assembled texts whose melodies represent a second stage of Beneventan composition.

A clue is given by the ingressa of the first mass, *Gaudeamus*, which adapts the melody used for the ingressae of Sts Peter and Paul and the Assumption.[100] Its text, of Byzantine origin,

[95] It is unfortunate that we can no longer read the Beneventan Pentecost mass of Ben38 itself, which has been erased and written over.
[96] See Leclercq, "Pentecôte", and Dix, *The Shape of the Liturgy*, pp. 340–1, 358.
[97] The ingressa, based on the book of Revelation, shares its text with part of a Milanese offertory for Christmas: see Appendix 2.
[98] It is not included in any of the eighth–ninth century graduals surveyed in *Sextuplex*. On the adoption of the feast, possibly in 835 under Gregory IV, see *Sextuplex*, p. CIX, n. 1; and Leclercq, "Toussaint," esp. col. 2679.
[99] For texts used in other liturgies, see table 5.2 and Appendix 2.
[100] See Chapter 4, p. 114, and ex. 4.10.

probably was intended originally for the feast of St Agnes at Rome.[101] Its Roman text (the Milanese version is *Laetemur*) suggests a borrowing from that quarter. These Beneventan texts, however, share no melodies with Rome; such a borrowed text is fitted with a suitable melody in local style.

The second ingressa, *Isti sunt sancti*, has a text used both at Rome and Milan, but its melody bears a close resemblance to the Milanese transitorium. It may be that these two masses are adapted from different sources, the first Roman and the second Ambrosian. The division is difficult since the two masses have three pieces in common, but the first mass begins with the Roman *Gaudeamus*, and its two other texts not shared with the second mass are used in the Gregorian liturgy (but not at Milan) as antiphons of martyrs.

Beyond the ingressa, the second mass's offertory, *Ad honorem*, is also musically related to Milan – but this piece also appears in the first mass, as a communion. The mass repeats the communion *Gaudent in celis*, which has no Ambrosian counterpart, and concludes with an antiphon (*Hodie exultat celum*) not known elsewhere. Hence, though this second mass has some musical connections with Milan, it is not a complete formulary derived from the Milanese chant as it survives.[102]

These two masses reflect an amalgam of sources brought together, perhaps as late as the ninth century, to celebrate the new feast of All Saints (a feast that may itself have come from Rome). But why are there two masses? We cannot be sure, but we can at least point out differences in them. For one thing, the first mass in Ben40 is unusually festive: it contains cues for *Gloria in excelsis* and *Kyrie*, and the offertory and the three (!) communions all have psalmodic endings attached. The record of Ben40 may represent a real need for two masses with different degrees of festal elaboration, or it may be the result of independent efforts in this direction, the one assembling existing liturgical materials and the other adapting Roman texts and dressing them in the local musical garb. In either case, the resulting formularies share much material in a way that makes it difficult to sort out the exact nature of their origins.

Feasts of the Holy Cross

Another pair of Beneventan masses in Ben40 follows the Gregorian mass for the Exaltation of the Holy Cross (14 September). The presence of two masses here, in a manuscript which contains Gregorian masses both for the Exaltation and for the Invention of the Holy Cross (3 May), raises the possibility that these two masses may be designed for two feasts of the cross.

The two Western feasts of the Holy Cross have origins that are geographically distinct. The Exaltation, on 14 September, is derived from the festival celebrating the Constantinian basilicas of the Anastasis and the Martyrion of Jerusalem. Associated with this feast was the adoration of

---

[101] We cannot tell whether the Beneventan mass arrived at its ingressa in the same way, since we have no Beneventan mass for Agnes; any mass for this Roman saint would have appeared in the now missing portions of Ben38 and Ben40.

[102] The gradual, *Anima nostra*, of the second mass is perhaps not borrowed from elsewhere in the Beneventan liturgy. At least it is written out in full here, and hence was not present earlier in the calendar. Elsewhere, however, the text is used for feasts that precede All Saints in the calendar: the Holy Innocents (28 December) in Gregorian and Old Roman liturgies, and for Sts Nabor and Felix (12 July) at Milan.

the cross, which soon overshadowed the dedications in importance; the feast can be traced in Rome from at least the end of the seventh century. The "Gallican" feast of the Invention (3 May), centering on the recovery of the relic of the cross, is found in extra-Roman sources of the eighth century.[103] Later Roman books contain both these feasts as the result of an amalgam of two separate traditions, each with its own date, for a feast of the Holy Cross. And it is just such a combination that may produce the double mass of Ben40.

Each Beneventan mass has its own focus, though they share the same Alleluia. The first is centered on the adoration, and apparently repeats two of the Good Friday adoration antiphons as offertory and communion.[104] The second includes a series of texts recounting the recovery of the true cross by Heraclius, and it includes two narrative verses attached to the ingressa (*Defuncto Chosroe* and *Gaudentes itaque omnes populi*) – the only such verses in the Beneventan liturgy.

The ingressae suggest that their masses are later compilations, for each ingressa shares its music with (and presumably is modeled on) another ingressa in the repertory. *Michi autem absit* is modeled on the ingressa for Sts Simon and Jude, doubtless owing to the similarity of their texts. *Venite omnes* shares its music with the ingressa for St Martin.

The first mass of Ben40 is designed quite likely for the feast of the Invention (3 May). This feast, generally said to be "Gallican," is attested at Naples in the seventh century[105] and hence cannot be said to be absent from the Beneventan region. Benevento's sister liturgy at Milan celebrates the Invention, but not the Exaltation, and it repeats for that feast two antiphons for the adoration of the cross on Good Friday – much as Benevento seems to repeat two of the same antiphons as the offertory and communion of this mass.[106] And, in the series of palimpsest ingressae present in Vall. C 9, the ingressa of the first mass in Ben40 (*Michi autem absit*) precedes that for St Michael (8 May), and hence is doubtless intended for the Invention on 3 May.

This would suggest, then, that the two masses of Ben40 are intended for the two successive feasts of the Holy Cross, 3 May and 14 September, presented in order of calendar. Their placement together after the Gregorian feast of the Exaltation – even though both feasts are present in Ben40 – is evidence that the Beneventan materials in Ben40 may have been assembled from more than one source, and that the Beneventan masses are not entirely fixed in the calendar. Indeed, one piece from the second (Exaltation?) mass is found as an alternative offertory in the Gregorian mass of the Invention in Ben38.

[103] See Cattaneo, "Croce"; *Sextuplex*, pp. LXXXII–LXXXIII; and Leclercq, "Croix."

[104] The cues *Adoramus* and *Crucem tuam* are presented in the manuscript without notation. That they are identical with the corresponding Good Friday pieces must remain in doubt.

[105] Two Anglo-Saxon gospel books (London, BL, Cotton Nero D. IV, and Royal I.B. VIII) were marked with pericopes intended for liturgical use in seventh-century Naples. One of these has the indication "Inuentione crucis domini nostri ihesu xpi": see Morin, "Capitula Evangeliorum." The mid-ninth-century *Liber pontificalis* of Naples reports that Bishop Leontius (alive in 649) made a cross to be used for the adoration on Good Friday, and also on the feast "inventionis seu exaltationis sanctae crucis." Both titles (perhaps both feasts?) were known there in the ninth century, if not by Leontius: see Mallardo, "La Pasqua," p. 20.

[106] Oxford, Bodleian, MS Lat. liturg. a. 4 contains the Invention (for which it provides the Good Friday antiphons *Crucem tuam* and *Laudamus te* on f. 116), but not the Exaltation. The feast of the Exaltation was instituted at Milan only in 1053: see Magistretti, *Beroldus*, p. 141, n. 48. Compare also the calendar in Magistretti, *Manuale*, I, 186 and 192. For the use of all three Good Friday adoration antiphons in what appears to be the newer feast of the Exaltation, see Magistretti, *Beroldus*, p. 126.

Thus, these are two relatively late Beneventan compilations, designed to respond to a calendar (perhaps the received Gregorian one) in which two feasts of the Holy Cross were celebrated. Though both feasts are of relatively late institution, it seems that the Invention (3 May) may be the earlier one celebrated at Benevento.

HOLY WEEK

The rites of Holy Week have been examined so thoroughly by Dom Hesbert[107] that we can do no better than to refer the reader to his magisterial studies. The sources and texts for these days are detailed in Appendices 1 and 2, and the arrangement of the sources has been studied in Chapter 2.

In the triduum, the Beneventan chant is preserved differently from a system in which each mass is a separate Beneventan unit; the Beneventan materials are combined with Gregorian music for the same days. Here, although the Beneventan music may be more complete than for other feasts (remember the frequent omission of graduals, for example, in Ben38 and Ben40), the manuscripts preserve it with considerable variation of repertory and placement.

Maundy Thursday is relatively straightforward. Our only surviving source (Ben40) provides a doublet mass[108] along with a separate group of Beneventan antiphons.

For Good Friday, in fact, we are also relatively well informed, since the Good Friday rite of Benevento itself is detailed in an *ordo* of Vat. lat. 10673. The scribe first wrote a series of rubrics and chants mixing Roman, Beneventan, and other materials. This series, incomplete at the beginning, extends from folios 27 to 33, with a lacuna after folio 27, and it includes tracts, lessons, the *Trisagion* in Greek and Latin with *Popule meus* and improperia, and a substantial collection of music for the adoration of the cross (including the Beneventan Greek–Latin antiphons, *Pange lingua*, and the antiphons *Cum fabricator*, *Cum rex glorie*, and *Ego sum alfa et ω*).

Evidently displeased with his hybrid result, and aware that his compilation was not useful as a service book, the scribe began again, and produced a long rubric ("Likewise how the services of Good Friday should be performed according to the Ambrosian rite") which precisely details the order and content of the Beneventan rite for Good Friday.[109] The musical pieces called for in this *ordo* are precisely those provided both in Ben33 and Ben40, though both these latter manuscripts include some non-Beneventan material as well.[110] Later manuscripts present hybrid compilations including progressively fewer Beneventan pieces, as we have seen in Chapter 2.

The Good Friday rite, however, is relatively clear. It consists of:

1 Two separate but similar functions, at the third hour and the ninth hour, each consisting of:

a   The adoration of the cross (for which three bilingual antiphons are provided)
b   A foremass with a first lesson (at the sixth hour a lesson from Daniel incorporating the elaborate canticle *Benedictus es domine*) followed by a responsory (gradual) and the reading of the passion.

---

[107] PM XIV, 275–446; and "L'antiphonale" (3)–(6).

[108] Fragments of it are preserved also in Vall. c 9 and Vat. lat. 10657.

[109] "Item qualiter peragatur officium sexta feria in Parasceben secundum ambrosianum." The full texts are transcribed in PM XIV, 290–5, and the same volume reproduces the manuscript in facsimile.

[110] Both add material at the place where the "Ambrosian" *ordo* calls for repeating the three Greek/Latin antiphons for the second adoration of the cross, and Ben40 has additional chants, including *O quando in cruce*, before the Beneventan music. Details of the ordering of materials in these manuscripts can be seen in the table in PM XIV, 296–7.

2 The solemn prayers and the communion of the presanctified, for which only rubrics remain.

3 The singing of vespers.

There is also a bilingual processional antiphon (*Panta/Omnes gentes*) for moving from the church (nave?) to the choir after the second adoration. And in Lucca 606 an opening antiphon (*Tristis est anima mea*) serves the same quasi-introit function as the opening antiphon of Holy Saturday.

For Holy Saturday we have no such *ordo* detailing a single vision of the Beneventan rites for that day, and in the mixed sources that survive, the Beneventan chant has been made to fit, sometimes in awkward Gregorian spaces. There is a considerable lack of unanimity in transmission, for example:

1 There are varying attempts to fit four Beneventan tracts into a Gregorian series of twelve lessons.[111]

2 The scribe of Vat. lat. 10673 acknowledges the impossibility of reconciling the two rites when he adds the rubric "The reading *Hec est hereditas*, which is placed fifth according to the Roman rite should be read here; according to the Ambrosian it should be read after the blessing of the candle."[112]

3 The place of the blessing of the paschal candle and the Exultet are transmitted with much confusion, owing to the incompatibility of the Roman practice (which places the Exultet at the beginning of the vigil) with the Beneventan (where the blessing of the new fire, the proclamation of the *Lumen christi*, and the *Exultet* take place before the last lesson *Hec est hereditas*). But the order survives nowhere correct and complete in the chant manuscripts. Vat. lat. 10673 breaks off during the Exultet; Ben40 somehow omits the Exultet and the twelfth lesson; Ben33, the clearest in this respect, omits the collect *Deus qui tribus pueris*, which should follow the lesson from Daniel with its canticle of the three children (*Benedictus es*); and in Ben38, the blessing of the paschal candle is placed after the eleventh lesson with its canticle,[113] but before the collect *Deus qui tribus pueris*, thus separating the lesson and canticle from the collect which belongs with it and which refers to the three children in the fiery furnace.[114]

The only clear presentation of this element of the Beneventan liturgy is in the early twelfth-century pontifical from the city of Benevento (now Macerata, Biblioteca comunale, MS 378). This is curious not only because the manuscript is a pontifical, but also because it retains almost nothing of the old Beneventan chant. Although the Holy Saturday liturgy of Macerata has only six lessons, it has several Beneventan peculiarities: the vigil begins with a litany;[115] tracts are provided after each lesson;[116] it has the abbreviated Daniel lesson characteristic of Benevento,[117]

---

[111] See Chapter 2, p. 54; PM XIV, 339–60; Hesbert, "L'antiphonale" (6), pp. 154–71.

[112] *Lectio Hec est hereditas que quinta est ordinata secundum rom*[*anum*] *legatur hic. Secundum ambr*[*osianum*] *legatur post Ben*[*edictionem*] *cerei* (ff. 34–34v). This lesson in the Beneventan rite precedes the procession to the font and includes the text of the processional antiphon *Omnes sitientes*; it is found in that position in Ben38, Ben33, and Ben39. See PM XIV, 346; Hesbert, "L'antiphonale" (6), pp. 157–8.

[113] Hesbert (PM XIV, 341) expands *deīde seqī̄ ben* (Ben38, f. 45v) as "deinde sequuntur benedictiones"; while this is perhaps the more usual way of referring to the canticle, the manuscript actually reads "deinde sequitur ben [edictio?]."

[114] See the tables in PM XIV, 340–1, 344–5.

[115] *In primis faciant letanias* (Ben38); *In primis letanias faciat* (Ben40); *In primis letania* (Ben33).

[116] The tracts here seem to be Gregorian, judging from the cue *Vinea*, whose Beneventan version begins with *Cantabo*.

with its canticle[118] and collect; and it places the lesson *Hec est hereditas* at the end, preceded by the blessing of fire, *Lumen christi*, and Exultet.

Some Beneventan elements of Holy Saturday persisted for a long time in southern Italy, to judge from the fourteenth-century Capuan missal now Paris, Bibliotheque nationale, latin 829. In the course of a "standard" Holy Saturday rite of twelve lessons and four Gregorian tracts, two rubrics describe an alternative practice still in use in some places:

a   Then are read the lessons; but in some places first the candle is blessed and then the lessons are read. (f. 28: Deinde leguntur lectiones; sed in aliquibus locis primo benedicitur cereus et postea leguntur lectiones.)

b   When the baptism is completed, in some churches is read the lesson *Hec est hereditas*. (f. 31: Completo baptismo, in aliquibus ecclesiis legitur lectio *Hec est hereditas*.)

4   The placement of the Beneventan litany (*Domine defende nos*, etc.) varies considerably. Ben38 (palimpsest) and Ben39 place it at the beginning of the procession to the font; in Ben40, Ben33, Ottob. 576, and Vall. C 32 it follows the antiphon *Omnes sitientes*; the Farfa fragment places it after the baptism during the returning procession.[119]

5   The bilingual antiphons *Doxa en ipsistis/Gloria in excelsis* are sung at the font, according to Ben38 (and probably also Ben40); while in the Farfa fragment it is sung after the antiphon *Transivimus*, and after the procession has arrived at the altar.

The original order of the Beneventan Holy Saturday rite is a matter of great complexity. It seems, however, that a reduced number of lessons (Macerata and Ben33 both have six) is a likely possibility for Benevento, and perhaps the use of a chant to follow each lesson is the Beneventan norm, which becomes garbled when combined with an imported Gregorian practice using twelve lessons.[120] The four surviving Beneventan tracts, along with the *Benedictus es*, in fact may suggest the original number of lessons at Benevento. If the tract *Sicut cervus* is a processional piece rather that a quasi-gradual,[121] the original number of lessons at Benevento may have been four. For confirmation of this, however, we must await new discoveries.

ORDINARY CHANTS

Some Beneventan masses include indications of chants for the ordinary. These do not occur frequently, or regularly, but they are sufficient in number to give evidence of all the ordinary chants which are familiar from the Roman mass. They are distributed as follows:

Gloria in excelsis
    Rome, Vall. C 9, f. 170v. Preceding Kyrie; feast cannot be determined.
    Ben38, f. 53. Intonation only (Gloria VII? Gloria I?) in Beneventan Easter mass.

[117] See PM XIV, 343, 353, n. 1.

[118] Cued only, with the beginning of the Beneventan melody.

[119] See PM XIV, 424–5.

[120] The rite of Milan, which we shall see in Chapter 5 shares much with Benevento, also uses six lessons, and follows each of them with a *psalmellus*. The lessons and their chants do not, however, match those of Benevento. See Magistretti, *Beroldus*, pp. 110–11.

[121] And we have already a Beneventan chant related to the lesson *Hec est hereditas*: the antiphon *Omnes sitientes*.

Ben40, f. 133v. Cued without notation (before Kyrie) in first mass of All Saints.

Ben40, f. 138v. Cued without notation in mass for St Martin.

Kyrieleyson

Vall. c 9, f. 170v. Threefold Kyrie following *Gloria in excelsis*; mass uncertain.

Ben40, f. 133v. Kyrie cued without notation after *Gloria in excelsis* for first mass of All Saints.

[Ben40, f. 18. Threefold Kyrie included in litany of Holy Saturday; also in Ben39, Farfa.]

Credo

Ben35, f. 202. Concluding phrase only, preceding Christmas offertory.

Vall. c 9, f. 14v. A brief section is visible in the palimpsest ([*consub*]*stantialem patri per quem omnia facta sunt qui propter nos homine*[*s*]); its context in a mass cannot be determined.

Vall. c 9, f. 167. Final portion only (palimpsest), preceding Easter offertory.

MC 361, p. 126. Palimpsest fragment of 8 lines ([*i*]*terum venturus. . .iudicare vivos et. . .regni non er*[*it*] . . . *sanctum dominu*[*m*]. . .[*proce*]*dit qui cum. . .adoratur et c*[*onglorificatur*]. . .*qui locutus est per.* . .), followed by an offertory; feast cannot be determined.

Sanctus

Ben35, f. 202. After offertory of Christmas mass.

Agnus Dei

Ben35, f. 202. After Sanctus, preceding communion of Christmas mass.

The melodies in all cases are relatively simple, and do not match those of ordinary chants from the Roman liturgy; to judge from the sources, there is a single melody for each text.[122]

The recording of ordinary chants is not a regular procedure in the surviving sources. Major feasts may indicate chants of the ordinary (the incomplete Christmas mass in Ben35 has Credo, Sanctus, and Agnus Dei; Easter masses include evidence of Gloria (Ben38) and Credo (Vall. c 9)). Except for these, the only identified masses with ordinary chants are St Martin (a Gloria in Ben40) and the unusually elaborate second mass for All Saints (Ben40) with Gloria and Kyrie (in that order).

The Kyrie at mass follows the Gloria; this is evident in the first mass for All Saints in Ben40, and in the Gloria-Kyrie succession in Vall. c 9, f. 170v (though in this latter case it is possible, though not likely, that the context is not that of a mass).

This Kyrie in Vall. c 9 is the only notated version we have; we can decipher a threefold *Kyrieleison* (there is no Christe petition). The threefold Kyrie (without Christe) is found elsewhere in the Beneventan liturgy as part of the litany for Holy Saturday in Ben40, Ben39, and Farfa. The music for this threefold invocation, however, is not that of Vall. c 9.

This usage, both as to the order of pieces (Kyrie following rather than preceding Gloria) and the threefold Kyrie without Christe, is precisely that found in the Ambrosian liturgy.[123]

For the *Gloria in excelsis* we have no surviving music, except for the intonation provided for

---

[122] But there is a Sanctus in the Kyriale of Ben35 which has Beneventan characteristics: see pp. 130–1.

[123] See the *Ordo missarum* in Magistretti, *Beroldus*, p. 49: "magister scholarum incipit ingressam, qua finita archiepiscopus aut presbyter ebdomadarius dicit *Dominus vobiscum*. Sequitur *Gloria in excelsis Deo*, et magister scholarum canit totam *Gloriam*, excepto in praecipuis solemnitatibus, quando canit tantum usque ad *suscipe deprecationem nostram*, a qua lectores canunt excelsa voce usque in finem; tunc magister scholarum dicit ter *Kyrie* cum pueris suis. Sequitur oratio super populum . . ." The threefold Kyrie is often mentioned in the Beroldus ordinal: for example pp. 41, 43, etc.

the Beneventan Easter mass in Ben38; this looks rather like the intonation of Gloria VII or Gloria I of the modern Vatican edition, and we cannot be sure that its melody is really Beneventan.[124]

Sanctus and Agnus Dei are found only in the Christmas mass of Ben35. The following mass of St Stephen has no evidence of the ordinary; the fragment breaks off at the Alleluia, so we cannot tell about Sanctus and Agnus, but the Gloria and Kyrie would have appeared if they were wanted. Evidently, the chants of the ordinary are used here either for Christmas only, or for principal feasts. Ordinary chants are not included for Easter in either Ben38 or Ben40, however (though there is a Credo in the Easter mass of Vall. C 9). Perhaps the Easter mass of the Ben35 fragment's parent manuscript included ordinary chants for Easter (and for other principal feasts as well?). But although this is clearly not the style for Ben38 and Ben40, which present limited collections of masses for principal feasts (and sometimes these are incomplete), there are still a few indications of Gloria and Kyrie in masses, for what may have been special occasions.

The creed is found surprisingly often. Though no indication of it survives in Ben38 or Ben40, portions of the Credo are found four times elsewhere – in three sources that contained nothing but Beneventan chant, and which thus represent a fuller tradition, less cramped for space. Only two of these appearances can be assigned to specific feasts: they are for Christmas (Ben35) and Easter (Vall. C 9, f. 167).[125]

That the creed should be a regular feature of the surviving liturgy of Benevento in the earlier eleventh century suggests its adoption in the region as least as early as elsewhere in the West. It was only in the eleventh century that the creed was incorporated as a regular feature in the Roman mass.[126] But the creed was in earlier use elsewhere: it was adopted by the council of Toledo in 589, and was used, with a text different from that used elsewhere, in the Mozarabic rite preceding the *Pater noster*.[127]

The creed was adopted in the late eighth century for use at the imperial chapel of Charlemagne; only later in the ninth century was it used more widely among the Franks.[128] The Carolingian usage places it after the gospel and before the offertory. It has been thought that the Carolingian usage must have been borrowed from Spain. According to Dom Capelle, it is to Paulinus of Aquileia that we can attribute the present text of the "Nicene" creed.[129]

But the creed is present in the Beneventan mass – and only in those sources, not contaminated by Gregorian tradition, which best represent the ancient usage. The early use of the creed

[124] The intonation of Ben38 is the same as that found in Ben34, f. 122, for the Holy Saturday mass; the intonation does not match any of the Glorias appended to Ben34, ff. 279–82, but this section is incomplete at its beginning, and might have included more Glorias. The Beneventan Easter mass in Ben40 is incomplete, and lacks the portion that might have included the Gloria.

[125] The text is that of the modern Nicene creed, as far as we can tell from the surviving fragments. The reading "et uitam *futuri* seculi" varies from modern usage, but it is the standard text in the region, and is undoubtedly the older reading. See Capelle, "L'origine," p. 14 and n. 26. Some south Italian sources that use this reading are the following: Rome, Vall. C 32, f. 21v (Odermatt, *Ein Rituale*, p. 269); London, BL, Add. MS 18859, f. 83v; Vat. lat. 4928, f. 188v; Vatican Borg. lat. 21.

[126] Berno of Reichenau reports that Emperor Henry II persuaded Pope Benedict VIII (1012–24) to adopt the usage: see PL 142, col. 1060.

[127] Capelle, "L'origine," p. 7. On the history of the adoption of the creed see also Jungmann, *Missarum sollemnia*, I, 569–84.

[128] See the text of Walafrid Strabo (d. 845) cited in Capelle, "L'origine," p. 11.

[129] Capelle, "L'origine," pp. 10–13. For a discussion of whether the use of the creed may have passed to Ireland, and have been suggested to Alcuin by his experience of the use at York, see Capelle, "Alcuin."

at Benevento doubtless had the same purpose that the use of the creed always has: to profess the orthodox faith. It is particularly needed, of course, when there is a possibility of heresy, and the Lombard tradition of Arianism is one that must have made the danger felt early at Benevento.[130] The Beneventan dismissals on Holy Saturday (*Si quis catechuminus est procedat*) includes prohibitions of pagans, heretics in general, and specifically excludes Arians.[131] That this is an old usage cannot be doubted; Arians were not so much a problem in the eleventh century as in the eighth. And the use of the creed serves the same purpose of ensuring orthodoxy. This series of monitions is used also in other churches of Italy, and it may be that the creed was a regular part of a non-Roman practice which included not only Benevento, but other churches in the north.

Surely the Beneventan creed was not borrowed in the ninth century from the Gauls. It seems more likely that a non-Roman Italian tradition, in which the creed had its place after the gospel, may have been the source of the Carolingian creed. It was nearer at hand than Spain, and had the same place in the mass.[132]

If the creed represents the early use of Benevento, we may surmise that the Agnus Dei, likewise, is not a later addition, but an early form of this acclamation. It appears that the Agnus Dei was regularly used in the Roman mass in the eighth century. According to the *Liber pontificalis* it was introduced into the mass by Pope Sergius I (687–701), and its text was just as we have it in the surviving Beneventan fragment:

Hic statuit ut tempore confractionis dominici corporis *Agnus Dei, qui tollis peccata mundi, miserere nobis* a clero et populo decantetur.[133]

Early sacramentaries prescribe a threefold repetition of this text. The Agnus Dei was used in the Frankish kingdom by the end of the eighth century, to judge from its appearance in the so-called sacramentary of Hadrian, the *ordines romani*, and Carolingian *Expositiones missae*.[134] But in its earliest Frankish musical sources, in cantatoria and tropers, it is provided with verses. It does not appear in Gregorian graduals until the eleventh century.[135]

The Beneventan Agnus Dei has all the marks of antiquity. The text, just as in the *Liber pontificalis*, is presented once only, with no threefold repetition, and no alteration to "dona nobis pacem."

The relatively simple melody, in fact, may be related to one originally sung by the congregation, *a clero et populo*. Of this we cannot be certain, but it bears a certain relationship to

---

[130] See Chapter 1, pp. 8–9.

[131] See the text "Si quis catechuminus" in Appendix 2; and Hesbert, "L'antiphonale" (6), pp. 197–201.

[132] The Beneventan text is so incomplete that we cannot be sure that it is identical with that of Paulinus. But it seems to be (characteristic is *et vitam futuri seculi*), and if it is, either the text was adopted at Benevento from Carolingian sources (not before the early ninth century), or else Paulinus produced a text already known to him from his Italian background: a creed already in use at Aquileia and, presumably, at Benevento. That the creed is found often in the Beneventan mass, but not in the Gregorian portions of contemporaneous manuscripts, suggests that the Beneventan usage is not borrowed from the received Carolingian recension of the Roman liturgy. For further discussion, see Hesbert, "L'antiphonale" (1), pp. 36–40; and Capelle, "L'introduction," esp. pp. 1021–3.

[133] Duchesne, *Le Liber pontificalis*, I, 376. The text is from Lucca, Biblioteca Capitolare Feliniana, MS 490, from the second half of the eighth century.

[134] On the early history of the Agnus Dei see Atkinson, "The earliest Agnus Dei melody," pp. 1–11.

[135] Atkinson, "The earliest Agnus Dei melody," p. 12, n. 32 and table, p. 13.

the palimpsest Old Roman Agnus Dei of Vat. lat. 5319, which also has only a single invocation, though a threefold repetition is specified.[136] We cannot be sure whether the Agnus Dei (and other items of the ordinary) were congregational chants in the eighth century at Benevento, nor whether, if so, our surviving sources represent this tradition accurately. Surely simple congregational melodies are not normally included in graduals. The fact that ordinary pieces are included for Christmas in Ben35 may indicate that these are not the usual melodies, or perhaps they indicate some special usage with regard to major feasts, which escapes us now.

OFFICE MUSIC

We have seen in the preceding chapter that the preservation of Beneventan office music is sporadic: pieces to fill a void in the received Gregorian repertory, a few canticle antiphons, occasional Beneventan turns of phrase in a Gregorian office. The melodies of the surviving music are considered in the next chapter.

For information on the structure of the Beneventan office we have only the vespers of Good Friday preserved in a few graduals, and the Beneventan vespers of St John the Baptist in fragments of a Gregorian antiphoner (the Solesmes flyleaves).

The Good Friday vespers (found in Ben38, Ben40, Ben39, Lucca 606, and Subiaco XVIII) consist of four antiphons, for three psalms and Magnificat, each with a following *versus ad repetendum*.[137] But the vespers of John the Baptist includes six antiphons, a responsory, and a final antiphon without psalmody;[138] the first four antiphons are accompanied also by *versus ad repetendum*.[139]

Unfortunately the psalms are not indicated for John the Baptist, nor is the Magnificat, and as a result the exact plan of this vespers remains imprecise. The final antiphon is so enormous, with its huge melisma and no psalmody, that it may be a special occasional or processional piece standing outside the normal vespers. This antiphon is a bit unusual anyway, since it is a communion in Ben40 – though long melismas are not typical of communions either. The Good Friday vespers gives no special treatment to the Magnificat antiphon *Velum templi*: it is similar in size and scope to the psalm antiphons and is certainly not analogous to the grand *Zacharias pater*. If the last antiphon has a special function, then the six other antiphons for John the Baptist are for five psalms and the Magnificat.

We cannot say, of course, whether a distinction existed in the Beneventan liturgy between monastic and secular usage. We do not even know that the Beneventan use was regular from day to day, judging from the discrepancies between Good Friday and John the Baptist. But clearly, the general shape of vespers is similar to the Roman: five psalms, or possibly six, each with its antiphon; on occasion a responsory; and the Magnificat with its antiphon – shapes and musical forms with which we are familiar. The similarity to Gregorian form and structure is

---

[136] The melody is palimpsest, but is partially recoverable, and is closely akin to one of the melodies of the Old Roman gradual of Saint Cecilia. See Boe, "Gloria A," pp. 19–21.

[137] For the use of *versus ad repetendum* with introits in Beneventan manuscripts, see PM XIV, 207.

[138] This office is treated in detail in Kelly, "Une nouvelle source."

[139] The first three antiphons have metrical verses that may be drawn from an unidentified poetical text: (1) *Seni patri nasciturus quem predixit angelus*; (2) *Condiditque cuncta verbo et in lucem protulit*; (3) *Criminaque auferentem mundi christum cecinit*.

more striking when we remember the significant differences between the two liturgies in the music of the mass.

The Beneventan liturgy, as we have it, contains enough music to give a clear notion of its special character (which we shall study in the next chapter); enough texts to show its particular euchological flavor; and enough formularies to allow some notion of the unique aspects of its liturgical practice.

The liturgy as it survives, however, is impure, incomplete, and variable. It is impure in that it survives largely in a hybrid formulation alongside the Gregorian liturgy, by which it is inevitably influenced; and in that there are various levels of antiquity within the Beneventan music itself: later feasts adapted from earlier ones and music borrowed from other rites. It is incomplete as to its calendar: we know that not all the existing music has survived, and we can identify some specific lacunae. And it is incomplete as to the formularies in the mass, which often lack a gradual, and sometimes other elements as well. Finally, it lacks fixity: many pieces are used in more than one mass, or in more than one liturgical category. There is no evidence of the codification and uniformity found in the Gregorian repertory, or in the Ambrosian chant as it is preserved in the documents of the twelfth century.

Nevertheless, the surviving elements of the Beneventan liturgy give clear evidence of an independent liturgical practice, whose required coexistence with Gregorian chant in a single document has affected its transmission. Hapless scribes have been faced with the difficulty of conserving two liturgies when both cannot be used on the same occasion; when custom, conservatism, or loyalty may urge the preservation of the Beneventan usage, while political or ecclesiastical authority press for the new orthodoxy.

4

BENEVENTAN MUSICAL STYLE

The Beneventan chant is a highly unified repertory with a remarkably constant melodic style. Although there are relatively simple melodies to be found among the surviving office antiphons, and a few extensive melismas, the music proceeds generally at a regular, rather ornate stepwise pace. Unlike the situation in Gregorian chant, there are few stylistic distinctions to be made in the repertory on the basis of liturgical placement or modal category, no clear differences between music for the cantor and music for the choir.

This is an archaic repertory, though it is not always easy to define what is meant by such a term.[1] Generally understood characteristics of archaic Western chant dialects include a relatively restricted melodic fund, a melodic prolixity with an underlying simplicity of structure, the frequent re-use of melodic fragments, a modality unaffected by the fully developed system of eight modes, and a relatively unsophisticated relationship of melody to text. And though many such characteristics are to be found in the Beneventan chant, this kind of definition is based more on a comparison with more "evolved" repertories (that is to say, with Gregorian chant) than on the archaic repertory itself. Here, we shall prefer to let the Beneventan chant be understood on its own terms, where possible without holding it up to the Gregorian yardstick by which students of the chant almost invariably measure deviation.

Though the surviving repertory is surely smaller than the original body of Beneventan music, many melodies are recorded in several manuscripts, and in these cases the sources disagree with only the smallest discrepancies. The melodic tradition as we have it is much more stable than that of the Ambrosian, Mozarabic, or Old Roman chants. This fixity of transmission may result, of course, from the simple fact that the sources represent very limited geographical and chronological bounds. The surviving repertory was written down in the eleventh century, though its origin is certainly much earlier, and the sources come from a relatively narrow area. In its development, of course, this music may have varied more through time and space than we can now determine. What survives to us surely is limited in its reference to other places and earlier times. It is difficult to believe that a chant so ornate, so full of the formulas which recall oral transmission, written down so long after its development and regular use, by scribes who

---

[1] The best discussion of archaisms is that of Bruno Stäblein in MMMA, II, pp. 31*–39*. See also Baroffio, "Le origini," esp. pp. 41–52; and Connolly, "Introits and Archetypes."

must have known the Gregorian chant better, could preserve in the eleventh century a state that represents unaltered that of the eighth century and before.

But what is preserved is written with care and, often, not a little effort in the face of challenging circumstances. It may have been of mostly antiquarian interest in the eleventh century and is not complete, but it is not garbled or misunderstood. What is left, then, is a musical and liturgical document of real worth, permitting a highly focused view on a very narrow field. It is only after we recognize the limitations of these documents, both for their value in what they permit, and for the dangers of attempting what they cannot, that we can derive the greatest benefit from their study.

The chief sources of the repertory are graduals, and the music they preserve is designed for the mass. These sources distinguish the repertory from Gregorian chant, either in separate books or as masses set apart from their Gregorian neighbors (see Chapter 2). This music is the most carefully preserved, and will be considered first as exemplary of the general'style of the chant. Music for the office, which survives almost entirely as antiphons preserved in Gregorian contexts, presents additional problems of transmission, as well as a few new stylistic ones, and will be considered separately. A special case is Holy Week. Here the sources vary substantially in their separation of Beneventan from Gregorian; much of the music falls into one of the other two categories, and it has been studied in detail in volume 14 of *Paléographie musicale*.

GENERAL STYLE

The first thing that strikes the eye and the ear in the Beneventan style is a richness of surface detail. Such a prolixity is to be found in other dialects of non-Gregorian chant, but seldom with the Beneventan fixity of detail. A substantial number of unvarying melodic contours are peppered throughout the repertory with formulaic regularity; they give it an immediate flavor.

These small melodic formulae are a surface decoration typically Beneventan in their shape, but universal in their function. Melodic formulae tend to occur repeatedly in similar contexts: they serve as springboards for a musical phrase, as modes of procedure, or as moments of repose. By looking at these formulae as functional elements articulating larger formal structures, we can begin to see how musical phrases are made, and how longer pieces come into existence, or at least are written down, as a combination of these procedures.

Closing formulae

Final cadences are among the most important of musical formulae. And in Beneventan music only two patterns account for almost all the conventional cadences in the repertory – some examples are shown in example 4.1.

Formula G (so called for its ending pitch) appears most often as in lines A and B; its many other forms become more regular as they approach the cadence. It is never used for the end of an entire piece, but serves only to articulate the ends of intermediate phrases ending on G. Some regular final cadences on G can be seen in the discussion of office antiphons below.

The second cadence, however, whose various forms occupy the rest of example 4.1, can be

Ex. 4.1 Beneventan cadences

A
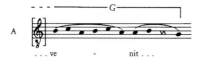
. . . ve - nit . . .

B

. . . Do-mi - nus . . .

C

. . . no-mi - nis . . .

D

. . . om-ni - um . . .

E

. . . et _____ nos . . .

F

. . . allelu - ia . . .

G

. . . est . . .

H

. . . respi - cientes . . .

I

. . . lig - no.

Legend:

A Ben38/110, Ing. *Lumen* (compare plate 26)
B Ben40/138v, Ing. *Stolam*
C Ben40/142v, Gr. *Constitues*
D Ben40/139, Com. *O quantus*
E Ben40/134v, Gr. *Anima*

F Ben40/121v, Ing. *Sancti* (plate 29)
G Ben38/93v, Ing. *Ecce* (compare plate 23)
H Ben40/125, Off. *Miraculo*
I Ben40/124v, All. *Dicite*

Ex. 4.1 (cont.)

M   ... sanc - tis   su -   is.

N   ... alle - lu -   -   ia.

O   ... manduca - ve -   -   rit ...

P   ... suorum ___   di -   -   -   cens ...

Q   ... me___   ma -   -   -   net ...

R   ... ti - bi   e - nim   tra -   -   -   -   di -   dit ...

S   ... lu - pi   ra -   pa -   ces.

Legend:

M   Ben40/134v, ant. *Hodie*
N   Ben38/93v, Com. *Psallite* (compare plate 24)
O   Ben38/53, Com. *Qui manducaverit* (plate 18)
P   Ben40/4v, Ing. *Postquam*
Q   Ben38/53v, Com. *Qui manducaverit* (plate 19)
R   Ben40/99v, Com. *Ut cognosceret*
S   Ben40/139, Com. *Dixerunt*

more variously structured, and appears in many longer and shorter forms, depending on the importance of the cadence and, sometimes, its accentuation. Each version here concludes in the same way with the basic formula *a*, and each is found throughout the repertory. The effect of these cadences is of increasing regularity and fixity as the phrase approaches its final point of rest. These two figures can each be seen many times in the plates and they will be pointed out in the transcriptions to follow.

Opening formulas

Like arrivals, departures are often conventional. Examples 4.2 and 4.3 show two opening procedures found throughout the Beneventan chant. Example 4.2, drawn from eight pieces, shows a phrase opening (never used at the beginning of a piece) which makes two substantial and characteristic leaps. The leap of a fourth generally occurs on an accented syllable (note the adjustment for the word "Laurenti"), and the melody rises to F, from which a variety of descents is possible. In their downward course most phrases pause (within the dotted lines of the example) to embroider the C that was the goal of the initial leap.

Example 4.3 shows a stylized opening for the beginning of a piece, beginning with a recitation on a repeated podatus. From this recitation (which occurs always on this pitch), there are three conventional ways of proceeding. The first group (beginning with the offertory *Omnes qui in Christo*) moves immediately to a five-syllable cursive cadence, emphasizing the pitches between A and C, and concluding with a standard closing formula before continuing, often at a higher pitch. The cadence *A* in each case concludes the first sense-unit of the text, and the music departs from recitation five syllables before the end of this unit, regardless of the accentuation. Hence, even though, in *Omnes qui*, the accent of *Christo* is emphasized, the word *baptizati* does not depart from the recitation, as we might expect from the accentuation of the other examples, on its accented syllable.

The melodies of the next group (beginning with the ingressa *Postquam surrexit*) all move from recitation to a melisma closing directly on a typical G-cadence. After this opening phrase, each piece goes its own way, generally with a gradual ascent from the lower part of the range.

The first three lines here are all phrases from *Postquam surrexit*; the second and third show a phrase that goes twice through the recitation before arriving at the cadence. The musical shape of this double phrase echoes the text with its parallel nouns coupled by the conjunction *et*: two parallel phrases, the first without its cadence to propel it onward, and the second – syntactically parallel – abbreviating the repetition to substitute the closure which the first had lacked.

The third group in example 4.3 leaves the recitation in the same way as group 2, but without that group's regular melodic turns; without arriving at a cadence they proceed directly to the higher part of the range. Note the transposition of the recitation formula to the upper fourth in the last line.

These opening formulas launch themselves from firm ground towards open sea; a given beginning, as we see, does not imply a certain continuation, and likewise we cannot always predict in the center of a phrase what the cadential port will be. What is recorded in the surviving repertory is a variety of single versions of many possible musical journeys. To begin a piece,

Ex. 4.2 A standard opening

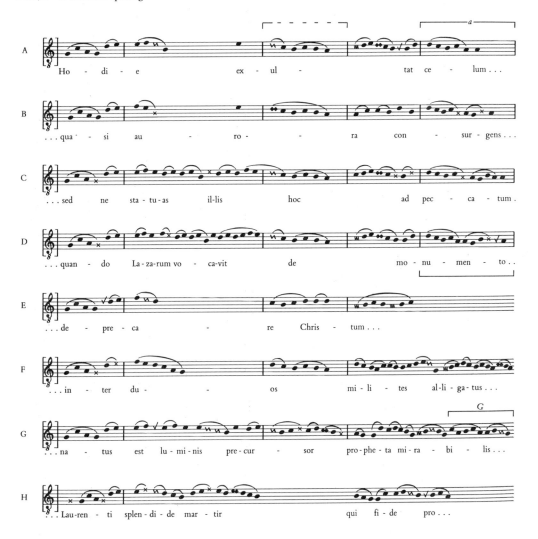

Legend:

A Ben40/134v, ant. *Hodie*
B Ben40/118v, Off. *Que est*
C Ben35/202v, Ing. *Stephanus* (plate 14)
D Ben38/37v, Ing. *Testificata*
E Ben40/61, Com. *Celestis*
F Ben38/116, Ing. *Petrus*
G Ben38/110, Ing. *Lumen* (compare plate 26)
H Ben40/112v, Com. *Clare* (plate 28)

Ex. 4.3 Initial recitation on repeated podatus

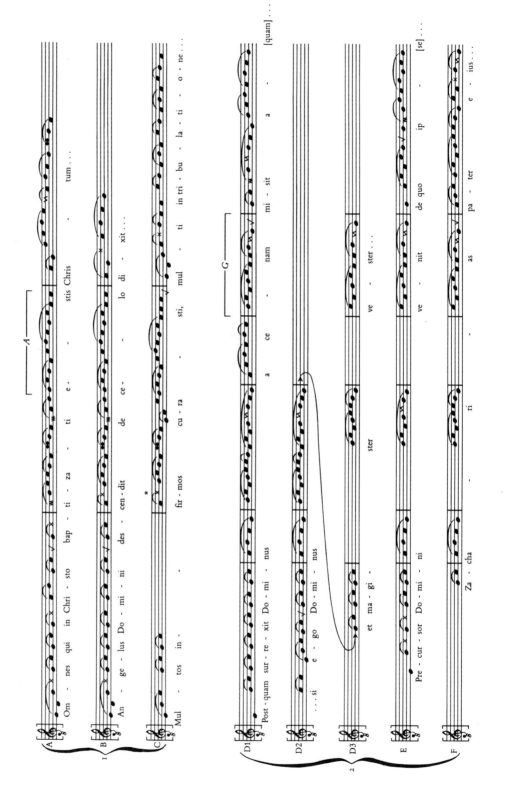

Ex. 4.3 (cont.)

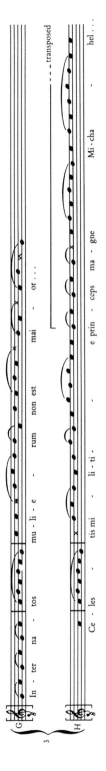

* Appears to be a second here, but this reading is confirmed by Ben38 and by context.

Legend:

A Ben38/47, Off. *Omnes* (compare plate 22)
B Ben38/53, Off. *Angelus* (plate 18)
C Ben40/61, Com. *Multos*
D1 Ben40/4v, ant. *Postquam*
    (D2 and D3 are from same piece)
E Solesmes/3, Resp. *Precursor*
F Ben40/89v, Com. *Zacharias* (plate 27)
G Ben40/89v, Off. *Inter* (plate 27)
H Ben40/61, Com. *Celestis*

or a phrase, the creators of this chant kept in mind several linked determinants: the possible syntactical divisions of the text into phrases, the accentual pattern of the opening syllables, and the intended destination of range.

Mid-phrase procedures

Naturally, much of what happens in the space between formulaic openings and stylized cadence cannot be predicted with accuracy. These places of transition, of continuation, and of extension, are the flexible areas in a musical shape. But a few melodic figures give some notion of flexibility within the bounds of an understood procedure: a means of moving forward (or standing still) in a stylishly consistent fashion.

One example of such a medial procedure can be seen in example 4.4. In its plainest form this consists of a three-element recitation on the note E inflected with the notes a step above and a fourth below, as shown in 4.4AI. All three elements are not always present, as can be seen in 4.4B and 4.4C.

In example 4.4C, the torculus-shaped decoration of the E from below (bracketed in the example) is an important aspect of the use of this formula. In 4.4D and 4.4E this torculus figure is combined with the basic shape to produce a variety of figurations. Part E shows that the torculus figure is not simply added for the delivery of additional text, but may be used in a purely melodic fashion for the melismatic elaboration of a single syllable.

This procedure may be used more than once, either melismatically, or for delivering text; it may in fact become a static recitation formula on its own, as in part F.

This decorated recitation on E is found throughout the repertory, but it exists in two forms: the one we have seen, and the same procedure operating one step lower. Occasionally the two pitch-levels are found in the same phrase, as in example 4.4G.

Recitation

The repeated figure descending from E in example 4.4F is one of many mid-phrase static procedures. Simpler recitations on single pitches are relatively rare in the Beneventan mass. In addition to the recitation on a podatus seen in example 4.3 (a recitation found also in the tracts of Holy Saturday), only a few further instances can be found, like those in example 4.5A and B. More common is a static procedure reiterating a more complex melodic figure, as in example 4.5C–E. Here a melody is halted in mid-course in order to repeat, as often as desired, one of its dynamic elements to accomodate text, or to achieve a static effect.

Recitation on a repeated quilismatic figure is found throughout the repertory. This is perhaps best seen as the expansion of a simpler melodic movement, like that in example 4.4. Example 4.6, showing a variety of forms of this movement, draws its examples from all categories of mass chants as well as from an office responsory:[2] the repertory is highly uniform. In example 4.6A, drawn from an offertory, a simple quilismatic figure rises to an elaborated C and descends

---

[2] Lines D and E are drawn from ingressae which share the same melody, adjusted for different texts.

Ex. 4.4 Recitation formula

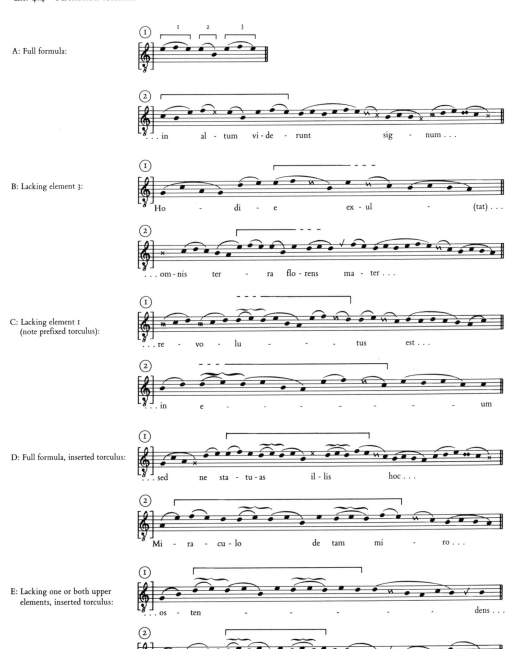

Ex. 4.4 (cont.)

F: Multiple, other inserted material:

① . . . quan - ta   pre - ci - pu -   e . . .

② Que est is - ta que pro - - gre - di - tur . . .

③ Ste - pha - nus   au - tem dum la - pi - da - re - tur a Iu - de - is . . .

④ . . . ad   im - mo - lan - dum . . .

G: With lower transposition:

. . . con - gre - ga - mi - ni . . .

Legend:

A   2: Ben38/79, Off. *Miraculo*

B   1: Ben40/134v, ant. *Hodie*
     2: Ben40/134v, ant. *Hodie*

C   1: Ben38/53, Ing. *Maria* (plate 18)
     2: Ben38/53v, Com. *Qui manducaverit* (plate 19)

D   1: Ben35/202v, Ing. *Stephanus* (plate 14)
     2: Ben38/79, Off. *Miraculo*

E   1: Ben38/110, Ing. *Lumen* (compare plate 26)
     2: Ben40/71, Ing. *Ecce* (plate 23)

F   1: Ben40/139, Com. *O quantus*
     2: Ben40/118v, Off. *Que est*
     3: Ben35/202, Ing. *Stephanus* (plate 13)
     4: Ben40/5, Gr. *Vadit.*

G   Ben40/134, Ing. *Isti*

Ex. 4.5　Recitations

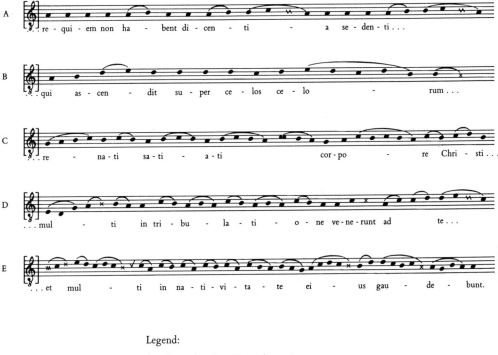

Legend:

A　Ben40/71, Ing. *Ecce* (plate 23)
B　Ben38/93v, Com. *Psallite* (compare plate 24)
C　Ben38/47v, Com. *Ymnum*
D　Ben40/61v, Com. *Multos*
E　Solesmes/2, ant. *Iohannes*

stepwise to G. Lines B through F show a variety of elaborations on this basic motion, while lines G–J alter the ending to conclude with a standard A-cadence. Of the variety of possibilities of inflection, a few are:

1　a double figure to begin (column B)
2　an extension of the quilismatic figure to adjust to varying text (column C)
3　a variety of elaborations on C with optional inclusion of neighboring tones (cols. D and E)
4　an optional rise to E (col. F)

Many more examples of recitation using the quilisma can be seen in examples 4.9 and 4.13.

Ex. 4.6   Recitation using quilisma

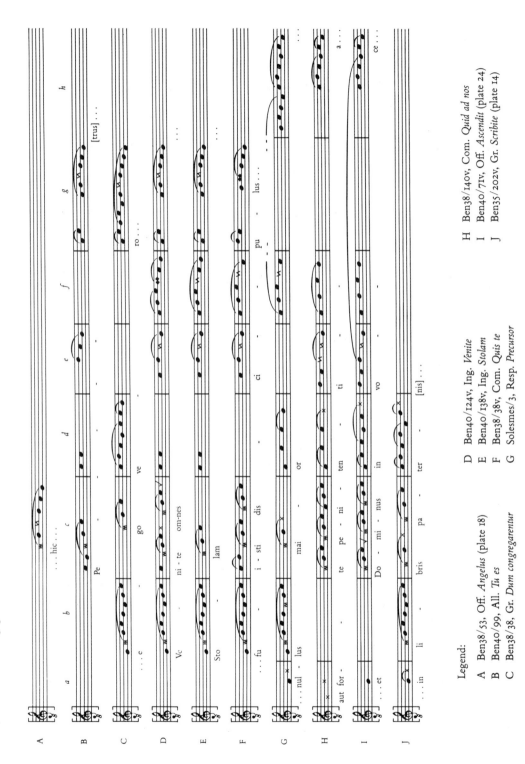

Legend:

A   Ben38/53, Off. *Angelus* (plate 18)
B   Ben40/99, All. *Tu es*
C   Ben38/38, Gr. *Dum congregarentur*

D   Ben40/124v, Ing. *Venite*
E   Ben40/138v, Ing. *Stolam*
F   Ben38/38v, Com. *Quis te*
G   Solesmes/3, Resp. *Precursor*

H   Ben38/140v, Com. *Quid ad nos*
I   Ben40/7rv, Off. *Ascendit* (plate 24)
J   Ben35/202v, Gr. *Scribite* (plate 14)

Larger forms

We have sampled initial, medial, and terminal procedures for Beneventan musical phrases; we now consider how these work together with a given text to produce entire pieces.

Example 4.7 shows a relatively elaborate antiphon from the office of St John the Baptist in the Solesmes fragments. An opening melisma, based on straightforward cadence formulas, underlines the important opening word and its accent; a brief second member, *est nomen eius*, balances the first in length, but proceeds through the entire range. The second half of the antiphon is a single phrase which recites on a decorated c and concludes with a standard cadence. Some other pieces of this kind are to be found among the offertories and communions of the mass. Most mass chants, however, are longer and more elaborate, and involve some degree of repetition.

Ex. 4.7   Antiphon *Iohannes est nomen eius*

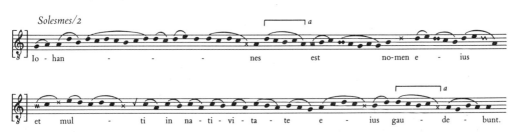

Repetition is very important in understanding this music – if by repetition we mean the use of music for more than one text. The Beneventan repertory is sometimes viewed as being full of repetition to the point of monotony: and we shall see the kind of piece that gives rise to such criticisms. But repetition comes in a great variety of forms, and about half of the repertory has no internal repetition at all.

There are several levels of repetition: firstly, a tendency to repeat particular patterns immediately, usually to extend a phrase without making a new one; to add a subordinate clause, a modifying or parallel element of text too short to be a phrase in itself. We have seen this in examples 4.4 through 4.7, and it is also shown in example 4.8, where the first phrase is extended by repeating the intermediate and cadential formulae to produce the short setting of *in auribus meis*, which completes the subordinate clause and prepares for the main verb which begins the second half of the antiphon.

Secondly, many pieces are made on a pattern of phrases repeated more or less exactly. One such piece, whose repetitions are not so exact as some we shall see, is *Inter natos* (see example 5.7), which serves variously as offertory, communion, and antiphon (see Appendix 2). The text is divided into two lengthy periods, each again subdivided:

> *Inter natos mulierum non est maior*
> *Iohanne baptista*
> *maior prophetis et minor angelis*
> *qui preparavit corda fidelium.*

Ex. 4.8 Antiphon *Ut audivi*

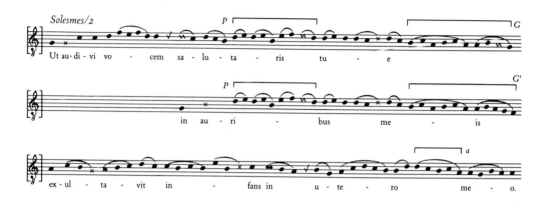

The first part of each member is set to the same music, with an additional opening formula to begin the piece. The words *Iohanne baptista* make a second phrase which is paralleled only at its beginning and end by the much longer final phrase *qui preparavit corda fidelium*.

A further level of repetition is to be found in those pieces which are made from successive iterations of a single melody; this procedure is the source of many of the longest pieces in the repertory. As in Gregorian practice, this technique is found in the tracts of Holy Saturday, and in certain other repetitive pieces like the *Benedictus es domine*.[3] But it is found much more widely than in multi-verse texts, and it seems to grow, not from a repertory of standard melodies which are shared by a liturgical genre or by a mode, but from individual phrases appearing only within a single piece (though perhaps repeated many times within that piece).

Though this reprise structure is found throughout the repertory, it is most characteristic of the ingressa, and examples of it will be seen in the discussion of ingressae below. These repetitions are generally well matched to units of the text; there are no cases in which a repeated phrase is allowed to begin in the middle of a syntactical unit, or in which the musical unit is left incomplete when the text ends.[4]

The adoption of a single melody for more than one text is a further aspect of musical repetition. To the listener, of course, this is a matter very different from the reiteration of a phrase within a single piece, but from the point of view of the singer or notator the process is a similar one, involving the re-use of musical material for new text. Melodies are recast among the antiphons; in several cases texts share the same melody, a phenomenon familiar to students of the Gregorian chant. The same melodic shape is to be seen in the three pieces (offertory and communions) of example 4.13. On a larger scale there is the re-use of ingressa melodies for other feasts. Three of these are seen in example 4.10.

---

[3] For transcriptions of these pieces see PM XIV, 320–3 (for the *Benedictus es*) and 362–71 (for the tracts).

[4] In the case of the Alleluia there is a melody which is variable in length depending on the text, though it does not involve repetition. See below, p. 119–22.

MUSIC FOR THE MASS

The multiple uses of pieces like *Inter natos* show that a chant's liturgical function is no sure determinant of its musical style, and it is with this caution in mind that we make some observations about each of the liturgical categories of the mass.

Ingressa

The ingressae, of which nineteen survive, include many of the longest and most elaborate Beneventan chants, though some (like *Gaudeamus* for All Saints) are of very modest scope. Unlike the Gregorian entrance chants, they have no psalmodic verses, and hence are probably not intended to be repeated.[5]

An ingressa of larger proportion is *Maria vidit angelum* for Easter (example 4.9). The piece is tailored in six repetitions of a single melody, which use different openings and endings. These can be further grouped into two larger cycles of three phrases each. Lines 1 and 4 open with a gesture not found in the other phrases, and lines 3 and 6 close the two cycles with a standard G-cadence unique to these phrases. Two final *alleluia* stand outside the repetition structure and close the piece. Relatively lengthy opening melismas (marked M1) set off the first accent of each line, and another melisma (M2) concludes the first sense-unit of each line on its final syllable.

Within each phrase we recognize formulas which link this piece to the repertory as a whole. Two formulas (P and A) appear each at two pitch levels. These transpositions occur throughout the repertory (though the presence of the cadence-formula A at the upper fourth is rare), and they are helpful in determining a suitable pitch-level for transcription. The untransposed versions of both formulas appear to fall on accented syllables, but this is not true of these melodies throughout the repertory, and while in the case of final A-cadences this accentuation may be the fortuitous result of a strongly rhythmical text, the adjustment made by quilismas preceding formula P place it, not on an accent, but on the third syllable from the end of its phrase (for example *interrogavit*).

Generally speaking, reiterated melodies of this kind are unique to the pieces in which they occur, although similar repetition plans are found in other pieces – using different repeated phrases which include many of the same formulas.

Among the nineteen surviving Beneventan entrance chants, five are adapted from those for another feast. These adaptations are as follows:

1 The ingressa *Maria vidit angelum* shares its melody with *Sancti uidentes angelum* for the feast of the Holy Twelve Brothers of Benevento. This latter piece, like the Easter ingressa, is arranged in two larger cycles, though its six lines, in groups of four and two, are no longer evenly divided.

[5] But in the series of ingressae included in Vall. C 9 two pieces have a psalmodic ending attached; the ingressae here may be serving as antiphons. One ingressa (*Venite omnes*, for the second Beneventan mass of the Holy Cross) is followed by two verses (*Defuncto Chosroe* and *Gaudentes itaque*); these are not psalmodic verses (like the *versus ad repetendum* for the antiphons of Good Friday) though they share the same music for the second half of their melodies. Owing to their position between ingressa and Alleluia, these verses might be mistaken for a gradual with the first verse mislabeled, but their musical style is markedly simpler than that of the surviving graduals.

Ex. 4.9 Ingressa Maria vidit angelum

Ben38/52v–53 (plates 17–18)

Ex. 4.9 (cont.)

* MS: splendorem.

2 *Stolam iocunditatis* for St Martin shares its melody with *Venite omnes*, the second ingressa for the Holy Cross. The latter is adapted evidently from the longer melody of the former by omitting a central section of the melody. The resulting adaptation is perhaps not entirely felicitous, including a substantial G-cadence (which in *Stolam iocunditatis* comes at the end of its first member (*Stolam iocunditatis induit eum DOMINUS*)) placed awkwardly in the midst of a sense-unit (*per quos nos CHRISTUS sacro redemit sanguine suo*).

3 *Petrus dormiebat* for Sts Peter and Paul shares its melody with two other ingressae: *Surge propera* for the Assumption, and *Gaudeamus omnes*, the first ingressa for the Holy Cross. This last group, transcribed as example 4.10, shows highly stylized and repetitive melodic structures: but the procedure is not the simple repetition of a single phrase. The three ingressae are presented in columns to show their repeated melodic elements. *Petrus dormiebat* is the simplest, using the same music three times, except that the second and third lines substitute alternative music (in column D) for that in column E. This element D is found in neither of the other ingressae. Similarly, *Surge* and *Gaudeamus* include a melodic element (column B) not found in *Petrus dormiebat*.

Thus, though *Surge* and *Gaudeamus* are very closely related – the latter is the first three lines of the former – they cannot be derived from *Petrus dormiebat*, nor can it be derived from them. Perhaps there is a lost melody from which all three of these ingressae descend. But more likely is that these ingressae represent written versions of a Beneventan melodic procedure; a process in which a unique melodic path is varied in its repetitions, sometimes to adjust to varying phrase-lengths, by altering the melodic content of less fixed portions. The music of columns B and D is not unique.[6] What sets these ingressae apart as a group is the particular assemblage of known melodic elements, and the special turns of phrase within them which are reproduced with particular fidelity.

Terminal Alleluias

Certain of the ingressae are linked by the melodies of their final Alleluias. The final Alleluia of example 4.9 is found with the ingressa of the Holy Twelve Brothers with which this piece shares its melody, but also as the final Alleluia of two other ingressae. But the situation is still more complicated, as the chart below shows.

Ingressa text	Feast	Final Alleluias
Maria vidit	Easter	A–B–C
Sancti videntes	XII Fratres	A–C*
Factus est repente	Pentecost	[B] M–C
Michi autem absit	Holy Cross	X–C (Ben40)
Michi autem absit	Holy Cross	X–Y–Z (Vall. C 9)
Michi autem nimis	All Saints	X–Y–Z (Ben40)

---

[6] That in column B is found in almost precisely the same form as the beginning of the ingressa *Lumen quod animus cernens* for St John the Baptist. Column D's music may be found, for example, in the offertories *Milia milium* (St Michael) and *Adhesit* (St Lawrence).

The first two ingressae are modeled on the same melody, which includes melody A within the repetition scheme. To this *Maria vidit* adds two Alleluias (B and C), *Sancti videntes* only one (C). Two other ingressae use the same final Alleluia, but precede it with different penultimate Alleluias; one of these (*Factus est*) concludes with music that matches melody B. It appears that melody C is a wanderer, attachable to melodies otherwise not closely related: its opening is found also in MC 361 (p. 189), though we cannot tell to what chant it is attached there.[7]

Two other ingressae – both beginning *Michi autem* – share the same melody throughout, except that their final Alleluias (as found in Ben40) are arranged differently: the first Alleluia (X) is the same in both pieces, but one continues with the "Easter" Alleluia (C), while the other adds two further Alleluias (Y and Z).

What may be the more usual form of *Michi autem absit* appears in Vall. c 9, whose Alleluias match, not the version in Ben40, but the Alleluias of the companion ingressa *Michi autem nimis*. Since these Alleluias have melodies that recur throughout both ingressae, we may surmise that Ben40 has altered *Michi autem absit* by substituting the "Easter" Alleluia for the original, integral, final Alleluias.

The transmission of these Alleluias is evidently somewhat flexible. And the fact that they may sometimes be cued suggests that to the scribe some of them are independent melodies which may be recalled by an abbreviated reminder.

The series of three Alleluias which conclude the Ascension ingressa *Ecce sedet in medio* (at least in the version of Vall. c 9, and probably of Ben38) is not found elsewhere among the ingressae, but it serves as a link with the wider repertory in that the same series concludes three communions (*Ymnum canite* for Holy Saturday, *Qui manducaverit* for Easter, *Ut cognosceret* for Sts Peter and Paul) otherwise not musically related, either to each other, or to the ingressa.

Again, there is a transmission problem. The chart below shows the arrangement of Alleluias in the sources (the Easter communion is example 4.15).

Text	Feast	Ben38	Ben40	Vall. c 9
Com. *Ymnum canite*	Holy Sat.	Q–R–S	Q–R–S	
Com. *Qui manducaverit*	Easter	Q–R–S	Q	?
(after V. 1):		Q*	Q	Q S
(after V. 2):		Q*	Q	?
Ing. *Ecce sedet*	Ascension	Q–R[S?]	Q	Q–R–S
Com. *Petrus ap.*	Peter & Paul	–	Q–R–S	

The final two Alleluias (R and S) of the series are not always present. For *Ecce sedet* the scribe of Ben38 apparently intends the singing of both R and S, cuing their beginning as they may be found earlier in the same manuscript for the Easter and Holy Saturday communions. The singer would have to know these melodies by heart, or at least be familiar enough with the repertory

---

[7] The connection of Alleluia C to the preceding piece is not always consistent; it appears to begin sometimes on G, sometimes on A. A comparison of its presentation at the end of *Maria vidit* in Ben38 and Ben40 is enough to confirm the problem of its pitch-level, but it is symptomatic of the notation of Beneventan chant in general, particularly in Ben40, that scribes feel free to place the pen at a new convenient place when beginning a new phrase.

Ex. 4.10 Three ingressae

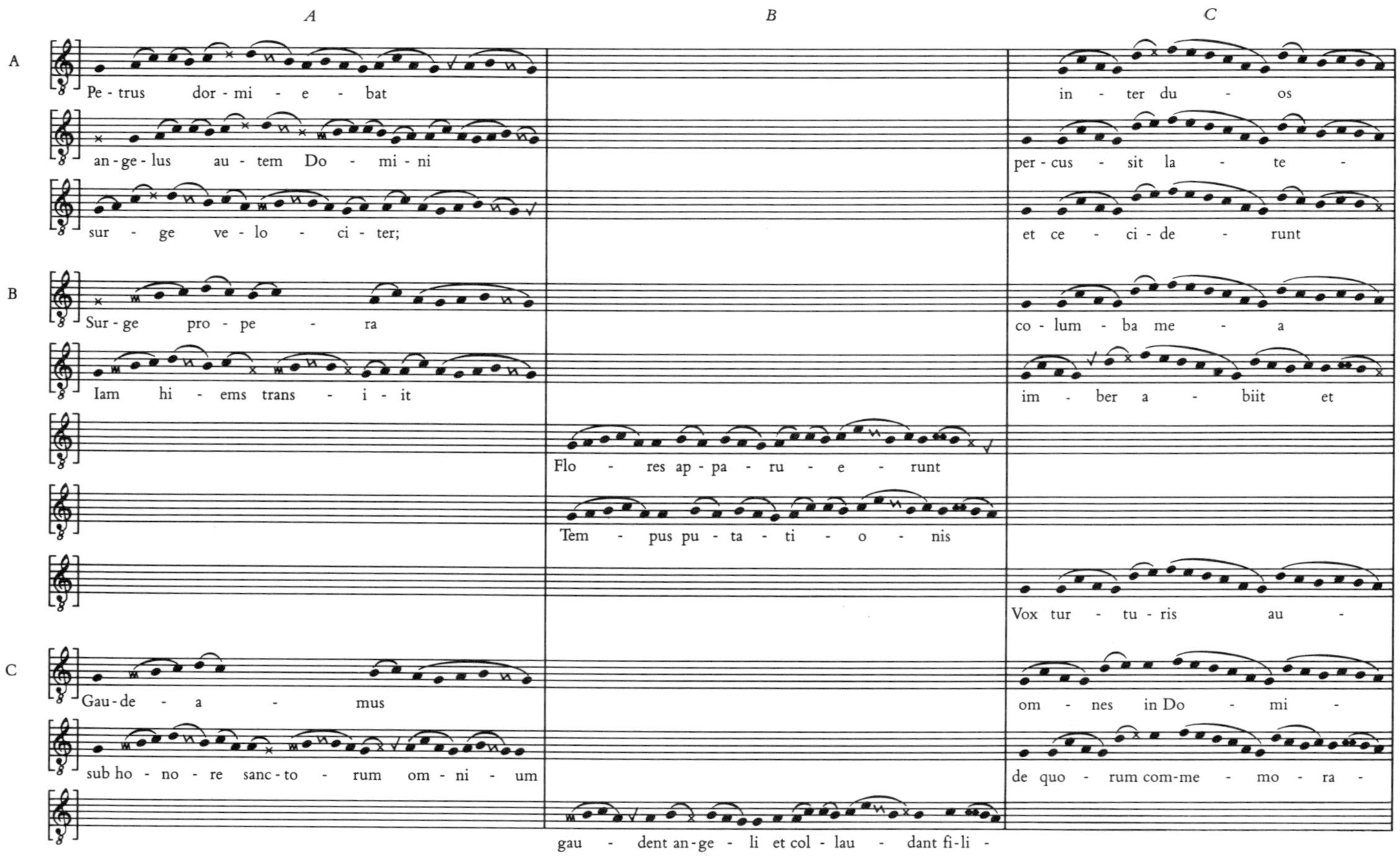

Ex. 4.10 *(cont.)*

Legend:
A Ben38/115v–116, Ing. *Petrus*
B Ben40/118, Ing. *Surge*
C Ben40/133v, Ing. *Gaudeamus*

to know that this cued melody is to be sought among the communions rather than the ingressae. But Ben40 apparently intends only the first Alleluia to be sung for the ingressa and for the Easter communion, though all three Alleluias are used elsewhere in the manuscript. Vallicelliana c 9 presents a curious truncated version of the three Alleluias for the Easter communion, moving as by homoioteleuton from a point in melody Q to an identical place in s, thus bypassing a central section. This melody is difficult to read, and cannot be controlled by reference to the two other times in which it should appear, owing to the difficulty of reading the palimpsest.

These final Alleluias, variable as to their content and their placement, serve as a link among sometimes unrelated melodies, and among liturgical categories. Taken together they are a written representation of choice in performance, of a detail not entirely fixed even in the written tradition.

Gradual

The very limited survival of what may have been a feature of every Beneventan mass makes it difficult to draw general conclusions about graduals. They are in some ways inconsistent, and they are only sporadically represented. Of the twenty-one masses in Ben38 and Ben40, only six have graduals. Nothing replaces the gradual in the other masses: the ingressa is followed directly by the Alleluia (or, where the Alleluia is missing, by the offertory). In other sources, however, there is evidence that the gradual is a more regular feature of the Beneventan mass than appears from Ben38 and Ben40.[8]

The graduals are extensive chants, each with a verse no less elaborate than the refrain. There is no evidence here of the repetition structures of the ingressa.

Three of the graduals (for Palm Sunday, All Saints, and Saint Andrew) include the sort of long melisma that we expect in Gregorian graduals, especially in their verses; these melismas are generally applied to the last syllable of the verse or (in two cases) the respond. Two verses open with melismas, either on the first syllable (NON *me conclusisti*, Palm Sunday) or the first accent (*Pro* PA–*tribus*, St Andrew).[9]

Two of the six graduals (*Scribite hunc* for Saint Stephen and *Vadit propitiator* for Maundy Thursday) include a final cue for partial repetition of the respond, while the others give no evidence of repetition, partial or total. That the respond is not to be repeated is perhaps suggested by the gradual *Anima nostra*, which provides a musical rhyme; the end of its verse *Laqueus contritus* duplicates the final melisma of the respond, making a rounded musical form even without a return to the respond. An incomplete musical rhyme is found in the gradual *Constitues eos*, where the verse ends with the opening portion of the respond's final melisma – the rest, perhaps, to be supplied in order to close the form.

These inconsistencies among the graduals may reflect the adaptation of an older style to a

---

[8] See Chapter 3, p. 75.

[9] Melismas are found more often on final syllables of words than on accents; they are used to close all the Holy Saturday tracts. The longest melisma in the repertory, however, is used on the penultimate accent of *Zacharias pater* (used both as a communion and as an antiphon): *PLE-bis sue*.

newer Gregorian fashion without partial repetition. In Ben38 and Ben40 Gregorian graduals are written with no evidence of repetition. However, if a partial repetition had been customary in the older Beneventan gradual, we should expect to find verses (like the Gregorian gradual-verse *Priusquam te formarem* which ends with *et dixit mihi*) requiring additional text, but such texts are not among those that survive, and indeed, the two partial repetitions that are indicated are not required by any incompleteness in the sense of their verses.[10]

Although neither the responds nor the verses appear to be based on psalmodic recitation tones, two verses (for the graduals of St Stephen and St Martin) share the same melody, though the responds to which they are attached are not similarly related. With only these two verses we cannot deduce much about the relation of music to varying texts in this situation, but the presence of a passage of recitation in the verse for St Martin has the effect of delaying the following music so that it falls on the final syllables and thus has a closing function in each verse. This is a perfectly normal procedure, but is at variance with the means we shall see in the Alleluia for adapting texts of varying lengths to a single melody.

We have suggested that the responsories found in the repertory, together with the graduals, may be part of a single larger category not clearly differentiated in their function between mass and office. Moreover, the two groups are linked by a phrase from the Palm Sunday gradual *Vadit propitiator* ("reliquit eum"), which is virtually identical with the phrase "et circa horam nonam" for the Beneventan responsory *Tenebre facte sunt*.

Alleluia

In the Beneventan chant all the Alleluias have the same melody, with the exception of one (*Posuisti*) for Saint Stephen and one (*Resurrexit tamquam dormiens*) for Holy Saturday,[11] which have unique melodies (two others are not notated).

The adaptation in the remaining Alleluia verses of many texts to the same music may be seen in example 4.11.

The Alleluia's melody is not repeated in the verse. The verses are of three lengths, depending on the size and shape of the text to be accommodated, and they end at three different places in the course of the same melody. By Gregorian standards these pieces are not all in the same mode; the two longer versions end on A, but the majority end a step lower. Perhaps the piece is rounded with a repetition of the Alleluia, though there is no mention of this in the sources.

The verses are divided into two, or occasionally three, phrases. The first phrase is relatively stable, and creates a sort of melismatic motto. The first few words that can stand alone (*Tu es*

---

[10] One of the surviving responsories, however, includes just such an incomplete verse text: *Amicus meus* for Good Friday has a verse that concludes *qui simul mecum*, leading back to the reprise *manducasti panem meum*. For the full text see Appendix 2.

[11] Another melody for this text, found in Ben38, f. 47, is based on the Gregorian Alleluia *Justus ut palma*: see Schlager, *Thematischer Katalog*, no. 38 (pp. 86–7). An Alleluia V *Pascha nostrum* appears in the Easter masses of Beneventan graduals (Ben35, f. 69v; Ben38, f. 50; Ben39, f. 30v; Ben40, f. 23v); though essentially Gregorian in style, it uses neither the Beneventan nor the Gregorian melody for this text. In the Gregorian mass for Easter in Ben38 and Ben40 this setting of *Pascha nostrum* is the second of two Alleluias using this text; the first, in both cases, is the melody familiar in the Gregorian tradition. The same text appears a third time in these two manuscripts, however, in the Beneventan mass, to the standard Beneventan Alleluia melody (see example 4.11).

Ex. 4.11   Alleluia verses

*   Appears to begin on C.
†   Bracketed music written separately in margin, perhaps accounting for the misplaced final syllable of *Andreas*.
‡   Appears to begin one step lower.

Ex. 4.11 (cont.)

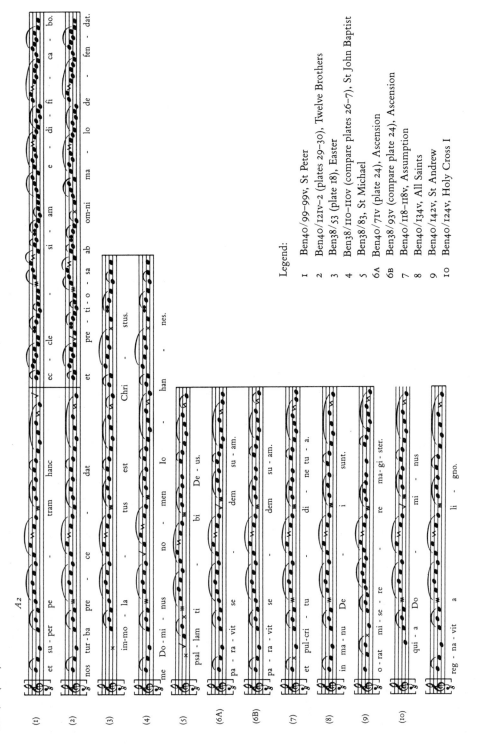

Legend:

1   Ben40/99–99v, St Peter
2   Ben40/121v–2 (plates 29–30), Twelve Brothers
3   Ben38/53 (plate 18), Easter
4   Ben38/110–110v (compare plates 26–7), St John Baptist
5   Ben38/83, St Michael
6A Ben40/71v (plate 24), Ascension
6B Ben38/93v (compare plate 24), Ascension
7   Ben40/118–118v, Assumption
8   Ben40/134v, All Saints
9   Ben40/142v, St Andrew
10 Ben40/124v, Holy Cross I

petrus, *Pascha nostrum*, etc.) are set to the opening music, which is designed around two long melismas: the first melisma begins on the last accented syllable, and the second begins on the last syllable (at least it does in Ben40; the scribe of Ben38 places the last syllable earlier. Apparently the two scribes disagree as to the tradition, or they are reporting slightly different practices). These melismas are stable as regards their notes, but in one case (6A) melisma 1 is abbreviated, and melisma 2 in some cases is omitted altogether. Number 9 omits both melismas in the main text (they are present in Ben38, f. 140v), but provides them in the margin. The scribe may have intended an abbreviated version like 6A, but misplaces the last syllable of *Andreas*, perhaps by overlooking the first neume of melisma 2.

After the opening phrase, the remaining text goes by much more quickly; there are no more long melismas. In numbers 1 and 2 the remaining text is divided into two phrases; these together balance the opening phrase in musical length, though they bear twice as much text. Verses 3 and 4 (*Pascha nostrum* and *De ventre matris mee*) extend the second phrase by using part of the music of the third, but without observing the pause that comes at the end of phrase 2 in all other verses.

Verses 5 through 9 present the shortest, and most usual, version of the melody: their second phrase is half as long as the first, though it usually bears more text. Like all the second phrases, these begin with a recitation of at least two syllables and align the following accented syllable on a five-note figure (marked accent 2). Verse 2, however, does not observe accent 2, doubtless because neither available accent (TUR-ba, pre-CE-dat) would permit both the obligatory two-syllable figure preceding the accent and a remainder of a least two syllables.

Two verses do not quite fit the pattern. Number 10 deals with a lengthy text in an unusual way. Having omitted melisma 2, and completed the music of the second phrase (*quia Dominus*), there remain six syllables (*regnavit a ligno*) – perhaps not enough to use the whole third phrase, and too many for the extension used by verses 3 and 4. Whatever the reason, the omitted second melisma is attached to the last syllable of phrase 2, and the whole second phrase is repeated; but there are not enough syllables remaining to allow the proper placement of the accent.

Number 4 (*De ventre matris mee*) also presents problems. This is the only verse whose first phrase is not a self-contained grammatical unit, and it misplaces the accent of phrase 2. Another possible setting for the first phrase – *De ventre matris mee* – would apparently leave a text too long for a single second phrase, and too short for two balanced phrases, *vocavit me dominus* and *nomen Iohannes*.

Evidently, this procedure for singing verses is based on the structure of the text, and on a strongly disciplined melodic opening.

The two "free" Alleluias (those not using the standard verse-melody) are similar in scope to the standard melody. An opening Alleluia is followed by a jubilus of moderate length. The following verse, moderately elaborate but without extended melismas, does not repeat any of its phrases, nor does it recall music from the opening Alleluia. One of these Alleluias, *Posuisti* for St Stephen (from Ben35, sadly incomplete (see plate 14); cued also in Ben40 for St Lawrence), is in the mainstream of the Beneventan melodic style.

The other "free" Alleluia (example 4.12) has a special placement that sets it apart from the core of the repertory, and it is musically distinct as well. The Alleluia *Resurrexit tamquam*

Ex. 4.12   Two versions of Alleluia *Resurrexit*

Ben34/126

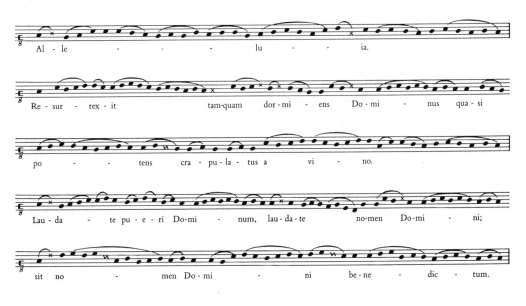

Ben40/19v (plate 22)

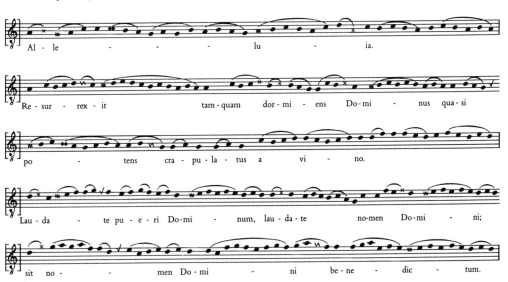

dormiens (a text used also in the Ambrosian rite) appears, in both Ben38 and Ben40, in a Holy Saturday rite that is a mixture of Beneventan and Gregorian styles. This Alleluia, which precedes a clearly Beneventan offertory and communion, is related to the repertory, particularly through the use of a standard cadential formula. The two verses, though they are entirely distinct from one another, are based on similar melodies, and neither repeats music from the Alleluia.

There are two possible endings for the verse *Resurrexit* resulting from the placement of the final cadence, which in some sources (Ben30, Ben33, Ben38, Ben40) is written a fourth higher than in others.[12] In cases where there is a second verse *Laudate pueri*, this following verse is pitched so as to match the ending of the first verse. Thus it appears a fourth higher in Ben38 and Ben40 than it does in Ben34, Ben35, and Ben39. The pitch of the second verse, however, does not seem to be the purpose of this alternative ending for the verse *Resurrexit*, since it appears in both its low (Montecassino Compactiones v) and high (Ben30, Ben33) versions in sources which do not have the second verse. The lower ending is used in the adaptations of this melody in Ben39, f. 121 (where it lacks the final six notes) and f. 140v (where it is followed by a second verse modeled on *Laudate pueri*). The version in Baltimore, Walters 6 perhaps acknowledges the problem when it omits the ending of *Resurrexit* (and of the adaptation *Hodie natus*) altogether.[13]

This piece, whose placement, preservation, and adaptation to other texts give it a special place in the Beneventan manuscripts, is so independent melodically of the style shared by the core repertory that we may suspect that its style is like its placement: bridging the stylistic space between Gregorian and Beneventan. This is the only chant associated with the Beneventan liturgy to be permeated by the rich body of tropes that flourished at Benevento in association with Gregorian chant. The Alleluia is frequently accompanied by a prosula (see Appendix 2).

Offertory

The offertory is often the shortest piece in the mass. Although they include a fair share of the musical formulas of the repertory, offertories do not generally have a larger reprise structure; they are similar in style to many communions. Sixteen offertories are notated, and five additional masses refer the singer elsewhere for the offertory: two masses cue offertories used elsewhere, two cue pieces otherwise unknown, and one cues a piece used in another mass as a communion.

The connection between offertory and communion is made also in other cases: two offertories in Ben38 serve as communions for the same feasts in Ben40.[14] And the very brief Ascension offertory (in Ben40, the first of two), *Ascendit Deus*, shares a melody with a number of communions and antiphons – several of these pieces are seen in example 4.13. These pieces have

---

[12] See PM XIV, 442.

[13] This transposition, and a possible connection with the change of ordinary mode in Byzantine chant between Holy Week and Easter, is discussed in Levy, "The Italian neophytes' chants," pp. 218–20.

[14] *Inter natos mulierum* for St John the Baptist, and *Petrus apostolus* for Sts Peter and Paul. On the relation of offertory and communion, see Chapter 3, p. 78.

Ex. 4.13 Four pieces with similar melodies

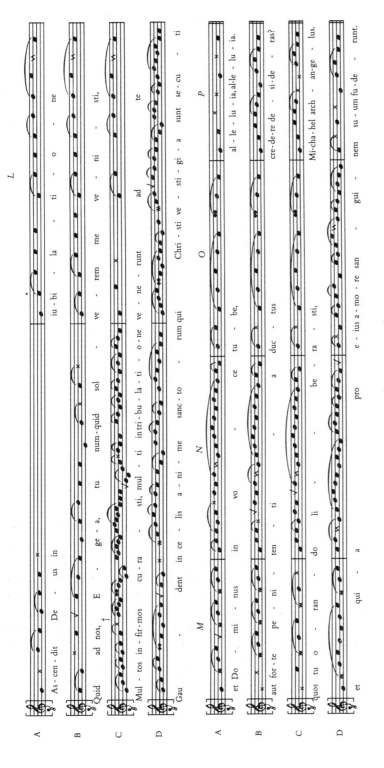

* A tiny custos placed before the syllable *bi* one note higher than its opening pitch may suggest that the entire piece to this point should be pitched one step lower (beginning on F).
† Appears to be a second in Ben40, but a third in Ben38.

Legend:

A Ben40/71v (plate 24), Ascension Off.
B Ben40/143, Holy Cross II Com.
C Ben40/61, St Michael Com.
D Ben40/133v, All Saints Com.

varying openings, but they all arrive at the same medial cadence, and all continue with a lengthy period which begins on a quilismatic recitation.

Another offertory (*Miraculo de tam miro*, for St Michael) shares much of its musical material with an antiphon (possibly intended as a second communion) following the communion of the second mass of All Saints (Ben40, f. 134v). And the offertory *Inter natos* has the same melody as the communion *Sancta maria exora*.

Generally, offertories have no verses, and no evidence of psalmody. One (*O quam pretiosum*) has a noted EUOUAE (Ben40, f. 133v); this is part of an especially festive mass for All Saints, including Kyrie, *Gloria in excelsis*, and three communions with psalmodic endings. One offertory (*Adhesit anima mea* for St Lawrence, Ben40, f. 112v) has a verse (*In craticula*) which goes twice through the same melody; it does not appear to be based on a psalmodic recitation, nor is its melody shared by other pieces in the repertory. Far less elaborate than any of the Gregorian offertory verses, it is closely related to a pair of Gregorian antiphons, and may in fact be a Beneventan borrowing from the Gregorian liturgy.[15]

Communion

Communions provide the widest variety of style in the Beneventan chant, ranging from relatively simple settings (example 4.14) to elaborately structured compositions like the Easter

Ex. 4.14   Ascension Communion *Pacem meam*

Ben40/71v (plate 24)

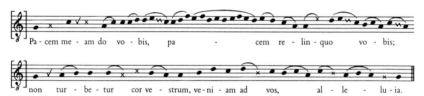

Pa - cem me - am do vo - bis, pa - cem re - lin - quo vo - bis;
non tur - be - tur cor ve - strum, ve - ni - am ad vos, al - le - lu - ia.

communion (example 4.15). Example 4.14, the communion used both for Ascension and Pentecost, is a freely structured melody in four distinct phrases, with no musical repetition and very little appeal to the usually abundant repertory of musical formulas. Example 4.15, however, is a long and elaborate structure based on reprises. Versions of the same cadence are repeated many times, both within text phrases (lines 1, 6, 9) and as final cadences (lines 5, 8, 11). This communion has two verses forming a doxology. They are based on the same music and the same structure as the communion itself, but rather than repeating music from the opening phrase in order to accommodate text beyond the opening gesture (as in line 2), they include a decorated recitation (lines 7 and 10) before proceeding to a close including the final Alleluias.

Some music is shared among communions. Example 4.13 above shows three communions and an offertory which share a similar melodic shape. Likewise, the Alleluias which close the Easter

---

[15] See the discussion and transcription in Chapter 5, p. 178–9.

communion and its verses (see example 4.15) are also used to close communions for Holy Saturday and for Saints Peter and Paul, though these pieces do not otherwise share the same melody.

Tract

As we have seen in Chapter 3, there are no Lenten tracts surviving in the Beneventan repertory, and little evidence that they existed. There are, however, four "tracts" for Holy Saturday, three serving as canticles after lessons and a fourth (*Sicut cervus*) for the procession to the font. These are uniformly called tracts in the rubrics,[16] and they share a number of musical traits. These pieces have been studied in detail by Hesbert in *Paléographie musicale* XIV, and the reader can find transcriptions and analyses there.[17] All these tracts are made of repeated psalmodic verses, generally in two halves with two periods of recitation (*Sicut cervus*, however, has short verses with a single period). All verses include recitation on repeated podatus (three beginning from G, *Sicut cervus* from A). The verses are briefer, and more strictly formulaic, than those of tracts in other Latin rites. All four tracts end with the same terminal melisma, which is repeated also at the ends of occasional interior verses (*Cantabo*, ℣ *Vinea*, *Sicut cervus* ℣ *Ita desiderat*) in Ben38, but these interior repetitions are not present in the version of Ben40, nor in the *Sicut cervus* of the Bari benedictional roll.

Two tracts begin with an unmatched period preceding the verses. In the case of *Domine audivi* the opening refrain is related to the Gregorian tract, but it also includes music later found in each of the verses.[18] *Cantabo* opens with a text which is an introduction to the verses to follow, and it is set to music which does not recur in the verses.

It is true, as Hesbert points out, that the two "responsorial" tracts have opening verses, whose texts serve as introductions, which could be repeated after the subsequent verses with no resulting harm to the sense of the text. He suggests that they were probably sung responsorially, using the opening verse as a refrain.[19] I think, however, that responsorial performance is unlikely in these two tracts with special openings. The canticles of Holy Saturday in the Roman rite are musical continuations of lessons sung to a special melody, and though the confused transmission of the Holy Saturday rite makes it impossible to know what readings were intended for the Paschal Vigil in the Beneventan rite,[20] all the Beneventan tracts except *Sicut cervus* have texts which are continuations of scripture lessons (from Habakkuk, Isaiah, and Deuteronomy) which are used on occasion for Holy Saturday. They are thus in the Beneventan tradition of *lectio cum cantico*,[21] and seem unlikely candidates for responsorial performance with a repeated refrain, owing to the necessity of delivering, *during* a reading (as opposed to the musical response *following* a reading), the scriptural lesson as it stands in the text.

[16] They are called *tractus ambrosianus* in Ben38 (the same label is used for *Sicut cervus* in Vat. 10673), and *Tractus* in Ben40. The only other rubric visible is a letter "T" attached to the palimpsest *Domine audivi* in Vat. 10657, f. 2v.

[17] PM XIV, 360–75.

[18] This shared music is treated differently in the opening period; the music for the words *consideravi opera* is used in the subsequent verses as the ending (*consideravi*) of the first psalmodic period and the beginning (*opera*) of the second. See chapter 5, example 5.3.

[19] PM XIV, 368, note 2.

[20] These matters are studied in detail in Hesbert, "L'antiphonale" (6), pp. 155–82; PM XIV, 337–75.

[21] For other examples of *lectio cum cantico* at Benevento see below, pp. 132, 156–60.

Ex. 4.15   Easter Communion

*Ben38/53–53v (plates 18–19)**

* Bracketed portions are cued in the manuscript.

Ex. 4.15 (*cont.*)

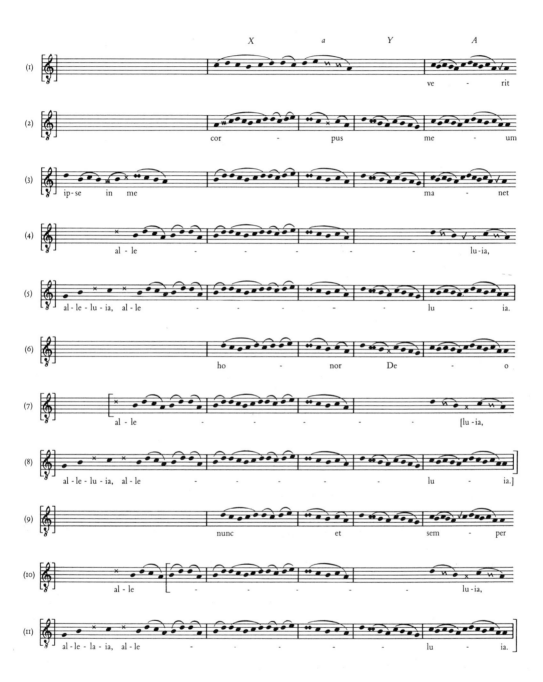

Chants of the ordinary

The surviving music for Beneventan chants of the ordinary of the mass is scant, although we have seen in Chapter 3 that there is considerable evidence for their use. The remaining music is transcribed in example 4.16. The melodies are relatively simple, and do not match those of the Gregorian repertory.[22] The Gloria intonation in the Beneventan Easter mass of Ben38 is the same as that found in the Gregorian Easter mass of Ben34. Though it appears to resemble the

Ex. 4.16   Chants for the ordinary of the Mass

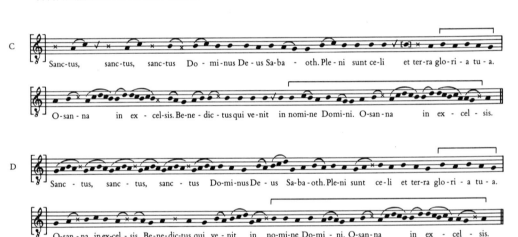

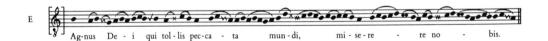

Legend:

A   Ben38/53 (plate 18)
B   Ben35/202 (plate 13)
C   Ben35/202 (plate 13)
D   Ben35/195v
E   Ben35/202 (plate 13)

[22] For possible parallels with the Old Roman chant, see Boe, "Gloria A."

intonation of Gloria I in the Vatican Edition, the regrettably few neumes visible at the end of the Gloria in Vall. c 9, f. 170v are certainly not those of Gloria I; this intonation may be that of a purely Beneventan piece. The Kyrie which follows this Gloria in Vall. c 9 (as apparently the Kyrie always does at Benevento: see Chapter 3) is almost indecipherable, though we can see that it is a relatively simple threefold Kyrie (with no following Christe).

The only clearly readable portion of a Credo is the ending found in Ben35, f. 202; this, however, matches the neumes visible in Vall. c 9, f. 167. Additional palimpsest Credos in Vall. c 9 and MC 361 have so far resisted efforts to extract useful readings, though it would appear that a single melody is the rule in the Beneventan rite.

The single melodies for Sanctus and Agnus Dei are found in the Christmas mass of Ben35, f. 202, and are attested nowhere else. Included in the Kyriale of Ben35 (f. 195v) is a melody for the Sanctus that resembles the Beneventan Christmas Sanctus (compare *gloria tua* and the final *osanna*). This melody also bears some resemblance to the reciting tones about to be considered.

Reciting tones

Some surviving reciting tones undoubtedly belong to the old Beneventan liturgy. While we cannot reconstruct the ordinary tones for lections, prayers, and the like,[23] there are a few elements, preserved, no doubt, precisely because they are not the usual manner of singing a text, which contribute to our knowledge of the music of the Beneventan liturgy.

A number of lections, monitions, versicles, etc. with notation probably are a part of the Beneventan liturgy, and they should be named here, though they cannot be considered in detail. These include:

1   The gospel "Mane facto" for Good Friday, cued with notation in Ben40, f. 11v (PM xiv, plate xiv).
2   The deacon's and subdeacon's "Flectamus genua" and "Erigamus nos" for the prayers of Good Friday in Ben38, f. 43 and Ben39, f. 25. See PM xiv, 334–5.
3   The reading "In principio creavit" for Holy Saturday, whose incipit has a few neumes in Ben40, f. 15v (PM xiv, plate xviii).
4   The litany "Domine defende nos" for Holy Saturday, found in slightly different forms in Ben39, f. 27, Ben40, ff. 18v–19 (PM xiv, plate xxi); and the Farfa fragment (PM xiv, plate xxvii). These center on a major third (c, d, e in Ben39) that may relate them to the Exultet and prayer tones discussed below.
5   The monition "Si quis catechuminus est procedat," warning catechumens, Jews, pagans and heretics to remove themselves from the rites of Holy Saturday. See PM xiv, 429–32; Hesbert, "L'Antiphonale" (6), pp. 197–201; Chapter 5, p. 186, and n. 56; Appendix 2.
6   The announcement of "Lumen christi" and the response "Deo gratias," which precede the singing of the Exultet.
7   The threefold Easter announcement "Iam christus dominus resurrexit" with its response "Deo gratias," found in the Beneventan mass of Easter of Ben38, f. 53, and in the Gregorian Easter masses of Ben34 and Ben39. That this may not be the announcement's proper place, and that it may have originated elsewhere, are discussed in Huglo, "L'annuncio pasquale."

The Exultet itself gives us the widest estimate of the geography of Beneventan chant, since it

[23] Evidently, there was a specifically Beneventan gospel tone, to judge from the "Ambrosian" Good Friday *ordo* of Vat. lat. 10673 (f. 34): "reliqu[a] (of the Matthew passion beginning "Hiesus stetit") in sono evg secundum ambrosianum."

is preserved in so many decorated Exultet rolls. Its melody is related also to other rites in Holy Week. Closely related is a tone used for prayers when they are part of a sung reading; a special tone, used within a normal lection, to which the lector turns when the text is appropriately solemn. This tone is preserved for a number of lections of Holy Week, and is essentially that used also for the Exultet. Though the Exultet is not in itself a lection – it is not a quotation of a biblical prayer, like those of Jonah, Jeremiah, or the children in the fiery furnace – it is, of course, a prayer, and is perhaps the source of inspiration for the singing of the following biblical prayers to the same solemn tone:

1   The reading of the book of Jonah, found in three manuscripts (Ben33, Vat. 10673, Lucca 606) for Maundy Thursday, and in many others among the lessons for the paschal vigil; this includes Jonah's prayer beginning *Clamavi de tribulatione*.
2   A reading from the book of Daniel, including the canticle of Azarias and that of the Three Children, used in Beneventan manuscripts (Ben33, Ben40, Ben39, and Vat. 10673) for Good Friday, and at Montecassino and elsewhere for Holy Saturday.
3   The prayer of Jeremiah preserved as a lection for matins of Holy Saturday in Rome, Vallicelliana R 32, f. 22v and in Naples, Biblioteca nazionale, MS VI A A 3 (ff. 219v–20; facs. in PM, II, plate 24).[24]

The survival of the Jonah and Daniel lessons is summarized in an appendix to this chapter. This tone is surprisingly widespread, being found also in Roman and central Italian manuscripts: it may represent a very old layer of Italian chant.

Example 4.17 compares this tone in various versions. An essential feature is its recitation on the central pitch of a major third (originally doubtless C–D–E, though in later manuscripts with clefs notated as F–G–A). Only the Exultet tone, however, is limited to these three pitches.[25] The termination on G at the end of example 4.17D is the standard close for verses not only in the prayer of Jeremiah, but also for those in the Jonah and Daniel readings. In these cases the more elaborate ending on F is used for introductory and closing verses.

This tone has been studied in detail by Hesbert, where more extensive transcriptions may be found.[26] The Beneventan Exultet has also received close study, both by Hesbert and Mocquereau.[27]

Another recitation, used for two readings in Holy Week, is recorded in the Beneventan manuscripts probably because of its unusual elaboration (see example 4.18). It is used for the reading from Wisdom at the first adoration of the cross on Good Friday, where notation

[24] The Lamentations of Jeremiah are sometimes found noted in Beneventan manuscripts (see the melody from Rome, Vallicelliana R 32, ff. 21–22v, facs. in PM XIV, plates XXVIII–XXIX, transcribed p. 417, n. 1), though the melody reciting on G gives no clear reason to associate it with the Beneventan liturgy. A fragment in Vatican, Rossi 297, ff. 2–3v (tenth–eleventh century) preserves a tone, reciting on A, which seems more closely related, at least by its cadences, to the Beneventan recitation tone.
[25] A few sources have Exultet tones more elaborate than the usual one listed here. As it is not our purpose to study these later developments, we will only list these manuscript sources, hoping that further study can learn much from these developments. Elaborated Beneventan Exultet melodies are to be found in Troia Exultet Roll 2; Bari Exultet roll 3; Berlin, Staatsbibliothek Preussicher Kulturbesitz, MS Lat. Fol. 920 (facs. in Huglo, "L'ancien chant," p. 290); Oxford, Bodleian Library, MS Canonici liturg. 342 (studied at length in PM XIV, 399–417); a Salerno missal of 1431 whose Exultet is transcribed in part in Latil, "Un Exultet"; see also one of the Exultet melodies in the Farfa fragment (studied in PM XIV, 390–9), which does not, however, seem to be a development of the Beneventan melody.
[26] PM XIV, 271–3, 318–21, and 417 note 1.
[27] PM XIV, 375–90; PM IV, 171–85.

Ex. 4.17 A recitation tone

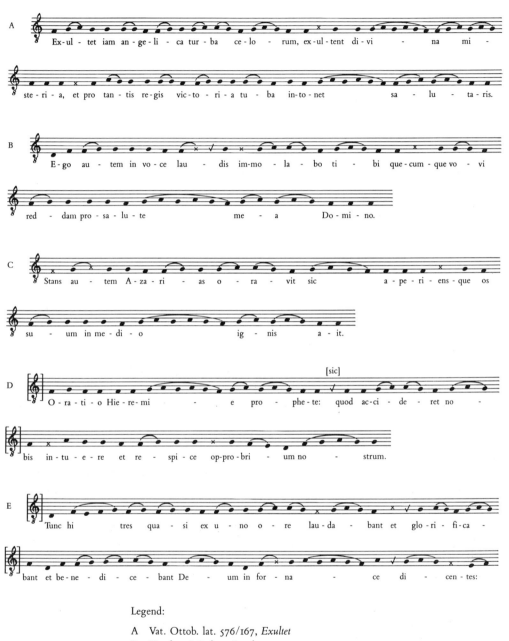

Legend:

A Vat. Ottob. lat. 576/167, *Exultet*
B Vat. lat. 6082/130, Jonah
C Vat. lat. 6082/132v, Daniel, introduction to canticle 1
D Rome, Vall. R 32/22v, Jeremiah
E Ben40/12v. Daniel, introduction to canticle 2

Ex. 4.18   Lection tone

Legend:

A   Ben40/11 (plate 21), Wisdom lesson
B   Ben40/14v, Matthew passion

survives only for the introductory *Dixerunt impii de deo* (example 4.18A), and also at the second adoration, for the passion according to St Matthew, for which four manuscripts provide both the opening words and the cry "Heli heli lama sabathani" with its Latin translation (example 4.18B).[28]

We cannot be certain whether the whole reading is sung in this tone, nor how, if so, it is arranged.[29] But there is a kinship of this tone with the preceding one; though example 4.17 does not show the descent of a third which closes most of the phrases in this second tone, this drop can be seen at the beginning of the lesson from Jonah, which is notated only in the Lectionary of St Cecilia.[30]

These two systems, then, may be aspects of a single procedure reciting in the center of a major third (i.e, on G or D), with a variety of possible ending pitches, and a variety of means of accentuation and cadence. That a larger system existed, including simpler tones for readings and prayers, cannot be doubted – there are rubrics that refer to returning from these tones to the

---

[28] Vat. lat. 10673 notates the passages twice, once in the Good Friday music and again in the ordo which follows. Hesbert reports that "Heli . . ." is notated in the margin of the twelfth-century evangeliary of Zadar (Berlin, Staatsbib. Theol. Lat. Quart. 278, f. 65), but the plate he provides does not show the margin in question: see Hesbert, "L'évangéliare," p. 202 and plate 21. The passage *Hely hely* is, of course, widely notated elsewhere for the reading of the passion.

[29] There is some discrepancy in the placement of music after the opening quilisma (on "impii de deo" and "[ste-]tit ante presidem").

[30] Transcribed in PM XIV, 272.

previous one, and occasional neumes in the readings give us evidence that these too were sung.[31] But we cannot, from the evidence at hand, do more than list these special tones, preserved, no doubt, not because they were typical, but because they were not. The simpler melodies had no need to be written, and as a result they are lost to us.

OFFICE MUSIC

For the Beneventan office the chief surviving music is that of some forty antiphons, to which may be added about nine antiphons for processional and occasional use (these are listed in Appendix 1). There are five surviving great responsories, mostly for exceptional occasions.

Responsories

There is no surviving evidence of a Beneventan night office featuring readings and responsories.[32] Although five pieces called "responsory" survive, only one is attached to the office (℟ *Precursor domini* for vespers of St John the Baptist); the other four are in the special rites for Holy Week. Three function as graduals, serving as a musical response to a liturgical reading (℟ *Ante sex dies* for Palm Sunday, *Amicus meus* and *Tenebre* for Good Friday), and *Lavi pedes*, not appended to a lesson, is found among the *mandatum* music for Maundy Thursday.[33]

Though these responsories serve a variety of functions, they have certain similarities. Each presents the responsorial form familiar from other contexts, including a respond, a verse, and a cue for the partial repetition of the respond.[34] The melodies of the responsories are ornate, and often present the sort of internal repetition we have seen in the more elaborate pieces for the mass.

The verses of the responsories might be expected, like their Gregorian counterparts, to give us a view of an elaborated psalmodic and modal structure. In fact four of the five surviving verses show substantial melodic similarities (example 4.19).[35]

---

[31] See the Appendix to this chapter.

[32] Some unique responsories in Beneventan manuscripts may preserve elements of Beneventan melody, but their placement in Gregorian offices gives little evidence that the same pieces ever served elsewhere, see note 35.

[33] On the liturgical placement of these pieces, see Hesbert, "L'antiphonale" (3), pp. 169–71; and (5), pp. 117–19, 127–33. See also Chapter 3, p. 75. A somewhat elaborated version of *Ante sex dies* with a second verse (*Gloria patri*) survives in the twelfth-century fragments at Zadar.

[34] This partial repetition is noted by Amalarius of Metz in the ninth century as being a Roman trait. See Hanssens, *Amalarii episcopi opera*, III, 55. Perhaps Amalarius would have characterized it as an Italian trait if he had known the Beneventan chant and, if it was the same in the ninth century as in later books, the Ambrosian.

[35] The opening (melody c) of *Magister dicit* and *Homo unanimis* is found in many seventh-mode responsories in later office books of the Beneventan region. In view of the fact that many of the responsories are for feasts of local significance (St Barbatus, St Benedict, St Scolastica, St Mercurius, etc.) this melody perhaps represents a survival of the earlier Beneventan practice represented in example 4.19, but it is part of a more stylized melody. A list of many of these verses follows:

    Accipe ℣ Hec sint: Ben22, f. 121

    Astante beato Barbato ℣ Eorumque: Ben21, f. 86

    Audi Israhel ℣ Observa igitur: Naples XVI A 19, f. 29v

    Convertimini ℣ Scindite: Ben19, f. 215v; Ben21, f. 96; Ben22, f. 173v; Ben37, f. 18v; Naples, XVI A 19, f. 27

    Cumque viri ℣ Ut qui: Ben21, f. 85v

Ex. 4.19   Responsory verses

Legend:

A   Solesmes/3, Resp. *Precursor*
B   Ben40/14v, Resp. *Tenebre*
C   Ben38/32v, Resp. *Ante sex*
D   Ben40/6v, Resp. *Lavi pedes*

Each verse shares a significant amount of melodic material with others. Though one text (*Qui autem*) is very short and one (*Ecce terremotus*) very long, there is some evidence of an intermediate and a final cadence of five syllables (marked B and E). For each of these cadences we have an example of a verse marking time with recitation before launching into the final decorated syllables: *Ecce terremotus* delays on the second word, and V *Magister* pauses on *facio pascha cum dis[cipulis]* before approaching the end.

In the verse *Magister*, the setting of text to a slightly different version of melody B is possibly a scribal flaw (the scribe of Ben38 is not always adept at understanding the needs of the text). A better arrangement might be to use the five syllables *meum prope est* which close the sense of the first phrase. This would necessitate an additional punctum at the end as in the other two versions of this melody.[36]

These verses represent a sort of highly decorated psalmody in two phrases. The small number of surviving examples, though, leaves many questions unanswered. The fifth responsory verse has no surviving melodic mates,[37] but perhaps with a larger sample we could see it as something more than an elaborate four-phrase melody.

Some of these verses also include music from the preceding responsory. The close of *Qui autem* matches the music preceding the beginning of the repetenda, and the long unmatched additional phrase of *Ecce terremotus* includes melodic figures from the preceding R *Tenebre*. Note also the striking repetitive figure with which *Ecce terremotus* begins. This sort of immediate repetition, like that found in some later Gregorian music, is extremely rare in the repertory.[38]

Dixit Jacob V Deus Abraham: Ben21, f. 103v; Ben22, f. 187v; Naples XVI A 19, f. 28v

Dum dormitet V Tollens ergo: Ben21, f. 102; Ben22, f. 182v; Vat. lat. 7818, f. 6v

Dum Ioseph V Videntes: Ben21, f. 105v; Ben19, f. 249v

Fratres Ioseph V Videns Iacob: Ben21, f. 108v

Hic est vir sanctus V Cumque: Ben21, f. 86

Hi pro dei amore V Laverunt stolas: Ben21, f. 285

Iste est sacerdos (Ambrosian) V Hic est doctor: Ben20, f. 229

Josue animadverte V Audi igitur: Ben21, f. 112v

Mons Gargane V Non licet vobis: Ben21, f. 162

Nursia provincia V Ne fide scientia: Ben21, f. 91v; Ben19, f. 89; Ben22, f. 153

Per beatum Clementem V Hoc domine: Ben21, f. 264v

Respice domine V Et nunc domine: Ben21, f. 276v; Ben22, f. 38v

Sancti monialis V Tanta fuit: Ben21, f. 74; Ben19, f. 58; Ben22, f. 143v; Paris, Bibl. nat. lat. 744, f. 171 (Fourteenth century)

Sepultus extat V Omnes igitur: Ben21, f. 302v; Ben37, f. 8v

Sicut precessit V Angelus qui fuit: Ben21, f. 242; Ben20, f. 83v

Simile est regnum V Venientes autem: Ben21, f. 297; Ben37, f. 3v; Capua, Bibl. Arcivescovile VI. F. 32, f. 112v

Summe regis archangele V Audi nos: Ben21, f. 162

Vidi civitatem V Vidi celum: Ben21, f. 253v, 276v

Vir dei Barbatus V Cumque eodem: Ben21, f. 85

Vir dei mundum V Tribus: Ben21, f. 92; Ben19, f. 91

Vir dei Silvester V Benedicto itaque: Ben21, f. 35v

[36] Note the similarity of this phrase B with a phrase found several times in ingressae, compare example 4.9, lines 2 and 3.

[37] Though it is full of typical formulas, see the transcription in PM XIV, 314.

[38] But note the melisma for the antiphon *Zacharias pater* mentioned above, p. 118, note 9, and the elaborated version of *Ante sex dies* from Zadar.

The question of modality naturally arises here. But, as elsewhere, the repertory as it survives defies any clear modal classification. These verses end on a variety of pitches, but their responsories all end on A and have roughly the same range. An important exception, though, is ℞ *Ante sex dies*, which is apparently one of very few pieces in the repertory which end on B.[39] Though its verse matches the end of the responsory, the same music ends the verse *Ecce terremotus*, whose responsory ends on A. The question of Beneventan modality, as we shall see at greater length later, almost invariably presents puzzles of this kind when approached with the preconceptions of the Gregorian octoechos.

Antiphons

Of the antiphons for the office itself, the sources are of three kinds:

1 Two entire offices preserved in a fashion that sets them apart in their sources as Beneventan music – vespers of St John the Baptist in the Solesmes flyleaves, and Good Friday Vespers in Ben38, Ben40, Ben39, and Lucca 606.

2 Substantial series of antiphons for local saints preserved in antiphoners of the twelfth century and later: in these sources the Beneventan music is not consciously distinguished from the Gregorian music alongside which it appears, and thus is in some sense not purely Beneventan. Such series survive for The Holy Twelve Brothers (8 antiphons, Ben21, Ben20, fragments in Melk 1012/1027 flyleaves), Saints Barbatus (6 antiphons in Ben21 and Ben22), Apollinaris (5 antiphons in Ben21 and Ben20 mixed with Ambrosian music), and Saint Nazarius (5 antiphons in Ben21 and Ben20 mixed with Ambrosian).[40]

3 Individual antiphons in Beneventan style among the Gregorian offices of later antiphoners (chiefly Ben19, Ben20, Ben21); such pieces are found in the offices of Saints Silvester, Xistus, John and Paul, Vincent, and Benedict. Additional antiphons, with and without psalmody, are found in the special rites of Holy Week,[41] and others are included among processional and occasional antiphons.[42]

The nature of many of these sources forces us to consider whether their transmission is contaminated by their late date and their proximity to Gregorian neighbors. Indeed, in some cases there are clear borrowings in these manuscripts from other rites, and there are antiphons

---

[39] See note 53 below.

[40] On the Ambrosian music in these offices see Chapter 5.

[41] Six antiphons with psalmody are found outside the normal round of office. They are used for the Lenten scrutiny (*Dum sanctificatus fuero*: see PM XIV, 243–8) and for special rites of Holy Week: the opening antiphons for the vigils of Holy Saturday (*Ad vesperum*) and Pentecost (*Ipse super maria*), *Dominus hiesus postquam cenavit* for the Maundy Thursday *mandatum*, and four bilingual Greek and Latin antiphons of Good Friday. Perhaps we should omit here the music and psalmody for Greek antiphons, which may suggest sources in Byzantine chant which set these pieces apart from the "pure" Beneventan chant. Musically, at least, these bilingual antiphons are in the stylistic mainstream of the Beneventan chant (they are discussed at length in Chapter 5).

[42] Antiphons in Beneventan style without psalmody are largely processional pieces for Rogations and the Purification, but antiphons without psalmody are found also for the ceremonies of Holy Week (*Cum recubuisset* for the Maundy Thursday *mandatum*; *Tristis est anima mea* at the beginning of the Good Friday rites in Lucca 606; and the Greek/Latin *Doxa/Gloria* for Holy Saturday). There are five "antiphons" for the monastic *mandatum* preserved in Vatican Ottob. 145, which doubtless represent the reuse of communions or offertories.

that dress an Ambrosian or a Gregorian melody in Beneventan garb. But for the most part, the melodic style in our earliest and least contaminated sources (category 1 above) is the same as that found in later Gregorian antiphoners. The Beneventan style as we have it does not change substantially when it comes in direct contact with the Gregorian: it is simply included more or less unchanged in the later sources, generally as parts of accepted official "Roman" liturgy.[43]

But it is difficult to draw a firm line of division, and some melodies of other offices (Sts Vincent, John and Paul, Scolastica) might have been included here if only there were slightly more evidence, musical or stylistic, of their close affinity with the Beneventan chant.[44] It is far too easy to see "Beneventan symptoms" in much south Italian office music; indeed, many echoes of earlier styles survive there. But although much remains to be learned from the study of the unique melodies of the Romano-Beneventan repertory, this must be left for another occasion. We have been limited here to music with a clear affinity with the Beneventan rite. Hence, we can feel confident when we discuss the melodic style of the antiphons as a group that we are not including in the Beneventan granary an excessive amount of neo-Gregorian chaff.

Beneventan antiphons range in melodic style from the very simple to the highly ornate. The simplest surviving melodies are those of the first two antiphons of the Holy Twelve Brothers, shown in example 4.20. Each is a very simple melody, clearly divided into melodic phrases matching those of the text; each is restricted to a range of a fifth and has the falling-third cadence to D (as pitched in Ben21) typical of many Beneventan antiphons. The antiphon *Hec est vera fraternitas* is curious in the extent to which it resembles a hymn strophe, with its quasi-metrical text and its four-phrase melody with musical shape A B A B'.[45]

Though the surviving sample may not be representative of the Beneventan office as a whole – we have no evidence, for example, of the ferial office – the musical style of the antiphons is considerably more developed generally than that in example 4.20, both in range and in musical complexity. As we have seen earlier in this chapter, they share, to the extent of their limited size, in the repertory of melodic formulas and structures common to the repertory as a whole.

In some cases, like the Gregorian antiphons, several texts use the same melody. From these we can learn much about the relation of text to music in the Beneventan aesthetic. Example 4.21 shows four antiphons from earlier sources. They share the same range of a seventh, and all have a characteristic falling-third cadence; two (A and B) have the same melody. All include examples (marked p, g, and a) of melodic formulas seen already in mass chants. Another cadence familiar from many antiphons is the series of descending podatus seen in examples 4.22 (B and D) and 4.23; note the similarity of these final cadences even though they are directed towards different notes.

[43] A clear example of this intact survival is the inclusion of the communion *Hos duodecim* (Ben40, f. 122) as a Magnificat antiphon in Ben21.

[44] The office of Sts John and Paul, though its antiphons are in many cases related to some cited in this chapter, is distanced at least from the earliest surviving layer of Beneventan office music by its placement in the Solesmes fragments. For there, the Vespers of St John the Baptist are separately labeled as "Ambrosian," while the remaining music – including the opening of Sts John and Paul – is not. The Solesmes fragments assemble music from two layers, two different sources, and though John and Paul may have music derived originally from the Beneventan rite, it has been filtered through Gregorian transmission, as the "Ambrosian" music in the same source has not.

[45] Another such hymn-like melody is the antiphon *Velum templi*.

In example 4.22 four antiphons share the same basic melody.[46] Each has four musical phrases, but the last, *Nursia provincia* for Saint Benedict, has a text which is not well adapted to the musical structure of the melody. The first phrases generally rise to a high C on an important accented syllable before falling to G. The second phrase expands the range and brings the first half to a close on B; the third phrase reaches the melody's high point with an accented syllable on E, and the antiphon concludes by echoing in the final phrase the simpler melodic shape of the opening. The antiphon *Clamabat beatus Barbatus*, example 4.22B, alters the normal four-phrase pattern characteristic of this melody: the second phrase is substantially lengthened, and the third and fourth are elided to make the single phrase *et Christo domino subicite colla*. Example 4.22C is the tersest statement of this theme, yet it does not represent the standard melody as clearly as does *Expletis missarum sollemniis* (4.22A), for it opens in a very low range with the cry "Heloy heloy."[47]

Example 4.23 shows three antiphons attracted to the same melody by the similarity of their opening words. Here the four-phrase melody is somewhat more elaborate, appending brief melismatic flourishes to the ends of phrases. In each phrase adjustments of text are made near the beginning, and the closes are relatively fixed. With the few examples available we cannot say whether the cadences here are based on syllable-count or on accentuation.

A group of rather complex melodies from two Beneventan offices have texts attracted to the same melody, such as those in example 4.23, by the similar superlatives with which they begin (example 4.24). Opening and closing phrases are clear, but central phrases, where they exist, vary substantially. Antiphon 4.24B is an unusual adaptation of this melody. The opening phrase is stretched significantly to span what is essentially two phrases of text. And although this text is long enough to accommodate a central phrase focused on D for *et catholica suscepta est fides Christi*, this clause is set instead to an overlong recitation anticipating the final phrase. This is a four-member text, attracted by its opening superlative to a three-phrase melody, and adjusted to it with less than consummate skill.

The only antiphon which displays any striking musical peculiarities is the *Zacharias pater eius* which closes the vespers of Saint John the Baptist in the Solesmes fragments. This is a highly ornate piece which concludes with an extraordinarily long melisma – by far the longest in the repertory – which is built on a "sequence-like" series of immediate repetitions. This piece is also found as a communion in Ben40, f. 80, where its style is arguably more suitable. It is perhaps imported to the office as an addendum, a final flourish standing outside the structure and style of a normal vespers.

---

[46] This melody type, which is similar to one used for Gregorian antiphons (see *Convertere*, AMon 216; *Cum his*, AMon 431, etc.) is found regularly among the unique offices of the Romano-Beneventan liturgy, and it may represent there a survival of Beneventan practice. Some examples: *Numquam ad salutationem* and *Reversus est Terentius* for Sts John and Paul (Ben21, ff. 193–193v; Ben20, ff. 203v–204); *Valerius episcopus* for St Vincent (Ben21, f. 66; Ben19, f. 33); *Rogavi te* and *Quid est quod loqueris* for St Scolastica (Ben21, ff. 73v–74v; Ben19, f. 62); *Silvester beatissimus* (Ben21, f. 36v; Ben19, f. 12).

[47] The psalmody for this last antiphon, confirmed from the twelfth-century gradual Ben39, f. 25, recites lower than the others; no doubt the psalmody on C was chosen to match the lower opening of the antiphon. One wonders, however, whether the scribe of Ben21, faced with this antiphon, would not have chosen the D-recitation of its melodic mates. A similar discrepancy is found with the antiphon *Reversus est Terentius* for Sts John and Paul, which uses this same melody type (see the preceding note); the psalmody is on C in Ben20 (f. 204), but on D in Ben21 (f. 193v).

Ex. 4.20 Antiphons for the Twelve Brothers

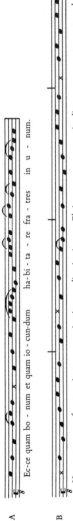

Legend:

A   Ben21/235v (plate 11)
B   Ben21/235v (plate 11)

Ex. 4.21 Antiphons

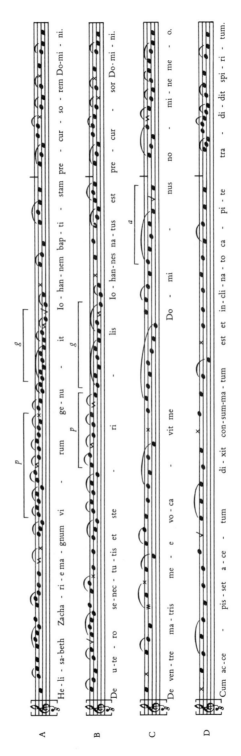

Legend:

A   Solesmes/2, St John Baptist
B   Solesmes/2, St John Baptist
C   Solesmes/2, St John Baptist
D   Ben38/43v (plate 16), Good Friday

Ex. 4.22 Antiphons

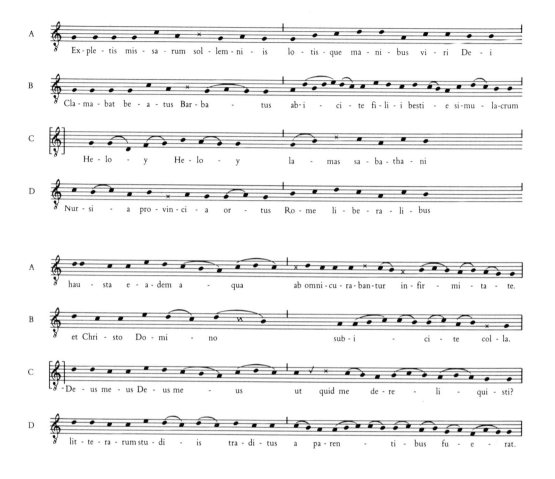

Legend:

A Ben21/87v (plate 8), St Barbatus
B Ben21/87–87v (plates 7–8), St Barbatus
C Ben38/43–43v (plates 15–16), Good Friday
D Ben21/90, St Benedict

Ex. 4.23   Antiphons

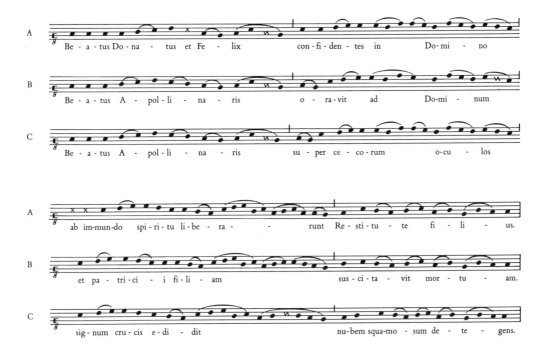

Legend:

A   Ben21/235v (plates 11–12), Twelve Brothers
B   Ben21/211v, St Apollinaris
C   Ben21/211r–v, St Apollinaris

Psalmody

There are many Beneventan antiphons with psalmody, but since much of this music is filtered through manuscripts devoted to Gregorian chant, we must proceed with care in any attempt to reconstruct the older Beneventan usage. Therefore, we begin by considering only examples of psalmody preserved in separate collections of Beneventan chant: the "Ambrosian" office of St John the Baptist in the Solesmes flyleaves and the psalmody of the antiphons of Holy Week in Ben38, Ben40, and elsewhere. We can then see that the practice as it is adapted in later Gregorian office books matches the earlier sources in many ways.

For most of the antiphons in the Good Friday and John the Baptist offices, a fully notated *versus ad repetendum* gives the whole psalm-tone; for the others we have only the ending of the final syllables of the doxology. Example 4.25 shows the psalm-tones or endings with the adjoining portions of the antiphon. To this example have been added the few psalm-tones found in the

Ex. 4.24 Antiphons

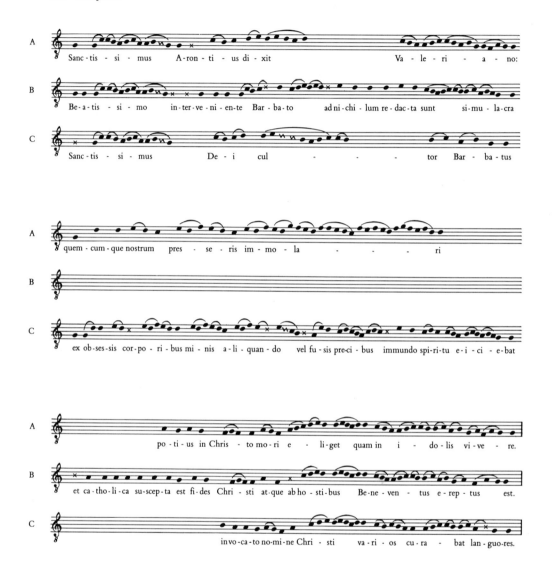

Legend:

A Ben21/236 (plate 12), Twelve Brothers
B Ben21/87v (plate 8), St Barbatus
C Ben21/87v (plate 8), St Barbatus

Ex. 4.25B   Psalmody on D

Legend:

A   Solesmes/2
B   Solesmes/2
C   Solesmes/2
D   Ben38/43v (plate 16)
E   Ben38/43v (plate 16)
F   Solesmes/2
G   Solesmes/2
H   Ben38/43v (plate 16)
I   Ben40/133v (Communion, All Saints)

* This piece may end on E and have psalmody on A. See Chapter 5, note 68.

† Psalmody as here in Ben33, Ben40, Vat. lat. 10645. Ben35 has a later version of c-psalmody (ex. 4.28, line 1, Ben21); Ben39 same as here, but the antiphon ends on G.

Ex. 4.25c Psalmody on C

Legend:

K Ben40/14v-15 (compare plates 15-16)   N Ben40/6v (original psalmody written over)   Q Ben40/11 (plate 21)   T Rome, Vall. c 9/168v
L Ben40/15v (plate 4)   O Ben40/16v (plate 20)   R Ben38/95   U Rome, Vall. c 9/168v
                                                                                          S Ben40/

mass: one for a communion, and two attached to ingressae in Vallicelliana c 9 (that attached to the final antiphon (*Ad honorem*) for All Saints I in Ben40, f. 134, is unclear as to its pitch).

Each fully written out psalm-tone has intonation, mediation, and termination; in two cases the second half-verse also has an intonation. All tones have the same tenor in each half of the verse, and for each reciting-note there is a variety of endings, presumably related in part to the melody of the antiphon to follow. The final cadences apparently fit notes to the final syllables of text without regard to their accentuation; comparing the antiphons which preserve both the verse melody and the *differentia* for the doxology[48] shows that no changes are made when the accentuation differs. At least one of the medial cadences, however, is accentual, judging from the additional note for the second syllable of *solveret* (line 5).

Among these examples from earlier sources there are three reciting pitches which account for all the psalmody. I have transcribed them here as being on E, D, and C, though the question of pitch does not arise in these sources without clefs. These pitches, determined with respect to the whole of the Beneventan repertory, situate their antiphons properly among their melodic brethren.

Benevento 39 includes six of these antiphons, and Benevento 35 has four, with clear indications of pitch. Those ending on G agree with my transcription, but the two ending on A (*Cum accepisset* and *Velum templi*) are presented a fifth lower, using an F-clef, matching these two pieces to the second Gregorian mode. This practice is regularly followed in the later sources, thus avoiding a mode ending on A. But despite the later evidence, the strong melodic relationship among almost all the Beneventan chants suggests that Ben39 creates a Gregorian modal distinction which is not characteristic of the Beneventan chant. The repertory uses the same limited range and formulaic construction throughout, and these antiphons must remain in this relationship to their fellows in the repertory.

For the psalmody reciting on C we have mainly the *differentiae*; some end on A, the rest on G. These G-endings, which show a variety of decorated descents to the final pitch, are more regular in Lucca 606, which records all these *differentiae* as ending on G. For *Ad vesperum*, Lucca has exactly the ending in example 4.25, but the four others all use the same ending as that for *Heloy* in example 4.25.[49]

The modal system here is clearly not organized along Gregorian lines. All the antiphons except for two end on A, and antiphons on A use all three reciting pitches. The two finishing on G use the same psalmody on C that is shared by antiphons ending on A. For most Gregorian antiphons we would have little difficulty in applying modal principles to select a suitable psalmody. But these Beneventan antiphons are not part of such a system, and the arrangement of the surviving evidence suggests a modality that has never known the imposition of the octoechos. Clearly the final note is not sufficient in itself to prescribe a category of psalmody in this protomodal repertory. In some cases, a relationship can be seen between the opening of the antiphon and the choice of psalmody. With one exception, all the antiphons using the highest

---

[48] The final syllables of the doxology are not present in the manuscripts, but the pattern of liquescence in the neumes indicates that they are for the syllables of *seculorum amen*.

[49] Other manuscripts preserving these endings match closely those transcribed here. Benevento 33, which preserves the three bilingual Adoration antiphons and *Ad vesperum*, and Vat. lat. 10673, which preserves one ending, match the endings in Ben40.

psalmody open rather high in the limited Beneventan range. Likewise, antiphons with low beginnings tend to use the low psalmody on C. But these observations are not without exception, and the choice of psalmody on D is a puzzle given the variety of openings.

The Beneventan psalm-tones themselves are very similar to the Gregorian. In each group there is an intonation, a single reciting note, and a variety of endings. It might be, of course, that this is a "Romanized" version of an earlier Beneventan psalmody. After all, our sources for psalmody, even the earliest ones, are books whose principal purpose is to record Gregorian chant. One exception is the palimpsest psalmody in Vallicelliana c 9. However strange it may be to find psalmody attached to pieces that elsewhere function as ingressae, the fragments are from a pure Beneventan book, and the psalmody itself matches that of the other sources. And the many liturgical and musical archaisms carefully preserved in the Beneventan repertory of all these documents suggest that the Beneventan chant resisted remodeling. More likely, I think, is that the Beneventan psalmody behaved much as we see it for a long time before the eleventh century.

When we expand our view of psalmody to include antiphons with Beneventan melodies in later sources, the picture becomes somewhat clearer and more systematic, and it is here that we can detect the influence of the modal codification operated on the Gregorian repertory.

The same three reciting pitches account for all the psalmody in later sources.[50] Examples 4.26, 4.27, and 4.28 present the psalmody which accompanies antiphons with Beneventan melodies in sources of the twelfth century and later, arranged according the psalmodic tenor. A glance will confirm that psalmody on E always accompanies antiphons ending on A (in these manuscripts the antiphons are written so as to end on D with psalmody on A), and psalmody on D is used for antiphons ending on G. Thus, these are arranged like two authentic modes, protus and tetrardus, with psalmody at the fifth. Recitation on C serves both finals as a sort of plagal psalmody.

The psalmody in example 4.26 uses always the same ending, but whereas the endings in Ben21 and Ben22 descend to D, Ben19/Ben20 (which records six of these antiphons) regularly uses an ending which descends only to C (as in line 3). The psalmodic endings do not exactly match any of those given in the earlier sources, and the way they are recorded gives no information about intonations or medial cadences. Unlike the antiphons in the earlier sources, many of which begin high in the range, all the antiphons in example 4.26 begin either a fifth or a sixth below the recitation.

Example 4.27 is equally regular. With few exceptions, the endings of Ben21 descend to A. Ben19/Ben20 generally uses the same endings in those antiphons which it records, but Ben22 usually has a higher version ending on C. Even though Ben21 has a choice of endings for this psalmody – note the higher ending used in lines 1 and 2 – seemingly, they are not always chosen to match the opening of the antiphon. The high ending is used for *Nursia provincia* – the only antiphon in this group that begins high – but also for *Vir dei Silvester* which begins low. In this group all the antiphons end on G; in the earlier psalmody the antiphons with psalmody on D all cadence one step higher (see example 4.25).

These two psalmodic tenors group the antiphons according to their final note. The same

---

[50] Except for the Greek/Latin antiphon *Panta ta etni/Omnes gentes*, which appears to have psalmody on B, see note 53.

Ex. 4.26 Psalmody on E in later manuscripts†

Legend:

A Ben21/87 (plate 7)
B Ben21/90v
C Ben19/86v
D Ben21/93v
E Ben21/192

F Ben21/211
G Ben21/211v
H Ben21/213 (plate 10)
I Ben20/236 (plate 6)
J Ben21/235v (plates 11–12)
K Vat. Reg. lat. 334/72

† Psalmody in other manuscripts containing these antiphons (Montecassino 542, Montecassino Compactiones V, Ben22) matches that given here, except for Benevento 19–20, which in those cases marked with an asterisk (*) gives the psalmody in line 3 above.

Ex. 4.27 Psalmody on D in later manuscripts

Ex. 4.27 (cont.)

Legend:

A Ben21/90
B Ben21/36
C Ben21/87 (plates 7–8)
D Ben21/87v (plate 8)
E Ben21/87v (plate 8)
F Ben21/87v (plate 8)
G Ben21/211
H Ben21/216
I Ben20/236 (plate 6)

J Ben21/90
K Ben21/236 (plate 12)
L Ben21/211v
M Ben21/66v
N Ben38/21
O Vat. Reg. lat. 334/71v
P Vat. Reg. lat. 334/74
Q Vat. Reg. lat. 334/76v

Ex. 4.28   Psalmody on c in later manuscripts

Legend:

A   Ben21/67
B   Ben21/192v
C   Ben21/236 (plate 12)
D   Ben21/236 (plate 12)

E   Ben21/236 (plate 12)
F   Ben21/236 (plate 12)
G   Ben21/235v (plate 11)
H   Ben21/235v (plate 11)
I   Vat. Reg. lat. 334/57

division is echoed, as it were, in plagal modes in the psalmody on c (example 4.28). For there are two c-endings, descending to final notes G or A (in these sources, D), which match the cadences of their antiphons. In the first group, at least, the opening notes of the antiphons are substantially lower than normal, fitting well with a low psalmodic ending.

It is not easy to discover the basis on which psalm-tones are selected. To some degree the melody itself is a determinant; the groups of antiphons sharing the same melody-type always use the same psalmody. Clearly also, the final note of the antiphon determines the choice of psalmody, and within each of the two *maneriae*, ending on adjacent scale-steps (before the transposition of the protus pieces), there is a choice of recitation either a fifth above the final, or on the c a third or a fourth above the final.

Some exceptional pieces have psalmody chosen for clear reasons: two antiphons with a range of a fourth lying low in the compass use the "plagal" c-psalmody; all three pieces that start above c have the high psalmody on E; those that start below G have the "plagal" c-psalmody; and the majority of the pieces using the extremes of the high range use the highest psalmody.

From the antiphons of the office and their psalmody, then, we can dimly see the shape of a two-tiered modal structure, with the conception of plagal and authentic modes, based on facts of range and melodic behavior at critical moments, becoming gradually clearer as the psalmody is recorded, and perhaps to some degree reorganized, in later sources.

PITCH AND MODALITY

The foregoing discussion of developing modality is based, to a large extent, on later sources. In the earlier manuscripts, notated without clear pitch reference, questions of pitch and mode are more difficult, but probably far more significant for the study of the Beneventan chant in a purer form. Students of Mozarabic chant know the frustration of having an important repertory under their eyes, but not quite available. In the case of the Beneventan chant, the careful study of the notation, along with the analysis of the formulaic nature of the music, can yield significant results, even though they must remain to some degree hypothetical.

The notation in the earlier sources is in some ways very accurate and in others unclear. The diastematic quality is good at short range: from note to note the relationship is usually clear, but from left to right across a page there is not always the uniform heightening that the more modern concept of a pitch-line would ensure. Larger intervals are more uncertain than seconds and thirds. An interval larger than a third seems often to imply a standard-sized sign which has the advantage of not wasting valuable diastematic maneuvering room.[51] The experiment of comparing Gregorian pieces transcribed from these manuscripts with other sources yields generally good results, with a few disastrous exceptions: the scribes occasionally change pitch-level at the end of a phrase without any corresponding heightening of the notation at the beginning of the next phrase; and physical limitations between lines of text occasionally require compressions or alterations, which are not readily apparent unless the piece in question is

---

[51] Aware of the problem, the scribe of Ben38 (or perhaps a later user) sometimes heightens with red ink neumes indicating larger intervals.

already known. Hence the occasional unclarity, especially as regards wider intervals and the starting points of new phrases, can sometimes result in a transcription in which melodically identical phrases appear on successively higher or lower pitches: a sort of Baroque sequence-technique which is inconsistent with all we know of the esthetics of formulaic Western chant.[52]

The transcription of these pieces is facilitated by the presence of much repetition; though the sources are few, it is possible to find for many of the small melodic formulae literally hundreds of comparable appearances. Likewise, pieces made in recurrent phrases present multiple copies of the same music. A careful study of formulae, beginning with the cadences, makes it clear that Beneventan chant generally employs a single pitch-level for a recurrent formula or phrase, and it is possible, both to establish the relationship of formulae to one another, and gradually to establish relationships over long stretches of music. But we still cannot sing this music: we do not know where to begin. There still remains the question of interval content, or, to put the question anachronistically, on what pitches do these pieces begin and end? Leaving aside, for the moment, the few pieces transmitted in later sources with clefs, and assuming the use in this music – at least in its eleventh-century garb – of the essentially diatonic gamut shared alike by all the known varieties of Western chant, we can by experimentation discover that there is only one pitch-level that accounts successfully for virtually all the repertory.

In example 4.9 above, the presence of two formulae, each of which appears in two transpositions, helps us to discover the single pitch-level at which this piece functions; a pitch which by the careful study of melodic formulae can be extended to the repertory as a whole.

When the repertory is considered in this fashion, it becomes apparent that all the pieces share the same general range, and that they conclude either on A or a step lower on G. We have seen in the study of the antiphons that this pair of finals accounts for that repertory, and the music for the mass likewise uses these two finals, though a final on A is much more common than that on G.[53]

This might appear to divide the Beneventan repertory into two distinct archaic modes, with major or minor thirds above the finals. We should expect the two modes to behave differently, to have separate repertories of formulae, melodies, melismas, and the like. But, in fact, there is little distinction to be made in the repertory on the basis of final note. In some cases we can clearly document this indifference to the final note. In the Alleluia verses the standard melody

---

[52] An example of scribal laxity in transcribing can be seen in Ben40, f. 133v: the communion *Gaudent in celis* begins with two identical phrases, but it is written in such a way that a slavish modern transcription will produce two phrases a step apart. A noteworthy example of a modern transcription which seeks to resolve these problems in another way is the modulating transcription of *Ante sex dies* in PM XIV, 261–2.

[53] There are a few pieces in the repertory that clearly end on notes other than A and G. One is the Greek/Latin antiphon *Panta ta etni*, which ends on B and is followed, in its Latin version, by what may be a psalmodic cadence, reciting and ending also on B (see PM XIV, plate XV). This piece, though it appears among the mixed Beneventan–Gregorian music for Good Friday, is melodically unusual and, in fact, may not belong to the Beneventan repertory. The responsory *Ante sex dies pasche*, however, is clearly part of the repertory, and its respond ends, like its verse (transcribed in example 4.19), on B, with a formula that is found not only throughout both parts of this piece but in many other pieces as well – although never as a final cadence. Though this ending is unique in the surviving repertory, it does not create a sense that this piece stands modally apart from its brethren. Although when it appears in the early twelfth-century Vatican, Reg. lat. 334 it is transposed so as to end on D, its clear kinship to three other melodies (example 4.19) makes the ending on B actually likely. The antiphon *Ton stauron* (example 4.25c and 5.11) may also belong to the small group of pieces on B: see Chapter 5, note 68. A further late example is the antiphon *Accepta secure* whose ending on E seems to be affected by Gregorian modality.

ends, depending on its length, either on A or G. And the ingressa *Michi autem absit* appears in two manuscripts with different closing Alleluias, ending in Ben40 on G and in the palimpsest Vallicelliana C 9 on A.

The same formulae appear throughout the repertory regardless of the closing note; the *finalis* does not affect the modal quality of a Beneventan melody any more than the modality of a Gregorian psalm tone is affected by its different endings. Although the repertory can be divided into A-pieces and G-pieces, the division does not teach us anything; we cannot see any other distinction between the two groups. We are in the presence of a sort of pre-modal music which operates within a single family of melodic procedures.

The antiphoners of the twelfth century, however, in adapting Beneventan music to Gregorian books, make a Gregorian distinction between the two finals, transposing pieces with the higher final down a fifth, and adapting the antiphons to authentic or plagal psalmody. The result is that the surviving Beneventan antiphons all appear as chants in modes 1, 2, 7, and 8.[54] This distinction is not so clear in the psalmody which survives from earlier sources. If, one day, we were to discover a substantial amount of Beneventan office music unaffected by Gregorian modal procedures, we might well be able to discern patterns of differentiation which are now obscure. But what we can see is a musical system of limited means, whose relationships are based on facts of melodic procedure, of formulaic adaptation, operating within a single universally available repertory of possibilities.

The Beneventan chant has a uniform central range, extending from the two finals G and A upward through the three reciting pitches C, D, and E. Both ends of this central scale may be extended, at the bottom by a note below the final, and at the top by rising to high F.[55]

The three psalmodic reciting pitches are identifiable also in the more elaborate music as focal pitches for recitation. The most common final cadence reiterates C (see example 4.1, and also examples 4.5 and 4.6); for recitation on D see examples 4.9 and 4.19; E is used as a repeated culminating pitch in example 4.2 and 4.4. Between the finals and the reciting pitches, the note B is often treated as an adjunct to the C above (as in the final cadence of example 4.1 and elsewhere), suggesting its use as a sort of flexible tone within the minor third. Though there is no evidence in the repertory of the availability of B-flat as an alternative pitch in this space, the transposition of formulas sometimes results in the alteration of the minor third's central pitch.

In a few of the more elaborate pieces the range is extended, both low and high, by the addition of a tetrachord. A gapped tetrachord is often used below the central range, using the notes

---

[54] With the exceptions given in note 53 above.

[55] This arrangement is a remarkable confirmation of the "échelle archaïque développée" posited by Dom Jean Claire as an early stage of modal development in Western liturgical chant, and it is worth quoting his description of this system, which he developed from a wide observation of archaic melodies in Western responsorial and antiphonal chant:

    – un *terme grave* de la composition (qui n'est encore jamais finale): *fa*

    – deux *finales*: *sol* et *la* (le *sol* pouvant servir de terme grave à une composition finissant en *la*)

    – la *corde mobile*, d'abord uniquement ♮, ensuite ♭

    – les trois cordes-mères, maintenant dominantes: *do, re, mi*

    – un *terme aigu* (qui n'est encore jamais dominante): *fa*

A ce stade, nous ne trouvons, en fait des modes évolues par déscente de la finale, que les modes de *la* et de *sol*, c'est-à-dire les modes qui dans la future organisation de l'octoéchos, recevront les noms de Protus et Tetrardus.

(Claire, "L'évolution modale," p. 240)

D, E, and G (frequently omitting F), in a gesture used at the beginning of pieces or of phrases (examples may be seen in example 4.3). This lower range rarely is developed beyond this intonation procedure, but a notable exception is the ingressa *Dum sacra misteria* (example 4.29), which twice uses the gapped opening (on *archangelus* and *accipere*), but precedes it each time with an unusual passage making significant melodic use of this unusually low range.[56]

In the upper region the range is likewise extended by the use of a tetrachord, which transposes to the upper fourth music found more often at the pitch of the finals. This extended upper range can be seen in example 4.9, where the music of the usual cadence formula A is found three times transposed a fourth higher (column A trs.).

These extensions are a sort of temporary transposition to the upper or lower fourth. The entire extended range presents a picture of three overlapping symmetrical pentachords (example 4.30B) – a satisfyingly tidy systematic exposition, but one that is not really an accurate description of the repertory: for these extensions, except for the gapped intonation below F, are quite rare in the repertory, and in no case are the low and high extensions used in the same piece. The essence of the repertory is its central limited range, shared alike by almost every piece, regardless of its final. The occasional movements outward do so by providing echoes, at a different pitch, of the essential marker of the repertory, which is the minor third between A and C.

We can describe the essentials of this system, but these observations must not be taken for prescriptions followed by the makers and preservers of the Beneventan chant. What survives is a musical style that has not been subjected to the later theoretical revisions and codifications that impose absolute uniformity. As such, the Beneventan repertory is of great value in appreciating the nature of chant dialects prior to the codification of systematic theory. The rearrangement of Gregorian chant according to the modes of the octoechos, while providing a superb theoretical basis for the description and elaboration of the chant, did much to obscure the original nature of Gregorian melody, and provides a systematic barrier which is penetrated only with difficulty. With the Beneventan chant, incomplete as it is, we can see a simpler, and perhaps less systematic, means of melodic unity, and one which can tell us much about the earlier stages of chant development.

APPENDIX: SOURCES OF *LECTIO CUM CANTICO*

A special Beneventan melody for the Exultet and other recitations is used also for prayers included within certain lections for Holy Week. These survive in many manuscripts not only from the Beneventan region but from Rome and central Italy as well.

JONAH: the reading of the Book of Jonah is assigned in three manuscripts (Ben33, Vat. 10673, Lucca 606) to Good Friday; elsewhere it appears among the readings of the Easter vigil. Jonah's prayer *Clamavi de tribulatione* is often set to the Beneventan tone.

---

[56] A similar phrase is found at the beginning of the Palm Sunday communion *Quis te supplantavit*.

Ex. 4.29   Ingressa *Dum sacra misteria*

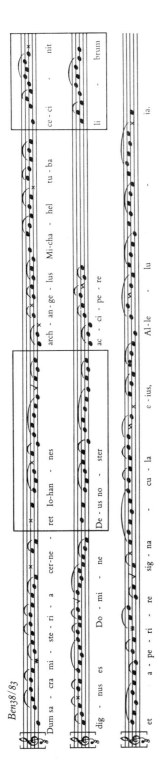

Ex. 4.30   Beneventan ranges

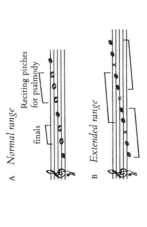

A   *Normal range*

Reciting pitches
for psalmody

finals

B   *Extended range*

DANIEL: Many of the same manuscripts preserve the reading from Daniel including the canticles of Azarias and of the Three Children, sung to special tones. Four Beneventan manuscripts (Ben33, Ben39, Ben40, Vat. 10673) assign this reading to Good Friday, the rest to the Easter vigil.

I Manuscripts which assign both readings to Good Friday and which use the elaborate Beneventan melody for the second canticle from Daniel.

Ben33 Jonah, ff. 63–64v: occasional neumes in text; canticle notated (ff. 63v–64), preceded by *hic mutat sonum*.

    Daniel, ff. 69v–71: a few neumes in the three sections of non-canticle text. The first canticle, notated, lacks the introduction *Stans autem Azarias*. . . the second canticle is abbreviated, including only a few (sample?) verses. Before and after the canticles are the following rubrics in order: *hic mutas sonum*; *hic rede in primo sono*; *deinde dicat excelsa voce*; *deinde leg[atur]*.

Vat. lat. 10673 Jonah, f. 27v: canticle only, notated, incomplete owing to a lacuna. The reading is cued also for Holy Saturday by a rubric on f. 35.

    Daniel, ff. 29v–30v: only the canticles are given, the opening of the lesson itself being indicated by a cue *Nabuchodonosor rex*: usque huic loco: *Stans autem*. . . The first canticle (notated) is followed immediately by the second, which is incomplete owing to a lacuna after f. 30. Detailed instructions for this lesson are given in the *ordo* for Good Friday on f. 33v. They make it clear that the elaborate second canticle – but not the first – is intended to be sung by cantors, rather than by the subdeacon who sings the rest of the lection:

Deinde legatur lectio danihelis prophete cum cantico. In diebus illis nabuchodonosor rex fecit statuam auream, usque: Stans autem azarias oravit sic. Finito, incipiat idem ipse in sono cantici sicut retro scriptum et notatum est. Expleta canticum [sic] redit ad pristinum sonum ubi incipit: et non cessabant qui miserunt; quo dicto, ascendens cantores gradum, pronuntiet unus excelsa voce hunc versum: tunc hi tres; quo expleto, cantent pariter benedictiones: benedictus es, domine. Deinde ipse subdiaconus sumet lectionem in sono pristino: Tunc Nabuchodonosor rex obstipuit.

Lucca 606 Jonah only, ff. 151–151v. Occasional neumes in text, canticle (notated) preceded by *muta sonum* and followed by *hic redi ad sonum priorem*. Facsimile in PM XIV, plates XXXV–XXXVI. Impossible to tell whether this MS originally also had the reading from Daniel.

Ben40 Daniel only, ff. 12v–14 (facsimile in PM XIV, plates XV–XVI). Only the elaborate second canticle, with its introduction *Tunc hi tres*, is notated, preceded by the rubric *Tunc unus cantor in alta voce dicat*. This book is evidently designed for singers and not for readers (explaining the absence of the Jonah lesson), and the second canticle must be intended for soloists.

Ben39 Daniel only, f. 23 (PM XIV, plate XXIII). The lesson is cued (*Lectio In diebus illis Nabuchodonosor*), but no text is present, and the first canticle is omitted. Only the introductory verse to the second (*Tunc hi tres*) is written and notated, without either the elaborate canticle, or the two concluding verses usually set to the same tone as *Tunc hi tres*. No indication of the Jonah lesson (perhaps because special singers were not required).

II Manuscripts preserving only the Daniel lesson, using it for Holy Saturday with the elaborate version of the second canticle.

Macerata, Archivio di stato, Tabulario diplomatico 645: a fragment (in Beneventan script, twelfth century) containing the end of the first canticle, intervening text, and the beginning (*Tunc hi tres*) of the second.

Macerata, Biblioteca comunale, MS 378 (pontifical from Benevento, twelfth century), f. 127v, cues a few neumes of the elaborate second canticle (the first is omitted) to conclude the fifth lection of the Easter vigil.

III Manuscripts (mostly from Montecassino and its orbit) which assign both lessons to Holy Saturday, omitting the second canticle from the Daniel lesson.

Vatican lat. 6082 Jonah, ff. 129–130v: canticle notated, no neumes in surrounding text. The introduction *Lectio ione prophete cum cantico* is not present.
    Daniel, ff. 131v–134: only the first canticle, beginning with *Stans autem Azarias*, is noted, the second omitted.

Vatican, Ottoboni lat. 576 Jonah, ff. 179–181v: the canticle only is notated, but it is incomplete owing to a lacuna after f. 180v. The lesson is labeled *Lectio danielis cum cantico*!
    Daniel, ff. 184–189: *Lectio danielis prophete cum cantico* is not notated, nor is any of the non-canticle text. The first canticle, without its introduction *Stans autem*, is notated, followed by the rubric *Hic mutat sonum sicut prius*. The introduction *Stans autem* is notated in the margin of f. 186 in a later hand.

Montecassino, MS 127 (missal, late eleventh century, generally without notation) Jonah canticle notated, p. 126, without label or rubrics.
    Daniel first canticle, beginning *Stans autem*, notated pp. 102–4.

Montecassino, Compactiones XXII, in a folder marked "Breviario con note scr. Long. Casin.," seven leaves from a missal or lectionary containing Holy Saturday lections Jonah: on a leaf marked "86" in pencil, the beginning of the canticle, notated. Facsimile in *Presenza musicale*, plate 15.
    Daniel: a leaf marked both "90" and "93" in pencil contains the beginning of the first canticle with notation. See Dold, "Umfangreiche"; this fragment is part of Dold's "Compactura VI."

London, British Library, MS Egerton 3511 Jonah: f. 153, the lesson is written out with the canticle notated, no rubrics.
    Daniel, f. 156v: the first canticle and its introduction are noted.

Berlin, Staatsbibliothek, MS Lat. Fol. 920 (Dalmatian missal, twelfth century) Jonah: the full lesson is present, only the canticle (which is labeled *or[atio]*) being notated, ff. 131v–133v.
    Daniel, ff. 134v–138: the first canticle is preceded by the rubric *can.*, and followed by *in sono lec.* On this manuscript see Huglo, "L'ancien chant," pp. 288–90.

IV Manuscripts, not in Beneventan script, which set the second Daniel canticle to the same tone as the first, often with the addition of polyphony.

Rome, Biblioteca Angelica, MS 1383 (lectionary of the eleventh century in ordinary minuscule, Italian notation) Jonah, ff. 75v–77v: the opening text is cued only – a *require* was perhaps present in the now-erased bottom line of f. 75v. The canticle is notated, as is its label *Oratio ione prophete*. The canticle tone continues through one further verse (Jonah 2, 11), but the remaining text (which continues through Chapter 3) is notated only at its end; Hesbert (PM XIV, 273) mistakenly thought the lectionary included only the canticle.

Daniel, ff. 79–86: the two canticles are notated, as are the beginnings and ends of the read portions preceding the first canticle and following the second. Rubrics precede and follow the canticles: *Hic mutat tonum*; *Hic mutat tonum in priore voce*; *Hic mutat vox*; *Hic mutat vox in priore tono.*

"Lectionary of St Cecilia" (formerly belonging to Sir Sidney Cockerell, and once on deposit at the Fitzwilliam Museum, Cambridge; currently in a private collection) Jonah: the opening of the lesson (*Lectio ione prophete cum cantico*) and several further verses are notated; occasional neumes are supplied in the text up to the canticle, which is fully notated. The remaining text, introduced by *Incipit legere in priore sono*, has occasional neumes.

Daniel: the canticles are notated, as are the beginning of the lesson and occasional cadences throughout. After the opening *Lectio danihelis prophete cum cantico*, the opening *In diebus illis* has a second voice, in a different ink, indicating a descent to the lower fifth: an indication of polyphonic performance? Though the preface *Tunc hi tres* is set to the somewhat elaborated version of the canticle tone used for this introduction at Benevento, the second canticle itself is not the elaborate Beneventan melody. The canticles are prefaced and followed by the rubrics: *Hic mutat sonus in cantu*; *Hic legatur in sono priori*; *Hic incipiat cantare cum organis*; *Tunc legatur in primo sono.*

Vatican lat. 4770 Jonah, ff. 106–106v: the full lesson including the canticle is present but without notation; the canticle, however, is followed by *incipit legere in sono*.

Daniel, ff. 107v–109v: though there are occasional neumes throughout the lection, the canticles are not fully notated. Before and after the canticles are the following rubrics: *Hic mutat sonus in cantico*; *Tunc incipit legere in primo sono*; *Tunc incipit canere cum organis clericis*; *Tunc incipit legere in priore sono*. The presence of cantors singing *cum organis* suggests a more elaborate performance for the second canticle, but the notation does not suggest the elaborate Beneventan melody.

Vatican, Barb. lat. 560 (missal, eleventh century, in ordinary minuscule) Jonah, ff. 64v–65v: the lection is not noted, but rubrics indicate that the reading is arranged so as to have two portions sung as canticles, the second beginning with the prayer of Jonah in Chapter 4. The rubrics are: INCIPIT CANTARE; HIC MUTAT SENSUS QUASI LECTIO; INCIPIT CANTARE; there is no indication of a return to the normal lection tone to close the reading.

Daniel, ff. 66–68v: no notation, but rubrics surround the two canticles: HIC MUTAT SONUM IN CANTICO; ET INCIPIT LEGERE IN SONO PRIORE; HIC CANERE INCIPIT CLERUS CUM ORGANIS; (within second canticle: ET RESPONDENT OMNES IN CHORO AMEN); POST ISTA BEN. INCIPIT LEGERE IN PRIORE SONO.

5

BENEVENTO AND THE MUSIC OF
OTHER LITURGIES

INTRODUCTION

A central question, perhaps the most difficult one, in the study of the Beneventan liturgy is this: where did it come from? Seeking the answer, however, only raises further questions. To what extent is the rite of Benevento independent of other Christian liturgies? How much of what survives there is part of a very old body of material shared alike by all or some of the Western liturgies? Do its texts and melodies reflect borrowings from elsewhere? Only by attempting answers to such questions can we arrive at an assessment of the core of the Beneventan rite itself, and an evaluation of its place in the spectrum of Western musical tradition.

However, in making comparisons we must be aware of an almost inevitable difference of approach: with Gregorian chant we seek distinctions within the repertory, but for other, "local" liturgies we often look for kinship with Gregorian chant. How can we not give a privileged place to the Gregorian chant, which for so many centuries has been viewed as the universal musical language of the West? Though this latter question is viewed differently nowadays, we must still contend with the fact that, at Benevento, as almost everywhere in Europe, Gregorian chant appears, in its fully developed form, with the earliest music-writing in the region.

Despite the significant information we gain from melodic comparison, we must again be cautious. When is one melody like another? The answer could not be simpler: when they sound alike to me. But another question is not so easy to answer: can you show me how these two melodies are alike? For here, although we recognize the need for some objective means of describing and measuring similarity, we generally have to answer in subjective terms.

When melodies are intended to be identical, we look for differences, and we learn much: we can sometimes detect differences between a composer's score and a printed edition. Even with such melodies as the medieval body of Gregorian chant – to the extent that it seeks to be uniform – we can apply the principles of textual criticism and learn much about sources and transmission.

When we compare melodies that are not "the same," and are not meant to be, our needs change. For here we look for similarities, not differences. And what seems similar to me may not seem so to my neighbor. When we deal with distinct bodies of chant, written a thousand years ago in places far apart, we especially have trouble equipping ourselves for the job. Such melodies in their written form, of course, may represent a tradition older still by hundreds of years, and the very fact of their writing tells something about a change in that tradition.

In the past century of vigorous study of Gregorian chant, many researchers have tackled the problem of describing melodic style, and of analyzing similarities in groups of melodies,[1] and the study of oral transmission in epic, folk music, and the music of other cultures has added much to our understanding of the melodic process in chant repertories and of the nature of ecclesiastical chant.[2] Indeed, there have been notable efforts at comparing the music of one liturgy with another.[3]

But the problems are evident: we find it easy to disagree, and terms of comparison may vary. When two chants have phrases that come to rest on the same notes, we posit an underlying melodic or modal identity. And when they do not, we remember that cadences, after all, are among the most characteristic moments of any body of chant, and cannot be expected to be the same from one place or time to another. Perhaps we notice a similarity of detail at certain points, and speak of the "surface" of the melody, of ornamentation and embellishment – terms which imply that we can distinguish some melodic kernel, some nodal points, some bones onto which a medieval Ezekiel has prophesied a melodic flesh; a surface whose physiognomy tells of local musical taste, while the skeleton beneath reveals heredity and ancestry.

Clearly, our methods of comparison and description remain woefully inadequate. In the preceding chapter we compared melodies within a single tradition – melodies that are "the same," though adapted to different texts; repeated melodic forms within a single text; families of melodies which seem adaptable to a variety of texts; and recurring identical melodic moments – and we have used the vocabulary and many of the terms which have been developed over the years to describe such music. But the terminology is not systematic, and we still lack the tools for comparison and description that we might wish in order to be "scientific." We have much to learn, and far to go.

Though many areas of liturgical comparison can tell us much about shape and structure, the chants themselves are inseparable from their texts. We must remember, of course, that we do not have the entire Beneventan repertory at our disposal, so that we can make only partial comparisons, yet they have much to teach us.

Textual similarities can be deceiving. When a widely known biblical text, for example, at Benevento matches one in the Ambrosian liturgy, but not that of the Roman liturgies, we can suggest that the Beneventan-Roman relation is tenuous at best, and we should perhaps remove it from the list of close connections. The following example illustrates this:[4]

[1] Of many that might be mentioned, some classics are: Wagner, *Einführung*, III; Frere, *Antiphonale sarisburiense*, I, 3–61 on responsories; Suñol, *Introduction*; Gevaert, *La melopée antique* on antiphons; Ferretti, *Estetica*.
[2] Recent studies dealing with the relation of music writing to oral tradition include Hucke, "Towards a new historical view," and Treitler, "Homer and Gregory."
[3] Wellesz, *Eastern Elements*; Levy, "The Italian neophytes' chants," and "The Byzantine Sanctus;" and Bailey, "Ambrosian chant."
[4] Details of the textual situation may be found for all cases in Appendix 2.

Beneventan	Ambrosian	Gregorian and Old Roman
Qui manducaverit	Qui manducaverit	Qui MANDUCAT
corpus meum	corpus meum	CARNEM (O-R: carne) MEAM
et biberit	et biberit	et BIBIT
sanguinem meam	sanguinem MEUM	sanguinem meam
ipse in me manet	ipse in me manet	in me manet
et ego in eum	et ego in eum	et ego in EO (O-R: eum)
alleluia alleluia	DICIT DOMINUS	DICIT DOMINUS
alleluia		

On the other hand, certain texts which differ between liturgies are nevertheless clearly related. Ecclesiastical compositions, or those involving substantial rearrangement of biblical texts, can show a common origin even when the texts themselves differ, for it seems impossible that the same combination should be reached independently in two places. Examples of such pieces are the responsory *Tenebre facte sunt* and the communion *Dicite pastores quem vidistis*.[5]

When we remove the pieces whose relationship is in doubt, and those which cannot be compared because the Beneventan text is incomplete, the list of related texts, and of similar melodies, is what appears in table 5.1. This table compares only texts of Beneventan chants preserved as a separate repertory in the oldest sources. Thus, it does not include the many antiphons in later office books. A glance at the table is enough to establish Benevento's independence from Rome. Musical similarities between the two are few, and we look in vain for any series of shared texts for similar liturgical functions. There are only a very few cases where Gregorian and Old Roman are not related to Beneventan in the same way. The Gregorian counterpart to a Beneventan chant generally has a partner in the Old Roman liturgy, which uses the same text and serves the same function in the liturgy and the calendar.

---

[5] The communion *Dicite pastores* is a particularly interesting example, even if it gives us no clear insight into the relation of the Beneventan with the Roman liturgies. Hesbert has devoted a long study to this text ("L'antiphonale" (1), pp. 41–66), which shares much of its non-biblical text with a Gregorian antiphon and responsory. He finds no witnesses outside Benevento for the Beneventan readings "Dicite pastores quem vidistis, annunciate nobis quis in terra apparuit" (the Roman text is invariably "Quem vidistis pastores, dicite, annunciate nobis in terris quis apparuit"), but for the end of the Beneventan offertory ("Natum vidimus in choro angelorum salvatorem nostrum venite adoremus") he is able to establish that the Gregorian antiphon had, as its original version, the reading "Natum vidimus in choro angelorum salvatorem dominum," despite the large number of manuscripts which give the now official text of the Vatican edition. Likewise the reading *venite adoremus*, which replaces the more usual double Alleluia in a very few Gregorian manuscripts of French and insular origin, must nevertheless represent an early stage of the text: how else could it appear in two places so removed from each other?

Hesbert does not attach much importance, however, to the witness of the Old Roman antiphoners with their "leçons évidemment postérieures – comme l'organisation d'ensemble à laquelle elles appartiennent" ("L'antiphonale" (1), p. 65, n. 38). These give the readings of the majority of Gregorian manuscripts: "et choros angelorum collaundantes dominum," without either *venite adoremus* or the double Alleluia. And one of them, Vatican B 79, adds the unique ending *mundi salvatorem* to the antiphon. Given what we now know about the importance of the Old Roman chant, we cannot but give more weight to these manuscripts than Hesbert was inclined to do, but the fact that they include the widely attested Gregorian reading, while including a textual variant of their own, added to the fact that their melodies are similar to those of Gregorian chant for these pieces, suggests that the history of this text is even more complex than Hesbert thought. Its common origin, however, is beyond doubt, and the unique Beneventan version, which has echoes in some Gregorian (but not Old Roman) sources, must stem from a time of common origin, before the standardization of liturgies, and in particular before the differentiation of Gregorian and Old Roman chant.

Table 5.1 *Beneventan mass chants with related texts in other repertories*

For expanded form of abbreviations used, see notes at end of table.

Feast / Function / Text	Type of text	Gregorian		Old Roman		Ambrosian	
Christmas							
Off. Hodie xpistus	N	Greg	a	Rom	a		
Comm. Dicite pastores	N	Greg	a,R	Rom	a,R		
Stephen							
All. Posuisti	B					Mil	A
Palm Sunday							
Ing. Testificata	N					Mil	Pl
Grad. Dum congregarentur	N					MIL?	R
Off. Popule meus	N	GREG	a	ROM	a		
Maundy Thursday							
Ing. Postquam surrexit	C	Greg	a,a			MIL	T
Grad. Vadit propitiator	N	Greg	R	Rom	R	MIL?	R
ant. Cum recubuisset	C	Greg	a				
ant. Dominus hiesus	C	GREG	C,a	ROM	C,a		
Resp. Lavi pedes	N			Rom	R		
Good Friday							
ant. Adoramus crucem	N					MIL	a
ant. Crucem tuam	N	Greg	a	Rom	a	MIL	a
ant. Laudamus te	N					Mil	a
Resp. Amicus meus	C	Greg	R				
ant. Omnes gentes	B	Greg	a	Rom	a	Mil	a
Cant. Tunc hi/Benedictus	B					MIL	
Resp. Tenebre facte sunt	C	Greg	R	Rom	R	MIL?	R
ant. Cum accepisset	B	Greg	a			MIL	a
ant. Inclinato capite	C					MIL	a
ant. Velum templi	C					Mil	a
Holy Saturday							
ant. Ad vesperum	B					Mil	a
Tract Domine audivi	B	GREG	T	ROM	T		
Tract Cantabo	B	Greg	T	[Rom]	T		
Tract Attende	B	Greg	T	[Rom]	T		
Tract Sicut cervus	B	Greg	T				
ant. Gloria in excelsis	B					MIL	a
All. Resurrexit tamquam	B					Mil	A
Off. Omnes qui in xpisto	B	Greg	C	Rom	C		
Comm. Ymnum canite	N					MIL	T
Easter							
All. Pascha nostrum	B	Greg	A	Rom	A	Mil	A
Off. Angelus domini	C	Greg	O	Rom	O	Mil	O
Comm. Qui manducaverit	B					Mil	T
Michael							
Ingr. Dum sacra misteria	C	Greg	a				
Comm. Celestis militie	N					MIL	Pl
Comm. Multos infirmos	N					MIL	Pl
Ascension							
Ingr. Ecce sedet	C					MIL?	O
Off. Ascendit deus	B	Greg	O+	Rom	O+	Mil	A
Comm. Pacem meam	C					Mil	I

Table 5.1 (*cont.*)

Feast / Function / Text	Type of text	Gregorian		Old Roman		Ambrosian	
Pentecost							
ant. Ipse super maria						Mil	a
Ingr. Factus est repente	C	GREG	C	ROM	C	MIL	I
John the Baptist							
Ingr. Lumen quod animus	B					MIL	Pl
Off.(Comm.) Inter natos	C					MIL	Pl
Peter and Paul							
Off. Petrus apostolus	N	Greg	a	Rom	a		
Comm. Ut cognosceret	C					MIL	Pl
Lawrence							
Ingr. Gratias ago	N	GREG	a,R	ROM	R	MIL	a
Off. Adhesit	C	GREG	a,a	ROM	a,a	MIL	a,Pl
Assumption							
Off. Que est ista	B	Greg	a				
Simon and Jude							
Ing. Michi autem nimis	B	Greg	I	Rom	I		
All Saints I							
Ingr. Gaudeamus	N	Greg	I	Rom	I	Mil	I
Off. O quam pretiosum	N	Greg	a	Rom	a		
Comm. Gaudent in celis	N	Greg	a				
Comm. Omnes sancti	N	Greg	a				
Comm. Ad honorem	N			Rom	a	MIL	Pl
All Saints II							
Ingr. Isti sunt sancti	N	Greg	a,R	Rom	a	MIL	T
Grad. Anima nostra	B	Greg	G	Rom	G	MIL?	Pm
Martin							
Ingr. Stolam iocunditatis	B	Greg	R	Rom	R		
Grad. Ecce magnum	N			Rom	R	MIL?	R
Off. Martinus abrahe	N	Greg	a,R+	Rom	R,a	Mil	a
Comm. Dixerunt discipuli	N	Greg	a,R+	Rom	a,R	Mil	Pl
Comm. O quantus luctus	N	Greg	a	Rom	a	Mil	Pl
Andrew							
Gr. Constitues eos	B	Greg	G	Rom	G	MIL?	Pm
Off. Salve crux	N	Greg	a			MIL	a
Comm. Quid ad nos	N					MIL	a

Type of text:
  B Biblical text
  C Cento, rearrangement of biblical text
  N Non-biblical text
Functions:
  I(ntroit) or Ingressa
  O(ffertory)
  G(radual)
  A(lleluia)
  T(ract)
  C(ommunion)
  a(ntiphon)
  R(esponsory)
  Pm Psalmellus
  Pl Psallenda
  + several functions
Capital letters (GREG, ROM, MIL) indicate a musical relationship with the Beneventan melody.

Many more texts are shared with the Ambrosian liturgy, and the Ambrosian parallel is much closer than the Roman. Where three liturgies use the same or similar texts, the Beneventan melody is often related to the Ambrosian, but not to the Gregorian. A few pieces shared among three liturgies may belong to a deep layer of pan-Italian liturgical usage; others result from the Ambrosian adoption of Gregorian melodies.

And there are relations with the Byzantine liturgy (not shown in the table) which will be considered presently.

Very few texts indeed serve the same liturgical function on the same feast-day in several rites. In these four Latin liturgies there are only the following (and there is more to be said about the use of some of these):

Antiphon	Crucem tuam	(Good Friday)
Responsory	Tenebrae	(Good Friday)
Alleluia	Pascha nostrum	(Easter)
Offertory	Angelus domini	(Easter)
Ingressa	Gaudeamus	(All Saints)
Gradual	Constitues eos	(Andrew)

This is really a very short list. There is no clear pattern of functional relationships; no series of entrance chants, Alleluia verses, or the like. The absence of such a wide-ranging relationship is a measure of distance among these liturgies. The shared material, except where it is a late direct borrowing, must come from a time before its standardization, before texts were invariably fixed as to feast and liturgical function, and before the separation of the Gregorian and the Old Roman versions of Roman chant.

GREGORIAN AND OLD ROMAN CHANT

The relationship of the Beneventan chant to the rites of Rome is not a particularly close one, despite the sharing of similar or identical texts. We do not have to look far to find differences in the two rites: the very fact of the use of different texts, the frequent Beneventan use of non-scriptural texts, the virtual absence of psalmody in the Beneventan mass, the paucity of Beneventan Alleluia melodies, the absence of offertory verses.

Almost all the texts which the Beneventan liturgy shares with the Gregorian repertoire are also found in the Old Roman, and in these cases, the relationship of Gregorian to Old Roman is very close, almost invariably closer than that of either "Roman" repertory to the Beneventan. The relation of Gregorian to Old Roman chant is a question of intense interest to scholars, and one that cannot be resolved here,[6] but the examples to follow show that the Roman melodies generally are much closer to each other than either is to the Beneventan, and that the intersections of the Beneventan repertory with the Roman dialects are almost inevitably through the medium of the Gregorian repertory. Old Roman chant, as it survives now in purely Roman books of the twelfth century and later, probably was not known in southern Italy.

The Gregorian chant, of course, was known at Benevento from an early date, and its trans-

---

[6] For an introduction to the subject with bibliography, see Hucke, "Gregorian and Old Roman."

mission is the principal purpose of most of the surviving sources of Beneventan chant. Although there is some evidence of later interactions of the two liturgies – in both directions – the two repertories are well insulated despite their proximity. The Gregorian chant may be a Frankish recension of Roman chant, and clearly Rome is nearer to Benevento than is Aachen, or Metz. But the Carolingian urge to uniformity in the later eighth century sought to impose the chant we now call Gregorian, and it was that music which soon arrived at Benevento.

At that time, however, the Beneventan chant was already in place. The fact that it survives alongside its Gregorian rival for several centuries attests to the tenacity with which it is preserved, and the clear separation that is intended between the local liturgy and the imported. Those elements, therefore, which are shared between the Beneventan and the Roman liturgies are either quite recent borrowings, or they are descended from an earlier common stock, having grown apart at a time earlier than the eighth-century confrontation. Indeed, such common elements can be supposed to date from a time before the question arises of the relation of Gregorian and Old Roman; a time before the revisions and standardizations of Western liturgies which seem to have been a feature of later medieval times.

From the small number of Beneventan-Roman relations in table 5.1 we can isolate only a few areas of significant textual sharing. These are the masses for St Martin and All Saints, the three final days of Holy Week, and the Beneventan offertory of St Lawrence.

St Martin

The Beneventan mass for St Martin has texts, most of them non-biblical, which are widely used in the Roman liturgies – and also in the Ambrosian – as antiphons or responsories for the office. The Beneventan melodies are not related to any of the others.

Though St Martin was venerated from the very earliest days of Montecassino,[7] and probably elsewhere in the region,[8] the Roman liturgy gave place to St Martin relatively late, judging from the absence of a firm textual tradition for the chant pieces, and from the fact that the formulary for St Martin in the earliest sources consists largely of pieces drawn from a pool of "common" chants.[9] It is only in the eleventh century that a variety of proper masses for St Martin begins to appear in Gregorian manuscripts, with texts often drawn from hagiographical materials.[10] Some of these texts are those used in the Beneventan mass of St Martin. The text *Martinus abrahe sinu* is the communion of the Gregorian mass *O beatum virum*, appearing in the early eleventh century in manuscripts from Italy, southern France, and Spain.[11] And the text *Dixerunt discipuli* is used as the gradual of the Gregorian mass *Beatus Martinus* found in a number of Italian sources.[12] As antiphons (or psallenda) and responsories these texts are used

---

[7] An oratory of St Martin was established by St Benedict himself (*Gregorii magni dialogi*, p. 96), expanded by Petronax (Chron. mon. cas., I, 4), spared in the extensive building campaigns of Desiderius (Chron. mon. cas., III, 34), and finally destroyed by earthquake in 1349. See Pantoni, "L'identificazione"; and Morin, "Pour la topographie," pp. 277–303.

[8] The antiquity of his cult (though not, of course, of the Beneventan mass propers) is suggested by the hagiographical mass lection provided in Ben33, which may be the remnant of an older practice: see Gamber, "Väterlesungen."

[9] See *Sextuplex*, no. 164, and pp. CIX–CX.

[10] See Oury, "Formulaires anciennes."

[11] It is found, for example, in Rome, Vall. C 32; Lucca 606; Oxford, Bodleian, misc. lit. 366; Paris, BN, lat. 903.

[12] Including Ben34; Vat. lat. 6082; Vercelli 56; Torino F. IV. 18; and Ivrea 60; the gradual is found in Modena O. I. 7.

also in the Gregorian, Old Roman, and Ambrosian offices. The melodies in all three liturgies are so similar, and so different from the Beneventan pieces using the same texts, that we must posit the Beneventan adoption of these texts, not from the other liturgies, but from readily available hagiographical materials.

This Beneventan mass provides one of only two texts shared with the Old Roman, but not the Gregorian, chant (their melodies are not related). The almost complete absence of connections elsewhere, except through the intermediary of Gregorian chant, suggests that a literary source, rather than a musical borrowing, accounts for the presence of the text *Ecce magnum* in both rites.

The relatively late adoption of the feast of St Martin in the Roman liturgy, and the lack of fixity of its mass texts, supports the notion that the Beneventan mass antedates the liturgical formularies for St Martin adopted elsewhere.

All Saints

We have seen in Chapter 3 that the two Beneventan masses for All Saints are probably relatively late compilations.[13] They employ a series of ecclesiastical texts known and used elsewhere for the office. (The Beneventan liturgy is much freer with the use of non-biblical texts in the mass than is the Roman rite.) The presence of two masses at this place may indicate a desire to salvage, from other places in the Beneventan liturgy, more suitable pieces than can be conveniently grouped into a single mass – but fewer than will make two masses, judging from the repetition of three pieces in each. To these are added new adaptations of widely used texts. In any case, the lack of fixity, at Benevento and in the other liturgies, makes it clear that we should not seek here to discover the deep evidence of an early Italian common ground.

Maundy Thursday

The Beneventan ingressa and gradual have strong melodic links to Milan,[14] though versions of their texts appear also at Rome. The Beneventan pieces for the *mandatum* ceremony, however, have texts used at Rome, but not at Milan.[15] The *mandatum* is one of those flexible places in the liturgy resulting from relatively late adoption, where sometimes each rite, and indeed each church, preserves local or favorite materials for its own use.

One of the Beneventan *mandatum* pieces has a Roman melodic counterpart, and it is one of the few instances of Beneventan music used also in the Roman mass. The Beneventan antiphon *Dominus hiesus postquam cenavit* is similar to the Maundy Thursday communion of the Gregorian and Old Roman rites (see example 5.1).

In one sense the Gregorian melody is the most organized: phrases 2, 3, and 4 have the same

[13] See Chapter 3, pp. 85–6.
[14] The ingressa is compared in example 5.9 below.
[15] This is the other case where Beneventan and Old Roman share a text not known in the Gregorian liturgy: the responsory *Lavi pedes*. This text, which might seem to be of Byzantine provenance, is found in the Old Roman matins of Maundy Thursday.

Ex. 5.1 Versions of *Dominius Iesus*

Legend:

BEN: Ben40/6v
GREG: Ben34/115v
ROM: Vat. lat. 5319/79

music, and the word *dominus* has the same music each time.[16] This is not true of the Old Roman melody, though it is melodically very close to the Gregorian. The Beneventan melody, however, has its own logic and structure, quite different from that of the Gregorian communion. Note that phrases 5 and 7 are alike. Although the Beneventan piece does not show the strict repetition often encountered in the repertory, it is composed of three parallel periods with the same medial pauses (*cenavit, vobis, vobis*) and final cadences (*ait illis, et magister, faciatis*), and it shares material with other pieces in the repertory (compare example 4.13).

Which of these melodies is the "original"? We cannot judge on the basis of a musical development that could proceed in only one direction, nor can we adduce firm liturgical evidence. But the fact that the Roman piece is found in the mass, while the Beneventan antiphon is used for a ceremony with music less fixed, is not a strong argument, for the Roman mass for Maundy Thursday is not part of the original layer of Roman chant. Its introit and offertory are borrowed from elsewhere in Lent; its non-psalmic gradual is likewise not primitive.[17] The communion, serving admirably as a transition from the mass (*postquam cenavit*) to the *mandatum* (*lavit pedes eorum*), is nevertheless part of an amalgam of pieces brought together for this purpose. The antiphon was available, possibly in a collection of *mandatum* pieces (where it is still to be found in some Gregorian manuscripts (see Appendix 2)), and appropriated to this function. Was it borrowed from Benevento? Not in the Beneventan antiphon's present form, surely, nor was the Beneventan music adapted from the Gregorian as it stands. But the relation between the two points to a fund of common material.

Good Friday[18]

The two non-biblical responsories used as graduals in the Good Friday rite of Benevento have texts found in the Gregorian office. One of them, *Tenebre*, is known throughout the West.[19] The other, *Amicus meus*, has a non-biblical text with a strong "Byzantine flavor"; it is not used in the Old Roman rite. There are, however, no noticeable similarities in the various musical versions of these pieces.

The Beneventan offertory *Popule meus* for Palm Sunday[20] has a musical parallel in the Roman liturgy of Good Friday. The modern Roman combination of *Popule meus* with the *Trisagion* and the reproaches is an amalgam of originally separate items, of which only *Popule meus* has a

---

[16] This phenomenon of textual affinity is to be seen in many genres of chant, and may be the result of subsequent changes to a melody based on how a scribe "hears" the melody he is writing. For some examples from the Beneventan office, see examples 4.23 and 4.24.

[17] See *Sextuplex*, p. LIX. See also Chapter 3, pp. 84–5.

[18] For the music of Good Friday, a recent series of articles by Johann Drumbl ("Gli improperi," "Die Improperien," and "Zweisprachige Antiphonen") has done much to unravel the complex situation of the liturgy at Benevento, first explored in detail by Hesbert (PM XIV, 290–337, and "L'antiphonale" (5)). Many of these matters will be considered in connection with the Ambrosian and Byzantine liturgies below.

[19] See Hesbert, "Le répons Tenebrae."

[20] On the relationship of the Good Friday antiphon *Omnes gentes* at Benevento to Gregorian and Old Roman melodies, see example 5.15 below.

place also in the Beneventan liturgy.[21] This offertory is compared with its melodic mates in example 5.2.

The Gregorian and Old Roman melodies, though clearly related to the Beneventan, are so similar as to set them apart as a group. The Beneventan music is essentially the same melody twice, with adjustments for varying lengths and accents in the text. The same characteristic cadence is used at the middle and end of each phrase.

Both versions of the Roman melody also show roughly this parallel structure, but they diverge from it in two ways. Firstly, the ending (*salvatori tuo*) is not parallel with the phrase *responde michi* as it is in the Beneventan version, nor do the medial cadences match each other or the final cadences. And secondly, the Roman melody in its second period repeats music (marked B) used only once in the earlier period. This repetition suggests an adaptation of the Roman melody from the Beneventan, based on a misreading of the music. Melody B in the first half marks the beginning of the second sub-phrase (*aut in quo contristavi te*), and its repetition serves the same purpose in the second half of the Beneventan music. But the Roman adaptor seems to have mistaken the structure of the second half. Coming too early to the melody marked A, he uses it for *eduxi vos*, and continues with the music that followed A in his first half; arriving too soon at the end of the musical phrase, he was obliged to repeat B for *parasti crucem* before concluding. He was doubtless confused by the fact that the Beneventan melodies for both A and B begin with the thirds G–B–D, so that his continuation from the misplaced A in the second half for a moment seemed correct.

We cannot be certain, of course, that a hypothetical Roman adaptor had before him the Beneventan melody preserved for us only in Ben38. But it is difficult to imagine a process of adaptation in the other direction, Rome to Benevento, for we can posit no process that would result in the Beneventan version, and indeed the Beneventan melody has a clearer and simpler parallel structure, without the repetition in the second half, which is justified by no syntactical structure in the text.

Holy Saturday

Holy Saturday has four tracts in the Beneventan rite. Three are clearly independent, textually and melodically, from their Gregorian counterparts, though both series derive their texts from the same pre-Vulgate biblical sources.[22] The fourth Beneventan tract, *Domine audivi*, has a

---

[21] Neither the Trisagion (usually combined with *Popule meus*), nor the Improperia, were originally a part of the Beneventan liturgy, to judge from the "Ambrosian" ordo of Vat. lat. 10673, but the same manuscript's mixed Beneventan–Gregorian rite contains all these pieces, including the Gregorian *Popule meus*. Likewise the version of *Popule meus* used for Good Friday in Lucca 606, though it is not written out in full, can be seen to be the Gregorian version from the intonation on f. 155v. Drumbl has shown that the long series of reproaches ("improperia") which follow the Trisagion/*Popule meus* complex in these and other Beneventan manuscripts cannot have originated in southern Italy, though their combination is first witnessed there (Drumbl, "Gli improperi", and "Die Improperien"). The earliest testimony of this union of Trisagion with Improperia, from Beneventan books, already shows a melodic version which, though originally adapted from a Beneventan chant for Holy Week, represents the received "Gregorianized" melody later adapted by the church at large. That the Old Roman melody is virtually identical with the Gregorian suggests either a borrowing of great antiquity, or that the Old Roman liturgy borrowed from the Gregorian, as with the tracts of Holy Saturday.

[22] See PM XIV, 360–75.

Ex. 5.2 *Versions of* Popule meus

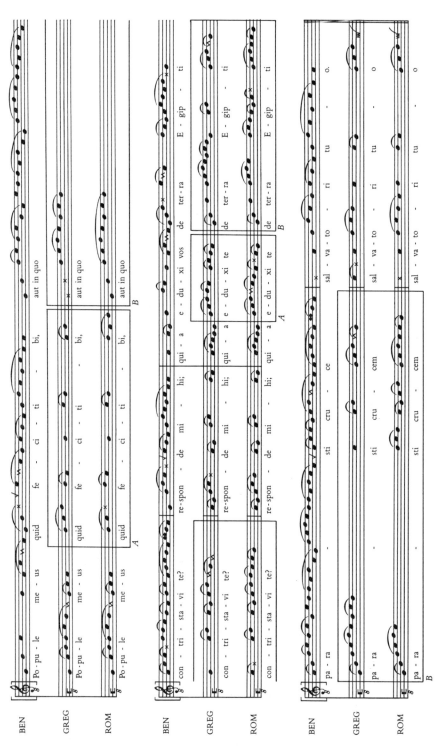

Legend:

BEN: Ben38/38
GREG: Ben34/118
ROM: Vat. lat. 5319/80

Ex. 5.3   Versions of *Domine audivi*

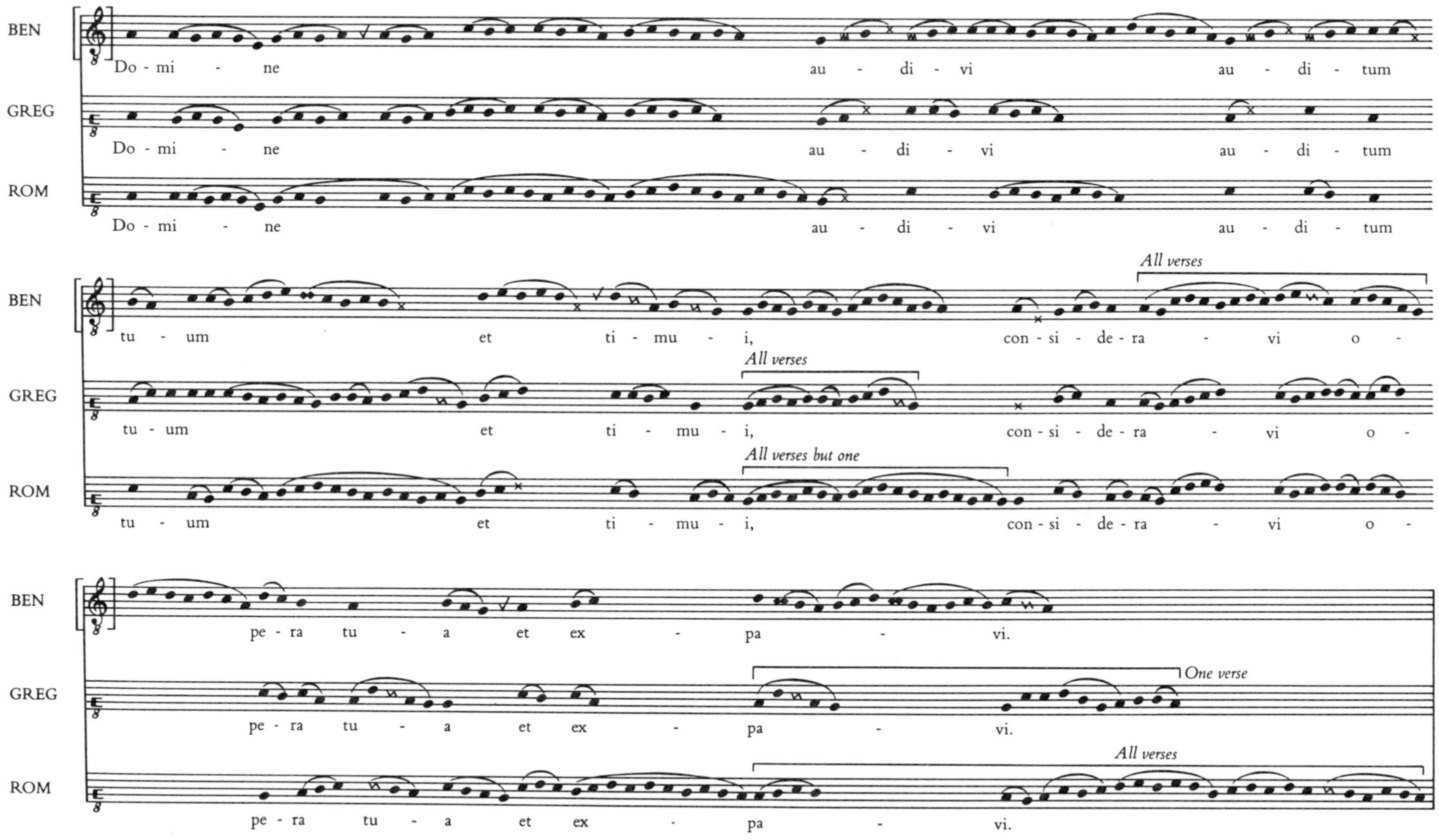

Legend:

BEN: Ben40/15v
GREG: Ben34/116
ROM: Vat. lat. 5319/79v

Ex. 5.4   Versions of *Factus est repente*

Ex. 5.4 (*cont.*)

Legend:

BEN: Ben40/79v (plate 25)
GREG: Ben40/79v (plate 25)
ROM: Vat. lat. 5319/108
MIL: Oxf. Bodl. lat. lit. a.4/99

curious relationship with its Gregorian counterpart. The Gregorian tract (which in the Roman rite is used, not for Holy Saturday, but for Good Friday) uses a pre-Vulgate text, but the Beneventan version uses verses from the Vulgate, set to a typically Beneventan recitation, and related melodically to the other three tracts. These Vulgate verses are preceded, however, by the introductory verse *Domine audivi*, whose text does not match that of the Vulgate to follow: it is borrowed, text and music, from the Roman version of the tract using the older text. This introductory verse is transcribed in example 5.3.

The Beneventan, Gregorian, and Old Roman versions are very similar at their openings, but they soon diverge. Each melody includes elements (marked in brackets) which will be repeated in the subsequent verses of each tract: the melismas on *(timu-)i* and *(ex-)pavi* in the Roman tracts are repeatedly used in their respective verses. The Beneventan verses follow a much stricter repetition scheme than the Gregorian and Old Roman verses, and they use an entirely different melody; within the Beneventan introductory verse transcribed here the music on *(conside-)ravi o(-pera)* is repeated in each subsequent verse.

This tract may be a relative newcomer to the Beneventan repertory; its verses have a Vulgate text, though their melody is structured like that of the other Beneventan tracts. The introductory verse, however, is evidently inspired from the Gregorian and Old Roman versions of the tract, at least for the opening words, and the borrowing of this opening has brought along with it the curious use of the pre-Vulgate text for this portion only.

Additional points of musical contact between the Beneventan and the Roman liturgies are few. A notable case is the Beneventan ingressa for Pentecost, which has echoes in Rome and Milan (example 5.4). Most noticeable here is the remarkable outline of a fifth for the opening words *Factus est repente*, common to all versions (though the Old Roman narrows it). Beyond this, although the basic shapes and the cadences point to a common origin, the Beneventan melody stands apart from the others, which form a relatively close melodic group.[23] Each melody, however, concludes with its own version of the final Alleluia.

It appears that the Ambrosian melody is closer to the Gregorian than is the Old Roman. Like many Ambrosian pieces, this ingressa may well be borrowed by the Ambrosian repertory from the Gregorian.[24] And, as Huglo has argued for the Ambrosian repertory as a whole, the melodic source of Ambrosian adaptations is the Gregorian repertory, not the Old Roman.[25] Benevento's musical connection with this communion, whether through Rome or Milan, is clearly most distant from the Old Roman version. The opening notes, for example, and the recitation on "et repleti sunt omnes" clearly align the Beneventan melody more nearly with the Gregorian and Ambrosian than with the Old Roman.

Another point of contact with the Roman liturgy, and one which has no Ambrosian parallel, is the Holy Saturday communion *Omnes qui in Christo*, example 5.5. This text is the communion for Easter Saturday in the Gregorian and Old Roman rites; it appears also in two manuscripts

---

[23] The Ambrosian melody, relative to all the others, effects an upward transposition of a fourth for the words "et repleti sunt omnes spiritu sancto loquentes," but returns to the common pitch for the end; such Ambrosian transpositions are not uncommon: see Huglo, Agustoni, Cardine, and Moneta Caglio, *Fonti*, pp. 67–9.

[24] On the substantial adaptation of Gregorian music into the Ambrosian rite, see Huglo, *Fonti*, pp. 127–8.

[25] Huglo, *Fonti*, pp. 128–34.

Ex. 5.5   Versions of *Omnes qui in Christo*

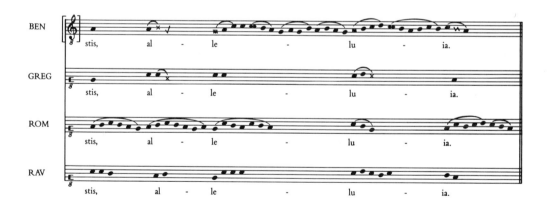

Legend:

BEN: Ben38/47 (compare plate 22)   ROM: Vat. lat. 5319/95v
GREG: Ben34/144v   RAV: Levy, "Neophytes," p. 191

of Ravenna. Clearly connected with the ceremonies of Christian initiation culminating in the Holy Saturday baptisms at Benevento and the putting off of the neophytes' albs in Roman ceremony, this piece is placed by Kenneth Levy in a complex of chants for neophytes from an early layer of Italian liturgy.[26] The lack of an Ambrosian witness is interesting here, particularly as the Ravenna usage might have served as an intermediary between Milan and Benevento. Beyond the low opening and the identity of mode, the variety of melodies here is considerable.

St Lawrence

A final musical parallel in the Roman and Beneventan repertories is *Adhesit anima mea* for St Lawrence, the only Beneventan offertory to which a verse (*In craticula*) is attached. Both the offertory and its verse have musical parallels in the Gregorian and Old Roman office, but whereas the Beneventan offertory with its verse is presented as a single, albeit unusual, chant, the Roman version is two separate antiphons, *Adhesit* and *In craticula*, in different modes. The Ambrosian liturgy also has the psallenda *In craticula* in a similar musical version, but there is no *Adhesit anima mea*. These musical versions can be seen in example 5.6.

In the opening section, *Adhesit*, each antiphon concludes on a different pitch. The Old Roman antiphon, while it is clearly related to the Gregorian melody, is substantially different from the Beneventan version.

The Beneventan offertory-verse *In craticula* is melodically quite distinct from the related antiphons: it is highly structured, having essentially a repetition, in the second half (*probasti*) of the melody of the first. This repetition is not evident in the other versions.

Perhaps the Beneventan melody is a drastic reworking of a non-repetitive melody. The Beneventan version is highly unusual in at least two ways. Firstly, there are no other surviving Beneventan offertories with verses. Secondly, in a piece of this length and melodic elaboration it is unusual to find so little reference to the characteristic formulas of Beneventan chant. Possibly, it is significant that there are no musical references between the offertory and the verse: or rather, if such references were present, we could be less assured in recognizing two separate sources for this unusual offertory.

The great antiquity and solemnity of the feast of St Lawrence at Rome (with its vigil and octave) make it unlikely that Rome would borrow its music from elsewhere. The Ambrosian version is surely not the original: only one of the antiphons is present, and it has unique textual variants. The Beneventan offertory, too, seems to be a local adaptation of borrowed music.

That some pieces used at Benevento may have been adapted into later stages of the Roman liturgy as a *mandatum* antiphon for Maundy Thursday, or as part of the assembled liturgy for Good Friday, suggests not that Beneventan chant was known and practiced at Rome, but simply that there existed a repertory of widely used "pan-Italian" pieces, possibly of great

---

[26] Levy, "The Italian neophytes' chants." Additional evidence of the neophytes' connection is the fact that the final Alleluia of the Beneventan version reproduces the melody of the Beneventan Alleluia connected with baptisms. Used on Holy Saturday (along with *Omnes sitientes*), it includes the Easter verse *Resurrexit tamquam dormiens* and the neophytes' verse *Laudate pueri dominum*. On this Alleluia see Chapter 3, p. 77.

Ex. 5.6   Versions of *Adhesit* and *In craticula*

Ex. 5.6 *(cont.)*

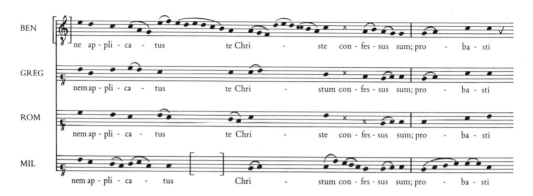

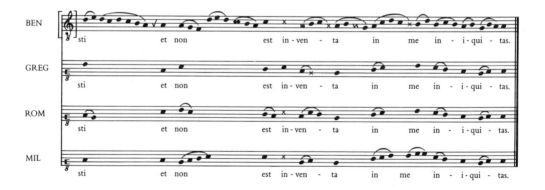

Legend: *Adhesit*   *In craticula*

BEN: Ben40/112v (plate 28)   BEN: Ben40/112v (plate 28)
GREG: Lucca 601/440   GREG: Lucca 601/441
ROM: Vat. San P. B 79/147v   ROM: B 79/147
                                      MIL: Oxf. Bodl. lat. lit. a.4/140

antiquity, which occasionally found places in the liturgies of more than one rite. We have seen in Chapter 4 that many Beneventan antiphons share their melodic shape with melody-types familiar from Gregorian chant (and from other repertories as well). These melodies, too, may represent a musical level that antedates the differentiation of Western liturgies.

Nevertheless, the liturgical and musical relationship of the Beneventan chant to that of Rome is a rather distant one. Generally speaking, common texts, even where they are identical, do not serve the same liturgical function. And the most stable part of the Roman chant, the music of the mass, generally does not share material with the Beneventan mass. Where pieces in Benevento are related to similar texts in Rome, the Roman texts are found in the office.

The musical relations we have seen here are unusual in one way or another: a late composition at Benevento, drawing for inspiration on a Roman tract, or an antiphon for a specifically Roman saint. And, in at least one case (*Popule meus*), the original may be Beneventan, not Roman. The melodic relationships that can be found, moreover, connect the Beneventan chant with the Gregorian version of the Roman chant; the Old Roman chant is musically farther from Benevento than the Gregorian. Whatever the age of the Old Roman chant as it is now preserved, it is not, at least, at the source of these musical relationships with Benevento. If Benevento is to be influenced by, and to give material to, the rite of Rome, it is surely by means of the Roman liturgy as it is known to those at Benevento, and that version is what we now call Gregorian.

AMBROSIAN CHANT

Backgrounds

In 1058 Pope Stephen IX strictly forbade the singing at Montecassino of "Ambrosian" chant: "Tunc etiam et Ambrosianum cantum in ecclesia ista cantari penitus interdixit."[27] By this act the Pope prohibits the local non-conforming chant, the music we call Beneventan, which is at variance with the practice of Rome. Stephen IX, long a leader in the papal reform movement of the eleventh century, was doubtless no friend of deviant local practices with which, as a foreigner, he was unfamiliar.[28]

"Ambrosian" is in fact the only name that Beneventan scribes ever use to distinguish their local chant from the Gregorian norm. It is used in a number of our Beneventan sources, and in each case the scribe attempts to distinguish "Ambrosian" from "Roman" chant, the local dialect from the official received Roman liturgy.

1 MC Compactiones XXII: "Ali. cō ambrō" labels the alternative Beneventan Communion *Gloriosus confessor.*
2 Vat. lat. 10673:
   a "officium sexta feria in Parasceben secundum Ambrosianum" (f. 33), introduces the Beneventan ordo for Good Friday

[27] Chron. mon. cas., II, 94.
[28] On Frederick's career as related to Montecassino, see Bloch, MMA, I, 32–40; "Monte Cassino, Byzantium," pp. 189–93; and Gay, *L'Italie méridionale*, pp. 509–11. Frederick had opportunities to hear the "Ambrosian" chant not only at Montecassino, but also at Benevento and Tremiti: see Kelly, "Montecassino," pp. 80–2.

   b "antifonas gregas latinasque ante crucem sicut in ambrosiano scripte sunt" (f. 33), labels the Greek/Latin antiphons for the adoration of the cross

   c "Lectio hec est hereditas que quinta est ordinata secundum romanum legatur hic; secundum ambrosianum legatur post benedictionem cerei" (ff. 34–34v), an explanation of the divergence in lessons for Holy Saturday between the Roman and local rites.

   d "Tractus amb." labels the Beneventan *Sicut cervus* (f. 34v).

3 Lucca 606: "Deinde responsorium ambrosianum" (f. 153), for the Maundy Thursday responsory *Lavi pedes*.

4 Ben33: "Officium in parasceve secundum ambrosianum" (f. 68v).

5 Ben38: "Tractus ambrosianus" is used four times for the Beneventan tracts *Domine audivi, Cantabo, Attende*, and *Sicut cervus* (ff. 44–46, the last is palimpsest).

6 Solesmes flyleaves: "vig. s. iohis bapt. a[nt.] ambro. ad vesp." for Beneventan vespers of St John the Baptist.[29]

7 Vat. Ottob. 145: "Item quando non canimus ipse ā secundum romano. quo modo supra scripte sunt canimus secundum ambro[siano] hoc modo," introducing a series of Beneventan antiphons for the *mandatum* ceremony.[30]

8 Macerata, Bibl. comunale, MS 1457.XII: "al[iae antiphonae?] sec[undum] ambro[sianum]," follows a series of Gregorian antiphons for Lauds of Lent II; the antiphons to follow do not survive.

There are, of course, many places where Beneventan chant is preserved with no label at all, but these are generally either duplicate masses where the distinction is clear, or substantial stretches of Beneventan music for Holy Week. We should not think that the scribes mean to label only a few Beneventan pieces as Ambrosian, the rest being something else. The "Ambrosian" chant of southern Italy as understood by these scribes is a rite, a usage, and not simply a few isolated pieces. Note the many references to "secundum Ambrosianum," that is, according to the Ambrosian manner or rite. They use this label when they think there may be some confusion as to the use of music which, of necessity, is written in close proximity to a Gregorian counterpart. It is a means of explaining apparently unnecessary and confusing duplication.

Some of these "Ambrosian" labels have attracted scholarly attention for some time,[31] and the nature of possible connections between the rite of Benevento and that of Milan has been discussed in the literature.[32] And indeed there was concern in southern Italy in the eleventh century about the same question: is what we call Ambrosian in the south the same as that found in the north in the city of Saint Ambrose?

At Montecassino the question seems to have been a real one (as of course it should have been; the Pope would not forbid what does not happen). As we have seen in Chapter 1 (pp. 23–4), Montecassino 318 includes a poem on the conflict of Roman and Ambrosian chant in Italy, which an eleventh-century scribe of Montecassino thought it fitting to include in a book of materials related to liturgical music, with a certain sympathy for the now-vanishing Ambrosian chant.

The concern with Ambrosian chant at Montecassino in the eleventh century went further

[29] See Kelly, "Une nouvelle source."
[30] See Boe, "Old Beneventan chant."
[31] Bannister, "Ordine Ambrosiano"; Avery, "The Beneventan lections."
[32] Bailey, "Ambrosian chant," is the first serious study of musical relations in the two liturgies; see also Odermatt, *Ein Rituale*, pp. 66–9; Baroffio, "Le origini," pp. 44–6; and PM XIV, 453–6.

still: there survives a leaf of genuine Milanese chant, in a Beneventan hand, perhaps of the late eleventh century, as the front flyleaf in the Cassinese martyrology Vatican Ottob. lat. 3.[33] That a Cassinese scribe copies Ambrosian chant means both that he had access to the Milanese liturgy, and that there was some use for such a document. Whether an entire manuscript was copied cannot be known, nor what the exemplar was.[34]

If the scribe knew that he was copying Ambrosian music from Milan (the document nowhere uses the term "Ambrosian"), he must have noticed the difference between what he copied and what he presumably already knew of the local rite. We know that the Beneventan liturgy was present at Montecassino, and that it was there called "Ambrosian." A scribe would surely note that the Milanese music was different. Was this what he wanted to know? It may be for just such research purposes that the Ambrosian flyleaf was copied: to add a reference work to the important library of Montecassino, to find out what the "pure" Ambrosian music was, to seek the source of what presumably was a local representative. It may have been a surprise to see the great distance between Milan and Benevento.

Elsewhere in the region, at what may have been the center of Beneventan chant, Ambrosian chant was occasionally used as a resource. At Benevento itself, Ben40 includes a mass for the Milanese saints Nazarius and Celsus, whose chants are cued from the common of saints with the addition of a local Alleluia.[35] This mass is followed, however, by an alternative (*alia missa*) in much grander style, including ordinary tropes and sequence, which borrows music from the Ambrosian rite.[36] The Ambrosian ingressa *Reddidit justus*[37] is fitted out with a psalm-verse to serve as a Gregorian introit, and the mass continues with an Ambrosian *Gloria in excelsis*.[38] The rest of the mass is in Gregorian style.[39] Benevento also borrowed Ambrosian antiphons for the offices of Sts Nazarius and Celsus and for St Apollinaris.[40] Hence, the Ambrosian chant was occasionally imported at Benevento as an aspect of the Milanese origin of certain saints. This borrowing seems to be relatively recent; the music is essentially identical with that of Ambrosian manuscripts.

The eleventh-century interest and research in Milanese chant, and its relationship to the local dialect, reflects a period of change, perhaps an attempt to gather materials to authenticate a local tradition at a time of renewed threat.

[33] Facsimile in PM XIV, plates XXXII, XXXIII, and in Bannister, *Monumenti*, II, plate 72 (see also I, no. 354, p. 124). These two pages contain music for Tuesday and Wednesday of the second week of Lent in the Ambrosian rite. All the pieces on this leaf are to be found, in the same order, in the Ambrosian Gradual-Antiphoner London, BL, Add. MS 34209, pp. 174–5 (facsimile in PM V, transcription in PM VI, 204–5).

[34] Evidently his model was not in Beneventan notation: the scribe uses the "Ambrosian" climacus not found in Beneventan notation: see Huglo, *Fonti*, no. 40, pp. 21–3.

[35] The mass begins on f. 102v: Int. *Clamaverunt*; Gr. *Clamaverunt*; All. *Sancti mei*; Of. *Anima nostra*; Comm. *Justorum animae*. For the Italian Alleluia *Sancti mei*, see Schlager, *Thematischer Katalog*, no. 273, p. 196. The same mass is found in Ben38, f. 118v, but with two other Alleluias: *Sancte Nazari vir dei* (a Beneventan product: Schlager, no. 262, pp. 189–90) and *Te martyrum* (cued only: Schlager, no. 397, pp. 347–8).

[36] For a facsimile see Kelly, "Beneventan and Milanese."

[37] AMed, p. 503; Oxford, Bodleian, MS Lat. liturg. a. 4, f. 171. The melody is used for St Nazarius also in Ben39, f. 132v.

[38] The melody is that printed in AMed as "Tonus Solemnior," pp. 607–9. For Ambrosian manuscript sources of this Gloria see the sources listed in Huglo, *Fonti*, p. 241.

[39] Gr. *Anima nostra* (cued); All. *Sancte Nazari*; All. *Sancti mei*; Seq. *Laetetur celum humus*; Sanctus with *Osanna plasmatum populum*; Of. *Anima nostra* (cued); Comm. *Justorum* (cued).

[40] See below, pp. 197–203, and Kelly, "Non-Gregorian music."

When we study the same question we must proceed like the monk of Montecassino, by studying the sources of Milanese music and comparing them with the local Beneventan chant. When we do so, we find that there is indeed a close relationship between Benevento and Milan, far closer than the connections of the Beneventan liturgy with the Gregorian or the Old Roman. But they are not identical. The scribe of Ottoboni 3 may have been surprised at the degree of difference; we are not.

Liturgical connections

Though the two liturgies are closely related, the incompleteness of the Beneventan sources makes a full comparison with the Ambrosian rite impossible, and the relatively late date of the Milanese musical manuscripts – the earliest is from the twelfth century – presents problems of transmission similar to those we encounter in Beneventan chant. But the parallels in the two liturgies are unmistakable.

On a physical level, there survives at Benevento a pair of manuscripts which correspond in their makeup to the Ambrosian model. Ben19 and Ben20 are a combined breviary and missal, divided into winter (Ben19) and summer (Ben20) portions between Holy Saturday and Easter. These features are typical of the arrangement of the surviving Ambrosian manuscripts: combination of mass and office, division of the liturgy into winter and summer portions at Easter.[41]

Liturgical comparisons may be grouped into three areas: firstly, general similarities in the shape of the liturgy; secondly, details of Holy Week rites, whose comparison is possible since we are relatively well informed on the Beneventan ceremonies of these days; and thirdly, certain unusual practices in the Gregorian liturgy of southern Italy which have marked Ambrosian analogies.

1 A number of general features of the Beneventan mass suggest parallels with the Ambrosian rite. Benevento uses an entrance chant for the mass which is called "ingressa" and which is used without psalmody. The same sort of entrance chant, with the same name, is used at Milan – a chant which varies substantially from the Gregorian introit with its psalmody. Benevento, like Milan, uses a threefold Kyrie (without *Christe eleison*) following the *Gloria in excelsis* rather than preceding it.[42] The Beneventan use of a single melody for all the Alleluia verses (except for two with special melodies) is an archaic feature, and one that can be seen to some extent in the Alleluias of Milan. The presence in many of the surviving Beneventan masses of two communions suggests the possibility that the Beneventan rite once regularly included two chants, corresponding to the Milanese *confractorium* and *transitorium*.[43] Unlike the Gregorian repertory,

---

[41] Of course, the correspondence may be accidental. Naturally, when a book is overlarge it is convenient to divide it, as is often done with lectionaries and breviaries. But this is not the only Beneventan book arranged in this way. Vat. lat. 10645, a collection of fragments taken from bindings, includes, as folio 63, a single leaf from a combined missal-breviary with musical notation of the twelfth century. With a single leaf we cannot say whether the book was divided (though it would probably have needed to be), nor whether the dividing point was at Easter. We have noted above (p. 51) that the scribe of Ben38 seems to have used a Beneventan "totum," combining mass and office, as his source for Beneventan melodies. On the use of mixed missal-breviaries elsewhere in Italy, in the Mozarabic rite, and very occasionally elsewhere, see Salmon, *L'Office divin*, pp. 64–7.

[42] See p. 91.

[43] On the Alleluias see Bailey, *The Ambrosian Alleluias*, p. 46f.; on communions see above, p. 79.

which uses for the mass almost exclusively scriptural texts, almost half the Beneventan chants for the mass are of ecclesiastical creation. A similar proportion is found in the mass chants of Milan and, as we shall see, many of these non-biblical texts are used in both repertories.

2 The rites of Holy Week provide many Ambrosian–Beneventan parallels. The book of Jonah (most often read in the Roman rite on Holy Saturday), is read at Milan on Maundy Thursday,[44] and on the same day in the Beneventan rite.[45]

Good Friday has many elements familiar in both rites. The reading from the book of Daniel, with the canticle of Azarias and that of the three children, appears on Good Friday in both Beneventan and Ambrosian rites[46] in versions remarkably similar as to their texts, their performance, and, as we shall see, their music. The responsory *Tenebrae factae sunt* serves in both liturgies as a quasi-gradual in a pro-anaphora for Good Friday.[47] In both rites there is a double adoration of the cross on Good Friday; essentially the same ceremony repeated at different hours. At Milan the second adoration is the public exhibition of the cross to the people; this may be the function of the second adoration at Benevento also, though we cannot be certain from the surviving rubrics.[48] The three bilingual Greek/Latin antiphons for the adoration in Beneventan manuscripts are used for the same ceremony at Milan in a Latin version (they will receive further attention below).[49] Of the four antiphons for Beneventan vespers of Good Friday three are also used at Milan, two of them with related melodies.[50]

Though the ceremonies of Holy Saturday differ markedly in the two rites, there are a few important parallels. The unusual phenomenon (noted by Hesbert) in the Beneventan manuscripts of providing tracts after each lesson of the paschal vigil is characteristic of those manuscripts which preserve the tracts of the old Beneventan rite,[51] and thus may be the

[44] It is mentioned as being read on that day by St Ambrose himself, see PL XVI, col. 1002.

[45] See PM XIV, 271–4.

[46] Vat. lat. 10673, Ben33, Ben40, Ben39: see PM XIV, 318–21; Hesbert, "L'antiphonale" (5), pp. 120–6; Cagin, *Codex sacramentorum*, pp. 198–9; PM V (BL, Add. MS 34209, pp. 248–50).

[47] Hesbert, "L'antiphonale" (5), pp. 127–33; PM XIV, 326–31.

[48] Benevento (from the Beneventan Good Friday ordo of Vat. lat. 10673, ff. 33–33v):

    Facta hora tertia congregentur omnes in ecclesia et cantet unusquisque tertiam in secreto cordis sui. Post hec incipiat canere antiphonas gregas latinasque ante crucem sicut in ambrosiano scripte sunt cum psalmis. . . Dum clerici canunt et legunt omnes adorent sanctam crucem juxta ordinem suum et finito evangelio discedant. Facta hora sexta iterum conveniant omnes in ecclesia et cantent sextam sibi in secreto cordis sui. Post hec incipiant canere ipsas antiphonas cum psalmis quod ad tertiam cantaverunt et omnes adorent sanctam crucem sicut jam diximus.

    Milan (from the twelfth-century "Beroldus" ordinal of Milan, ed. Magistretti, *Beroldus*, pp. 106–7):

    Tunc egrediuntur de secretario in camisio portando honorifice crucem in medio ecclesiae, adorante archiepiscopo prius cum omni clero, subdiaconibus canentibus hanc antiphonam: *Crucem tuam adoramus, Domine*. Aliam: *Adoramus crucem tuam. Beati immaculati*, usque ad *Legem pone*. Adorata vero cruce, revertuntur in secretarium, subdiaconibus reportantibus honorifice crucem, et cantando hanc antiphonam: *Laudamus te, Christe*. . . . Tunc custodes iterum portant crucem de secretario in medio ecclesiae, ad adorandum plebi, cantantes antiphonas: *Crucem tuam*; II. *Adoramus crucem*; III. *Laudamus te, Christe*, alternando cum versibus *Beati immaculati*; et quicquid ad crucem offertus, totum est custodum.

    This double ceremony is attested in most, but not all, Ambrosian books. The second adoration is not mentioned in Milan, Biblioteca Ambrosiana, MS, T 103 sup. (a manual of the eleventh century), Milan Biblioteca Ambrosiana, I 27 sup. (twelfth century), or Y 18 sup. (fourteenth–fifteenth century). See Cattaneo, "L'adorazione," pp. 181–5.

[49] On these antiphons in the Beneventan liturgy, see below, pp. 194–7; PM XIV, 308–13; and Hesbert, "L'antiphonale" (5), pp. 104–16. On their connections with the Byzantine liturgy, see below, pp. 209–14. On the use of these antiphons in both rites, for the feast of the Exaltation, see above, p. 87.

[50] See PM XIV, 335–7; and Hesbert, "L'antiphonale" (5), pp. 136–41.

[51] See PM XIV, 339–60 and table, p. 356; and Hesbert, "L'antiphonale" (6), pp. 154–71.

survival of an originally Beneventan arrangement. The Ambrosian rite also, though it provides only six lessons for the paschal vigil, follows each of them with a psalmellus or a canticle.[52] The Ambrosian arrangement, like the Beneventan, seems to have been disturbed since its original ordering. The order of lessons is not uniform,[53] nor is the ordering of chants clearly related to the lessons,[54] and at least two of the psalmelli are borrowed from elsewhere in the repertory.[55]

The Beneventan dismissal of catechumens, Jews, and heretics ("Si quis catechumenus est procedat," etc.) precedes the baptismal rite of Holy Saturday; a very similar form is found at Milan (and occasionally elsewhere) on the Saturday before Palm Sunday (*Sabbato in traditione symboli*).[56] A threefold announcement of the Resurrection is found both at Benevento and Milan.[57]

3 Many non-standard features in the Gregorian masses of Beneventan manuscripts already seen in Chapter 3 have noteworthy Ambrosian parallels. Lacking any old Beneventan lectionary or sacramentary we cannot be certain that these are features of the older Beneventan liturgy, but their exceptional quality merits attention, particularly in the context of their relationship to the rite of Milan. These include: a shared series of gospels for Sundays in Lent, which give their names to the weeks ("De Samaritana," etc.); a system of three readings at mass; a large number of proper prefaces, identical for Lenten Sundays; the Beneventan *oratio post evangelium* corresponding to the Ambrosian *super sindonem*; and the use of hagiographical lessons at mass.

The many texts shared in the two liturgies point to a close relationship. Table 5.1 above lists Beneventan mass chants with shared texts, indicating whether there is a demonstrable musical relationship. Most interesting, of course, is the case of non-biblical texts which are not shared by the Roman liturgy, for in these cases a strong presumption must exist that the pieces, at least for their texts, are closely related, since they can have no common source in universally available scripture.

Benevento shares more texts, and many more melodies, with Milan than with the Roman rites. But though Benevento and Milan have many texts in common, they never share a whole mass, though there are substantial musical connections in the feasts of Holy Week, Saint Michael, Saints Peter and Paul, Saint Lawrence, Saint Martin, and All Saints. But there is no textual basis for concluding that either liturgy is derived from the other – that the Beneventan liturgy, for

[52] Magistretti, *Manuale*, II, 202–4; and Magistretti, *Beroldus*, pp. 110–11; the lessons, but not the chants, can be seen in Cagin, *Codex sacramentorum*, p. 199.

[53] The order of the fourth (*Armati ascenderunt*, Exodus 13: 18–22, 14: 1–9) and fifth (*Hec est hereditas*, Is. 54: 17b, 55: 1–11) lessons is reversed between *Manuale* and *Beroldus*, and the confusion is present also in the *capitula lectionum* edited by Cagin (see previous note).

[54] The song of the three children (*Benedictus es, domine*) does not follow a reading from Daniel (none is present in the series), and the song of Moses (*Tunc cantabat . . . Cantemus*) follows the wrong (fourth) lesson in Magistretti, *Manuale*, II, 203.

[55] *Tui sunt celi* from the Christmas vigil and *Benedictus dominus deus israel qui facit mirabilia* from the Epiphany vigil.

[56] Hesbert, "L'antiphonale" (6), pp. 197–201; PM XIV, 429–32; PM V, facs. p. 219; and Borella, "La missa." An additional source of this dismissal, not noticed heretofore, is in Vatican, Barb. lat. 631, a late eleventh-century pontifical of Montecassino. On folio 75, after the pre-baptismal rite and before the propers of Holy Saturday is found the single dismissal "Si quis catecuminus est recedat," without musical notation.

[57] Oxford, Bodleian, MS lat. liturg. a. 4, f. 4: "Ad cornu altaris dicat presbiter tribus vicibus Xristus dominus resurrexit. ℣ Deo gratias." Ben38, f. 53: "Deinde dicat sacerdos III vicibus Iam xpistus dominus resurrexit. ℟ cleri simul cum populo Deo gratias." See Huglo, "L'annuncio."

example, might well be called "Old Ambrosian." We should not expect this, of course, when we can only compare two very dissimilar objects: the Beneventan liturgy, preserved only in part, in fragmentary form, with much evidence of fluidity of liturgical assignment, and probably much affected by the harassment of the Gregorian influx; and the Ambrosian in a form that reflects a codification (and probably some simplifications and some developments).[58]

In a few known cases, and perhaps others yet to be found, there is a recognizable source – like the Byzantine liturgy – from which both liturgies might have drawn independently. But for most of the non-biblical texts there are such close textual parallels that it is difficult to imagine anything other than a direct connection between the two liturgies. And indeed, many biblical texts are so arranged from the scriptures as to be musical libretti, adapted for musical performance, that would surely not have been invented in two places independently.[59]

From this we might posit a model in which an original common tradition undergoes independent development in two places. The kingdom of the Lombards, extending from the Milanese north to the Beneventan south could reasonably be expected to share common liturgical practices, indeed, to have exchanged chant books (which until the tenth century may have included only texts). But despite the ostensible unity of the Lombard kingdom, the pursuit of independence by the Lombard dukes of Benevento underscores the detachment which sheer distance and geographical hardships imposed on the south. The fall of the Lombard kingdom in the north at the advent of Charlemagne, and the taking up of the Lombard mantle by Arichis II in 774, only reaffirm the separation of tradition which must have been a continuing feature of Lombard relations.

So any original liturgical unity had every opportunity to develop along separate lines over the centuries that separate the Christianization of the Lombards from the ultimate suppression of the duchy of Benevento, and its local liturgy, in the middle of the eleventh century. Even in the presence of common texts, the development of separate liturgical traditions, in a time before the Carolingian urge to uniformity, and in places so distant from each other, is inevitable.

But matters seem somehow more complex than this. In such a situation we should expect to detect a deep layer of liturgical uniformity, revealed in matters of calendar, particularly in the chants (and lections) of the mass, and perhaps some evidence of a persistent melodic tradition. But whereas we can observe some of these things, they are not patterned in such a way as to indicate a general common origin of the liturgies: they are not as close, for example, as the Gregorian and Old Roman repertories. To be sure, there are some striking identities of text and of liturgical practice, but there are as many places that are entirely different. The rites of Holy Saturday, for example (many features of which Benevento seems to share with Rome), do not continue the close parallels to be seen in Good Friday. And the sporadic distribution of common texts does not seem to denote a fundamental common inheritance of entire mass formularies, much less a whole *antiphonal missarum*. A more direct liturgical connection might be argued if pieces with the same texts regularly served the same liturgical function in each

[58] The official ordinal produced by Beroldus early in the twelfth century (ed. Magistretti, *Beroldus*) is probably part of the same effort at codification that produced the earliest of the surviving complete chant books, also from the twelfth century. The principal early manuscripts are listed in Bailey, *The Ambrosian Alleluias*, p. 102. For a more complete catalogue, see Huglo, *Fonti*, and the additions noted in Baroffio, "Le origini," pp. 47–8, n. 85.
[59] Details of these textual relationships can be found in Appendix 2.

liturgy, graduals matching psallendae, ingressae matching ingressae, and so on. But in fact, most of the common texts serve different functions in each rite.

Clearly, much remains to be learned about the nature and the history of the relation of Beneventan and Ambrosian chant. Further study will necessarily involve a wide view of the liturgy, ranging far beyond the chant and its music to include calendar, sacramentary, lectionary, breviary, and their changes over the course of time. Our purpose here is more restricted, but it can contribute to a developing picture of a complex, but evident, relationship. Among the chants of the two rites there are many which share texts unique to these liturgies, and in these pairs there are often clear musical relationships. It is to these musical connections that we now turn.

Musical connections

Many Ambrosian melodies are extremely florid, and when their Beneventan counterparts are also elaborate the terms of comparison are difficult enough that we cannot safely claim a musical relationship. In these cases (but particularly in those where there seem to be similarities of structure and repetition) I have marked a possible musical relationship with a question mark in table 5.1.[60]

Many shared texts, however, have more than their structures to compare. Example 5.7 compares the Beneventan and Ambrosian melodies for *Inter natos mulierum*, which uses a version of the text not shared by other liturgies. The melodies display a similar contour, though the Beneventan version, as often happens, is more ornate. They have parallel cadences on *baptista* and *fidelium*, and similar phrases beginning with *Inter natos* and *maior prophetis*. But the structure is much clearer at Benevento. Except for adjustments for length of text, there are two strictly parallel phrases in the Beneventan piece, the second of which delays its ending to accomodate the syllables [*prepa-*]*ravit cor*[*-da*], while the Ambrosian phrases are only alike at their beginnings and their ends. It seems unlikely that Beneventan musicians should have fabricated a repetition where one was not present in an earlier way of singing this text. It is more likely that the Ambrosian music has not felt the need of preserving this rigor.

A further example is the communion *Multos infirmos* for St Michael, which appears in the Ambrosian liturgy as a psallenda (example 5.8). Here, a recitation begun twice from a low note in the Ambrosian psallenda (on *Multos* and *multi*) is echoed, but less clearly, in the Beneventan melody, which is far more elaborate than the Ambrosian. Note the longer (but typically Beneventan) melismatic cadence on *cu-RA-sti* and the Beneventan elaboration at the

---

[60] One such comparison can be made by the reader who has access to volumes 5 and 14 of the *Paléographie musicale*; there he may compare the Canticle of the Three Children (*Benedictus es, Domine Deus patrum nostrorum*), with its preface *Tunc hi tres* and its concluding verses. Though the elaborate melodies are not the same, the structures of the two canticles are in many ways closely parallel. The introduction and the final verses are alike in each version, though each rite uses its own recitation tone (on Beneventan recitation tones, see Chapter 4, pp. 131–5). And the melodic structures match in the canticle. The opening words *Benedictus es* (1) *domine* (2) *deus* (3) have the same melody three times (melody A), though the music of Benevento is not that of Milan. And in each rite another melody (B) appears on *laudabilis* and on *saecula. Amen.* These two melodies function throughout the canticle at parallel places: *Ymnum dicite* in each matches that canticle's melody B. In two other places melody A is used three times in each: *Benedicite* (1) *omnia* (2) *opera* (3), and *Benedicimus* (1) *patrem* (2) *et filium* (3). And other matching texts have matching music, as for *Domini dominum* (at Milan, *Domini domino*). The structure is the same, but the melodies are different.

Ex. 5.7   Versions of *Inter natos*

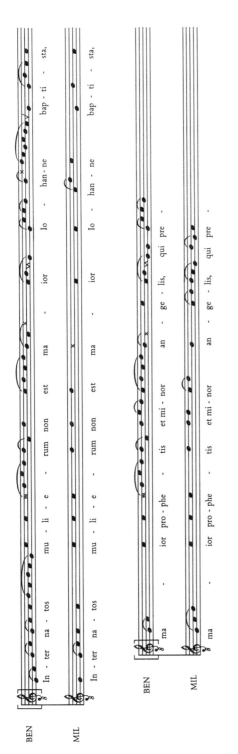

Legend:

BEN: Ben40/89v (plate 27)

MIL: Oxf. Bodl. lat. lit. a.4/140

Ex. 5.8   Versions of *Multos infirmos*

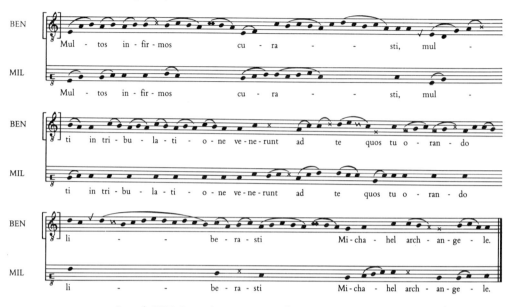

Legend: BEN: Ben40/10   MIL: Oxf. Bodl. lat. lit. a.4/204

point where the Ambrosian melody rises for the first syllable of *liberasti*. We can see, too, the Beneventan fondness for elaborated recitations: repeated podatus (*Multos infirmos*), quilisma (*orando*) and three-note figures (*tribulatione*) where the Milanese melody has single notes.

The Beneventan piece here, however, is an expanded version of a melody that occurs elsewhere in the Beneventan repertory; it is a member of a melodic family, and many of its melodic turns are dictated by that relationship. Example 4.13 shows some melodic mates which do not appear in the Ambrosian liturgy. The piece cannot have traveled from Milan to Benevento unless it was either in company with the others (which it apparently was not), or unless the other Beneventan melodies are derived from either the Ambrosian original or its Beneventan derivative (which is highly improbable).

Example 5.9, which compares the ingressa for Maundy Thursday at Benevento with the transitorium for Saturday *in albis* at Milan, suggests that Beneventan chant is closer to Milan than to Rome. The pieces have essentially the same text, though Milan uses a triple *alleluia* for Easter Week, while verbal quotation marks take their place for Maundy Thursday at Benevento ("dicens: Si ego . . . dicit dominus"); these are typical enough of liturgical texts, and useful as verbal cadences, though they are redundant in meaning.

The first four lines begin low and continue with one or more podatus; each line has a medial (on C) and final (on D) cadence (on G and A, to be more accurate for the Beneventan version). Despite its highly formulaic content, however, the Beneventan melody is not, like many ingressae, based strictly on repetitions of entire phrases. There is a loosely organized double cycle, in which the opening recitation is followed first by one continuation (melody A, line 1), then by another (melody B, line 2); the pattern is then followed in the second half of the piece for lines 3 and 4, the whole being completed by the final *dicit dominus*.

The Ambrosian melody is clearly related, but it does not follow this pattern. The effect is rather one of a freely repeated recitation, without the double cycle. All but one of the recitations continue with the melody α, and all but one of the medial cadences use the melody β, but these rarely parallel Beneventan elements; and the Ambrosian *alleluia* added to line 3 obscures the sense of two halves that would be marked if it were absent, leaving two *alleluias* corresponding to the Beneventan *dicens* and *dicit dominus*.

The Gregorian liturgy also uses this text, as two separate antiphons for the *mandatum*.

Benevento	Milan	Rome
Postquam surrexit	Postquam surrexit	1 Postquam surrexit
dominus a CENAM	dominus a CENA	dominus a CENA
misit aquam in pelvem	misit aquam in pelvim	misit aquam in pelvim
cepit lavare	cepit lavare	cepit lavare
pedes discipulorum	pedes discipulorum	pedes discipulorum
suorum	suorum	suorum
DICENS	ALLELUIA	HOC EXEMPLUM
		RELIQUIT EIS
Si ego dominus	si ego dominus	2 Si ego dominus
et magister vester	et magister vester	et magister vester
lavi pedes vestros	lavi pedes vestros	lavi VOBIS PEDES
	ALLELUIA	
quanto magis vos	quanto magis vos	quanto magis vos
debetis alter alterius	debetis alter alterius	debetis alter alterius
pedes lavare	pedes lavare	LAVARE PEDES
DICIT DOMINUS	ALLELUIA	

Such rearrangements of scripture, unlikely to have originated independently, are certainly derived from a common source.[61] The two Gregorian antiphons have essentially the same melody, and hence represent the same sort of double cursus as the Beneventan version. The Gregorian music, however (the antiphons do not appear in Old Roman sources), is substantially different from the Benevento–Milan pair. The fourth-mode melodies bear little resemblance to those in example 5.9. These widely used Gregorian antiphons can be found in the same sources that preserve the Beneventan version[62] – manuscripts that show the divergence and confluence of traditions in the juxtaposition of pieces which may once have been identical, but which in these mixed sources are preserved, and justly so, as representatives of separate and conflicting liturgies.

Particularly revealing of the antiquity of Benevento as compared with Milan is the case of several antiphons for Holy Week that occur, in at least some Beneventan manuscripts, in both

---

[61] For a more detailed study of these texts see Hesbert, "L'antiphonale" (4), pp. 70–3.
[62] Ben35, Ben39, Ben40, and Lucca 606; the first of them only is in Ben33 and Ben30.

Ex. 5.9 Versions of *Postquam surrexit*

Ex. 5.9 (cont.)

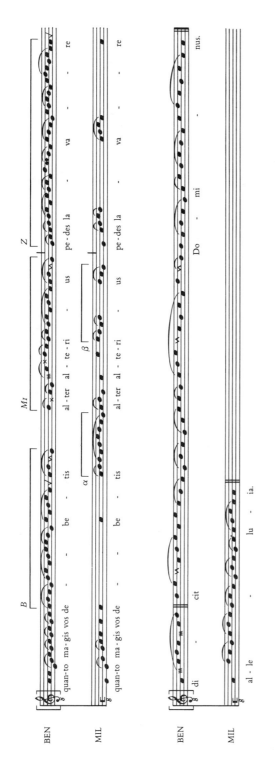

Legend:
BEN: Ben40/4v
MIL: Oxf. Bodl. lat. lit. a.5/31v

Ex. 5.10   Versions of *Gloria in excelsis*

Legend: BEN: Ben40/19   MIL: Oxf. Bodl. lat. lit. a.4/33

Greek and Latin versions. In such cases it seems likely that the Greek version is the original, by the very presence of a foreign (or at least liturgically archaic) language in the Latin liturgy.[63] And, just as the Greek version drops out in later Beneventan manuscripts, the Latin versions that alone survive at Milan represent a degree of distance from the bilingual original. This notion is strengthened by the surviving music in the two liturgies.

Example 5.10 compares the antiphon *Gloria in excelsis deo* (the Greek original in Benevento is *Doxa en ipsistis theo*) in its Latin versions from Benevento and Milan.[64] This is a famous text whose Latin translation is already available in the liturgy; a Greek original is not needed to explain the existence of similar texts in Milan and Benevento. But this text, in just this form, is not used elsewhere in the Latin liturgies, and the musical similarities in the two versions reinforce their common original.[65]

The music of the opening syllable is repeated for the beginning of the second phrase (*et*) in both pieces; in both, a musical A B A form structures the three concluding Alleluias, and most cadence points are identical. Here again, however, we see a higher degree of structural repetition in the Beneventan version. The end of the first phrase (*deo*) is repeated to close the middle Alleluia, and also closes the second phrase of text ([*ter-*]*ra pax*).

The three Greek/Latin antiphons for the adoration of the cross on Good Friday at Benevento have a close parallel at Milan, for all three are there used together for the same function. But there are important differences. Firstly, Milan preserves only the Latin texts. Secondly, though they are used together in both liturgies, they are not in the same order, and one of the Milanese antiphons uses only a part of the Beneventan text.[66]

---

[63] This assumption has been challenged, at least in the case of certain antiphons for the adoration of the cross. Johann Drumbl has seen these as simultaneous creations, in which the Latin text may well be the original: "Zweisprachige Antiphonen," and the discussion below, pp. 209–14.

[64] That the Milanese melody is also used as an antiphon *ante evangelium* in certain northern Italian manuscripts was pointed out by Borders in "The northern Italian." On these sources, see Appendix 2.

[65] The musical parallel is noted also in Huglo, *Fonti*, p. 122, and in Levy, "The Italian neophytes' chants," pp. 188–90, 192.

[66] This is related to differences in their Greek sources: see below, p. 209.

But even when we assume a Byzantine or other external origin our task is not changed. These are not the only pieces conceived outside and assimilated into the repertory. Used at Benevento and Milan from an early date, these antiphons have a close kinship: they are used in a similar double ceremony for the adoration, and their melodies are closely related, but differ substantially from other melodic versions.[67] From a common ancestor (the compilation of these three texts) the two rites have developed the group of antiphons in ways that allow us to see something of their relationship and their history.

That the Beneventan group of antiphons, whatever their possibly heterogeneous origin, is older than the Ambrosian, is suggested, first of all, by their bilingual form, and secondly by their use at Benevento in a uniform series in a single ceremony (where Milan separated one for processional use).

Musical comparisons can tell us even more (see example 5.11).[68] The melodies are compared here in the Beneventan order. There are musical similarities enough to make it clear that the melodies are related, at least for the first two antiphons. But for the third (*Laudamus*) the musical similarities are obscure at best, and there are additional problems. At Benevento the antiphon *Laudamus* is clearly related to *Adoramus*; their second halves are virtually identical ("et qui crucifixus est virtutem" and "quia per crucem redemisti mundum"). But this parallelism is not reflected in the Ambrosian versions. Indeed, there is some modal dislocation in the Milanese melody of *Laudamus*: it seems to be written a step too low and has needed adjustment with B-flats.[69] If the Ambrosian antiphon were written a step higher without B-flat (or, more likely in later manuscripts, transposed down a fifth to end on D rather than A) it would correspond more nearly with the pitches of the Beneventan antiphon, and, what is more, its closing phrase (from *per crucem*) would match exactly that of the Ambrosian *Adoramus*.

In the Ambrosian antiphons, then, there is a three-stage process of distance from the original – an original to which Benevento is closer. First, the Greek text is dropped. Then the two antiphons which clearly are related at Benevento become more differentiated at Milan, even in the "undislocated" form. (This is a process we have seen already.) And finally the Milanese version further distances the two antiphons by the transposition, accidental or not at its origin, of one of the antiphons.

We cannot compare here all the related melodies in the Beneventan and Ambrosian liturgies.[70] But even from these few examples some more general patterns can be observed. First,

---

[67] Compare the later versions from Ravenna and Nonantola in Drumbl, "Zweisprachige Antiphonen," p. 50.

[68] The central antiphon (*Crucem tuam*) is pitched ending on E (highly unusual for Beneventan chant) in Ben35 (see PM XIV, plate XXV) and Oxford, Bodleian, Can. lit. 342 (our only sources with clefs). However, the use of the same psalmodic ending for all three antiphons in Lucca 606 (PM XIV, plates XLII, XLIII) suggests a common final, and here I have transcribed the central antiphon as ending on the same pitch as the others (but see p. 154 n. 53). The Beneventan melody here is that of Ben40; there are some significant differences in the versions of Vat. 10673, which presents a number of cadences in forms more typically Beneventan. Compare PM XIV, plates 56–7 and XIII.

[69] B-flats in the British Library MS are added in an inconsistent way by the use of a green line, possibly added to the MS by a later, and not very artistic, hand. But the B-flat is confirmed by other readings.

[70] The reader who wishes to pursue matters on his own (and much research remains to be done) already has many further comparisons available in the *pars hiemalis* by consulting volumes XIV and V of the *Paléographie musicale*. That same series proposes to present, in the near future, both a complete set of facsimiles of the Beneventan chant, and the *pars estivalis* of the Ambrosian liturgy.

Ex. 5.11   Adoration antiphons

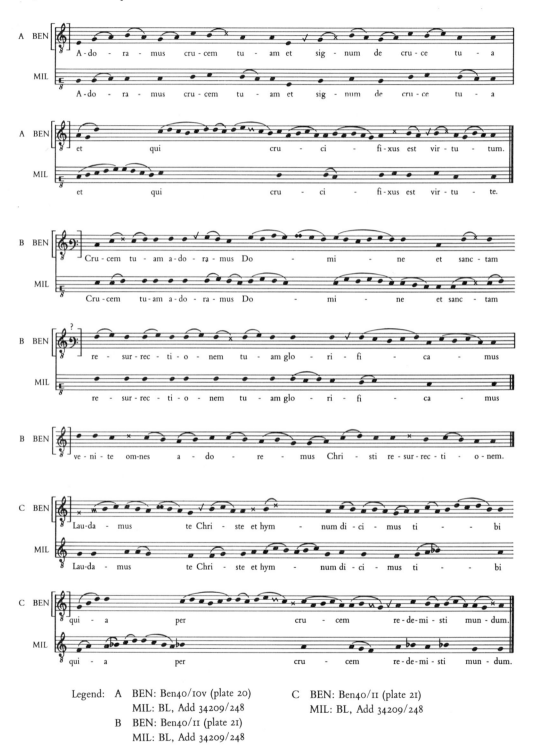

Legend: A BEN: Ben40/10v (plate 20)   C BEN: Ben40/11 (plate 21)
                MIL: BL, Add 34209/248   MIL: BL, Add 34209/248
           B BEN: Ben40/11 (plate 21)
                MIL: BL, Add 34209/248

many texts share similar melodies in the two repertories, but though they have common melodic roots, it is not possible to establish that one melody is derived directly from another. In no case are the melodies identical, or nearly so. Beneventan chant, by comparison with Ambrosian, uses melodies differently (if we can imagine a process that surely never happened so simply, whereby composers – or traditions – fashioned from identical musical "source material" melodies which were the "development" or the "improvement" of those sources). For one thing, Beneventan chant is more highly structured with formulas and melodic repetitions than is the Ambrosian (though the Ambrosian gives evidence of the same sort of repetitions in a less literal and more relaxed fashion). Beneventan chant, though it is not always more ornate than Ambrosian, seldom approaches the rigid syllabic quality of some portions of Ambrosian melodies; it prefers any of several highly ornamented reciting procedures to the single-note recitations of Ambrosian chant. And the presence of many small rigid melodic formulas in Beneventan chant makes of it a mosaic of many recognizable elements, a quality that is not so clearly a part of the Ambrosian esthetic.

In many of our comparisons we have suggested that the Ambrosian version of a melody is farther removed from a hypothetical common ancestor than the Beneventan. By this we do not mean that the presence of formulaic music, of small identical turns of phrase, or of highly regular cadences, indicate by their mere presence an archaic musical style. But the imposition of large internal musical repetitions on music that lacks such structure seems a less likely event, in music whose chief formal element is such repetition, than a process by which the more fluid member of the pair has over time relaxed the rigidity of the rules.

Office music

Although many Ambrosian melodies may appear to be looser versions of an original whose more rigid structure is preserved at Benevento, we can cite at least a few examples of Beneventan borrowings of Milanese melodies. And in these cases the process of adaptation to Beneventan norms is so carefully wrought that it is difficult, without additional information, to separate local from adopted chant.

Until now, we have not discussed the Ambrosian music in south Italian office books. Two feasts of particular importance in the rite of Milan have proper offices at Benevento: Saint Apollinaris, bishop of Ravenna, and Saints Nazarius and Celsus, whose remains were discovered in Milan by Saint Ambrose himself. In each case the Beneventan books provide substantial series of Milanese antiphons – antiphons which in some cases, at least, have been converted to Beneventan style.[71]

The antiphons for Saint Apollinaris (23 July) in Benevento 21 are essentially in two series, one Ambrosian and the other Beneventan, as seen in table 5.2.[72] All the antiphons for lauds and vespers are Ambrosian. That is, they are found in Ambrosian antiphoners, and in many

---

[71] One further example of a Beneventan–Milanese relationship in the office should be mentioned for the sake of completeness: this is the antiphon *Usque in senectam*, an antiphon for St Xistus in Ben20 and Ben21 found also at Milan, and with a similar melody. See Appendix 2.

[72] The antiphons of Benevento 66, an *ordo officii* of the twelfth century, are exactly those of Benevento 21.

Table 5.2 *Antiphons of Saint Apollinaris*

Benevento 21		Benevento 20
ad noct.		ad noct.
Accipe spiritum sanctum	BEN	Accipe spiritum
Beatus Ap. super cecorum	BEN	Beatus Apollinaris super
vig. ii		
Beatus Apollinaris oravit	BEN	Beatus Apollinaris oravit
Ap. martyris festa recolimus	MIL	LEX DEI EIUS
ad can.		ad can.
Vere cognoscent	[BEN]	Vere cognoscent
		AP. MARTYRIS FESTA LAUDAMUS
ad laudes et v.		ad mat. laud. et v.
Beatus Petrus apostolus	MIL	Beatus Petrus
Ap. egregius antistes	MIL	Ap. egregius
Super cecorum oculos	MIL	Super *cecati*
Ap. martyr per unigenitum	MIL	Ap. martyr per unig.
Ap. martyris festa laudamus	MIL	Ap. mart. festa recolimus
B/M		B
O martyr domini Apollinaris	MIL	O martyr domini Ap.

cases their melodies are widely used in the Milanese rite for other antiphons. In the Muggiasca manuscript (pp. 242–6), and in Oxford, Bodleian, MS lat. liturg. a. 4 (ff. 163–165v) – two related fourteenth-century Ambrosian sources[73] whose office pieces for Saint Apollinaris are almost identical – these six antiphons of Benevento 21 are all present, though not in the Beneventan order. Apparently the Ambrosian series is selected and adjusted to the needs of the liturgy at Benevento, and the Ambrosian psalmody is not used. The Beneventan series of antiphons for matins, however, is based on texts not used at Milan.[74]

One antiphon, however (*Apollinaris martyris festa recolimus/laudamus*), appears in both series. In Benevento 21 the antiphon appears twice with the same Ambrosian melody: first, among the Beneventan antiphons with the word *recolimus*, and later, with *laudamus*, in the Ambrosian series.[75] But Benevento 20 has both texts, and one antiphon is Beneventan, the other Ambrosian.[76]

The two versions of this text, *recolimus* for Milan and *laudamus* for Benevento, have become confused in Ben21. The displacement of the order in Ben20 also suggests that there is something special about this antiphon. At the place where *Apollinaris martyris* appears in the other manuscript, Ben20 substitutes the antiphon *Lex dei eius* (CAO 3611) – a piece, evidently not

---

[73] On these sources see Huglo, *Fonti*, nos. 62–4.

[74] The Ambrosian tradition itself is not of exemplary purity, since the antiphon *O martyr domini*, which appears in both manuscripts and at Benevento, is in fact a relative of the Gregorian O-antiphons of Advent.

[75] This same double transmission is apparently present in Benevento 66 also, and in the twelfth-century Santa Sofia ordinal Vatican, MS Vat. lat. 4928 (they indicate that the antiphons, cued only, are in the seventh mode, true only for the Ambrosian melody).

[76] Example 5.14D below; the Beneventan version of this antiphon unfortunately is partly illegible in Benevento 20. The Ambrosian antiphon is a version of the melody in example 5.14A.

from the Beneventan repertory, used in Ben21 also for Saints Xistus and Germanus of Capua (both local saints, with Gregorian music) – and places *Apollinaris martyris* at the end. So it appears that Ben21 really represents two pure series: Ambrosian antiphons for the day office, and Beneventan for the night, but similarity of text allowed the Beneventan version of *Apollinaris martyris festa laudamus* to drop out.

A similar confrontation of the Ambrosian and the Beneventan tradition is found in the office of Saints Nazarius and Celsus[77] (28 July; see table 5.3). The final antiphon of Ben21, for the canticles of lauds and vespers, is a substantial piece in clear Beneventan style. This antiphon also closes the series in Ben20.[78] The other antiphons in Ben21, except for the two with question marks, are Ambrosian,[79] but not used in the Ambrosian order, nor with Ambrosian psalmody. And, unlike the two series, Ambrosian and Beneventan, for Saint Apollinaris in Ben21, the music here is almost entirely Ambrosian, except for the final antiphon.

Table 5.3 *Antiphons of Saint Nazarius*

Benevento 21		Benevento 20	
ad M. et cant. et ad tert.			
Apparuit thesaurus	MIL		
ad noct.			
DEMONSTRA MIHI	MIL		
Religio matris	MIL		
vig. ii			
Annuit deus	MIL		
Incompositi iudices	MIL		
ad laud. et vesp.		ad laud. et vesp.	
Turbati sunt naute	MIL	DEMONSTRA MIHI	BEN
SANCTE VIR DEI	MIL	ACCESSIT NAZ.	BEN
Sancte Naz. vir dei	?	TURBATI SUNT	BEN?
Benedicimus te	MIL	Sanct Naz. vir dei	? (=Ben21)
Justi et sancti	?	SANCTE VIR DEI	BEN
M/B		ad B.	
BEATUS NAZ. UNA CUM	BEN	BEATUS NAZ. UNA	BEN

This final antiphon probably comes from an earlier stage in the relationship of Milan to Benevento. Perhaps it was already present at Benevento as a communion: there are other Beneventan office pieces with similar style and placement. When a full office was sought for Nazarius at some later time, it was not necessary to adapt a piece which already existed in the repertory, and which in fact shared the sort of melodic relationship to a common original we have already discussed. This antiphon does have a melodic mate at Milan (see the comparison in example 5.12), but the relationship does not suggest a recent borrowing from the Ambrosian liturgy. It is true that the Beneventan antiphon does not sit well at its present pitch, unless

[77] Benevento 21 does not include Celsus in the naming of the feast.
[78] It is also the final antiphon in Benevento 66: see Kelly, "Non-Gregorian music."
[79] Muggiasca, San Lorenzo, MS without shelf-number, pp. 249–59; Oxford, Bodleian, lat. liturg. a. 4, ff. 166–71.

Ex. 5.12   Versions of *Beatus Nazarius*

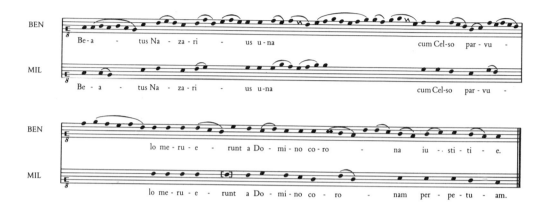

Legend:

BEN: Ben21/213 (plate 10; compare plate 6)
MIL: Oxf. Bodl. lat. lit. a.4/173v

B-flat is used throughout; its original pitch was probably on A. However, the remaining music in Ben21 does represent a wholesale borrowing of Ambrosian music to make a fuller office for an Ambrosian saint.

Ben20, however, gives this Ambrosian music a Beneventan dress; it presents a shorter proper of six antiphons, all but one of them known from Ben21[80] – or rather, their texts are known, but their melodies in several cases are Beneventan, where those of Ben21 were Ambrosian. In addition, the final Beneventan antiphon from Ben21, and a new Beneventan antiphon, *Accessit Nazarius* (on a text not duplicated in Milan), give this series a clearly non-Ambrosian flavor. One further antiphon (*Turbati sunt*) varies from Ben21 – though the version here is not distinctly Beneventan. And so, only one antiphon, *Sancte vir Dei*, retains the same melody as in Ben21,[81] and this one is not found in the Ambrosian office.

The antiphons which we know in both Ambrosian and Beneventan guise are versions of the same basic melody, presented in one or another style. But in this case the melodic original has surely come from Milan, and at a relatively recent date. Example 5.13 shows versions of *Sancte vir Dei*. Ben21 clearly had access to the Ambrosian office: its antiphon matches Muggiasca very closely. But the scribe of Ben20 has made the melodic shape a Beneventan one, with some melodic elaboration, a few specifically local turns of phrase, and a clear-cut Beneventan cadence (compare example 4.27).

[80] *Accessit Nazarius*, not used in Ben21, is indicated as the first antiphon for matins in the ordinal Benevento 66.
[81] While Ben21 presents an Ambrosian office and Ben20 a shorter Beneventan series, the ordinal Benevento 66 is a sort of middle ground mixing the two styles: evidently several of the Beneventan antiphons of Ben20 are included, though we cannot know which version of *Turbati sunt* is intended. See Kelly, "Non-Gregorian music."

Ex. 5.13   Versions of *Sancte vir Dei*

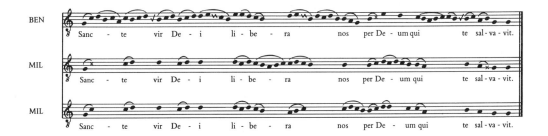

Legend:

BEN: Ben20/236 (plate 6)
MIL: Ben21/213 (plate 10)
MIL: Muggiasca/249

Example 5.14 shows, among other things, various versions of *Demonstra mihi*. In this latter case, though the Ambrosian and Beneventan melodies are clearly parallel, the Beneventan version shares its melody with other antiphons in the Beneventan repertory. The scribe of Ben21 transcribes faithfully (5.14B) the melody of the Ambrosian office (5.14A). The version of Ben20 (5.14C) follows the same melodic contours, but adapts them to Beneventan style in what appears to be the same manner as the previous example. But the situation is complicated here by the fact that the "new" Beneventan version of *Demonstra mihi* turns out to share a melodic shape with a number of other Beneventan antiphons (examples 5.14D, 5.14E).[82]

The Ambrosian melody, too, is representative of an Ambrosian melody-type (it is the model, for example, of the Ambrosian version of *Apollinaris martyris*). The fact that both versions, Beneventan and Ambrosian, belong strongly to their own repertories would seem to argue against any recent remodeling, were it not for the presence of the Ambrosian versions in the Beneventan manuscripts themselves. It is possible, of course, that the scribe of Ben21 has simply substituted an Ambrosian version wherever he could find one, but then why not substitute the Ambrosian version of *Beatus Nazarius* as well?

More likely is that there is in these offices a second and later encounter of Beneventan and Ambrosian; one which involves direct borrowing from Milan, but with a readaptation, in Ben20, of the Nazarius office in such a way that its antiphons not only ape the original Beneventan style, but in fact match the older style so closely that we cannot tell the newer adaptations from related melodies which have evolved over a long time.

And so the relation of these two musical repertories comes full circle. After growing apart from a substantial body of common material, adapting and changing music over several centu-

---

[82] Example 5.14E, *Dum sanctificatus*, is a Lenten scrutiny antiphon found among the Gregorian music of Benevento 38. See PM XIV, 243–8.

Ex. 5.14   Milanese and Beneventan antiphons

Legend:

A   Muggiasca/251
B   Ben21/212v (plate 9)
C   Ben20/236 (plate 6)
D   Ben20/226 (plate 5)
E   Ben38/21

ries, the two now distinct repertories confront each other in the eleventh century. For this seeking out of Ambrosian originals at Benevento, of course, is like the research conducted at Montecassino which resulted in the copying of the Ambrosian flyleaf of Vatican Ottoboni 3. In both places the indigenous chant was threatened, in both places there was a tradition of calling the local music "Ambrosian", and in both places there was an ancient memory of a common heritage which we are only now beginning to rediscover.

BYZANTINE CHANT

Backgrounds

Byzantine influence in the Beneventan manuscripts is evident in several ways: there are seven chants in Greek, some Beneventan texts are translations from the Byzantine liturgy, and many of the non-biblical chant texts have a "Byzantine flavor" in their poetical development and the personal nature of their language. Other elements that may be identified with Byzantine influence include Byzantine saints in the Beneventan calendar: St Michael, the great Lombard patron, St Mercurius, St Elijah.[83] And the presence of an *oratio post evangelium* in some Beneventan manuscripts has been seen as an Eastern symptom.[84]

Where do these influences come from? Although we know that southern Italy in the Middle Ages was in close contact – though not always amicable – with the Byzantine empire, it is not so easy to localize the nature of Greek influence in the Beneventan liturgy. Do these elements stem from a very early time when Greek, not Latin, was the liturgical language of the Western church? Are they created at home, or adapted from elsewhere in the West? Are they later accretions to the Beneventan liturgy from a time of pro-Byzantine sympathy? Even more basic, perhaps, is the question of whether we can consider these Greek influences as a single phenomenon, since they appear in various guises: Greek texts, Greek translations, and "Byzantine-style" liturgical texts.

We have seen in the historical sketch in Chapter 1 that the political interests of the Byzantine empire throughout the Middle Ages were opposed to those of the Lombards; southern Italy is viewed as an imperial dominion, and long-term imperial policy is always to subjugate or remove the Lombard invaders. From the Lombard point of view, however, the Byzantine empire is one of several powers that must be kept in balance: Lombard rulers are now allied, now opposed, to the empire, depending on how they saw the need to keep themselves independent from the Franks and from each other.

But we can be sure that Byzantine culture and art continued to be admired and emulated, from the time of Arichis II with his quasi-Byzantine court ceremonial to the substantial importation of Byzantine craftsmen under Desiderius at Montecassino.[85] The influence of Greek

---

[83] See above, pp. 11–12, 71–2 and n. 46.
[84] See Dold, *Die Zürcher*, pp. XXXI–XXXIII; and Martelli, "I formulari," esp. pp. 570–1. See also above, p. 65.
[85] Bloch, MMA, I, 40–71, and "Montecassino, Byzantium," pp. 193–218.

writing on the Beneventan script has been argued by several scholars,[86] as has the influence of Byzantine art on book-decoration painting, and other arts.[87] It is perhaps representative of these continuing currents that one of our sources of Beneventan chant, Wolfenbüttel 112, was erased in favor of a Greek liturgical text.[88]

Byzantine culture was clearly a reality in southern Italy, while Byzantine power, at least in the Beneventan region, was only occasionally present. It is remarkable how often a deposed duke flees to Constantinople; how gladly a Lombard prince accepts imperial titles; and how freely Byzantine styles and customs are imitated.

Greek influence on the church in southern Italy

For the church, the situation is deeper than politics. Greek was the language of the liturgy in Italy for the first three Christian centuries, and we know it was used at Rome up until the fourth century.[89] From the early history of monasticism in southern Italy, the honor and the influence of the East can be felt. St Benedict himself, in the Rule, recommends the rule of St Basil as worthy of study,[90] and indeed the rule of St Basil is found in almost all medieval monastic libraries, including Montecassino, in versions of Rufinus and others.[91] Peter the Deacon reports in his *Liber miraculorum monachorum Casinensium* the honored visit of St Basil and his Greek monks to St Benedict and his community.[92]

The liturgical use of Greek at Montecassino is documented in later centuries as well, albeit for special occasions. The Chronicle, describing ceremonies of Easter Tuesday in the mid-ninth century, mentions the singing of the mass *Venite benedicti* "cum cantu promiscuo, Grego videlicet atque Latino."[93]

Indeed, Montecassino had a tradition of singing in Greek, at least on this day, that may go back to the refounding of the abbey by Petronax of Brescia in 717 or 718. The Chronicle's source for the passage just cited is a ninth-century *ordo* from Montecassino MS 175 which describes this feast ("feria tertia in Albis quando monachis maior est festivitas")[94] in greater detail: the monks from the summit of Montecassino went in solemn procession, with cross, candles, and relics, to meet the brothers of San Salvatore below; the two choirs, joining, proceeded to the church of St Peter, where, after Tierce, the mass *Venite benedicti* was sung with music in Greek.[95]

---

[86] Most recently in Pratesi, "Influenze."

[87] See Bertaux, *L'Art dans l'Italie méridionale*, pp. 115–53; Guillou, in *Aggiornamento*, ɪ v, 293–301; and Toubert, "Le bréviaire."

[88] It is, in fact, a double palimpsest, both upper scripts being in Greek: see Dold, "Untersuchungsergebnisse"; on Greek-Latin relations as seen in manuscript production, see Cavallo, "Manoscritti"; Devreesse, *Les Manuscrits*.

[89] See Brou, "Les chants"; Bardy, "Formules liturgiques"; Klauser, "Der Übergang"; and Morin, "Formules liturgiques."

[90] "Necnon et Collationes Patrum et Instituta et Vitas eorum, sed et Regula sancti Patris nostri Basilii, quid aliud sunt nisi bene viventium oboedientium monachorum instrumenta virtutum?" de Vogüé, *La Règle*, ɪɪ, 672–4.

[91] See, for example, Montecassino MS 443, late eleventh century.

[92] See Inguanez, "Due frammenti"; and von Falkenhausen, "Il monachesimo," pp. 119–20.

[93] Chron. mon. cas., ɪ, 32.

[94] *Ordo casinensis II dictus ordo officii*, ed. Tommaso Leccisotti, in Hallinger, *Corpus consuetudinum*, ɪ, p. 119.

[95] "Inde incipiunt missam: Introitus *Venite benedicti patris mei* et lectio quae in feria sexta; item tonus *Alleluia*; psalmus tuus [probably a misreading of an exemplar that read 'ʟxxɪ' or 'cɪɪɪ'] David; responsorium; *Proscomaen*; in gradu *Alleluia*; versus *Caeli enarrant gloriam dei*; versus *Expectans expectavi dominum*. Et ipsi versi plani in grecu." Leccisotti, *Ordo casinensis II*, p. 120. On the ceremonial of this day, see Citarella, *The Ninth-Century Treasure*, pp. 111–16.

An anonymous – and not very literate – monk of the eleventh century has left an indication that this Greek tradition was known in his day, and adds that it goes back to the time of Petronax: "In the same tower of St Benedict every year on a portable altar a service was performed in Greek and Latin as Abbot Petronax ordained."[96] We have no further evidence that Petronax celebrated St Benedict in Greek and Latin. But two letters from the late eighth-century Abbot Theodemar suggest, at least, that this special rite of Easter Tuesday was celebrated, in some form, in his time.[97] Theodemar does not say that such ceremonies included Greek, nor that the tradition goes back to Petronax, but there is some tradition of Greek on this day, and the special nature of this Easter Tuesday can be traced at least to the eighth century.

The visit of St Nilus of Rossano to Montecassino in about 980 gives more evidence of the esteem in which at least one famous Greek monk was held.[98] He was received by the monks of Montecassino in procession at the bottom of their mountain, and invited to preside in Greek at the office; he used the hymns which he had composed in honor of St Benedict. St Nilus, with sixty companions, remained in a nearby monastery given him by Abbot Aligern until his break with the worldly Abbot Manso sometime after 985.

The use of bilingual singing is attested, too, in documents of the ninth and tenth centuries from the region of Naples. The translation of the remains of Bishop Anastasius from Naples to Montecassino in 877 occasioned bilingual singing: "In which the laity together with the clergy incessantly sing to God with common prayer in Greek and Latin, and together perform the due rites."[99] The transfer of the relics of Saint Severinus to a monastery named for him in Naples took place in 910, and there were similar incidents, of which one may represent liturgical singing: "and eagerly presenting their humble veneration with alternating Latin and Greek choirs they bore the holy ashes to the monastery of the well-known abbot with due solemnity and burning torches."[100] Another is perhaps more an indication of a heterogeneous population, though it is not without its interest in the estimation of the influence of Greek culture in the south: Now both sexes and all ages poured together and resounded songs of psalmody with sweet melody in either Greek or Latin as they could."[101]

That Greek culture and language were present, to some degree at least, in Lombard southern

[96] "In ipsa turre omni anno sci benedicti altare biariczo [=*viaritio*, portable?] faciebant officium greci et latini sicut praecepit petronax abbas." Montecassino, MS 175, p. 580, ed. in *Bibliotheca casinensis*, IV, Florilegium, p. 33. See also Schuster, "A proposito," pp. 66, 85–87; and Morin, "Pour la topographie", p. 480.

[97] Theodemar to "Theodoricum gloriosum" (778–97): "Tertia quoque feria [post Pascha], quia mos nobis est dies Quadragesimae apud sanctum Benedictum peragere, descendentes de monte veniunt fratres nostri, qui ad monasterium Domini Salvatoris in planicie commanent, cantando obviam nobis . . . et celebrata missa in sancto Petro imus sonoris concentibus resonando ad Domini Salvatoris coenobium." (Hallinger, *Corpus consuetudinum*, I, 130–1). Theodemar to Charlemagne (early ninth century): "In summis quoque festiuitatibus, hoc est in Natiuitate Domini, in Epyphania, in Pascha et tertia feria post Pascha, quando nobis grandis festiuitas est . . ." (Hallinger, *Corpus consuetudinum*, I, p. 164; this letter may date from the ninth century only, not the early ninth: see Hallinger, pp. 152–3).

[98] Life of St Nilus: PG, 120, cols. 123–6. See Gay, *L'Italie méridionale*, pp. 381–5; and Rousseau, "La Visite."

[99] "In qua layci simul cum clericis assidue Grecę Latineque communi prece psallunt Deo debitumque persolvunt iugiter officium" (MGH SS Lang., p. 440).

[100] ". . . et certatim supplicem exhibentes venerationem, alternantibus choris Latinis et Graecis, ad monasterium saepefati abbatis debito obsequio concinnatisque luminaribus cineres sanctos deducunt" (MGH SS Lang., p. 456).

[101] "Confluebant autem uterque sexus et aetas diversa, et qualiter poterant psalmodiae cantus utriusque linguarum Grecae et Latinae suavi modulatione resonabant" (MGH SS Lang., p. 451).

Italy in the period of the Beneventan chant seems certain. The extent to which the Byzantine liturgy itself penetrated the Latin liturgy of the area is less clear. Greek was sung at Montecassino and at Naples, but that the practice was still more widespread is suggested by the numbers of Greek monks and monasteries established in southern Italy by that time. It appears that there was a large influx of Greek monks in southern Italy in the eighth century, and Greek monasticism was never absent from Lombard territory thereafter.[102] It would be surprising, in fact, if this Greek presence did not make itself felt in the local Latin church.

Greek elements in the Beneventan liturgy

Greek elements in the Beneventan liturgy may be divided by their language: Latin translations of Greek originals, and original texts in Greek. Of the former type all the Western liturgies give ample evidence, and some of the Latin texts of the Beneventan liturgy, too, are related, more or less directly, to the Byzantine liturgy. An example is the Maundy Thursday gradual *Vadit propitiator*, which is the translation of part of a composition of Romanos. It is found, in a variety of liturgical settings, and with a number of melodies, in Ambrosian, Old Roman, and, only occasionally, Gregorian manuscripts.[103] The melodic transmission of the piece is complex, but the Beneventan version stands apart from the others textually, and its melody is characteristically Beneventan. This text, like many others, seems to represent the frequent practice of translating Greek texts for use in Western liturgy. Such texts at Benevento include some that are widely used in the West, and which bear a different melody in each tradition.[104] This is a widespread practice, dating in some cases from early in the history of the Latin rites.[105]

Other Beneventan chants, though no Greek source has been found for them, have such agreement of language and style that some Greek inspiration may be inferred. Among the non-biblical chants in the Beneventan liturgy are many texts commenting on scriptural situations in poetical and personal language.[106] Though, as yet, these are not identified as being

---

[102] Vasiliev, *Histoire de l'empire byzantin*, I, 348, says that some fifty thousand Greek monks had found refuge in southern Italy between 726 and 775. However exaggerated this figure seems, Lenormant, *La Grande-Grèce*, II, 387, says that there were a thousand Greek monks in the province of Bari by 733. On later Greek monastic establishments in southern Italy, see Gay, *L'Italie méridionale*, pp. 376-86; von Falkenhausen, "Il monachesimo"; Borsari, "Monasteri bizantini"; Ménager, "La Byzantinisation"; and Feine, "Studien", pp. 95-105. For a general discussion of Byzantine political influence see von Falkenhausen, *Untersuchungen*.

[103] See Appendix 2; Hesbert, "L'antiphonale" (4), pp. 73-8; PM XIV, 277-83; PM V, 6-9, 25-7; Drumbl, "Gli improperi," p. 80 Mezei, "Das Responsorium."

[104] An example is *Hodie christus natus est*: see Wellesz, *Eastern Elements*, pp. 141-9; and Baumstark, "Byzantinisches", p. 169.

[105] Kenneth Levy has been concerned for some years with relations of Byzantium to the West, and in a series of important articles has dealt with elements of the Beneventan liturgy in their relation to the East (see the Bibliography). We should not proceed without referring the reader, in particular, to his study of a complex of Italian music for initiation rites ("The Italian neophytes' chants") in which he is concerned with (among much else) the possibility that the two pitches for verses of the Beneventan Alleluia *Resurrexit* may be related to the Byzantine modal change between Holy Saturday and Easter (see esp. p. 196). Important also is his discussion of the possible relation of the Beneventan offertory *Omnes qui in christo* to a wider complex of neophytes' chants. In "The Byzantine Sanctus" (pp. 50-1) Levy discusses the possible relation of the Beneventan dismissal "Si quis catechuminus est" to a Byzantine melody.

[106] Such pieces include the following (full texts may be seen in Appendix 2): *Amicus meus*, *Gaudent in celis*, *Hodie exultat celum*, *Lavi pedes*, *Lumen quod animus*, *Quis te supplantavit*, and *Sancta Maria exora* – of particular interest are the groups of texts for All Saints, St Michael, and the Holy Cross.

derived directly from elements of Eastern liturgy, they are inspired to some degree by the Byzantine style.

The Greek language itself is used in the Beneventan rite for Holy Week, and these pieces may be divided into five elements:[107]

1 The antiphons *Otin ton stauron/O quando in cruce*, used for the adoration of the cross
2 A group of three bilingual antiphons, also used for the adoration: *Proskynumen/Adoramus, Ton stauron/Crucem tuam*, and *Enumen se/Laudamus*
3 The antiphons *Panta ta etni/Omnes gentes*, used for the second adoration at Benevento
4 The antiphons *Doxa en ipsistis/Gloria in excelsis* for Holy Saturday
5 The Greek sticheron *Pascha ieron*, appearing only in Ben40 at the end of the Easter mass

These pieces appear in the manuscripts as in table 5.4, and will be discussed in order.

1 The bilingual antiphon *O quando in cruce*, though it is transmitted in southern Italy is, like the *Trisagion*, not a part of the older corpus of the Beneventan liturgy. It is neither included in our oldest sources (Vat. 10673 and Ben33), nor mentioned in the *ordo* of Vat. 10673, and the variety of its placement in Beneventan manuscripts suggests its relatively recent arrival.[108]

This piece has been discussed and transcribed by Hesbert, and is the subject of an extended study by Wellesz.[109] Its original is a Byzantine troparion, still in use, which can be traced to the seventh-century rite of Jerusalem.[110] Like the Greek/Latin antiphons for the adoration, *O quando in cruce* appears, not only in Beneventan books, but also in sources from northern Italy, including one connected with Ravenna (Modena, O. I. 7). Wellesz has argued that the "Ravenna" version of the Western melody is older than the Beneventan, basing his theory both on the regularity of the Beneventan melody[111] and on the fact that the Beneventan version of the Greek melody (in Ben38) includes a melisma on μάννα which matches that on ὕδατος, but this parallelism is not matched in Modena, or in the Byzantine original (nor, for that matter, in the Beneventan Latin versions). Benevento, for Wellesz, has created a parallel that did not originally exist, and its version is a revision of a received original that lacked it.[112] Wellesz

[107] The *Trisagion*, now used in the Roman Good Friday adoration of the cross, is also found in some Beneventan manuscripts (Vat. 10673, Ben40, Ben33, Ben34, Ben35, Ben39, Lucca 606, etc: see the tables in PM XIV, 296–7, 300–1), though not among pieces from the Beneventan liturgy. It is a hymn of great antiquity in the East, and is widely used in the West, though it does not appear in the earliest Gregorian manuscripts. Its Eastern importation evidently does not come through Benevento; rather, it must have appeared at Benevento in company with the imported Gregorian repertory (see Brou, "Les chants," p. 171 and n. 1; Wellesz, *Eastern Elements*, pp. 20–1; and Drumbl, "Gli improperi," p. 87). But its combination with the *improperia* and its subsequent adoption into the modern Roman liturgy are connected with Benevento: see Drumbl, "Die Improperien."

[108] Details of this placement for southern Italian manuscripts can be found in the tables in PM XIV, 296–7, 300–1. Levy, "The Italian neophytes' chants," p. 209 n. 59, notes the appearance of this piece also in Pistoia, Biblioteca capitolare, MS C. 120, f. 67, in Latin and only partly noted.

[109] PM XIV, 305–8; Wellesz, *Eastern Elements*, pp. 68–77.

[110] It is the eighth of twelve troparia in the twelfth-century Typicon of Jerusalem (Papadopoulos-Kerameus, Ἀνάλεκτα, p. 153), and it appears in a Georgian version of a Kanonarium composed in seventh-century Jerusalem (see Baumstark and Klüge, "Quadragesima," p. 227, and Thibaut, *Ordre*, p. 99); these versions are compared in Thibaut, *Ordre*. On the attribution of these troparia to St Sophronios of Jerusalem (634–8), see Baumstark and Kluge, "Quadragesima," p. 205; Thibaut, *Ordre*, pp. 9–10. Also see PM XIV, 306–7; and Wellesz, *Eastern Elements*, pp. 21–2.

[111] "It seems that Codex Mod. represents the original version and Codex Benevent. a later adaptation; for we know from examples in Plainchant that absolute regularity in the structure of melodic phrases is always a sign of a later revision of melodies which formerly showed a greater variety" (*Eastern Elements*, p. 76).

[112] See transcriptions in PM XIV, 306–7; and Wellesz, *Eastern Elements*, pp. 105–8.

Table 5.4 Greek music manuscripts* in Beneventan manuscripts

	Ben40	Ben38	10673	Ben33	Ben35	1.606	4770	Ben39	Ben34	Oxf	Mod	Pad	c 52	Cas	s 62
Otin/O quando	L				L	L	G	L			G				
Proskynumen/Adoramus	GL	[ ]	GL	L	L	L	L			L	GL	GL	L	L	L
Ton stauron/Crucem	GL	[ ]	GL	L	L	L	L			L				L	
Enumen se/Laudamus	GL	[ ]	GL	L	L	L	L			L	GL	GL	L		
Panta/Omnes	GL	[ ]	GL	L	L	L	L	GL	GL						
Doxa/Gloria	GL	GL	[plus Vat. 10657, Farfa]						GL						
Pascha ieron	G														

* The following manuscript abbreviations are used:
Oxf   Oxford, Bodl., Can. lit. 321; Ravenna, twelfth century
Mod   Modena, Bibl. cap., MS o. i. 7, Ravenna, twelfth century
Pad   Padova, Bibl. cap, MS A 47, Ravenna
c 52   Rome, Bibl. Vallicelliana, MS C 52, Ravenna
Cas   Rome, Bibl. Casanat., MS 1741, Nonantola
s 62   Rome, Biblioteca nazionale, MS Sessorianus 62, Nonantola

may be right in this case, and there are further connections with Ravenna to be seen shortly. For our purposes, though, it may suffice to say that *O quando in cruce* was not a part of the old Beneventan liturgy, to judge from its musical style, its irregular placement, and its omission from the Good Friday *ordo*.

2 The three bilingual antiphons for the adoration of the cross on Good Friday are attested in the earliest Beneventan musical manuscripts,[113] and are called for in the *ordo* of Vat. 10673 as an element of the old Beneventan rite. The picture is complicated, however, by several factors: one of these pieces has a counterpart in the Byzantine liturgy, and other versions of it are used in the Gregorian and Old Roman rites; all three are used also at Milan; and there is another tradition using two of these texts at Ravenna. (The Beneventan and Milanese antiphons have been compared in example 5.11.)

The second antiphon at Benevento, *Crucem tuam*, is derived from the Greek church, and versions of it are found in the Ambrosian, Gregorian, and Old Roman rites as well (see table 5.5). But the Byzantine liturgy has two related chants, a longer one for Easter,[114] and a shorter one now used for the Sunday of the Cross in Lent and for the Exaltation of the Cross on September 14.[115] Evidently the longer text (Greek I) is the source for both the Gregorian and Old Roman versions, which use *laudamus et glorificamus* and which adapt section three of the Greek text in slightly different ways. The shorter Greek text parallels the Ambrosian version exactly, including the single verb of praise *glorificamus*. The Beneventan text follows the first two sections of the longer Greek version, but it, too, has the single δοξάζωμεν / *glorificamus* of the other Greek text and omits δι πιστοὶ both from the Greek and from the Latin translation. Clearly, several Greek originals have received a variety of translation in different rites. It is not possible to establish a clear melodic relation between the Western melodies and either of the surviving melismatic Greek melodies,[116] which in any case are substantially later than our Beneventan documents.

The other two Greek/Latin antiphons of the Beneventan adoration have, so far as we know, no original in the surviving Byzantine liturgy. But they are not unique to Benevento. In addition to their use at Milan in Latin versions, they are found together as a single antiphon in a few Italian manuscripts (including some from Ravenna), sometimes with a Greek version

---

[113] They are not present in Ben38 but may have appeared in the portion now lost after folio 11. For the Beneventan sources, see Appendix 1. They are also called for in an early *ordo* of Montecassino (MS 175, p. 587; printed in *Bibliotheca Casinensis*, IV, Florilegium, pp. 33–4). Among the Beneventan sources for the antiphons should be included Vat. lat. 4770. Though it is not from Benevento and lacks musical notation, the texts are clearly Beneventan, and the psalms specified for the antiphons match those of Beneventan sources. Related to Vat. lat. 4770 is the central Italian manuscript Vatican, Barb. lat. 560, an early eleventh-century missal whose rubrics for Holy Week have been erased and revised, but the three adoration antiphons survive the revision: "Quibus expletis dicatur ymnus *Crux fidelis* et ant. *Adoramus. Crucem tuam. Laudamus*" (f. 47v).

[114] This is Greek Text I in table 5.5. It is found in the Πεντηκοστάριον (Rome, 1887), p. 17, and in the Ὡρολόγιον τὸ μέγα (Rome, 1876), pp. 227–8; see Follieri, *Initia*, I, 103, under Ἀνάστασιν Χριστοῦ Θεασάμενοι, but note that there are two different chants beginning with these words.

[115] Found in the Τριῴδιον, p. 362, and elsewhere. See Follieri, *Initia*, IV, 233.

[116] Published transcriptions of the shorter text from the Byzantine liturgy can be found in Dragoumis, "The Survival," p. 21, from Athens, National library, MS 899, along with a neo-Byzantine version of the melody; and in Moran, *The Ordinary*, II, 73–80, from Mt Athos MS Lavra Γ. 3. Huglo ("Relations musicales," p. 278) notes that the Milanese intonation is similar to that of the first Greek melody in Mt Athos MS Lavra I. 185.

Table 5.5 *Versions of Crucem tuam*

Greek I	Greek II	Beneventan/Gk	Beneventan/Lat	Milan	Greg.	Old-Roman
Ἀνάστασιν Χριστοῦ θεασάμενοι προσκυνήσομεν ἅγιον Κύριον, Ἰησοῦν τὸν μόνον ἀναμάρτητον.						
1. Τὸν Σταυρόν σου, Χριστέ, προσκυνοῦμεν, καὶ τὴν ἁγίαν σου Ἀνάστασιν ὑμνοῦμεν καὶ σοξάζομεν	Τὸν σταυρόν σου προσκυνοῦμεν, Δέσποτα, καὶ τὴν ἁγίαν σου ἀνάστασιν δοξάζομεν.	Ton stauron sou proskynumen kyrie ke tin agian su anastasin doxazome deute pantes	Crucem tuam adoramus domine et sanctam resurrectionem tuam glorificamus venite omnes	Crucem tuam adoramus domine et sanctam resurrectionem tuam glorificamus	Crucem tuam adoramus domine et sanctam resurrectionem tuam laudamus et glorificamus	Crucem tuam adoramus domine et sanctam resurrectionem tuam laudamus et glorificamus
2. Δεῦτε, πάντες οἱ πιστοί, προσκυνήσομεν τὴν τοῦ Χριστοῦ ἁγίαν Ἀνάστασιν· ἰδοῦ γὰρ ἦλθε διὰ τοῦ σταυροῦ χαρὰ ἐν ὅλῳ τῷ κόσμῳ		proskynisumen tin tu xpistu anastasin	adoremus xpisti resurrectionem		ecce enim propter lignum venit gaudium in universo mundo.	quia venit salus in universo mundo.

Sources Greek I: Πεντηκοστάριον, p. 17.
Greek II: Τριῴδιον, p. 362.
Beneventan: Ben40 (Vat. 10673 proskynumen (proskynisumen))
Milan: London, BL, Add. MS 34209, p. 248.
Gregorian: CAO 1953
Old Roman: Vat. lat. 5319, f. 80.

as well.[117] And the first antiphon (*Adoramus crucem tuam*) is found in two manuscripts of Nonantola.[118]

The three antiphons are transmitted in the following order:

BENEVENTO	MILAN	RAVENNA	RAVENNA (Oxford)
1 Adoramus	2 Crucem	2 Crucem (GREG)	2 Crucem (GREG)
2 Crucem	1 Adoramus	1 Adoramus [+	1 Adoramus [+
3 Laudamus	3 Laudamus	3 Laudamus]	3 Laudamus]
			2 Crucem

We have seen that the Ambrosian series, though it is only preserved in Latin, and though its order is rearranged, is close, musically and textually, to the Beneventan antiphons, and that the series is used in a similar way for a double adoration on Good Friday. Despite their close relationship, however, the Ambrosian series has undergone its own development. Presumably the antiphons were once in use at Milan in Greek: one of the antiphons (*Crucem tuam*) is based on the shorter Greek original not used at Benevento. Drumbl's suggestion that the longer text was originally present, but was abbreviated at the point where it conflicted with the Gregorian version,[119] is reasonable, but a simpler solution is that Milan uses a Latin translation of a shorter Greek original (which, unlike the Gregorian version, has only *glorificamus* instead of *laudamus et glorificamus*).

The Ravenna tradition transmits the two antiphons for which no Byzantine original is known (1 and 3) as a single piece, changing *Laudamus* to a second *Adoramus* which parallels the local Greek text. However, the central antiphon (*Crucem tuam*) is not missing: it immediately precedes the combined "Greek" antiphon, but with the "Gregorian" text and its melody (concluding "ecce enim propter lignum venit salus in universo mundo," see table 5.5). But here, these three (or, at Ravenna, two) antiphons are not transmitted as a single series as at Benevento and Milan; the Ravenna manuscripts preserve a Greek version for the combined antiphons 1 and 3, but not for the preceding *Crucem tuam*. However, one Ravenna manuscript, Oxford 321, has both versions of *Crucem tuam*, the Beneventan version (with essentially the Beneventan melody) following the combined antiphon.

The Ravenna combination of antiphons 1 and 3 is based on a Greek original somewhat different from that of Benevento, and the resulting Latin translations reflect the differences in the original Greek (see table 5.6). Both versions make perfect, though different, sense in Greek: for the first antiphon, the Beneventan Greek might be translated: "We adore your cross, and the sign of your cross, and the power of the crucified one." The Ravenna Greek text, a somewhat

[117] Padua, Biblioteca capitolare, MS A 47, f. 126, and Modena, Biblioteca capitolare, MS O. I. 7, f. 97v, provide Greek and Latin texts; Oxford, Bodleian Library, MS Can. liturg. 321, f. 66, New York, Morgan M. 379, and Rome, Biblioteca Vallicelliana, MS C 52, f. 153, have Latin only.

[118] Rome, Biblioteca Casanatense, MS 1741, f. 152 (facs. in Vecchi, *Troparium*), and Rome, Biblioteca nazionale, MS Sessorianus 62. The melodies of the Ravenna and Nonantola antiphons (see Drumbl, "Zweisprachige Antiphonen," p. 50), though substantially simpler than the more elaborate Beneventan melodies, cannot be said to be unrelated, and a Greek melody linking all these Latin versions is not inconceivable.

[119] Drumbl, "Zweisprachige Antiphonen," p. 47.

Table 5.6 *Greek transliterations compared*

Benevento (Vat. 10673)	Ravenna (Modena O. I. 7)
Proskynumen ton	Prositnomen tu
stauron su	stauru¹ su
ke ton tipon	ke tu tipu
tus¹ stauru su:	tu stauron su
ke ton	ke tu
staurothentos	stauronthenta²
tin dinamin.	en dinami
Enumen se xpiste	prositnumen se xpiste
ke ymnologumen² se	ke ymmoympomen³ si
oti dia tu³ stauru	oti cia tu stauron su
exigorasas	elitroti
ton cosmon	tu cosmu

¹ tu: Ben40	¹ stauron: Pad. A 47
² imnologume: Ben40	² staurontenta: Pad. A 47
³ tus: Ben40	³ ymoypomen: Pad. A 47

more obscure transliteration, varies from the Beneventan version at its close:[120] "We adore your cross, and the sign of your cross, and him who was crucified in (by reason of) his power."

Though the versions are different, they both make sense. The difficulty comes in the Latin translation. In both, the locution "et signum de cruce tua" (or "crucem tuam") is awkward, but its purpose is, I think, clear, as Hesbert thought fifty years ago: in order to preserve the word order of the Greek in a text designed to receive identical music, it presents precisely the same number of syllables with the ideas in the same order.[121] Likewise the closing phrase of the first antiphon in both versions is curious. On the one hand, Benevento presents "et qui crucifixus est virtutum" (3 MSS), or *virtute* (Lucca 606) or *virtutem* (Ben35). This is awkward Latin, and perhaps what is meant is "et eius qui crucifixus est virtutem": "and [we praise] the power of him who was crucified" (a translation of the Greek text). Here the *eius* is left understood, and the accusative form of *virtus* is not the standard one. But the intention is clear: the number of syllables is precisely the same, and the word order is generally preserved, despite the difficulty of translating the aorist passive participle.

The Ravenna version translates its Greek differently, and no more smoothly than the Beneventan. The Latin text generally reads "et qui crucifixus est [or *es*, Padua, A 47, Vall. C 52] *in virtute*." Here, the Greek version seems to be τὸν σταυρωθέντα [an accusative, as compared to the Beneventan gentitive] ἐν δύναμι: "and [we adore] the crucified in (by reason of) his power." The Greek here is logical, but the Latin is awkward. The Greek accusative is replaced in Latin by *qui crucifixus est* – not an accusative, but perhaps including an understood *te* (or *eum*).

[120] If we can assume that *prositnomen* represents προσκυνοῦμεν, and that *tu tipu* may represent τὸν τύπον.
[121] For Hesbert's studies of these antiphons, see PM XIV, 309–13; and "L'antiphonale" (5), 104–16.

In view of the clarity of both Greek versions, and the equal infelicities of their Latin translations, I see no compelling reason to assign a priority to Ravenna, despite the fascinating evidence that the learned Johanicis performed composition and translation services at Ravenna in the seventh century.[122] Though Ravenna's participation in this tradition of bilingual adoration may be very old indeed (and there is every reason to believe that Ravenna's connections with the Byzantine East were early and strong), the surviving sources are later in date and somewhat confused in transmission. What seems clear is that, as with the antiphon *Ton stauron/Crucem tuam*, there is a variety of received Greek versions, which are translated into Latin in a variety of ways.

That Greek texts lie at the origin of these pieces seems the clearest explanation, both of the curious Latin translations, and of the discrepancies in transmission. Only one of these texts has been identified in the surviving Byzantine liturgy, but we cannot say that others did not exist. The source of these texts may well be an Eastern ceremony for the adoration of the cross, perhaps originally from the liturgy of Jerusalem. We know that such a ceremony was practiced at the third hour (that is, at terce, as in the Beneventan and Ambrosian rites) from very early times, though it was later suppressed in the Byzantine rite – which might account for the lack of Byzantine witnesses to two of the three antiphons.[123]

The ultimate origin in Italy of these three antiphons remains in doubt. That they came from Ravenna and were transmitted to Benevento and to Milan is difficult to reconcile with the close affinities between the latter, and with the threefold nature of the Milanese and Beneventan traditions. It may be that Ravenna's practice underwent substantial alteration. The presence of more than one version of *Crucem tuam* in Oxford 321 is indicative of multiple influences, and perhaps by the twelfth century Ravenna had rearranged the antiphons to cope with Gregorian influence, omitting the Beneventan doublet. The Greek source at Benevento may have been near to hand, among the many Greek settlements and monasteries of southern Italy; but that the original source was Ravenna, in a bilingual version, seems less likely. Perhaps a borrowed Byzantine melody served as a seed for the addition of more local products.

Far more needs to be known about these pieces before conclusions can be reached about their transmission in Italy. In particular, the widespread use of the many versions of *Crucem tuam* (all with related melodies) may one day provide an important clue about Byzantine influence

[122] Johann Drumbl has argued that, for these two antiphons, the Greek is the adaptation of a Latin original, and that they were composed, in Latin and Greek simultaneously, by a certain Johanicis the Grammarian in Ravenna in the year 711 ("Zweisprachige Antiphonen," p. 51). His argument is closely reasoned, based on the variants in the first antiphon, *Proskynumen/Adoramus*. The Beneventan version of the text, says Drumbl, though it may be older, is farther from the original than the group of later sources from Ravenna, two of which also transmit a Greek text. For Drumbl, the ablative *virtute* is surely the original reading, matched by the Ravennaic Greek *ke tu staurotenta en dinami* (Καὶ τὸν σταυρωθέντα ἐν δύναμι). Drumbl also suggests that the creator of this antiphon (and hence, presumably, of *Enumen se/Laudamus* as well) was much influenced by vernacular patterns when creating his Latin text: thus the use of *de cruce* for the genitive and the substitution of *qui crucifixus es* for the subject accusative. It is difficult, however, to be convinced that a writer of great repute, when asked by the bishop of Ravenna to provide antiphons in Greek and Latin (MGH SS Lang., p. 373: "Sapientissimus Iohanicis istius in temporibus claruit. Et rogatus a pontifice, ut omnes antiphonas, quas canimus modo dominicis diebus ad crucem sive sanctorum apostolorum aut martirum sive confessorum necnon et virginum, ipse exponeret non solum Latinis eloquiis, sed etiam Grecis verbis, quia in utraque lingua fuit maximus orator"), should produce such doubtful Latin. It is more likely that, as with the antiphon *Crucem tuam*, the Latin versions here derive from the Greek, and that they vary as the Greek texts themselves vary.

[123] Wellesz, *Eastern Elements*, pp. 19–20.

and transmission in Italy.[124] For the moment, we can conclude only that the source of these pieces is Greek, adapted to Latin in various places (sometimes only the Latin survives); that the three antiphons are not originally an entity, but were combined and recombined variously; and that at the heart of the matter, surely, is an ancient ceremony for the adoration of the cross, whose preservation, in one of its forms, is a central feature of the Beneventan liturgy for Good Friday.

3 The bilingual antiphon *Panta ta etni/Omnes gentes* (example 5.15) is used for Good Friday only in Beneventan manuscripts and in two (Lucca 606 and Vat. 4770) with close affinities to Beneventan Holy Week ceremonial. The piece is clearly a part of the Beneventan rite described in the Vatican *ordo*: it is sung three times in both languages at the end of the second adoration of the cross.[125] The text and its melody are, however, used widely in the West for other feasts. The Latin version is used in the Gregorian and Old Roman rites for Epiphany and at Milan for the dedication of the major church.[126]

The melody of this antiphon does not have a Beneventan aspect: it twice uses a cadence on B (or E as reported in Ben34 and Ben39) which resembles a psalmodic ending occasionally found in the Gregorian liturgy and which may be borrowed from Byzantine practice. (It is also similar to cadences in *O quando in cruce*.) The four-note syllabic cadence after recitation on B is identical in the two Greek appearances, but the Latin version alters both cadences, and there are occasional discrepancies between manuscripts. Evidently, the first Latin cadence (*adorabunt*) seeks to place the accent where the Greek accent is, but this results in leaving the recitation a note too late, with confusing results that miss the syllabic quality of the Greek melody; the second cadence (*coram te domine*) does not have enough syllables, and hence recitation and cadence are elided on the syllable *te*. It seems clear that the Greek version is the original, and that it is not composed in Beneventan style.

That a familiar psalm-verse should be widely used in Western rites is no surprise, but the melodic similarity in all versions denotes a common origin. The Greek versions of Benevento are likely derived from Byzantine liturgy rather than from some other Western rite, and although the other rites might have borrowed text and melody from Benevento (the adaptations of *adorabunt* and *coram te Domine* present similar problems), they might of course have borrowed directly from a Byzantine source and solved translation problems individually – at Milan, by discarding the old melody entirely.

4 Three Beneventan manuscripts contain a Greek/Latin antiphon *Doxa en ipsistis/Gloria in excelsis* for Holy Saturday. In Ben38 and Ben40 this serves for the procession returning to the altar after the baptismal rite; in the Farfa fragments this function is served by the antiphon *Transivimus per ignem et aquam*, specified in a rubric but not notated. The rubric is followed by the antiphon *Doxa/Gloria*, followed in turn by the Alleluia of the vigil mass. Possibly, the bilin-

---

[124] That this antiphon circulated in multiple versions is attested not only by Oxford 321; Oxford, Bodleian Library, MS Douce 222, f. 187, also contains side-by-side versions of the Gregorian and Old Roman texts, and Vat. lat. 4770, f. 91v, transmits both Beneventan and Old Roman (but without notation).

[125] "Finitis itaque psalmis: [i.e., the psalms accompanying the antiphons of the second adoration] ingrediantur chorum: euntes cantent ter antiphona grega seu latina. panta ta. alii romana. omnes gentes." (Vat. lat. 10673, f. 33v).

[126] See Appendix 2.

Ex. 5.15   Versions of *Panta ta etni/Omnes gentes*

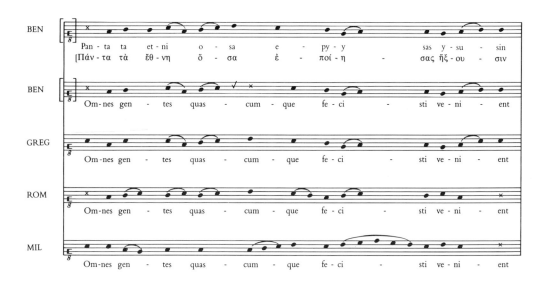

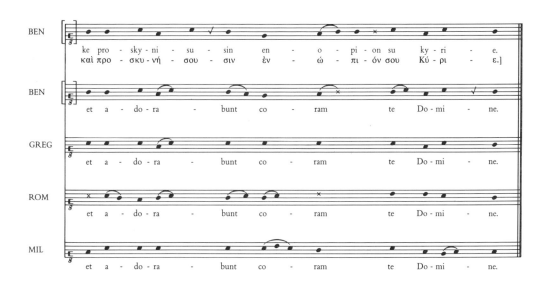

Legend:

BEN: Ben40/12v
BEN: Ben40/12v
GREG: Lucca 601/69
ROM: BL, Add 29988/35
MIL: Oxf. Bodl. lat. lit. a.4/214v

gual piece served as a second antiphon for the same processional function or, as Hesbert suggested,[127] it replaces the Gloria of the vigil mass.

The Latin text is a familiar one, as it begins the *hymnus angelicus* used in the mass, and is found in the Gregorian and Old Roman rites as an antiphon for Christmas. But there, the text includes the rest of the biblical angelic announcement: "et in terra pax hominibus bonae voluntatis."

The text of the Beneventan antiphon, preserved only for Holy Saturday, is not found in this form in the Roman liturgies, nor is it used alone in the Byzantine liturgy, so far as I know; but it does appear as part of a longer idiomelon for Christmas,[128] which is one of many Byzantine "Hodie" texts, and which bears a clear relation to the antiphon *Hodie christus natus est* used at Benevento and elsewhere.[129]

The melody of the Beneventan antiphon is essentially the same in both languages. Though it is in clear Beneventan style, it is related, as we have seen, to the Ambrosian *ante evangelium* for Christmas, which has precisely the same Latin text.

5 As the last item for Easter, after the Beneventan communion, the scribe of Ben40 (f. 28v) has written a Greek sticheron in transliteration. This sticheron is found, in almost this form (overlooking the curious Beneventan spellings) in the twelfth-century liturgy of Jerusalem[130] and in the modern Byzantine liturgy.[131]

Texts from Benevento and Jerusalem

Benevento 40:	Jerusalem:
	Papadopoulos-Kerameus, Ἀνάλεκτα II, 197.
Pascha yeron imin simeron anadedite	Πάσχα ἱερὸν ἡμῖν σήμερον ἀναδέδεικται
Pascha kenon agios	Πάσχα καινὸν ἅγιον
Pascha mysticos	Πάσχα μυστικόν
Pascha panthebasmye	Πάσχα πανσεβάσμιον
Pascha xpm tu litrotu	Πάσχα Χριστοῦ τοῦ λυτρωτοῦ
Pascha amomu	Πάσχα ἄμωμον
Pascha megas	Πάσχα μέγα
Pascha ton pisteon	Πάσχα τῶν πιστῶν
Pascha tas pus	Πάσχα τὸ πύλας ἡμῖν
tu paradysu aneote	τοῦ παραδείσου ἀνοῖξαν
Pascha panthe anaplatete	Πάσχα πάντας ἁγιάζον

[127] For the Latin version see example 5.10 above; and PM xIV, 433, where both versions are transcribed.
[128] Μηναῖα, II, p. 661. For facsimiles see Strunk, *Specimina*, plates 63, 81, 138, 148.
[129] On the influence of these texts on the Western liturgy, see Baumstark, "Byzantinisches."
[130] Papadopoulos-Kerameus, Ἀνάλεκτα, II, 197.
[131] Πεντηκοστάριον, p. 12; see Follieri, *Initia*, III, p. 295. For facsimiles see Follieri, *Triodium*, f. 127; Strunk, *Specimina*, plate 96.

In the manuscript there is no musical notation; the lines are spaced as if to receive it, but no space is left between syllables. If the text scribe knew what melody was intended, it must have been syllabic.

Curiously, this very piece is attested in the so-called *ordines romani* XI and XII of Mabillon, which detail the papal liturgy of twelfth-century Rome. The ceremonies of the day being concluded, the Pope and his retinue pause for refreshment:

Ordo XI: . . . and he drinks wine, and all the others drink. Meanwhile the cantors rise, and sing this Greek sequence: Πάσχα ἱερὸν ἡμῖν σήμερον, which sequence being finished they go and kiss the feet of the pontiff, and he gives them a cup of drink. Thus all happily depart.[132]

Ordo XII: Then is given to him claret wine to drink and to all those in attendance, by the archdeacon, and other things by the attendants. Meanwhile the primicerius rises with the singers, and sings the Greek prosa in this wise: Πάσχα ἱερὸν . . . [in extenso]. And when this has been sung, all return home.[133]

This Roman tradition, which is not attested in earlier documents, matches the Beneventan witness in some ways: its placement at the end of Easter, and the undoubtedly syllabic chant which led the Roman commentators to call it *sequentia* and *prosa*.

A piece so striking and joyous might well be adopted at Benevento from neighboring Greeks, whether by way of Rome or not, and included among the chants of Easter. Such a practice, however, is surely not of great antiquity and solemnity, to judge by the lack of uniformity of the Beneventan manuscripts. The presence of this piece at Benevento, in a single document, without music, and without a Latin version, suggests that it is not normally a part of the Beneventan rite.

Conclusions

These pieces in Greek in Beneventan manuscripts set themselves apart from their surroundings by the very fact of being in a language other than that of the local liturgy. Their transliteration in Latin characters shows the absence of a written Greek tradition in these manuscripts, and variations in spelling[134] suggest writing from oral memory. The Greek is written down as it is heard: it comes from an oral source, and hence presumably one nearby. At least two of these pieces (*O quando in cruce* and *Crucem tuam adoramus*) have parallels in the Byzantine liturgy, but they were undoubtedly adopted at Benevento, not directly from the East, but through the intermediary of some source relatively near at hand where such music could be heard. The other pieces in Greek may also have been features of an Italian Greek liturgy.

[132] ". . . et vinum bibit ipse, et omnes alii bibunt. Interim cantores surgunt, et cantant hanc Sequentiam Graecam, Πάσχα ἱερὸν ἡμῖν σήμερον, qua Sequentia finita, eunt, et osculantur pedes pontificis, et dat eis bibere coppam potionis. Sic omnes laeti recedunt." (PL, 78, col. 1045.)

[133] "Deinde propinatur sibi claretum vinum, et omnibus circumstantibus, ab archidiacono et alia pincernis. Interim vero primicerius cum cantoribus surgit, et canit prosam Graecam hujusmodi: Πάσχα ἱερὸν . . . [in extenso]. Et his decantatis, omnes ad propria revertuntur." (PL, 78, cols. 1079–80.)

[134] *ipsistis* (Ben40, Farfa): *ipsisti* (Ben38); *yrini* (Ben40): *irini* (Ben38): *kyrini* (Farfa); *ysusin* (Ben40, Ben39): *yxusin* (Vat. 10673); *ymnologumen so* (Vat. 10673): *ymnologume se* (Ben40); *tu stauri* (Vat. 10673): *tus stauri* (Ben40).

Not all pieces were adopted at the same time, or in the same fashion: some include melodic elements of their Greek version, some do not; some are included in the Beneventan liturgy, others in the Gregorian. We can presume that the Greek pieces included in Gregorian portions of Beneventan manuscripts (the Trisagion and *O quando in cruce*, as well as such Greek-inspired elements as the *improperia*) are later adaptations, either from the East or through a Western intermediary. A special case also is the Easter troparion *Pascha yeron* found only at Benevento, but witnessed later in Rome.

All the other Greek pieces have related versions in the liturgy of Milan: the adoration antiphons and *Gloria in excelsis* in melodically-related form, and *Omnes gentes* with matching texts. That the adoration antiphons appear also in manuscripts of Ravenna suggests that they derive from an ancient Italian practice, perhaps independent of Rome, which underwent subsequent development in various ways, the Beneventan and Ambrosian versions retaining a close relationship from which the Ravenna practice, at least as it is preserved now, varies substantially.

We can suggest a chronology for the adoption of these Greek pieces at Benevento only in very rough terms. The Greek/Latin material that Benevento shares with Milan (and to some extent, with Ravenna) was already in use in eighth-century Benevento (as elsewhere in Italy), in a liturgy not yet subject to the codification and systematization typical of later Carolingian pressure for uniformity. But the fall of the Lombard kingdom in the north to the Carolingians led to divergent liturgical developments, and the emphatic Byzantine emulation associated with the new dignity of Arichis II as leader of the Lombard south assured the preservation of the Greek versions which had disappeared from Milan by the time of its earliest documents. Good Friday, originally aliturgical, continued its development afterward.

Greek influence was always present at Benevento. The Byzantine garrison there at the end of the ninth century brought a substantial Greek population of officials, soldiers, and the necessary clergy for the Byzantine rite. Despite the hostility of the inhabitants, churchmen would be aware of one another's presence, and of the difference in their rites; and though the Greeks would hardly borrow materials from their subjects, the long tradition of Greek in the Western church at large, and in the Beneventan church in particular, might lead to the adoption of further Greek items. These would be received, not into the older Beneventan rite, by then under severe pressure from the Gregorian usage, but into the newer Roman music. This, combined in Holy Week with older Beneventan forms, results in the confusing melanges which are characteristic of the Beneventan manuscripts and witness to the continuing and varied cultural influences in the city itself.

1 Vatican City, Biblioteca Apostolica Vaticana, MS Vat. lat. 4939 ("Liber preceptorum S. Sophie"),
f. 26v: Duke Arichis II and the church of Santa Sofia

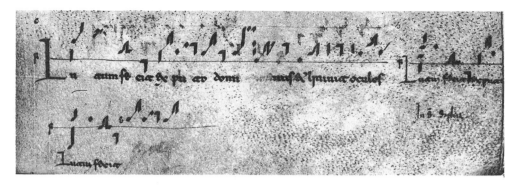

2 Benevento, Biblioteca capitolare, MS 34, f. 94 (detail): melodic version of Gregorian communion *Lutum fecit*, labeled *In s. Sophia*

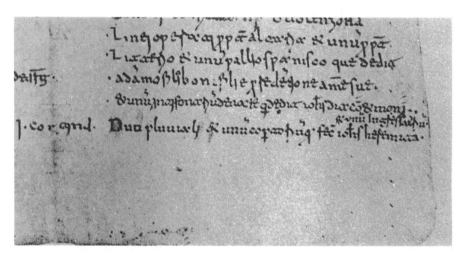

3 Montecassino, Archivio della Badia, Aula II, capsula CI, fasc. 1, no. 1: *Commemoratorium* of Theobald (detail)

4 (1) Vatican City, Biblioteca Apostolica Vaticana, MS Vat. lat. 10673, f. 34

4 (2) Lucca, Biblioteca capitolare Feliniana, MS 606, f. 156v

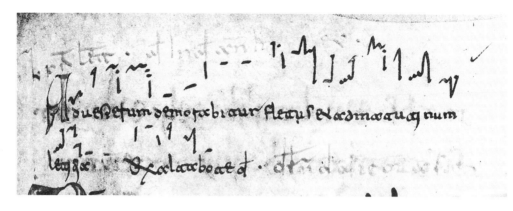

4 (3) Benevento, Biblioteca capitolare, MS 33, f. 73

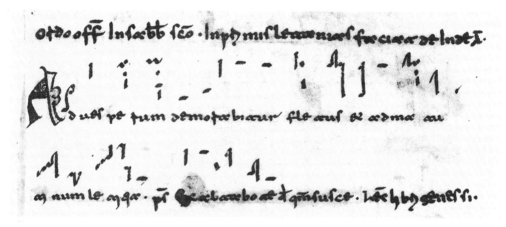

4 (4) Benevento, Biblioteca capitolare, MS 40, f. 15v

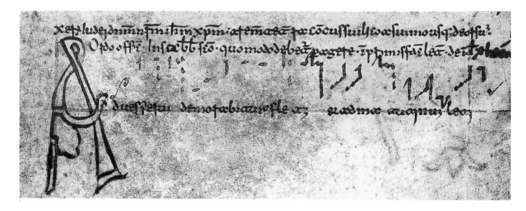

4 (5) Benevento, Biblioteca capitolare, MS 38, ff. 43v–44

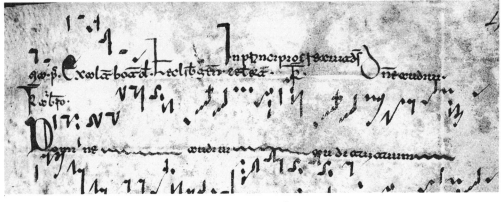

4 (5) *Continued*

4 (6) Benevento, Biblioteca capitolare, MS 39, f. 25v

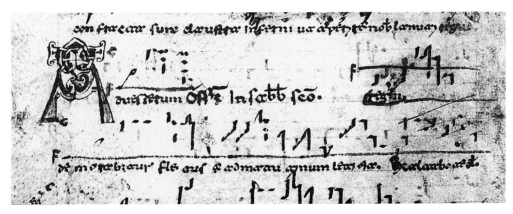

4 (7) Benevento, Biblioteca capitolare, MS 35, f. 66v

5 Benevento, Biblioteca capitolare, MS 20, f. 226: office of St Apollinaris

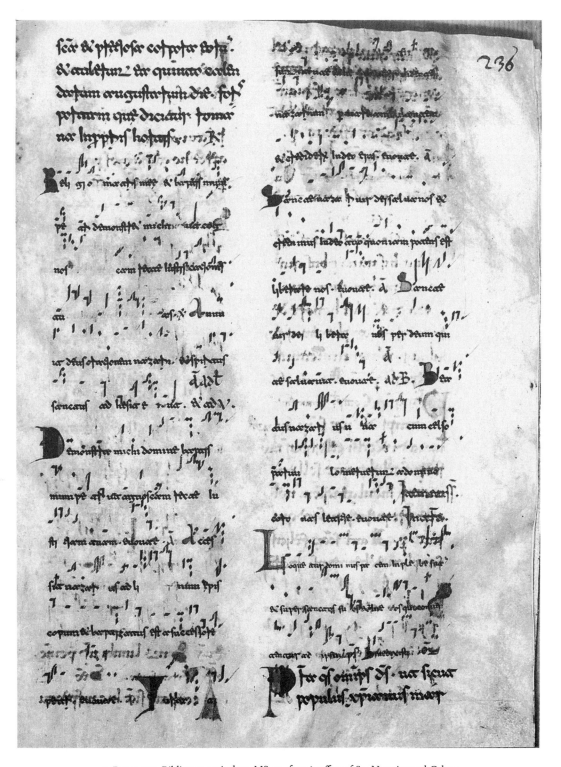

6 Benevento, Biblioteca capitolare, MS 20, f. 236: office of Sts Nazarius and Celsus

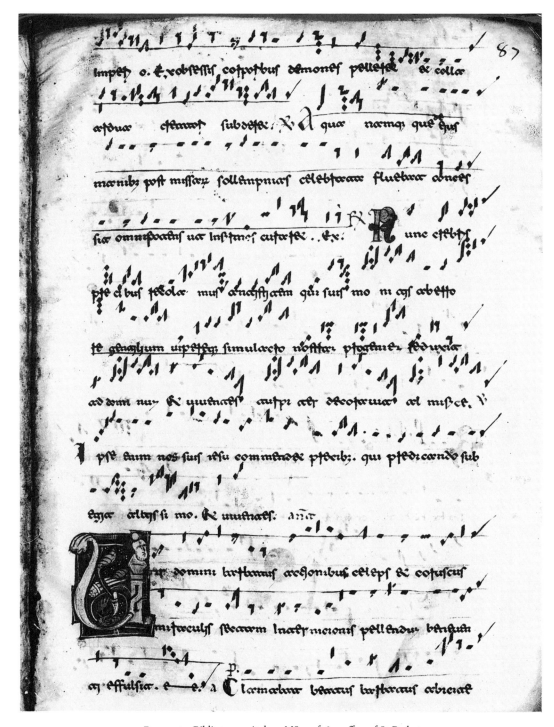

7 Benevento, Biblioteca capitolare, MS 21, f. 87: office of St Barbatus

8 Benevento, Biblioteca capitolare, MS 21, f. 87v: office of St Barbatus continued

9 Benevento, Biblioteca capitolare, MS 21, f. 212v: office of Sts Nazarius and Celsus

10 Benevento, Biblioteca capitolare, MS 21, f. 213: office of Sts Nazarius and Celsus continued

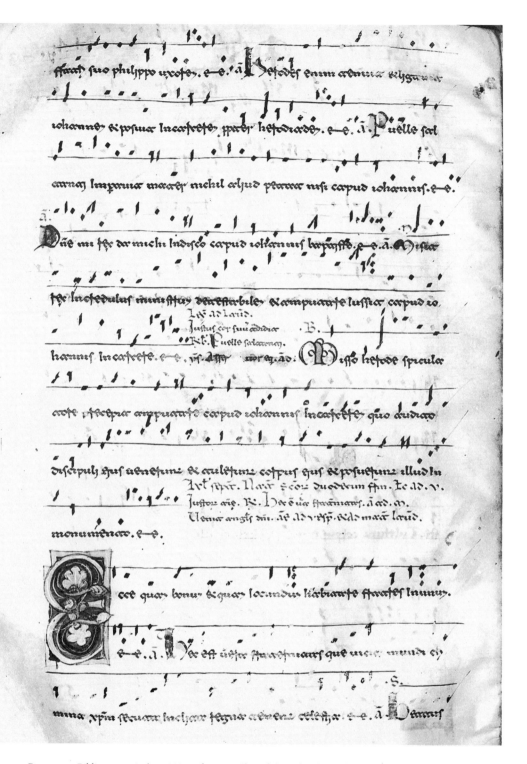

11 Benevento, Biblioteca capitolare, MS 21, f. 235v: office of the Beheading of John the Baptist concluded; office of the Holy Twelve Brothers

12 Benevento, Biblioteca capitolare, MS 21, f. 236: office of the Holy Twelve Brothers continued

13 Benevento, Biblioteca capitolare, MS 35, f. 202: mass of Christmas (concluded); mass of St Stephen

14 Benevento, Biblioteca capitolare, MS 35, f. 202v: mass of St Stephen continued

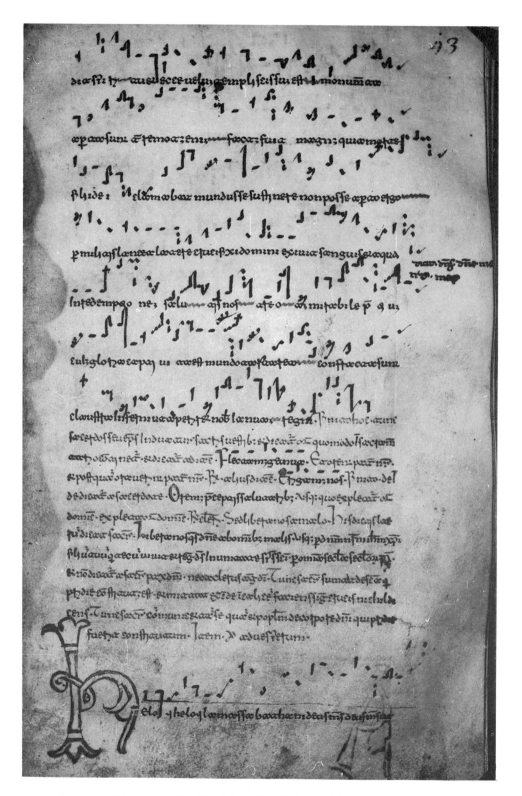

15 Benevento, Biblioteca capitolare, MS 38, f. 43: Good Friday, with beginning of Beneventan vespers

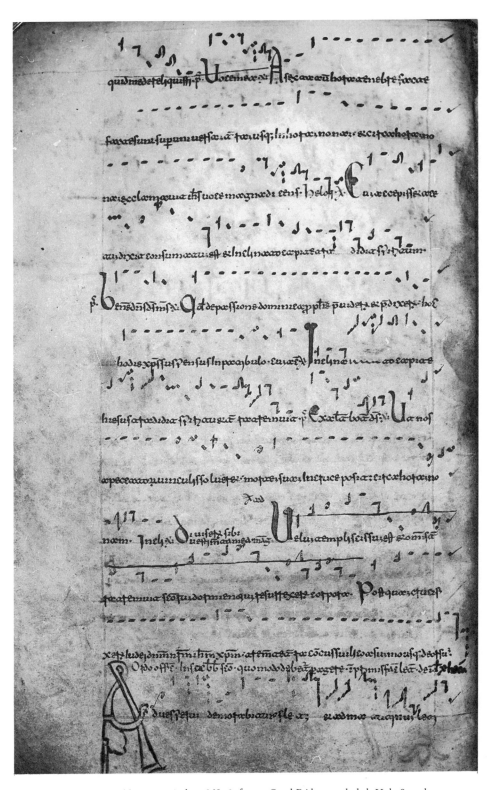

16 Benevento, Biblioteca capitolare, MS 38, f. 43v: Good Friday concluded; Holy Saturday

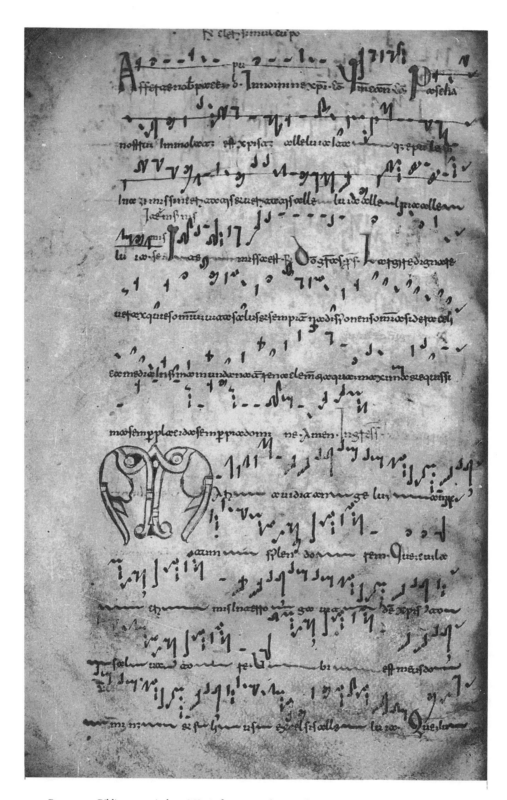

17 Benevento, Biblioteca capitolare, MS 38, f. 52v: conclusion of "Gregorian" Easter mass (with cued Beneventan communion *Ymnum canite*); Beneventan Easter mass begins

18 Benevento, Biblioteca capitolare, MS 38, f. 53: Beneventan Easter mass continued

19 Benevento, Biblioteca capitolare, MS 38, f. 53v: Beneventan Easter mass concluded;
Gregorian Easter Monday mass begins

20 Benevento, Biblioteca capitolare, MS 40, f. 10v: Good Friday,
with Greek/Latin adoration antiphons

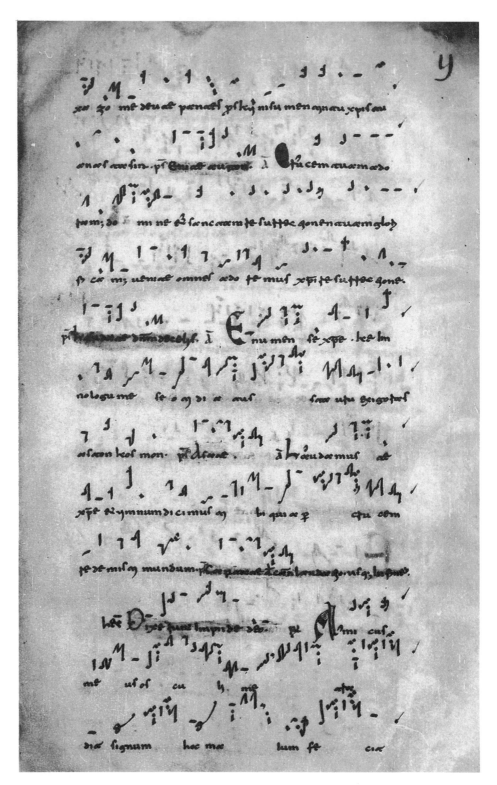

21 Benevento, Biblioteca capitolare, MS 40, f. 11: Good Friday; adoration antiphons concluded; Beneventan responsory *Amicus meus* begins

22 Benevento, Biblioteca capitolare, MS 40, f. 19v: Holy Saturday

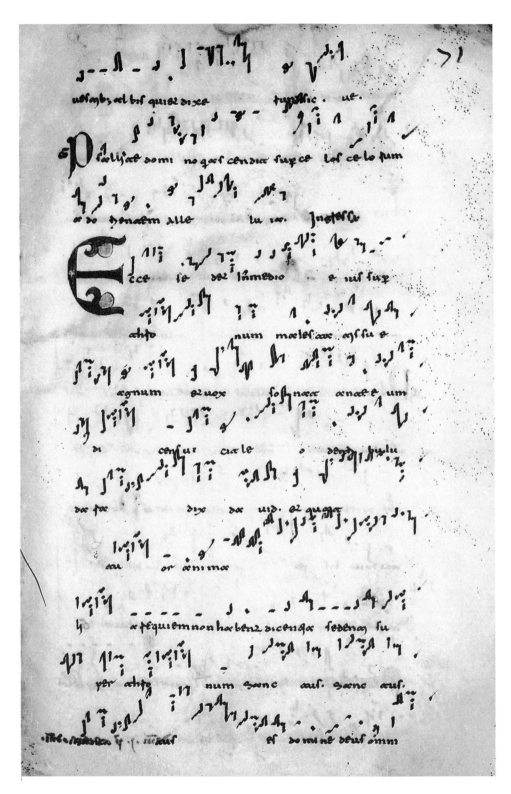

23 Benevento, Biblioteca capitolare, MS 40, f. 71: Gregorian Ascension mass concluded;
Beneventan Ascension mass begins

24 Benevento, Biblioteca capitolare, MS 40, f. 71v: Beneventan Ascension mass concluded

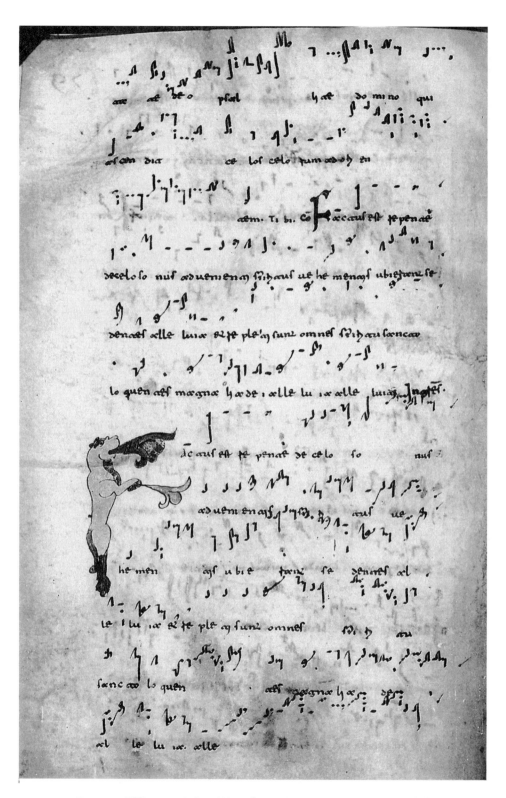

25 Benevento, Biblioteca capitolare, MS 40, f. 79v: Gregorian Pentecost mass concluded;
Beneventan Pentecost mass begins

26 Benevento, Biblioteca capitolare, MS 40, f. 89; Gregorian mass of John the Baptist concluded; Beneventan mass of John the Baptist begins

27 Benevento, Biblioteca capitolare, MS 40, f. 89v: Beneventan mass of John the Baptist concluded

28 Benevento, Biblioteca capitolare, MS 40, f. 112v: Beneventan mass of St Lawrence

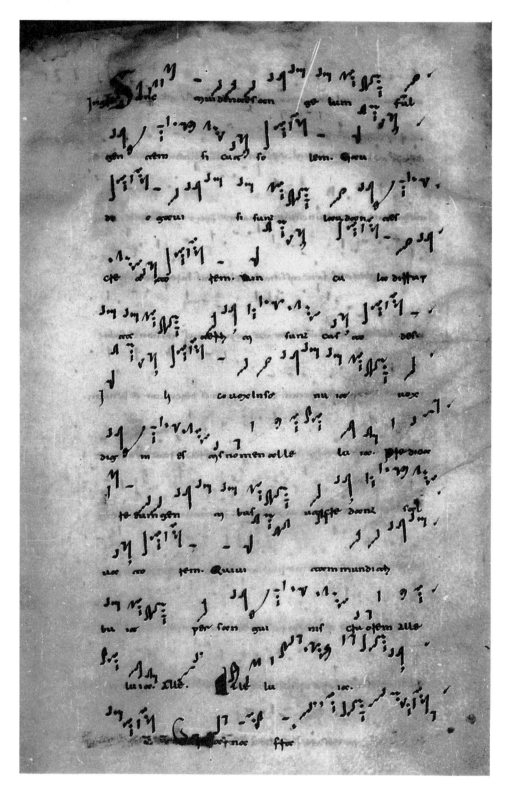

29 Benevento, Biblioteca capitolare, MS 40, f. 121v: Beneventan mass of the Holy Twelve Brothers

30 Benevento, Biblioteca capitolare, MS 40, f. 122: Beneventan mass of the Holy Twelve Brothers concluded; Gregorian mass of the Nativity of the Virgin Mary begins

THE BENEVENTAN REPERTORY

This table is a synopsis of the musical materials of the Beneventan liturgy. It does not include the evidence of ordinals where the musical text is incomplete; and it does not include a number of elements from the Beneventan liturgy which are essentially recitations. Notably absent here, therefore, is the Exultet, whose many witnesses are listed in Chapter 2; also missing are canticles, lections, and a few other elements which are detailed in Chapter 5. The following abbreviations are used here:

I	Ingressa	L	Latin version only
G	Gradual	*	cued only
T	Tract	sn	without musical notation
A	Alleluia	2h	written in a second hand
O	Offertory	g	found in Gregorian mass
C	Communion	pal	palimpsest, lower script
R	Responsory		
a	antiphon		

I Beneventan music found in manuscripts of music for the mass

	Ben40	Ben38	Other manuscripts
CHRISTMAS			
A Hodie natus est			Baltimore, w 6, f. 86 g
Credo (incomplete)			Ben35, f. 202
O Hodie christus natus			Ben35, f. 202
Sanctus			Ben35, f. 202
Agnus dei			Ben35, f. 202
C Dicite pastores quem			Ben35, f. 202
STEPHEN			
I Stephanus autem			Ben35, f. 202
G Scribite diem hunc			Ben35, f. 202v
A Posuisti (incomplete)			Ben35, f. 202v

I *Beneventan music found in manuscripts of music for the mass (cont.)*

	Ben40	Ben38	Other manuscripts
PALM SUNDAY			
Procession			
R Ante sex dies pasche		32v	Ben35, f. 55
			Vat. lat. 10673, f. 24
			Lucca 606, f. 150v
			Vat. Reg. lat. 334, f. 58v
			Zadar, Ord. 38 (in office)
Mass			
I Testificata		37v	Rome, Vall. C 9, f. 19 pal
G Dum congregarentur		38	
O Popule meus		38	
C Quis te supplantavit		38	
MAUNDY THURSDAY			
Mass			
I Postquam surrexit	4v		Rome, Vall. C 9, f. 19v pal
G Vadit propitiator	5		Vat. lat. 10657, f. 2 pal
O Popule meus	5* sn		
C Quis te supplantavit	5* sn		Vat. lat. 10657, f. 2* pal
[C? Accipiens. . .]			Vat. lat. 10657, f. 2 pal
Mandatum			
a Cum recubuisset	6		Ben33, f. 66v* sn
			Ben35, f. 62v
			Lucca 606, f. 152v
a Dominus ihesus	6v		Ben35, f. 62v
R Lavi pedes	6v		Ben30, f. 71
			Ben33, f. 66v* sn
			Ben35, f. 63
			Ben39, f. 21
			Lucca 606, f. 153
			Bologna 144 framm 3, recto (incomplete)
GOOD FRIDAY			
a Tristis est anima			Lucca 606, f. 155
First foremass, at third hour			
a Proskynumen/Adoramus	10v		Ben33, f. 68v L
			Ben35, f. 65v L
			Vat. lat. 10673, f. 28v
			Lucca 606, f. 155v L
			Vat. lat. 4770, f. 91v sn L
			Vat. Barb. lat. 560, f. 51* sn L
a Ton stauron/Crucem	10v		Ben33, f. 69 L
			Ben35, f. 65v L
			Vat. lat. 10673, f. 28v
			Lucca 606, f. 156 L
			Vat. lat. 4770, f. 91v sn L
			Oxford, Can. lit. 342, f. 51
a Enumen se/Laudamus	11		Ben33, f. 69 L
			Ben35, f. 65v L
			Vat. lat. 10673, f. 28v
			Lucca 606, f. 156 L
			Vat. lat. 4770, f. 91v sn L

I Beneventan music found in manuscripts of music for the mass (cont.)

	Ben40	Ben38	Other manuscripts
R Amicus meus	11		Ben33, f. 69
			Vat. lat. 10673, f. 31
Second foremass, at sixth hour			
a Panta ta/Omnes gentes	12v		Ben33, f. 69v L
			Ben34, f. 119
			Ben35, f. 65v* sn L
			Ben39, f. 23
			Vat. lat. 4770, f. 91v sn L
			Vat. lat. 10673, f. 29v
			Lucca 606, f. 156* L
Tunc hi/Ben. es, domine	12v		Ben33, f. 71
			Ben39, f. 23
			Vat. lat. 10673, f. 30v
			Macerata 378, f. 127v*
R Tenebre facte sunt	14		Ben33, f. 71v* (verse noted)
			Vat. lat. 10673, f. 31
			Benev. frag. B
Vespers			
a Heloy heloy	14v	43	Ben33, f. 72v* sn
			Ben39, f. 25
			Lucca 606, f. 156
			Subiaco XVIII, f. 77 sn
a Cum accepisset	15	43v	Ben39, f. 25
			Lucca 606, f. 156
			Subiaco XVIII, f. 77 sn
Inclinato capite	15	43v	Ben39, f. 25v
			Lucca 606, f. 156
			Subiaco XVIII, f. 77v sn
a Velum templi	15	43v	Ben21, f. 132
			Ben38, f. 46v (named, later hand)
			Ben39, f. 25v
			Lucca 606, f. 156
			Subiaco XVIII, f. 77v sn
			Vat. Ottob. 576, f. 166v* sn
HOLY SATURDAY			
Vigil			
a Ad vesperum	15v	43v	Ben33, f. 73
			Ben35, f. 66v
			Ben39, f. 25v
			Benevento frag. B
			Vat. lat. 10673, f. 34
			Lucca 606, f. 156v
			Vat. lat. 10657, f. 2v pal
T Domine audivi	15v	44	Wolfenbüttel 112, f. 136
			Rome, Vall. C 9, f. 19 pal, f. 32v pal
			Vat. lat. 10657, f. 2v pal
T Cantabo nunc	17v	45	Rome, Vall. C 9, f. 32v pal
T Attende	18	46v pal	
T Sicut cervus	18	46v pal	Vat. lat. 10673, f. 34v
			Bari benedictional
			Vat. lat. 10657, f. A pal

I *Beneventan music found in manuscripts of music for the mass (cont.)*

	Ben40	Ben38	Other manuscripts
a Omnes sitientes	18v	46v pal	Ben33, f. 78
			Ben35, f. 67v
			Ben39, f. 27
			Bari benedictional
			Rome, Vall. C 32, f. 30
			Vat. Ottob. lat. 576, f. 210
			Vat. lat. 10657, f. A pal
			Farfa A F 338, f. B (incomplete)
Si quis catechumenus	19	46v pal	Ben33, f. 78 sn
			Ben35, f. 67v
			Ben39, f. 27v
			Farfa A F 338, f. Bv (incomplete)
			Vat. Ottob. lat. 576, f. 211
			Rome, Vall. C 32, f. 31
			Vat. Urb. lat. 602, f. 99v (upper script)
a Doxa/Gloria	19	46v	Farfa A F 338, f. Bv
			Vat. lat. 10657, f. A pal

Mass
A ℣ Resurrexit

	Ben40	Ben38	Other manuscripts
℣ Laudate	19v	46v	Ben30, f. 75v g, ℣ 1 only
			Ben33, f. 79, ℣ 1
			Ben34, f. 126 g, ℣ 1
			Ben35, f. 68
			Ben39, f. 27v
			Vat. lat. 10657, f. A pal
			Baltimore W 6, f. 124v, 1
			Farfa A F 338, f. Bv (inc., ℣ 2 only)
			MC Comp. V, R in Greg.
			Easter fer. 2 Vespers, ℣ 1 only
O Omnes qui in Christo	19v	47	Ben33, f. 79v
			Ben35, f. 68
			Vat. lat. 4770, f. 113v sn
			Vat. lat. 10657, f. A pal
C Ymnum canite	20	47	Ben33, f. 79v
		52v g*	Ben35, f. 68
			Vat. lat. 4770, f. 114 sn

EASTER

	Ben40	Ben38	Other manuscripts
I Maria vidit angelum	159v	52v	
Gloria in excelsis		53*	
A Pascha nostrum		53	
Credo			Rome, Vall. C 9, f. 167 pal
O Angelus domini	27	53	Rome, Vall. C 9, f. 167 pal
C Qui manducaverit	28	53	Rome, Vall. C 9, f. 167 pal
Pascha yeron imin	28v sn		

MICHAEL (8 MAY)

	Ben40	Ben38	Other manuscripts
I Dum sacra misteria	61	83	Rome, Vall. C 9, f. 168v pal
A In conspectu		83	
O Milia milium	61	83	
C Celestis militie	61		Vat. Ottob. lat. 145, f. 124 (antiphon)
C Multos infirmos	61	83v*	

I Beneventan music found in manuscripts of music for the mass (cont.)

	Ben40	Ben38	Other manuscripts
ASCENSION			
I Ecce sedet in medio	71	93	Rome, Vall. C 9, f. 169 pal
A Dominus in celo	71v	93v	
A Hodie migravit			Ben39, f. 121 g
O Ascendit deus	71v	93v	
O Paraclitus autem	71v		
C Pacem meam	71v		
C Psallite domino	71v	93v	
PENTECOST			
a Ipse super (vigil)	73v	95	Ben33, f. 97v
			Ben35, f. 110v
			Ben39, f. 92v
			Vat. lat. 10645, f. 4v
I Factus est repente	79v	99 pal	Rome, Vall. C 9, f. 169 pal
			MC 361, p. 143 pal
A Spiritus domini sn	80		
O Paraclitus autem*sn	80		
C Pacem meam*sn	80		
JOHN THE BAPTIST			
I Lumen quod animus	89	110	Rome, Vall. C 9, f. 169v pal
			Vat. lat. 10657, f. 103 pal
A De ventre matris	89	110	
O Inter natos mulierum	89v		Solesmes flyleaves, p. 2 (as antiphon)
			Vat. Ottob. 145, f. 124 (as antiphon)
			(Ben38 Communion)
O Johannes est nomen		110v*	Solesmes flyleaves, p. 2 (as antiphon)
C Zacharias pater	89v		Solesmes flyleaves, p. 2 (as antiphon)
C Inter natos		110v*	(Ben40 Offertory)
PETER AND PAUL			
I Petrus dormiebat	99	115v	Rome, Vall. C 9, f. 169v pal
			Vat. lat. 10657, f. 100 pal
A Tu es petrus	99		
A In omnem terram		116*	
O Petrus apostolus	99v		Vat. Ottob. lat. 145, f. 124v (as antiphon)
O Tu es pastor		116*	
C Ut cognosceret	99v		MC 361, p. 150 pal
			Vat. lat. 10657, f. 101 pal
C Petrus apostolus		116*	(Ben40 Offertory)
LAWRENCE			
I Gratias ago deo meo	112v		
A Posuisti	112v* sn		(Stephen Alleluia)
O Adhesit anima mea	112v		
C Clare sacris	112v		
ASSUMPTION			
I Surge propera columba	118	128	
A Specie tue	118	128	
O Que est ista	118v	128	
C Sancta maria exora	118v	128v* sn	Vat. Ottob. lat. 145, f. 124 (as antiphon)
			Berkeley ff 2MS A2M2 1000:6

I *Beneventan music found in manuscripts of music for the mass (cont.)*

	Ben40	Ben38	Other manuscripts
TWELVE BROTHER MARTYRS (I SEPT.)			
I Sancti videntes	121v		
A Germana fratrum	121v		
O Circuierunt	122		MC 361, p. 166 pal
C Hos duodecim	122		MC 361, p. 166 pal
			Ben21, f. 236 (as antiphon)
HOLY CROSS I [INVENTION, 3 MAY?]			
I Michi autem absit	124v		Rome, Vall. C 9, f. 168v pal
A Dicite in gentibus	124v		
O Adoramus crucem*sn	124v		(Good Friday antiphon?)
C Crucem tuam*sn	124v		(Good Friday antiphon?)
HOLY CROSS II [EXALTATION, 14 SEPT.?]			
I Venite omnes	124v		
A Dicite in gentibus	125* sn		(Holy Cross I Alleluia?)
O Miraculo de tam	125	79 g	
C Tunc imperator	125		
SIMON AND JUDE			
I Michi autem nimis	128v		Rome, Vall. C 9, f. 173 pal
A In omnem terram*sn	128v		(Peter and Paul Alleluia?)
O Confortatus est*sn	128v		
C Nolite timere*sn	128v		
ALL SAINTS I			
I Gaudeamus omnes	133v		
Gloria in excelsis	133v* sn		
Kyrieleyson	133v* sn		
A Justorum anime	133v* sn		(All Saints II Alleluia?)
O O quam pretiosum	133v		
C Gaudent in celis	133v		
C Omnes sancti	134 sn		
C Ad honorem sanctorum	134		MC 361, p. 162 pal
			(All Saints II Offertory?)
ALL SAINTS II			
I Isti sunt sancti	134		
G Anima nostra	134v		
A Justorum anime	134v		
O Ad honorem	134v* sn		(All Saints I Communion?)
C Gaudent in celis	134v* sn		(All Saints I Communion?)
a (C?) Hodie exultat	134v		
MARTIN			
I Stolam iocunditatis	138v		
Gloria in excelsis	138v* sn		
G Ecce magnum et verum	138v		
O Martinus abrahe	139		
C Dixerunt discipuli	139		
C O quantus luctus	139		Vat. Ottob. lat. 145, f. 124v (antiphon)

I *Beneventan music found in manuscripts of music for the mass (cont.)*

	Ben40	Ben38	Other manuscripts
ANDREW			
I Prima predicationis	142	140	Rome, Vall. c 9, f. 172v pal
G Constitues eos	142	140v	
A Territus andreas	142v	140v	
O Salve crux que in	142v		
C Dum visitaret	142v	140v	
C Quid ad nos	143	140v	
BENEDICT			
C (or antiphon)			
Gloriosus confessor			MC Comp. XXII (Communion)
			Vat. Ottob. lat. 145, f. 124v (antiphon)
TRANSFIGURATION			
A Hodie transfiguratus			Ben39, f. 140v g
CHANTS OF THE ORDINARY WHOSE FEASTS CANNOT BE DETERMINED			
Gloria in excelsis			Rome, Vall. c 9, f. 170v
Kyrieleyson			Rome, Vall. c 9, f. 170v
Credo			Rome, Vall. c 9, f. 14
			Rome, Vall. c 9, f. 167v
			Montecassino 361, p. 126
Sanctus			Ben35, f. 195v (?)
PROCESSIONAL AND OTHER ANTIPHONS PRESERVED IN GRADUALS			
Purification			
a Lumen ad revelationem			Ben35, f. 15v
			Bologna, Univ. 2551, p. 34
a Congregamini omnes			Ben35, f. 15v
			Vat. Reg. lat. 334, f. 57
Feria 2 of Lent 3 (scrutiny)			
a Dum sanctificatus		21	Vat. Barb. lat. 697, f. 17 sn
ROGATION ANTIPHONS FOR LENT AND THE GREATER LITANIES			
a In tribulationibus		26v	Ben34, f. 157
			Ben35, f. 89v
			Ben39, f. 3
			Vat. Reg. lat. 334, f. 71v
			Naples XVI.A.19, f. 8
a Peccavimus domine		27	Ben35, f. 92
			Vat. Reg. lat. 334, f. 72
			Naples VI.G.34, f. 6
			Naples XVI.A.19, f. 9v
			Oxford, Can. lit. 277, f. 125 sn
a Respice cuncta	49	73	Ben34, f. 160v
			Ben35, f. 91v, 92
			Ben39, f. 62v
			Naples XVI.A.19, f. 8v
			Vat. Reg. lat. 334, ff. 74, 74v
a Gemitus noster			Ben35, f. 90
			Oxford, Can. lit. 277, f. 83 pal
UNKNOWN			
. . . alleluia alleluia			Leningrad F. 200, f. 83 pal

II *Beneventan music found in office manuscripts*

	Ben40	Ben38	Other manuscripts
GOOD FRIDAY			
a Velum templi scissum est	132	*See mass tables*	
Ses mass tables for other vespers antiphons			
JOHN THE BAPTIST			
a Helisabeth zacharie		Sol, f. 2	
a De ventre matris mee		Sol, f. 2	
a De utero senectutis		Sol, f. 2	
a Ut audivi vocem		Sol, f. 2	
a Iohannes est nomen eius		Sol, f. 2	Ben38, f. 110v* (as Offertory)
a Inter natos mulierum		Sol, f. 2	Ben38, f. 110v* (as Communion)
			Ben40, f. 89 (as Offertory)
			Vat. Ottob. lat. 145, f. 124 (antiphon)
R Precursor domini		Sol, f. 3	
a Zacharias pater eius		Sol, f. 3	Ben40, f. 89 (as Communion)
SYLVESTER			
a Vir dei Silvester	36	Ben19, f. 12	
		Ben22, f. 78v	MC 542, p. 31
VINCENT			
a Insigne preconium	67	Ben19, f. 35	MC 542, p. 86
		Ben22, f. 132v	MC Comp. v
BARBATUS			
a Vir domini Barbatus	87	Ben22, f. 146	Vat. lat. 14446, f. 38
a Clamabat Beatus Barbatus	87	Ben22, f. 146	Vat. lat. 14446, f. 38
a Sanctissimus dei cultor	87v	Ben22, f. 146v	Vat. lat. 14446, f. 38
a Expletis missarum sollem.	87v	Ben22, f. 146v	Vat. lat. 14446, f. 38v
a Accepta secure Barbatus	87v	Ben22, f. 146v	Vat. lat. 14446, f. 38v
a Beatissimo interveniente	87v	Ben22, f. 146v	Vat. lat. 14446, f. 38v
BENEDICT			
a Nursia provincia ortus	90	Ben19, f. 88	Vat. lat. 14446, f. 61v
		Ben22, f. 152v	MC 542, p. 106
a Ecce vir dei Benedictus	90v	Ben19, f. 86v	MC 542, p. 105
		Ben22, f. 153v	
a Dum famis inopia tristes	93v	Ben19, f. 93v	MC 542, p. 112
		Ben22, f. 156	Vat. lat. 10646, f. 51
JOHN AND PAUL			
a Mandaverunt Iuliano	192v	Ben20, f. 204	MC Comp. v
APOLLINARIS			
a Accipe spiritum sanctum	211	Ben20, f. 226	Vat. lat. 14733, f. 11v
a Beatus Apollinaris super	211	Ben20, f. 226	
a Beatus Apollinaris oravit	211v	Ben20, f. 226	
a Apollinaris martyris	211v [MIL]	Ben20, f. 226 [BEN]	
?a Vere cognoscent omnes	211v	Ben20, f. 226	Vat. lat. 14733, f. 11v

II *Beneventan music found in office manuscripts (cont.)*

	Ben40	Ben38	Other manuscripts
NAZARIUS			
a Turbati sunt nautae	212v [MIL]	Ben20, f. 236 [BEN?]	
a Sancte vir dei libera nos	213 [MIL]	Ben20, f. 236 [BEN]	
a Beatus Nazarius una cum	213	Ben20, f. 236	
a Demonstra michi domine	212v	Ben20, f. 236	
a Accessit Nazarius ad Linum		Ben20, f. 236	
XISTUS			
a Usque in senectam	216	Ben20, f. 249	
TWELVE BROTHER MARTYRS			
a Ecce quam bonum	235v	Ben20, f. 278	Melk 1012, f. Av MC Comp. v
a Hec est vera	235v	Ben20, f. 278	Melk 1027, f. Z MC Comp. v
a Beatus donatus	235v	Ben20, f. 278	Melk 1027, f. Z MC Comp. v
a Venit angelus domini	236	Ben20, f. 278	Melk 1027, f. Z MC Comp. v
a Sanctissimus arontius	236	Ben20, f. 279	Melk 1027, f. Z MC Comp. v
a Beatum vitalem satorum	236		MC Comp. v
a Hos duodecim misit	236	Ben40, f. 122 (as Communion) MC 361, p. 166 pal (as Communion)	
a Sancti vero uno ore	236	Ben20, f. 278	Melk 1027, f. Z
a Beatus hono/ / /			Melk 1027, f. Z
UNKNOWN			
a Sancti enim ducti			Venice B. 159 n. 28

BENEVENTAN TEXTS

This appendix presents the texts of Beneventan chants, along with references to the sources in which they appear. Manuscript citations are abbreviated: manuscripts of Benevento are preceded by Ben; L606 = Lucca 606. A diagonal line separates the manuscript reference from the folio number on which the piece begins: thus Ben22/24v is Benevento, MS 22, folio 24 verso.

Reference is also made to the use of these texts in the Gregorian, Old Roman, and Ambrosian liturgies. Abbreviations used in these citations are:

Ambrosian (MIL):

Mugg. Muggiasca, Ambrosian antiphoner without shelf number, the two volumes completed in 1387 and 1388. Huglo, *Fonti*, nos. 62–3
Oxf. Oxford, Bodleian Library, MS Lat. liturg. a. 4. A Milanese antiphoner, *pars aestiva*, completed in 1399. Huglo, *Fonti*, no. 64
BL London, British Library, Additional MS 34209. A twelfth-century Ambrosian antiphoner, *pars hiemalis*. Huglo, *Fonti*, no. 50; complete facsimile and transcription in PM v and PM vi
F.2.2 Milan, Biblioteca capitolare MS F.2.2. A twelfth-century *pars hiemalis*. Huglo, *Fonti*, nos. 55–6
Manuale Magistretti, *Manuale ambrosianum*
Beroldus Magistretti, *Beroldus*
Modern editions: LVesp, AMed (see Bibliography)

Gregorian (GREG): citations are from CAO and *Sextuplex* with occasional citations of other manuscripts; modern sources include GRom, AMon (see Bibliography).

Old Roman (ROM):

5319 Vatican, MS Vat. lat. 5319. Old Roman gradual, eleventh-twelfth century, perhaps from the Lateran; transcribed in MMMA2 listed below
F 22 Vatican, Archivio di San Pietro, MS F 22. An Old Roman gradual of the thirteenth century
Bodmer Cologne-Geneva, Biblioteca Bodmeriana, MS 74. A gradual from Santa Cecilia in Trastevere dated 1071
B 79 Vatican, Archivio di San Pietro, MS B 79; a twelfth-century antiphoner of the Old Roman rite from St Peter's basilica
29988 London, British Library, Additional MS 29988. An Old Roman antiphoner of the twelfth century, perhaps from the Lateran
MMMA: transcription of Vat. lat. 5319 (see Bibliography)

Spellings are carefully preserved for Beneventan sources, though I have differentiated between u and v. Elsewhere they are often taken from one or another source without comment, although significant variants are noted. Biblical texts are cited according to the *Vulgata* (see Bibliography); psalm texts are compared with the Roman (see Rom in Bibliography) and Gallican (Ga, printed in *Vulgata*) psalters; where no version is indicated, the two psalters are in agreement.

Accepta secure barbatus perrexit votum
et sacrilegam arborem suis manibus evellit radicibus.

Barbatus antiphon: Ben21/87v (C A O 1220); Ben22/146v; Vat. lat. 14446/38v

1   secure: Ben22
2   radicitus: Ben22; Vat. lat. 14446

Text: compare AA SS, Feb. III, 142, n. 2

Accessit nazarius ad linum episcopum
et baptizatus est a successore petri.

Nazarius antiphon: Ben20/236

M I L: ℟ (Muggiasca, p. 249, *Manuale*, II, 320) Oravit beatus naz . . . ℣ Accessit nazarius ad linum successorem petri postulans ab eo baptizatus est et exaudita est [Muggiasca adds *oratio*]

Accipe spiritum sanctum simulque pontificatum
surge perge ravennam multitudo populi ibi moratur
predicans eis hiesum quod vere sit dei filius.

Apollinaris antiphon: Ben20/226; Ben21/211 (C A O 1231); Vat. lat. 14733/11v (illegible)

1   Ben21: *sanctum*, omitted in error and supplied later
2   ravenna: Ben20
3   iesum: Ben20

Text: compare Mombritius, I, 117, ll. 37–9

M I L: antiphon (Mugg., p. 246; Oxf. f. 165v; *Manuale*, II, 317) Accipe spiritum sanctum simulque pontificatum et perge ad urbem que vocatur ravena

Accipiens dominus hiesus pa[nem?]. . .

Maundy Thursday [communion?]: Vat. lat. 10657/2 (palimpsest)

Adhesit anima mea post te
quia caro mea igne cremata est
pro te deus meus.
    ℣ In craticula te [MS:ne] deum non negavi
et ad igne applicatus te xpiste confessus sum
probasti cor meum et visitasti nocte
igne me examinasti et non est inventa in me iniquitas.

Lawrence offertory: Ben40/112v

Text: compare Ps. 62, 9A; Ps. 16, 3 (Rom); Mombritius, II, 94, ll. 12–13 and 95, ll. 17–18

M I L: compare psallenda (Oxf., f. 196; *Manuale*, II, 333; LVesp, p. 709) In craticula sanctum deum non negavi et ad ignem applicatus christum confessus sum; probasti (as above)

G R E G: antiphon (C A O 1271, AMon, p. 1006) Adhesit (compare C A O 1272); antiphon (C A O 3216, AMon, p. 1007) In craticula (ignem; christum)

ROM: antiphon (B 79/147v; 29988/116v) Adhesit: propter (pro); antiphon (B 79/147v; 29988/116v) In craticula: ignem; compare antiphon (B 79/33) Adhesit. . .lapidata: Stephen

> Ad honorem sanctorum occurrite populi videntes gloriam dei
> et ecce quid meruerunt qui dominum xpistum non negaverunt.

Communion: Ben40/134 (All Saints I); offertory: Ben40/134v cued sn (All Saints II); MC 361, p. 162, palimpsest, function and feast uncertain

MIL: psallenda, several martyrs (Oxf., f. 164v; *Manuale*, II, 388) 1: concurrite; 2: *om.* et (*Manuale*); *om* ecce (Oxf.); qui (quid)

ROM: antiphon, ded. eccl. (5319/135v, MMMA, 554) 1: concurrite; 2: *om.* et; qui (quid); domine hiesum (dominum)

> Adoramus crucem tuam
> et signum de cruce tua
> et qui crucifixus est virtutum.

Good Friday antiphon: Ben33/68v; Ben35/65v; Ben40/10v (cued as Offertory, f. 124); Vat. 10673/28v; L606/155v; Vat. 4770/91v sn; Vat. Barb. lat. 560/51 cued sn

2   de crucem tuam: Ben40, Ben35; tue: Vat. 4770

3   *om* et: Vat. 4770; es virtutem: Ben35; virtute: L606

Text: compare Proskynumen. See Chapter 5, pp. 209–14

MIL: antiphon (BL, p. 248; *Manuale*, II, 188; AMed, p. 182) 3: es (BL, AMed); virtute (BL), virtutem (*Manuale*, AMed)

GREG: (other Italian MSS) antiphon (Oxford, Bodl. Can. lit. 321, f. 66; Padova, Bib. cap. A 47, f. 126; Modena, Bib. cap. O. I. 7, f. 97v; Rome, Vall. C 52, f. 153; Rome, Casanat. 1741, f. 152; Rome, BNaz 1343, f. xx; New York, Morgan M. 379)

2   crucem tuam: Modena O. I. 7; Vall. C 52

3   es: Vall. C 52, Padova A 47; in virtute: Oxford 321, Padova A 47, Modena, Vall. C 52; virtute: Casanat., Rome, BNaz 1343; in virtute tua: New York, Morgan M. 379. Five manuscripts (Oxf. 321, Padova, Modena, New York, Vall. C 52) add the following text: adoramus te xpiste et hymnum dicimus tibi quia per crucem tuam redimisti mundum

> Adoramus crucem. . .

Holy Cross I offertory: Ben40/124v cued sn

> Ad vesperum demorabitur fletus
> et ad matutinum letitia.

Holy Saturday introductory antiphon: Ben33/73; Ben35/66v; Ben38/43v; Ben39/25v; Ben40/15v; Benevento fragment B (fragmentary); Vat. 10673/34; Vat. 10657/2v, palimpsest; L606/156v

Text: Ps. 29, 6B

MIL: antiphon in choro, common of Sundays (Oxf. 332, *Manuale*, II, 411 – cued also on p. 95, LVesp, p. 162): demoretur fletus domine

> Agnus dei qui tollis peccata mundi miserere nobis.

Ben35/202 Christmas

> Amicus meus osculi me tradit signum
> hoc malum fecit qui per osculum adimplevit homicidium
> et in finem abiens laqueo se suspendit.
>   ℣ Retulit triginta argenteis principibus sacerdotum et ait
>   peccavi domino peccavi tradidi sanguinem iustum. Et in fi[nem].

Good Friday ℟: Ben33/69; Ben40/11; Vat. 10673/31

2   occulum *corr. to* osculum: Ben33

3   habiens: Vat. 10673

5 peccavit: Ben40; tradidit: Ben33, Ben40

Text: for verse compare Matt. 27:3, 5; varies from Vulgate (argenteos; sacerdotum et senioribus dicens peccavi tradens; et abiens laqueo se suspendit)

GREG: Maundy Thursday ℟ (CAO 6083):
1 signo (3 of 6 MSS); *add* Quem osculatus fuero, ipse est, tenete eum!
2 fecit signum; *add* Infelix praetermisit pretium sanguinis; *om* abiens
4–5 *om*; MSS have ℣ Melius illi or ℣ Bonum erat ei

> Angelus domini descendit de celo dixit mulieribus
> quem queritis non est hic surrexit sicut dixit alleluia.

Easter offertory: Ben38/53; Ben40/27 (incomplete at beginning); Rome, Vall. C 9/167 palimpsest

Text: compare Matt. 28:2, 5–6

MIL: Easter offertory (Oxf. f. 10; *Manuale*, II, 214; AMed, p. 210):
1 et dixit
2 *om* non est hic
3 Adds verses ℣ Euntes, ℣ Jesus stetit

GREG: Easter Monday offertory (*Sextuplex*, pp. 100–1; GRom, p. 246). Text as in MIL

ROM: Easter Monday offertory (5319/87; F22/54v; MMMA, p. 388). Text as in MIL except *dixi* (5319)

> Anima nostra sicut passer erepta est de laqueo venantium.
> ℣ Laqueus contritus est et nos liberati sumus.

All Saints II gradual: Ben40/134v

Text: Ps. 123:7

MIL: Nabor and Felix, psalmellus (Oxf. 161v, *Manuale*, II, 313, AMed, p. 497)
1 Anima mea (*Man*)

GREG: Holy Innocents, gradual (*Sextuplex*, pp. 20–1, GRom, p. 41), offertory (*Sextuplex*, pp. 20–1, GRom, p. 43). Offertory as here; gradual adds "adjutorium nostrum in nomine domini qui fecit celum et terram"

ROM: Gradual, Holy Innocents (5319/18v, MMMA, p. 156), several martyrs (F22/88v). Text as in GREG gradual

> Ante sex dies pasche venit hiesus bethania
> ubi lazarum resuscitavit a mortuis
> et dixit discipulis suis
> desiderio desideravi manducare vobiscum antequam patiar.
> ℣ Magister dicit tempus meum prope est
> aput te facio pascha cum discipulis meis. Et dix[it].

℟ for blessing of palms: Ben35/55; Ben38/32v; L606/150v; Vat. 10673/24; Vat. Reg. lat. 334/58v; Zadar Ord. 38 (office ℟)
1 ihs: Ben38
2 lazarusm: Vat. 10673
4 desiderabi: Ben35
6 apud: Ben35, Vat. Reg. lat. 334, Zadar; pasca: Zadar. Zadar. *add*.: Gloria patri et filio et spiritui sancto

Text: compare John 12:1 "Iesus ergo ante sex dies paschae venit Bethaniam ubi fuerat Lazarus mortuus quem suscitavit Iesus"; Luke 22:15 "Et ait illis desiderio desideravi hoc pascha manducare vobiscum antequam patiar"; Matt. 26:18B "Magister dicit . . ."; for reading "suscitavit a mortuis" see Wordsworth-White, I, 591

GREG: compare antiphon (CAO 2161; AMon, p. 396) Desiderio desideravi hoc Pascha manducare vobiscum antequam patiar. And compare antiphon (CAO 3657, AMon, p. 396), text as in BEN verse

ROM: compare antiphon *Desiderio* (text as in BEN), B 79/89, 29988/59v. And compare antiphon *Magister* (text as in BEN verse), B 79/89, 29988/59v

Apollinaris martiris festa laudamus
qui pro xpisti nomine tormenta sustinuit.

Apollinaris antiphon: Ben20/226

MIL: Mugg., p. 243, Oxf. 163v, *Manuale*, II, 315, LVesp, p. 682, Ben20/229v, Ben21/211v (*recolimus*), Ben21/212 (*laudamus*).
CAO 1451 is MIL version in Ben21. Text as in BEN except *recolimus* (*laudamus*)

Ascendit deus in iubilatione et dominus in voce tube alleluia alleluia.

Ascension offertory: Ben38/93v; Ben40/71v

Text: Ps. 46:6 (Rom)

MIL: Ascension, V in Alleluia (Oxf. 53v, *Manuale*, II, 243, AMed, p. 242): no final Alleluias

GREG: Ascension, Alleluia (*Sextuplex*, pp. 120–1, GRom, p. 286), no final Alleluia; offertory (*Sextuplex*, 120–1, GRom, p. 287): om et; one alleluia; antiphon (CAO 1490, AMon, p. 1075): 1 final Alleluia; compare R̂ CAO 6122, 6123

ROM: Ascension, Alleluia (5319/105v, F22/61v, MMMA p. 182): no final Alleluia; offertory (5319/105v, F22/61v, MMMA, p. 322), 1 Alleluia; adds verse *Subiecit populos*

Attende celum et loquar et audiat terra verba ex ore meo.
Expectetur sicut pluvia eloquium meum et descendant sicut ros
verba mea.
Sicut imber super gramen et sicut nix super fenum.
Quia nomen domini invocabo.

Holy Saturday tract: Ben38/46 (palimpsest); Ben40/18

1   Adtende: Ben38

Text: Deut. 23:1–3A; not Vulgate: see PM XIV, 370; Hesbert, "L'antiphonale" (6), pp. 178–9

GREG: compare Holy Saturday tract (*Sextuplex*, pp. 96–9; GRom, p. 231). Same text as BEN plus more

ROM: MSS contain Gregorian tract: 5319/81v; F22/52v; MMMA, p. 243

Beatissimo interveniente barbato
ad nichilum redacta sunt simulacra
et catholica suscepta est fides xpisti
atque ab hostibus beneventus erepta est.

Barbatus antiphon: Ben21/87v (CAO 1600); Ben22/146v; Vat. lat. 14446/38v

3   catholice: Ben21; Vat. lat. 14446

4   ostibus: Vat. lat. 14446; ereptus: Ben21

Text: compare AA SS, Feb. III, 141–2, n. 17; 144, n. 16

Beatum vitalem satorum et repositum iussit valerianus
pro xpisto quasi in prandium iugulandos afferri.

Twelve Brothers antiphon: Ben21/236 (CAO 1607); MC Comp. v

Text: compare AA SS, Sept. I, 138, n. 3

Beatus apollinaris oravit ad dominum
et patricii filiam suscitavit mortuam.

Apollinaris antiphon: Ben20/226; Ben21/211v (CAO 1611)

Text: compare Mombritius, I, 119, ll. 29–48

Beatus apollinaris super cecorum oculos
signum crucis edidit nubem squamosam detegens.

Apollinaris antiphon: Ben20/226; Ben21/211 (CAO 1612)
1   oculis: Ben20

Text: compare Mombritius, I, 121, ll. 51–7

MIL: compare antiphon (Oxf. 163v, Mugg., p. 243, *Manuale*, II, 316) Super caecati oculos beatus Apollinaris signum crucis edidit, lumenque ei reddidit

Beatus donatus et felix confidentes in domino
ab immundo spiritu liberarunt restitute filium.

Twelve Brothers antiphon: Ben20/278; Ben21/235v (CAO 1622); Melk 1027/Z; MC Comp. v
1   dominum: Ben20
2   inmundo: Melk

Text: compare AA SS, Sept. I, 139, nn. 4–5

Beatus hono[ratus. . .]

Twelve Brothers antiphon: Melk 1027/Z (incomplete)

Beatus nazarius una cum celso parvulo
meruerunt a domino coronas iustitie.

Nazarius antiphon: Ben20/236; Ben21/213 (CAO 1650)
2   corona: Ben21; letitie: Ben20

MIL: antiphon Oxf. 153v, Mugg., p. 322, *Manuale*, II, 322: coronam perpetuam

Cantabo nunc dilecto canticum dilecte vinee mee.
℣ Vinea facta est dilecta in cornu in loco uberi.
℣ Et maceria circumdedi et circumfodi et plantavi vineam sorech.
℣ Et edificavi turrem in medio eius et torcular fodi in ea.
℣ Et sustinui ut faceret uvas fecit autem spinas.
℣ Quoniam sustinui ut faceret iudicium fecit autem iniquitatem
et non iustitiam sed clamorem.

Holy Saturday tract: Ben38/45; Ben40/17v; Rome, Vall. c 9/32v (palimpsest)
Text: Isaiah 5:1–2, 7B; not Vulgate: see Hesbert, "L'antiphonale" (6), pp. 176–7
GREG: compare Holy Saturday canticle *Vinea* (*Sextuplex*, pp. 98–9; GRom, p. 230), based on same textual version
ROM: MSS contain GREG canticle: 5319/81v; F22/51v; MMMA, p. 245

Celestis militie princeps magne michahel
deprecare xpistum pro afflictorum gemitum redemptorem mundi.

St Michael communion: Ben40/61; antiphon: Vat. Ottob. lat. 145/124
MIL: psallenda (Oxf. 203v; *Manuale*, II, 358; LVesp 755): gemitu
GREG: antiphon, CAO 1834 (Ben21 only)

Circuierunt sancti in melotis et pellibus caprinis
angustiati afflicti quibus dignus non erat mundus.

Twelve Brothers offertory: Ben40/122; MC 361, p. 166 (palimpsest)

Text: Hebrews 11:37B–38A: "circumierunt in melotis in pellibus caprinis egentes angustiati adflicti quibus dignus non erat mundus." For a tradition of *circuierunt* see Wordsworth-White, II, 751

> Clamabat beatus barbatus abicite filii bestie simulacrum
> et xpisto domino subicite colla.

Barbatus antiphon: Ben21/87 (CAO 1817); Ben22/146; Vat. lat. 14446/38

Text: compare AA SS, Feb. III, 143, n. 7

> Clare sacris meritis laurenti splendide martir
>   qui fide pro xpristi premia digna tenens:
> solve tuis precibus delictis vincula nostris
>   ut pateant famulis regna superna tuis.

Lawrence communion: Ben40/112v

Confortatus est. . .

Simon and Jude offertory: Ben40/128v (cued)

Text: compare Ps. 138:17

GREG: compare antiphon (CAO 1881, AMon, p. 627): "Confortatus est principatus eorum, et honorati sunt amici tui, Deus"

ROM: antiphon, Peter and Paul (B 79/136, 29988/107): text as in GREG except *honorificati* (*honorati*)

> Congregamini omnes et videte virtutem
> qualem dedit dominus matri sui.

Purification antiphon: Ben35/15v; Vat. Reg. lat. 334/57

2   matris sue: Ben35

Text: compare below, s. v. "Isti sunt sancti"

MIL: antiphon, martyrs (Oxf. 265v; *Manuale*, II, 388; LVesp, p. 782): videbitis; sanctis suis

> Constitues eos principes super omnem terram
> memores erunt nominis tui domine.
>   ℣ Pro patribus tuis nati sunt tibi filii
> propterea populi confitebuntur tibi.

Andrew gradual: Ben38/140v (cued); Ben40/142

Text: Ps. 44:17 (Rom), reordered

MIL: Psalmellus, Peter and Paul, Oxf. 151; *Manuale*, II, cued 309 (for Andrew, 16); AMed, p. 393 (Andrew)

GREG: Gradual, Andrew (*Sextuplex*, pp. 168–9; GRom, p. 393); Peter (*Sextuplex*, 138–9). Compare Peter offertory (*Sextuplex*, p. 139; GRom, p. 534); antiphon CAO 1902 (Constitues. . .domine); ℟ CAO 6329, CAO 6330, CAO 6331

ROM: Gradual, Peter and Paul (5319/115, MMMA, p. 130); Apostles (F22/86v)

[Credo in unum deum. . .]

Ben35/202 Christmas (. . . et vitam futuri seculi. Amen.)

MC 361, p. 126, palimpsest; feast uncertain. ([i]terum ventures . . . iudicare vivos et. . .regni non er[it])

Rome, Vall. C 9/14v, palimpsest; feast uncertain ([fi]lium dei unigenitum et ex patre natum ante omnia secula deum de deo lumen de. . .[consub]stantialem patri per quem omnia facta sunt qui propter nos homines. . .sub pontio pilato pas[sus]. . . tertia die. . .[mortu]os cuius regni. . . .)

Rome, Vall. C 9/167, palimpsest, Easter (final portion, text not legible)

> Crucem tuam adoramus domine
> et sanctam resurectionem tuam glorificamus
> venite omnes adoremus xpisti resurrectionem.

Good Friday adoration antiphon: Ben33/69; Ben35/65v; Ben40/11 (cued as Communion, f. 124v); Vat. lat. 10673/28v; Vat. Barb. lat. 560/15 cued sn; Vat. lat. 4770/91v; L606/156; Oxford, Bodl., Can. liturg. 321/65v

2   resurrectionen: Ben40; laudamus et glorificamus: Vat. 4770

3   venite gentes: Ben35; *om* omnes: Vat. 4770; resurrectione: Ben40, Vat. 4770

Text: on Greek origin, see pp. 209–14

MIL: antiphon, BL, p. 248; 29988/248; Oxf. 106 (Invention); *Manuale* II, 188; AMed, p. 181; LVesp, p. 354 (Invention). Text ends with *glorificamus*

GREG: compare Good Friday antiphon (*Sextuplex*, 97; CAO 1953; GRom, p. 217)

2   laudamus et glorificamus

3   ecce enim propter crucem venit gaudium in universo mundo

ROM: Good Friday antiphon F22/51 (cued), 5319/80, MMMA, p. 516; Invention antiphon B 79/117v; 29988/91

2   *om* et: B 79, 29988

3   quia (5319: *qui*) venit salus in universo mundo

> Crucem tuam. . .

Holy Cross I communion: Ben40/124v (cued sn: same as Good Friday antiphon?)

> Cum accepisset acetum dixit consumatum est
> et inclinato capite tradidit spiritum.
> ℣ Quod de passione dominica prophete previderunt et predixerunt
> hoc hodie xristus suspensus in patibulo. Cum ac.

Good Friday antiphon: Ben38/43v; Ben39/25; Ben40/15; L606/156; Subiaco XVIII/77

Text: Antiphon from John 19:30 ("Cum ergo accepisset Iesum . . .")

MIL: Holy Saturday, antiphon: BL, p. 256; *Manuale*, II, 197

2   reddidit (tradidit)

3–4   omitted

GREG: antiphon Good Friday (or occasionally elsewhere): CAO 1970; AMon, p. 444. Lines 3–4 omitted

> Cum recubuisset dominus hiesus in domo simonis leprosi
> mulier que erat in civitate peccatrix habens alabastrum unguenti
> et sedens retro secus pedes domini lacrimis pedes eius rigavit
> et capillis suis tergebat et unguento ungebat.

Maundy Thursday mandatum antiphon: Ben33/66v (cued sn); Ben35/62v; Ben40/6; L606/152v

1   symonis: Ben35, L606

2   alabaustrum: Ben35

3   rigabit: Ben35

4   unguebat: L606

Text: derived from Luke 7:37–38, but with additions from other gospels; see Hesbert, "L'antiphonale" (4), pp. 79–84

GREG: compare antiphon "In diebus illis mulier" (CAO 3224; AMon, p. 975); antiphon "Mulier quae erat. . .attulit" (CAO 3822, AMon, p. 978); "Mulier quae erat . . . stans retro" (AMon, p. 585)

Demonstra mihi domine baptismum petri
ut agnoscam recte iustitiam tuam.

Nazarius antiphon: Ben20/236 [Ben21/212v: MIL melody]

Text: compare Mombritius, II, 328, ll. 8–9

MIL: antiphon Mugg. p. 251; Oxf. 169; *Manuale*, II, 320; Ben21/212v (CAO 2147)
2   iustitias domini (Ben21: iustitiam tuam)

De utero senectutis et sterilis
iohannes natus est precursor domini.
℣ Criminaque auferentem mundi xpistum cecinit.

John the Baptist antiphon: Solesmes/2

GREG (lines 1–2 only): antiphon, CAO 2753, AMon, p. 921 (Ex utero); Alleluia-verse in s. Italian manuscripts only
(see Schlager, *Thematischer Katalog*, no. 38, pp. 86–7, to which may be added London, BL, Eg. 3511; Vat. lat. 4770; Oxford,
Canon. liturg. 342)

MIL: psallenda: Oxf. 141; *Manuale*, II, 303
1   de sterilis (sterili: Oxf.)
2   preco luminis (precursor domini)
3   omitted

Alleluia. ℣ De ventre matris mee vocavit me dominus nomen iohannes.

John the Baptist Alleluia: Ben38/110; Ben40/89

Text: compare Ps. 21:11; Ps. 70:6; Is. 45:4; Is. 49:1

GREG: compare introit (*Sextuplex*, 134–5; GRom, p. 523): De ventre matris meae vocavit me Dominus nomine meo: et posuit
os meum ut gladium acutum: sub tegumento manus suae protexit me, posuit me quasi sagittam electam

ROM: compare introit, F22/80v; 5319/111v; MMMA, p. 1. Text as in GREG

De ventre matris mee vocavit me dominus nomine meo.
℣ Condiditque cuncta verbo et in lucem protulit.

John the Baptist antiphon: Solesmes/2

Text: see entry above

MIL: (BEN verse not present) antiphon Oxf. 137v, *Manuale*, II, 301, LVesp, p. 646; psallenda *Manuale*, II, 303

GREG: compare introit (see entry above)

ROM: compare introit (see entry above)

Alleluia. ℣ Dicite in gentibus quia dominus regnavit a ligno.

Alleluia: Ben40/124v (Holy Cross I); Ben40/125 (Holy Cross II, cued sn)

GREG: Alleluia-verse, Easter Friday and feasts of the Holy Cross; see Schlager, *Thematischer Katalog*, no. 347, pp. 224–5;
.GRom, pp. 256, 491

Dicite pastores quem vidistis
annunciate nobis quis in terra apparuit
natum vidimus in choro angelorum salvatorem nostrum
venite adoremus.

Christmas communion: Ben35/202

Text: see Hesbert, "L'antiphonale" (1), pp. 41–66

G R E G: compare antiphon C A O 4455, AMon, p. 240 (Quem vidistis pastores dicite annunciate nobis in terris quis apparuit. Natum vidimus in choro angelorum, Salvatorem Dominum, alleluia, alleluia); ℟, C A O 7470 (Quem vidistis pastores dicite annunciate nobis in terris quis apparuit. Natum vidimus in choro angelorum, Salvatorem Dominum, alleluia, alleluia. ℣ Natus est or ℣ Dicite quindnam). Both these texts have important variants; see C A O and Hesbert

R O M: compare antiphon (B 79/29v; 29988/23v): Quem vidistis pastores dicite annuntiate nobis in terris quis apparuit; natum vidimus et choros angelorum collaudantes dominum [29988 *adds*: mundi salvatorem]. And compare ℟ (B 79/26v, 29988/22v): text as in R O M antiphon omitting *mundi salvatorem*; ℣ Dicite quindam (B 79); ℣ Natus est nobis (29988)

> Dixerunt discipuli ad beatum martinum
> cur nos pater deseris aut cui nos desolatos relinquis
> invadent enim gregem tuum lupi rapaces.

Martin communion: Ben40/139

Text: Sulpicius Severus, see Mombritius, II, 229, ll. 13–14

M I L: psallenda, F.2.2/2; *Manuale*, II, 4; LVesp, p. 509
3   eum (enim): F.2.2

G R E G: antiphon (C A O 2262; AMon, p. 1115); ℟ (C A O 6463, with ℣ Scimus quidem). For use of this text as a gradual in Italian sources (Ben34; Ben39; Vat. lat. 6082; Vercelli 56; Torino F. I V. 8; Ivrea 60; Modena O. I. 7), see Oury, "Formulaires anciens," pp. 31–2

R O M: antiphon, B 79/169v; 29988/138v (deseris pater; orphanos (desolatos)); ℟, B 79/168v; 29988/137v (deserit pater: B 79; orphanos (desolatos)); ℣ Domine si adhuc (B 79); ℣ Scimus quidem (29988)

> Domine audivi auditum tuum et timui
> consideravi opera tua et expavi.
>   ℣ In medio annorum notum facies
> cum iratus fueris misericordie recordaveris.
>   ℣ Deus ab austro veniet et sanctus de monte umbroso.
>   ℣ Operuit celos gloria eius et laude eius repletur terra.
>   ℣ Suscitans suscitabis arcum tuum iuramenta patribus
> que locutus es.
>   ℣ Egressus in salutem populi tui in salutem cum xristo tuo.
>   ℣ Viam fecisti in mare equis tuis in luto aquarum multarum.
>   ℣ Ego autem in domino gaudebo et exultabo in deo hiesu meo.
>   ℣ Et ponam pedes meos quasi cervorum
> et super excelsa mea deducet me victor in psalmis canentem.

Holy Saturday tract: Ben38/44; Ben40/15v; Vat. lat. 10657/2v (palimpsest); Rome, Vall. C 9/19 (Maundy Thursday) (palimpsest); Rome, Vall. C 9/32v (palimpsest); Wolfenb. 112/36 palimpsest
  3   in medioo (first o cancelled): Ben38; motum: Ben38
  6   laudes: Ben38
  7   suscitans suscitavi: Ben40; tribus (patribus): Ben38
  9   Egressus es: Ben40
 10   Quam (viam): Ben40; tui (tuis): Ben38; multtarum (first t cancelled): Ben38
 12   meo: Ben38
 13   deducit: Ben38

Text: Habakkuk 3:2–3, 9A, 13A, 15, 18, 19B. Verses are essentially Vulgate, while opening section is non-Vulgate. G R E G and R O M use older version throughout. See Hesbert, "L'antiphonale" (6), pp. 171–5; PM X I V, 361–5

G R E G: compare Good Friday gradual/tract: *Sextuplex*, 94–5; GRom, p. 206

R O M: Good Friday, F22/50; 5319/79v; MMMA, p. 228. Text essentially as in G R E G

Domine defende nos
Domine protege nos
Hemmanuhel nobiscum deus adiuva nos
Kyrieleyson. Kyrieleyson. Kyrieleyson.
Xpiste audi nos
Sancta maria ora pro nobis.

Holy Saturday litany: Ben39/27; Ben40/18v; Farfa/Bv
1 *om* Farfa
2 *add* Domine guberna nos: Farfa
3 emmanuhel: Farfa
4 Kyrieleyson. Xristeleyson. Kyrieleyson: Ben39, Farfa
6 *add* Xpiste audi nos: Ben39; *add* Xpiste audi nos; Sancte michahel ora pro nobis; Xpiste audi nos: Farfa

Dominus hiesus postquam cenavit cum discipulis suis
lavit pedes eorum et ait illis
Scitis quid fecerim vobis ego dominus et magister
exemplum dedi vobis ut et vos ita faciatis.

Maundy Thursday mandatum antiphon: Ben35/62v; Ben40/6v
1 *suis* written twice, the first cancelled: Ben35

Text: compare John 13:5, 13–15; see Hesbert, "L'antiphonale" (4), pp. 90–2

GREG: Maundy Thursday communion (*Sextuplex*, 94–5; GRom, p. 201), sometimes also as antiphon (CAO 2413)

ROM: Maundy Thursday communion, F22/49v; 5319/79; MMMA, p. 447

Alleluia. ℣ Dominus in celo paravit sedem suam.

Ascension Alleluia: Ben38/93v; Ben40/71v

Text: Ps. 102:19A

GREG: compare antiphon CAO 2408: Dominus in coelo, alleluia, paravit sedem suam, alleluia. Text, adding "et regnum eius omnium domina," used as alleluia-verse in Italian manuscripts (Ben35, Ben40; Modena O. I. 13; Rome, Angelica 123; Vat. lat. 10645); see Schlager, *Thematischer Katalog*, no. 271 (pp. 192–4); Dold, "Fragmente," p. 45

ROM: compare antiphon B 79/121, 29988/92 bis. Text as in CAO 2408

Doxa en ipsisti theo kepi gis irini
alleluia alleluia alleluia.

[Δόξα ἐν ὑψίστοις Θεῶ καὶ ἐπὶ γῆς εἰρήνη
ἀλληλούια ἀλληλούια ἀλληλούια.]

Holy Saturday antiphon: Ben38/46v; Ben40/19; Farfa/Bv; Vat. lat. 10657/Ar (palimpsest)
1 ipsistis: Ben40, Farfa; yrini: Ben40; kyrini: Farfa

Text: Greek (Septuagint) version of *Gloria in excelsis* (Luke 2:14); Greek antiphons in Beneventan manuscripts are accompanied by Latin versions: see *Gloria in excelsis*

Dum congregarentur inimicis mei simul adversus me
ut acciperent animam meam consiliati sunt
ego vero in te speravi domine.
℣ Non me conclusisti in manus inimici
et statuisti in spatioso loco pedes meos.

Palm Sunday gradual: Ben38/38

Text: Ps. 30:14B–15A, 9, Rom: "omnes (inim. mei); adversus; nec conclusisti me; loco spatioso" (but a tradition of BEN version exists, see Rom)

MIL: feria IV in Auth, ℟: BL, p. 234; *Manuale*, II, 179
1   inimici; adversum
4–5   ℣ In te speravi. . .

> Dum famis inopia tristes fratres cerneret beatus benedictus
> per prophetie spiritus eos ammonuit
> hodie minus habetis crastina vero habundanter habebitis.

Benedict antiphon: Ben19/93v; Ben21/93v (CAO 2454); Ben22/156; Vat. lat. 10646/51 (incomplete); MC 542, p. 112
1   panis: Ben22, MC 542
2   spiritu: Ben22; spiritum: MC 542
3   abundanter: Ben22

Text: Gregory the Great, compare Mombritius, I, 167, ll. 16–7

> Dum pateretur beatus vincentius ait ad datianum
> dominum hiesum fateor filium patris altissimi
> quem negare non possum quia que vera sunt confiteor.

Vincent antiphon: Ben19/35; Ben21/66v (CAO 2463); Ben22/132; MC 542/p. 88; MC Comp. v
2   iesum: Ben19
3   que (quem): Ben21

Text: compare Mombritius, II, 627, ll. 25–7

> Dum sacra misteria cerneret iohannes
> archangelus michahel tuba cecinit
> dignus es domine deus noster
> accipere librum et aperire signacula eius alleluia.

Michael ingressa: Ben38/83; Ben40/61; Rome, Vall. C 9/168v (palimpsest)

Text: compare Rev. 5:9 ("Dignus es accipere librum et aperire signacula eius"); 4:11 ("dignus es Domine et Deus noster accipere gloriam. . .")

GREG: antiphon CAO 2469 (4 MSS); compare AMon, p. 1057

> Dum sanctificatus fuero in vobis coram eis
> tollam quippe vos de gentibus
> et congregabo vos dicit dominus.

Antiphon ad scrutinium: Ben38/21; Vat. Barb. lat. 697/17, 20 sn; Rome, Vall. C 32/1, 2v sn
2   gntibus: Ben38

Text: Ezek. 36:23B–24A: "cum (dum); congregabo de universis terris"

MIL: compare Pentecost, post ev. (Oxf. 100v; *Manuale*, II, 273; AMed, p. 256): "Cum sanctificatus fuero in vobis congregabo vos de universo mundo dabo vobis cor novum alleluia alleluia"

GREG: compare feria 4 of Lent 4 introit: *Sextuplex*, pp. 76–7; GRom, p. 145

ROM: compare feria 4 of Lent 4 introit: F22/35v; 5319/62v; MMMA 2, p. 21. Text as in GREG introit

> Dum visitaret me oriens ex alto
> audivi vocem dicentem michi sequere me
> statim non quievit caro et animam
> sed tuli crucem meam secutus sum dominum meum.

Andrew communion: Ben38/140v; Ben40/142v

>Ecce magnum et verum sacerdotem
>ecce bonum dispensatorem
>qui clamidem suam dans pauperi
>xpistum induit et videre meruit.
>℣ Dispersit dedit pauperibus
>iustitia eius manet in eternum.

Martin gradual: Ben40/138v

Text: ℣, Ps. 111:9 ("manet in saeculum saeculi")

MIL: ℟, F.2.2/IV; *Manuale*, II, 3
3 et (qui): *Manuale*; om suam
4 xristum videre meruit
5–6 replaced with ℣ Gloria et divitiae

ROM: ℟, B 79/169; 29988/138
3–4 "et clamidem suam dans pauperi cristi cristum enim induit": B 79; "qui clamidem xpisto xpistum enim induit": 29988
6 seculum seculi (eternum)

>Ecce quam bonum et quam iocundum habitare fratres in unum.

Twelve Brothers antiphon: Ben20/278; Ben21/235v (CAO 2538); Melk 1012/Av-1027/Zr; MC Comp. v

Text: Ps. 132:1

MIL: psallenda, *Manuale*, II, 298 (Prot. and Gerv.)

GREG: gradual, *Sextuplex*, pp. 136–7 (John and Paul), pp. 196–7 (Pentecost XXII, XXIII); GRom, pp. 384, 455 (with verses ℣ Sicut unguentum, ℣ Mandavit)

ROM: gradual, Bodmer/515; 5319/112v (John and Paul), 133* (Pentecost XXI); F22/89v (Feasts of martyrs), 73v* (Pent. XXI); MMMA, p. 112. Text as in GREG

>Ecce sedet in medio eius super thronum maiestatis sue agnus
>et vox sonat ante eum dicens
>vicit leo de tribu iuda radix david
>et quattuor animalia requiem non habent
>dicentia sedenti super thronum
>Sanctus Sanctus Sanctus es domine deus omnipotens
>qui es et qui eras et qui venturus es alleluia. All[eluia].

Ascension ingressa: Ben38/93: Ben40/71; Rome, Vall. C 9/169 (palimpsest)
1 agnum: Ben40
4 requie: Ben38
6 est (es): Ben38

Text: compare Rev. 5:6 (et vidi et ecce in medio throni et quattuor animalium et in medio seniorum agnum . . .); 5:5 (ecce vicit leo de tribu Iuda radix David . . .); 4:8 (et quattuor animalia singula eorum habebant alas senas et in circuitu et intus plena sunt oculis et requiem non habent die et nocte dicentia sanctus sanctus sanctus Dominus Deus omnipotens qui erat et qui est et qui venturus est)

MIL: compare Christmas offertory (BL, p. 61; *Manuale*, II, 61; AMed, p. 44) Ecce apertum est templum tabernaculi testimoni et Jerusalem nova descendit de caelo, in qua est sedes Dei, et Agni: et servi eius offerunt ei munera, dicentes: Sanctus, Sanctus, Sanctus, Dominus Deus omnipotens, qui erat, et qui est, et qui venturus est.
℣ Et ecce sedet in medio ejus super thronum majestatis suae Agnus: et vox sonat ante eum, dicens: Vicit Leo de tribu Juda, radix David. Et quattuor animalia requiem non habent, dicentia sedenti super thronum. Sanctus. . .

Ecce vir dei benedictus reliquid nutricem suam secutus est dominus.

Benedict antiphon: Ben19/86v; Ben21/90v (CAO 2556); Ben22/153v; MC 542/p. 105

Text: compare Mombritius, I, 157, ll. 15–16
1 reliquit: MC 542; dominum: Ben19, MC 542

Enumen se xpiste ke imnologume se
oti dia tu stauru exigorasas ton kosmon.

[Αἰνοῦμέν σε Χριστέ καὶ ὑμνολογοῦμέν σε
ὅτι διὰ τοῦ σταυροῦ ἐξηγόρασας τὸν κόσμον.]

Good Friday antiphon: Ben40/11; Vat. lat. 10673/29
1 ymnologumen: Vat. 10673
2 tus: Ben40; cosmon: Vat. 10673

Text: Greek version of "Laudamus te"

Expletis missarum sollempniis lotisque manibus viri dei
hausta eadem aqua ab omni curabantur infirmitate.

Barbatus antiphon: Ben21/87v (CAO 2800); Ben22/146v; Vat. lat. 14446/38v

Text: compare AA SS, Feb. III, 140, n. 4
1 sollempnis: Vat. lat. 14446
2 austa: Ben21, Vat. lat. 14446

Exultet iam angelica turba . . .

For Beneventan sources of the Exultet see Chapter 2. Two versions of the text circulated in southern Italy: the Beneventan text was succeeded by the more usual Vulgate text (for these texts see Pinell, "La benediccíó")

Factus est repente de celo sonus advenientis spiritus vehementis
ubi erant sedentes alleluia
et repleti sunt omnes spiritu sancto loquentes magnalia dei
alleluia alleluia.

Pentecost ingressa: Ben38/99 palimpsest; Ben40/79v; MC 361 p. 143 (palimpsest); Rome, Vall. C 9/169 (palimpsest)

Text: compare Acts 2:2 (et factus est repente de caelo sonum tamquam advenientis spiritus vehementis et replevit totam domum ubi erant sedentes); 2:4 (et repleti sunt omnes Spiritu Sancto); 2:11 (audivimus loquentes eos nostris linguis magnalia Dei)

MIL: Pentecost ingressa (Oxf. 99; *Manuale*, II, 272; AMed, p. 253): text as here with only one final Alleluia

GREG: Pentecost communion, *Sextuplex*, pp. 124–5; GRom, p. 296. For use of this text as offertory, see Hesbert, "Un antique offertoire"; Levy, "Charlemagne's archetype." Compare also R, CAO 6717; antiphon CAO 2487

ROM: Pentecost communion, Bodmer/510; F22/63; 5319/108; MMMA, p. 500. Three final Alleluias

Gaudeamus omnes in domino
diem festum celebrantes sub honore sanctorum omnium
de quorum commemoratione gaudent angeli
et collaudant filium dei.

All Saints I ingressa: Ben40/133v

MIL: ingressa, Agatha (BL, p. 134; *Manuale*, II, 114; AMed, p. 444), All Saints (AMed, p. 557)
1 Laetemur (Gaudeamus)
2 ob honorem Agathe martyris (*or* omnium sanctorum)
3 de cuius tropheo (All Saints: de quorum tropheo)

GREG: introit, Agatha (*Sextuplex*, pp. 40–1; GRom, p. 436), All Saints (GRom, p. 647)

2   Agathae martyris (Agatha introit only)

3   de cuius passione (Agatha)

Compare also ℟, CAO 6760

ROM: introit, Agatha (Bodmer/460; F22/75v; 5319/31v; MMMA, p. 2), All Saints (5319/129, MMMA, p. 2)

2   agathe martyris (Agatha introit only)

3   de cuius passione (Agatha)

> Gaudent in celis anime sanctorum
> qui xpisti vestigia sunt secuti
> et quia pro eius amore sanguinem suum fuderunt.

Communion: Ben40/133v (All Saints I); Ben40/134v (All Saints II cued sn)

GREG: compare antiphon, CAO 2927 (Feasts of martyrs; All Saints): text as here, adding "ideo cum Christo regnabunt in aeternum" (4 MSS add "sine fine"). Compare with AMon, p. 653. Used also as "antiphona ante evangelium" in northern Italian MSS (Rome, Casanat. 1741; Rome, BNaz Sess. 62; Bologna 2824), according to Borders, "The northern Italian antiphons"

> Gemitus noster ad te non est absconditus
> cor nostrum conturbatum est in nos
> et deseruit nos fortitudo nostra
> exurge xpiste adiuva nos
> et libera nos propter nomen tuum.

Rogation antiphon: Ben35/90; Oxford, Can. lit. 277/125v sn

2   conturbatus: Ben35

4   adiuba: Ben35

MIL: Rogation antiphon, Oxf. 66v, *Manuale*, II, 253

1   Gemitus noster domine

2   nobis (nos)

3   desunt: Oxf.

> Alleluia. ℣ Germana fratrum nos turba precedat
> et pretiosa ab omni malo defendat.

Twelve Brothers Alleluia: Ben40/121v

> Gloria in excelsis. . .

Ben38/53 Easter, cued between ingressa and Alleluia; Ben40/133v All Saints I, cued sn between ingressa and Kyrie; Ben40/138v Martin, cued sn between ingressa and gradual; Rome, Vall. c 9/170v, palimpsest ("tu solus altissimus hiesu xprist. . .dei patris. amen.")

> Gloria in excelsis deo et in terra pax:
> alleluia alleluia alleluia.

Holy Saturday antiphon (accompanied by Greek version *Doxa*): Ben38/46v; Ben40/19; Farfa/Bv; Vat. lat. 10657/A (palimpsest)

Text: Luke 2:14 (Gloria in altissimis)

MIL: Christmas, antiphon ante evangelium (Oxf. 33; BL, p. 61; *Manuale*, II, 60; AMed, p. 43). This melody appears also as "antiphona ante evangelium" in northern Italian MSS (Verona 107; Rome, Casanat. 1741; Rome, BNaz Sess 62; Bologna 2824) according to Borders, "The northern Italian antiphons"

GREG: compare Christmas antiphon, CAO 2946, AMon, p. 243 ("pax hominibus bonae voluntatis, alleluia, alleluia")

ROM: compare Christmas antiphon, B 79/30, 29988/26; text as in GREG

> Gloriosus confessor domini benedictus
> vitam angelicam gerens in terris
> speculum divinum factus est mundo omnium
> et ideo cum xpisto sine fine iam gaudet.

Benedict communion: MC Comp. XXII, (lacks last three words); antiphon: Vat. Ottob. lat. 145/124v

GREG: antiphon, CAO 2965 (2 MSS, F and D only)
1 Hilarius: D
3 divinum (bonorum operum); *om* omnium
4 jam sine fine gaudet in coelis (D: coelo)
Compare ℟, CAO 6784

> Gratias ago deo meo quia hostia xpisti effici merui
> assatus non negavi et interrogatus xpistum confessus sum.

Lawrence ingressa: Ben40/112v

Text: compare Mombritius, II, 95, ll. 17–18

MIL: antiphon, Oxf. 185v; *Manuale*, II, 333; LVesp, p. 709
2 accusatus (assatus); *om* et

GREG: antiphon, CAO 2970; compare ℟, CAO 6763 (text as in ROM ℟)

ROM: ℟, B 79/146v; 29988/115; "Gaudeo plane quia ianuas tuas ingredi merui; Accusatus non negavi interrogatus te criste confessus sum assatus gratias ago. ℣ Probasti domine. . . ."

> Hec est vera fraternitas
> que vicit mundi crimina
> xpistum secuta inclita
> regna tenens celestia.

Twelve Brothers antiphon: Ben20/278; Ben21/235v (CAO 3004); Melk 1027/Zr; MC Comp. V
4 tenent: Ben21

GREG: Alleluia ℣, GRom, p. 495, used in Italian (and Dalmatian: Oxf. 342/82) MSS for the Twelve Brothers and other martyrs: see Schlager, *Thematischer Katalog*, no. 348 (pp. 227–8); and also Naples XVI A 19/46

> Helisabeth zacharie magnum virum genuit
> iohannem baptistam precursorem domini.
> ℣ Seni patri nasciturus quem predixit angelus.

John the Baptist antiphon: Solesmes/2

MIL: antiphon, Oxf. 138v; *Manuale*, II, 302
1 virum magnum
2 *om* precursorem domini
3 *om*
℟, Oxf. 139, *Manuale*, II, 302
1 virum magnum
2 *add* cuius nativitatis (*Manuale*: natalitio) letatur ecclesia
3 *om*; *add* ℣ Accipiens pugilarem. . .

GREG: antiphon, CAO 2639, AMon, p. 924 (no ℣); compare ℟, CAO 6652

ROM: antiphon, B 79/130, 29988/101 (no ℣)

> Heloy heloy lama sabathani
> deus meus deus meus ut quid me dereliquisti.
> ℣ A sexta autem hora tenebre facte sunt
> super universam terram usque in horam nonam
> et circa horam nonam exclamavit ihesus voce magna dicens. Heloy.

Good Friday antiphon: Ben33/72v cued sn; Ben38/43; Ben39/25; Ben40/14v; L606/156; Subiaco XVIII, p. 77
1 Heloy eloi: L606; lamassabathani: Ben38, Subiaco
3 facte written twice: Ben38
4 oram: Ben40; per (super): Subiaco
5 iesus: L606; hiesus: Ben39

Text: Matt. 27:46B; 45–46A (hoc est Deus meus . . .; dereliquisti me [but compare *Vulgata* variants]; ad horam; clamavit [compare Mark 15:34: exclamavit]

GREG: CAO 2640 (deus deus meus; without ℣); compare also Rome, Vall. C 5/148; Vall. C 13/403

> Hodie exultat celum et letantur omnis terra
> florens mater ecclesia de virtute et gloria
> qualem dedit dominus omnibus sanctis suis.

All Saints II, final antiphon (second communion?): Ben40/134v

> Alleluia. ℣ Hodie migravit ad dominum beatus petrus princeps apostolorum.

Peter Alleluia: Ben39/121
1 Second syllable of *migravit* written twice, the first *gra* cancelled. The Alleluia is accompanied by a prosula: "Vertex ter quaternorum ethera nunc conscendit fulgidum in cuiuc vos laude deicole hoc canite carmen"

> Alleluia. ℣ Hodie natus est nobis dominus
> gaudent omnes angeli in celo.

Christmas Alleluia: Baltimore, Walters 6/86

GREG: compare antiphon CAO 3111 (Ben21 only): Hodie natus est Christus, gaudent omnes angeli in coelo; gaudete et vos, fideles omnes, hymnum canite et dicite, Gloria in excelsis Deo, alleluia

> Alleluia. ℣ Hodie transfiguratus est dominus coram tribus discipulis.
> ℣ Moyses et helias hinc inde secum loquentes ascendit in maiestate.

Transfiguration Alleluia: Ben39/140v

> Hodie xristus natus est.
> Hodie salvator apparuit.
> Hodie in terra canunt angeli. Letantur archangeli.
> Hodie exultant iusti dicentes
> gloria in excelsis deo et in terra pax hominibus [b]one voluntatis
> alleluia alleluia.

Christmas offertory: Ben35/202

Text: on Byzantine elements of this text, see Wellesz, *Eastern Elements*, pp. 141–9; Baumstark, "Byzantinisches," p. 169; Baumstark, "Die Hodie-Antiphonen"

GREG: antiphon, CAO 3093, AMon, p. 249; ends "Gloria in excelsis deo, alleluia"

ROM: antiphon 29988/26v. Text as in GREG, except: in terris

Hos duodecim misit hiesus in mundum
predicare gentibus regnum dei.

Twelve Brothers antiphon: Ben21/236 (CAO 3139); communion: Ben40/122; MC 361, p. 166 palimpsest

Hymnum canite, *see* Ymnum canite

Inclinato capite hiesus tradidit spiritum et terra tremuit.
℣ Ut nos a peccatorum vinculis solveret
mortem suam in cruce positum circa horam nonam. Incli.

Good Friday antiphon: Ben38/43v; Ben39/25v; Ben40/15v; L606/156; Subiaco XVIII/77v sn
1   ihesus: L606; spiritu: Ben38
3   morte sua: L606, Subiaco; positus: Ben39, Ben40, L606

Text: compare John 19:30 (et inclinato capite tradidit spiritum), Matt. 27:51 (et terra motum est)
MIL: Holy Saturday antiphon, BL, p. 255; *Manuale*, II, 196. Omits verse
1   reddidit
2–3   omitted. Adds ℣ *Adhaesit pavimento*

Alleluia. ℣ In conspectu angelorum psallam tibi deus.

Michael Alleluia: Ben38/43

Text: Ps. 137:1 (Rom, Ga omit *deus*)

MIL: antiphon, common of martyrs, Oxf. 256; *Manuale*, II, 384; LVesp, p. 465 (compare LVesp, p. 765): In conspectu
sanctorum . . .

GREG: Offertory, Ded. sci. Michaelis, *Sextuplex*, p. 160; antiphon, CAO 3215, AMon, p. 146: text as here adding "meus";
for use of this text as Alleluia, see Schlager, *Thematischer Katalog*, nos. 119, 165, 397; compare ℟, CAO 6893, 6894

ROM: compare offertory, Ded. sci. Michaelis, 5319/128v; F22/85; MMMA, p. 356: "In conspectu angelorum psallam tibi et
adorabo ad templum sanctum tuum et confitebor nomini tuo domine. ℣ Confitebor. ℣ Confiteantur"

Alleluia. ℣ In omnem terram.

Alleluia: Ben38/116 (Peter, cued); Ben40/128v (Simon and Jude, cued)

Text: Ps. 18:5 (?)

GREG: compare gradual (vigil of St Peter), *Sextuplex*, pp. 136–7, GRom, p. 629; Alleluia (Philip and Jacob), *Sextuplex*, p. 115;
offertory (Simon and Jude), *Sextuplex*, pp. 162–3, GRom, p. 406; antiphon, CAO 3262; compare, ℟, CAO 6918, 6919

ROM: antiphon (apostles), B 79/175 (text as in CAO 3262)

[In omnem] terram exivit sonus eorum et in [fines] orbis terre
verba eorum . . .

Rome, Vall. C 9/173 palimpsest. Simon and Jude (?) or common of apostles (?), gradual or offertory (?)

Text: Ps. 18:5

Insigne preconium alme tue nobilitatis consona voce collaudantes
verbo fragili prosequamur
ave inclite martir vincenti angelorum consors apostolorum socie
prophetarum concivis et martirum coheres
intercede pro nostra omniumque salutem.

Vincent antiphon: Ben19/35; Ben21/67 (CAO 3355); Ben22/132v; MC 542, p. 86; MC Comp. v
3   martyr: Ben19, Ben22, MC Comp. v

4 concives: Ben19; martyrum: Ben19, MC Comp. v

5 omnium: Ben19, Ben22, MC 542; MC Comp. v; salute: MC 542, Ben19

MIL: Mauritius, post evangelium: Oxf. 109v; *Manuale*, II, 355; AMed, p. 536

2 supplici (fragili)

3 martyr: *om* vincentius; socius

5 sancte mauriti intercede; omnium; salute (*Manuale*, AMed)

GREG: antiphon, CAO 3355, with variants: text as here only in Ben21

Inter natos mulierum non est maior Iohanne baptista
maior prophetis et minor angelis
qui preparavit corda fidelium.

John the Baptist communion: Ben38/110v (cued); offertory: Ben40/89v; antiphon: Vat. Ottob. lat. 145/124; Solesmes/2 (incomplete: apparently a verse was attached, whose ending (. . . *baptizare dominum*) is found on f. 3, followed by cue to beginning of antiphon)

Text: compare Luke 7:28 ("inter natos mulierum propheta Iohanne baptista nemo est")

MIL: psallenda, Oxf. 140; *Manuale*, II, 303; compare LVesp. p. 647 ("Major prophetis et minor angelis qui preparavit corda fidelium")

GREG: compare antiphon, CAO 3369 (Inter natos mulierum non est major Johanne Baptista); CAO 3370, AMon, p. 925 (Inter natos mulierum non surrexit major Joanne Baptista); ℟, CAO 6979 (Inter natos mulierum non surrexit major Joanne Baptista, qui viam Domino praeparavit in eremo)

ROM: antiphon, Ben79/130; 29988/101; text as in CAO 3370

In tribulationibus exaudi nos
mitte nobis de celo auxilium
quia multa mala circumdederunt nos
libera nos domine deus noster.

Rogation antiphon: Ben34/157; Ben35/89v; Ben38/26v; Ben39/3; Vat. Reg. lat. 334/71v; Naples XVI A 19/8

4 *om* nos: Ben38

Iohannes est nomen eius et multi in nativitate eius gaudebunt.

John the Baptist offertory: Ben38/110v (cued); antiphon: Solesmes/2

Text: combination of Luke 1:63 and 1:14

MIL: antiphon, Oxf. 137v; *Manuale*, II, 301; LVesp. p. 649

GREG: compare antiphon CAO 3498, AMon, p. 920 (Johannes est nomen eius; vinum et siceram non bibet, et multi. . .); antiphon, CAO 3504, AMon, p. 924 (Johannes vocabitur nomen ejus, et in nativitate ejus multi gaudebunt)

ROM: compare antiphon B 79/130; 29988/101; text as in CAO 3504; Alleluia, Bodmer/514 (according to Cutter, *Musical Sources*)

Ipse super maria fundavit eam
et super flumina preparavit illam.

Pentecost vigil antiphon: Ben33/97v; Ben35/110v; Ben38/95; Ben39/92v; Ben40/73v; Vat. lat. 10645/4v

1 fundabit: Ben35; ea: Vat. 10645

2 illa: Ben38, Vat. 10645

Text: Ps. 23:2 (Rom: eam, illam; Ga: eum, eum)

MIL: Epiphany antiphon, BL, p. 103; *Manuale*, II, 88

1 eum

2 eum

Isti sunt sancti qui pro testamento dei sua corpora tradiderunt
et in sanguine agni laverunt stolas suas
congregamini omnes et videte virtutem
quantam gloriam dedit dominus sanctis suis.

All Saints II ingressa: Ben40/134

Text: compare Rev. 7:14 (hii sunt qui . . . laverunt stolas et dealbaverunt eas in sanguine agni); compare text "Congregamini" above

MIL: common of martyrs, transitorium: Oxf. 272v; *Manuale*, II, 390

1 *om* sancti

3 after omnes *add* qui timetis deum; *om* virtutem

GREG: ℞, CAO 7018 (text as in MIL, with ℣ Isti sunt qui contempserunt); compare antiphon CAO 3444, AMon, p. 651 (Isti sunt. . . stolas suas.)

ROM: compare antiphon B 79/138v; text as in CAO 3444

Alleluia. ℣ Iustorum anime in manu dei sunt.

Alleluia: Ben40/133v (All Saints I, cued sn); Ben40/134v (All Saints II)

Text: Wisdom 3:1 (*Iustorum autem*)

MIL: compare Alleluia (BL, pp. 83*, 122*, 139*; *Manuale*, II, 389; AMed, p. 357; text as here adding "et non tanget illos tormentum malitiae"); ℞ (Oxf. 259v; *Manuale*, II, 386; text as in MIL Alleluia plus ℣ Et si coram.); psallenda (Oxf. 161v; *Manuale*, II, 387; text as here adding "et non tanget illos tormentum mortis"). All pieces used for common or proper of several martyrs

GREG: compare gradual (*Sextuplex*, see index p. 237; GRom, p. 413: text as in MIL Alleluia, with ℣ Visi sunt); communion (*Sextuplex*, see index p. 250; GRom, p. 505: text as in MIL Alleluia plus "visi sunt oculis insipientium mori, illi autem sunt in pace"); compare antiphons CAO 3538; CAO 3539; ℞, CAO 7055, CAO 7056, CAO 7057. Used for feasts or common of several martyrs

ROM: compare gradual (Bodmer/512; 5319/110v; F22/89v; MMMA, p. 127; text as in GREG gradual), communion (Bodmer/504; 5319/104v; F22/91; MMMA, p. 438: text as in GREG communion (oculi) plus "alleluia alleluia"), antiphon (B 79/178v; 29988/146: text as in MIL Alleluia except: *Justorum autem*); feasts of several martyrs

Kyrieleyson kyrieleyson kyrieleyson

Rome, Vall. C 9/170v palimpsest; Ben40/133v, All Saints I, cued sn

Laudamus te xpiste et ymnum dicimus tibi
quia per crucem redemisti mundum.

Good Friday adoration antiphon: Ben33/69; Ben35/65v; Ben40/11; L606/156; Vat. Barb. lat. 560/15 cued sn; Vat. lat. 4770/91v sn; Vat. lat. 10673/29

1 ynnum: 4770; hymnum: 10673

2 crucem tuam: 4770

Text: compare with "Enumen se"

MIL: adoration antiphon, BL, p. 248; *Manuale*, II, 189; AMed, p. 182.

GREG: compare CAO 1287 (Adoramus te, Christe, et benedicimus tibi, quia per crucem tuam redemisti mundum); see above, entry "Adoramus crucem"

Alleluia. ℣ Laudate pueri domini *see* Alleluia ℣ Resurrexit.

Lavi pedes tuos discipule
feci te testem sacramenti mei
manducasti panem meum
et tu quare sine causa sitisti sanguinem meum.

℣ Homo unanimis dux meus et notus meus qui simul mecum.
Man[ducasti].

Maundy Thursday *mandatum* responsory: Ben30/71; Ben33/66v cued sn; Ben35/63; Ben39/21; Ben40/6v; L606/153 (unianimis); Bologna 144/framm. 3, incomplete

Text: verse is Ps. 54:14–15A (more usual reading, in both Rom and Ga, is "unianimis")

ROM: Maundy Thursday ℟, B 79/96v; 29988/66

1 *om* discipule
2 *add* paravi convivium
5–6 ℣ Homo pacis meae in quo sperabam, qui edebat panes meos, ampliavit adversus (29988: adversum) me supplantationem. Para[vi] (29988: Manducasti)

Lumen ad revelationem gentium et gloriam plebis tue israhel.

Purification antiphon: Ben35/15v; Bologna 2551/34

Text: Luke 2:32

GREG: antiphon, CAO 3645, AMon, p. 803

ROM: antiphon, B 79/62v

Lumen quod animus cernens non sensum corporeus
in utero vivens iohannes exultat in domino
natus est luminis precursor propheta mirabilis
ostendens agnum qui venit peccata mundi solvere.

John the Baptist ingressa: Ben38/110; Ben40/89; Vat. lat. 10657/103, palimpsest; Rome, Vall. C 9/169v (palimpsest)
1 cernit: Ben40; sensu: Ben40
2 exultas *corrected to* exultat: Ben40

MIL: psallenda, Oxf. 139v; *Manuale*, II, 303
1 animi cernunt; sensus
2 vidit (vivens); exultans
4 ostendit; tollere (solvere)
This text, in essentially the MIL version, is used as antiphon ante evangelium in Verona 107/98 and Bologna 2824/67v, according to Borders, "The northern Italian antiphons," and Planchart, "Antiphonae ante evangelium."

Magnus es domine deus noster quoniam tu castigas et salvas
deducis ad inferos et reducis
et post lacrimationem et fletum exultationem inducis.
℣ Benedictus es domine deus patrum nostrorum
qui cum iratus fuerit misericordiam facis.

Responsory: Ben20/81v; Ben37/9; Naples XVI A 19/34v
4 Benedictus dictus (at page turn): Ben37
Text: derived from Tobias 13:1–2; 3:22B; 3:13

Mandaverunt iuliano cesare
sancti viri iohannes et paulus dicentes
scias quia xpistum colimus
et ad tuam salutationem numquam veniemus.

John and Paul antiphon: Ben20/204; Ben21/192v (CAO 3689); MC Comp. V
1 cesari: Ben20, MC Comp. V
Text: compare Mombritius, I, 572, ll. 11–13

> Maria vidit angelum amictum splendorem
> Quem cum lacrimis interrogavit de xpisto salvatore
> Ubi est meus dominus et filius excelsis alleluia
> Quem iudas per osculum ut agnum crucifixit
> Lapis revolutus est ab ore monumenti
> Illum quem queris dominum surrexit sicut dixit alleluia
> Alleluia alleluia

Easter ingressa: Ben38/52v; Ben40/159v

1 splendore: Ben40

3 filius us excelsi: Ben40

4 agnus: Ben40

5 revolutum: Ben38

GREG: versions of this text used as processional antiphon in the ninth-century antiphoner of Compiègne (Paris, BN, lat. 17436, f. 29, ed. in *Sextuplex*, p. 223), in Vat. Reg. lat. 334/88v and in Oxford, Bodl. Douce 222/195; and as a Kyrie-trope in Ben34/123v (ed. AH, XLVII, 186–7; Chevalier, *Repertorium*, no. 34929) and Ben39/28v (first noticed by Alejandro Planchart and announced in "New wine in old bottles")

Compiègne: 1 splendore/ 2 interrogat/ 3 excelsis; *om* alleluia/ 4 follows line 5/ 5 quod lapis; monumento

Reg. Lat. 334: 1 indutus/ 2 interrogat/ 3 excelsis; *om* alleluia/ 4 agnus crucifixum/ 5 revolutus; monumentis/ 6 non est hic surrexit sicut dixit alleluia/ 7 4 alleluias

Douce 222: 1 splendore/ 2 interrogabat/ 3 excelsis; *om* alleluia/ 4 quem iudas osculum tradit ut agnum crucifixit alleluia/ 5 quem lapis/ 6 queritis

Ben34, Ben39:
Kyrieleison.
> Ad monumentum domini plorabant mulieres. Kyrieleison.
> Maria vidit angelum amictum splendore (Ben34: splendorem). Ky[rieleison].
> Cum lacrimis interrogat (Ben34: interrogant)de xpisto salvatore. Xpisteleison.
> Ubi est meus dominus et filius excelsi. X[pisteleison].
> Quem iudas tradidit osculum ut agnum crucifixit. X[pisteleison].
> Cum lapis revolutus est ab ore monumenti. K[yrieleison].
> Sedit desuper angelus mulieribus dixit. K[yrieleison].
> Illum quem queris mulier surrexit sicut dixit. K[yrieleison].
> In galileam pergitis ibi eum videbitis. K[yrieleison].
> Alleluia alleluia alleluia.

> Martinus abrahe sinu letus excipitur
> martinus hic pauper et modicus
> celum dives ingreditur
> ymnis celestibus honoratur.

Martin offertory: Ben40/139

Text: Sulpicius Severus, see Mombritius, II, 230, ll. 9–11

MIL: psallenda, F.2.2/2; *Manuale*, II, 4; LVesp, p. 510

GREG: antiphon, CAO 3711, AMon, p. 1116; ℟, CAO 7132, with ℣ *Martinus episcopus* or ℣ *Oculis ac manibus*. For the use of this text as a communion in the mass *O beatum virum*, see Oury, "Formulaires anciens," pp. 30–1; as Alleluia verse, see Oury, p. 34 and Schlager, *Thematischer Katalog*, nos. 38, 245, 318

ROM: antiphon B 79/169; 29988/138v; ℟, B 79/168v (℣, *Dum sacramenta*); 29988/137v (℣, *Oculis ac manibus*)

Michi autem absit gloriari
nisi in cruce domini mei hiesu xpristi alleluia.

Holy Cross I ingressa: Ben40/124v; Rome, Vall. c 9/168v (palimpsest)

Text: Galatians 6:14 (domini nostri; for early use of "domini mei" see Wordsworth-White, II, 404)

GREG: compare introit ("Nos autem gloriari oportet. . ."), *Sextuplex*, see index, p. 233; GRom, pp. 195, 490; antiphon, CAO 3953, AMon, p. 1041 ("Nos autem gloriari oportet. . ."); ℟, CAO 7152 (MS r only: ℟, "Mihi autem absit gloriari, alleluia, alleluia." ℣ "Nisi in cruce Domini nostri Jesu Christi.")

ROM: compare introit (Tuesday in Holy Week, Maundy Thursday, feasts of the Cross), Bodmer/487; F22/47; 5319/76v; MMMA, p. 42. Text: GREG introit

Michi autem nimis honorati sunt amici tui deus
nimis confortatus est principatus eorum
alleluia alleluia alleluia.

Simon and Jude ingressa: Ben40/128v; Rome, Vall. c 9/173 (palimpsest)

Text: Ps. 138:17, Rom (honorificati)

GREG: introit, Simon and Jude (*Sextuplex*, pp. 162–3), Andrew (*Sextuplex*, pp. 168–9; GRom, p. 392); offertory (*Sextuplex*, see index, p. 247 – Paul, Andrew, vigil of Peter; GRom, p. 394): texts as here without Alleluias

ROM: introit, Peter and Paul, vigil of Simon and Jude, Andrew, apostles (5319/115; F22/86; MMMA, p. 14); offertory, vigil of Peter and Paul, Paul, vigil of Simon and Jude, Andrew (5319/114v; F22/87; MMMA, p. 325): texts as here (except: honorificati) without Alleluias

Milia milium angelorum ministrabant ei
et decies centena milia assistebant ei.

Michael offertory: Ben38/83; Ben40/61
1   ministrabat: Ben40

Miraculo de tam miro cum omnes terrerentur
respicientes in altum viderunt signum sancte crucis
in celo flammeo fulgore resplendere.

Offertory: Ben38/79 (Holy Cross in GREG mass); Ben40/125 (Holy Cross II)
1   de tamnmiro: Ben38; terrenrentur: Ben38

Text: Rhabanus Maurus, see Mombritius, 1, 380, ll. 51–2

Multos infirmos curasti
multi in tribulatione venerunt ad te
quos tu orando liberasti michahel archangele.

Michael offertory: Ben38/83v (cued); communion: Ben40/61

MIL: psallenda, Oxf. 204; *Manuale*, II, 358. Compare *post ev.*, AMed, p. 551

Nolite timere . . .

Simon and Jude communion: Ben40/128v cued sn

Text: Matt. 10:28? compare antiphon CAO 3896 ("Nolite timere eos qui corpus occidunt. . ."), used for apostles, Paul, Hippolytus, and saints in paschal time. Also compare antiphon CAO 3897 ("Nolite timere: non separabuntur. . ."), used for Sebastian; also ROM antiphon (B 79/56v; 29988/48) for Sebastian and Fabian

Nursia provincia ortus rome liberalibus litterarum studiis
traditus a parentibus fuerat.

Benedict antiphon: Ben19/88; Ben21/90 (CAO 3982); Ben22/152v; MC 542, p. 106; Vat. lat. 14446/61v
1 hortus: Vat. lat. 14446; ortus over erasure: Ben21

Text: Mombritius, I, 156, ll. 40–41

GREG: antiphon, CAO 3982; compare ℟, CAO 7252

ROM: antiphon, B 79/187
1 exortus (ortus)

Omnes gentes quascumque fecisti venient
et adorabunt coram te domine.

Good Friday adoration antiphon: Ben33/69v; Ben34/119; Ben35/65v cued sn; Ben39/23; Ben40/12v; L606/156 cued; Vat. lat.
4770/91v sn; Vat. lat. 10673/29v cued

Text: Ps. 85:9A

MIL: antiphon, dedication eccl. maioris: Oxf. 214v; *Manuale*, II, 360; LVesp, p. 417

GREG: antiphon, Epiphany, CAO 4125; compare ℟, CAO 7315

ROM: antiphon, Epiphany: B 79/39v; 29988/35

Omnes qui in xpisto baptizati estis
xpistum induistis
alleluia.

Holy Saturday offertory: Ben33/79v; Ben35/68; Ben38/47; Ben40/19v; Vat. lat. 4770/113v sn; Vat. lat. 10657/A (palimpsest)
1 induisti: Ben38
3 *om*: Vat. 4770

Text: arr. from Gal. 3:26–27 ("omnes . . . quicumque enim in Christo . . ."); see Pietschmann, "Die nicht dem Psalter," p. 142

GREG: communion, Sabbato in albis: *Sextuplex*, 106–7; GRom, p. 261

ROM: communion, Easter Saturday: Bodmer/497; F22/58v; 5319/95v; MMMA, p. 429

Omnes sancti quanta passi sunt tormenta
ut securi pervenirent ad palmam martirii
alleluia.

All Saints I communion: Ben40/134 sn

GREG: antiphon, martyrs, CAO 4132, AMon, p. 647: no Alleluia

Omnes sitientes venite ad aquas
querite dominum dum inveniri potest dicit dominus.

Holy Saturday antiphon: Ben33/78; Ben35/67v; Ben38/46v (palimpsest); Ben39/27; Ben40/18v; Farfa/B (text missing);
Vat. lat. 10657/A (palimpsest) Vat. Ottob. lat. 576/210;
Bari benedictional; Rome, Vall. c 32/30

Text: Isaiah 55:1 (o omnes sitientes venite ad aquas), 55:6 (quaerite Dominum dum inveniri potest)

MIL: compare confractorium, Palm Sunday: BL, p. 227; *Manuale*, II, 174; AMed, p. 163 (sitientes venite ad aquas dicit
Dominus: et qui non habet pretium, venite, et edite, et bibite cum laetitia)

GREG: antiphon, Advent I (CAO 4133, AMon, p. 188: "alleluia" replaces "dicit dominus."); compare introit, *Sextuplex*,
pp. 80–1; GRom, p. 149

ROM: compare introit, Saturday of Lent 4: Bodmer/480; F22/38; 5319/65; MMMA, p. 19 (sitientes venite ad aquas dicit dominus et qui non habetis pretium venite et bibite cum letitia)

O quam pretiosum est regnum
in quo cum xpisto regnant omnes sancti
amictis stolis albis sequuntur agnum quocumque hierit.

All Saints I offertory: Ben40/133v; hieris *altered to* hierit

GREG: antiphon (All Saints, martyrs, Innocents), CAO 4063; AMon, p. 1107: *O quam gloriosum*. Alleluia ℣ (Ben35/150v, Ben39/169), see Schlager, *Thematischer Katalog*, no. 378

ROM: antiphon, B 79/164v; 29988/133v

1 gloriosum; *add* dei: 29988 in later hand sn
2 gaudent (regnant): B 79
3 amicti; secuntur (B 79); ierit

O quantus luctus omnium
quanta precipue lamenta monachorum et virginum chorus
quia pium est gaudere martino
et pium est flere martinum.

Martin communion: Ben40/139; antiphon: Vat. Ottob. lat. 145/124v

3 gaudere/re: Ottob. 145
4 flere/re: Ottob. 145

Text: Sulpicius Severus, compare Mombritius, II, 229, ll. 51–2; 230, ll. 2–3

MIL: psallenda, F.2.2/2; *Manuale*, II, 4

1 hominum (omnium): F.2.2
3 et pium; martinum

GREG: antiphon, CAO 4074; compare ℟, CAO 7295 (O quantus erat luctus)

ROM: antiphon B 79/169v; 29988/138v

3 martinum

Pacem meam do vobis pacem relinquo vobis
non turbetur cor vestrum veniam ad vos
alleluia.

Communion: Ben40/71v (Ascension); Ben40/80 (Pentecost, cued sn)

Text: compare John 14:27–8; there is however a long tradition for the first seven words here: see Pietschmann, "Die nicht dem Psalter," p. 139

MIL: ingressa, Sunday after Ascension, Oxf. 54v; *Manuale*, II, 244; AMed 244 (Pacem meam do vobis, alleluia; pacem meam relinquo vobis, alleluia; non turbetur cor vestrum donec veniam ad vos, alleluia alleluia)

GREG: compare communion, Thursday after Pentecost, *Sextuplex*, 126–7, GRom, p. 301 (Pacem meam do vobis, alleluia; pacem relinquo vobis, alleluia alleluia); compare antiphon, CAO 4204, 4205, ℟, CAO 7345

ROM: compare communion, Thursday after Pentecost, Bodmer/511; F22/64; 5319/109; MMMA, p. 469 (Pacem meam do vobis, alleluia; pacem meam relinquo vobis, alleluia alleluia)

Panta ta etni osa epyysas
ysusin ke proskynisusin enopin su kyrie.
[Πάντα τὰ ἔθνη ὅσα ἐποίησας
ἥξουσιν καὶ προσκυνήσουσιν ἐνώπιόν σου Κύριε.]

Good Friday antiphon: Ben34/119; Ben39/23; Ben40/12v; Vat. lat. 10673/29v

1 eni (etni): Ben34; epysa: Ben34; epyssas: Ben39
2 yxusin: 10673; proskinisusyn: Ben34; proskinisusin: Ben39

Text: Greek transliteration of Ps. 85:9. See the text *Omnes gentes*

Paraclitus autem spiritus sanctus
quem pater mittet in nomine meo
ille vos docebit
alleluia.

Offertory: Ben40/71v (Ascension); Ben40/80 (Pentecost, cued sn)

Text: John 14:26 (mittet pater; docebit omnia)

GREG: compare antiphon, CAO 4212 (Ben21 only): Paraclitus autem spiritus sanctus, quem mittet pater in nomine meo, ille vos docebit omnia, alleluia

Alleluia. ℣ Pascha nostrum immolatus est xpistus.

Easter Alleluia: Ben38/53

Text: I Cor. 5:7

MIL: compare Easter Alleluia ℣, Oxf. 9; *Manuale*, II, 214; AMed, p. 209 (Pascha nostrum immolatus est agnus qui est christus [AMed *add* ipse est] dominus deus noster); Easter confractorium, Oxf. II; *Manuale*, II, 214; AMed, p. 212 (Pascha nostrum immolatus est christus, alleluia; itaque epulemur in azymis sinceritatis et veritatis, alleluia alleluia)

GREG: Easter Alleluia, *Sextuplex*, pp. 100–1, 106–7, 199; GRom, p. 242 (with additional ℣ Epulemur); see ℟, CAO 7355

ROM: Easter Alleluia, Bodmer/492; F22/54; 5319/84; MMMA, p. 211 (with additional ℣ Epulemur); used also for Easter vespers, 29988/74; 5319/85; MMMA, p. 219

Pascha yeron imin simeron anadedite
Pascha kenon agios
Pascha mysticos
Pascha panthebasmye
Pascha x̄p̄m̄ tu litrotu
Pascha amomu
Pascha megas
Pascha ton pisteon
Pascha tas pus tu paradysu aneote
Pascha panthe anaplatete.

Ben40/28v sn, after Beneventan Easter communion

Text: transliteration of Byzantine sticheron: see p. 216

Peccavimus domine peccavimus
et peccata nostra congnoscimus
clementissime deus dona nobis veniam.

Rogation antiphon: Ben35/92; Ben38/27; Vat. Reg. lat. 334/72; Naples VIG 34/6; Naples XVI A 19/9v; Oxf. Can. lit. 277/125, sn
2   agnoscimus: Oxf. 277
3   pluviam (veniam): Reg. lat. 334

Petrus apostolus et paulus doctor gentium
ipsi nos docuerunt legem tuam domine.

Peter communion: Ben38/116, cued; offertory: Ben40/99v; antiphon: Vat. Ottob. lat. 145/124v; function not clear: Rome, Vall. C 9/169v (palimpsest)
2   tua: Ben40

Text: compare I Peter 1:1 (Petrus apostolus); I Tim. 2:7 (ego . . . doctor gentium)

GREG: antiphon, CAO 4284

ROM: antiphon, Peter and Paul, B 79/136; 29988/107

Petrus dormiebat inter duos milites alligatus catenis
angelus autem domini percussit latere petri suscitavit eum dicens
Surge velociter et ceciderunt catene de manibus eius.

Peter ingressa: Ben38/115v; Ben40/99; Vat. lat. 10657/100 (palimpsest); Rome, Vall. c 9/169v (palimpsest)

2   latera: Ben38

Text: see Acts 12:6–7 (erat Petrus dormiens inter duos milites vinctus catenis duabas . . . et ecce angelus Domini adstitit et lumen refulsit in habitaculo percussoque latere Petri suscitavit eum dicens surge velociter et ceciderunt catenae de manibus eius); for versions with "dormiebat," "alligatus," see Wordsworth-White, III, 45

MIL: compare psallenda, *Manuale*, II, 308: Angelus domini petrum suscitavit, et dixit, Surge velociter; et surrexit: et ceciderunt catenae de manibus eius. ℣ Eloquium Domini. . .

GREG: compare antiphon, CAO 1411 (Angelus Domini astitit, et lumen refulsit in habitaculo carceris; percussoque latere Petri excitavit (M: suscitavit) eum dicens: Surge velociter. Et ceciderunt catenae de manibus ejus); also see antiphon, CAO 5073 (Surge Petre velociter, quia ceciderunt catenae de manibus tuis); CAO 2660 (Erat Petrus dormiens inter duos milites, vinctus catenis duabus . . .), ℟, CAO 6090, CAO 7731

ROM: compare ℟, B 79/133; 29988/104: Surge petre et induete vestimenta tua Accipe fortitudinem ad salvandas gentes Quia ceciderunt catenis (B 79: catene) de manibus tuis. ℣ Angelus autem domini astitit et lumen refulsit in habitaculo carceris percussoque latere petri excitavit eum dicens surge velociter. Quia ce[ciderunt]

Popule meus quid feci tibi
aut in quo contristavi te
responde michi
quia eduxi vos de terra egipti
parasti cruce [sic] salvatori tuo.

Offertory: Ben38/38 (Palm Sunday); Ben40/5 (Maundy Thursday, cued sn)

Text: compare Micah 6:3–4 (populus [*or* popule] meus quid feci tibi et [*or* aut] quid molestus fui tibi responde michi quia eduxi te de terra Aegypti . . .)

GREG: verse for Good Friday adoration, associated with Trisagion; *Sextuplex*, p. 97; GRom, p. 211

4   te (vos)
5   crucem

ROM: verse for Good Friday adoration, associated with Trisagion; F22/51; 5319/80; MMMA, p. 517

1   qui: F22
4   te (vos)
5   crucem

Postquam surrexit dominus a cenam [sic]
misit aquam in pelvem
cepit lavare pedes discipulorum suorum dicens
Si ego dominus et magister vester lavi pedes vestros
quanto magis vos debetis alter alterius pedes lavare
dicit dominus.

Maundy Thursday ingressa: Ben40/4v; Rome, Vall. c 9/19 (palimpsest)

Text: compare John 13:4–5, 14–15

MIL: transitorium, Sabbato in Albis: Oxf. 31v; *Manuale*, II, 226; AMed, p. 228

1   cena
3   alleluia (dicens)
4   *add* alleluia
6   alleluia (dicit dominus)

GREG: compare antiphon, CAO 4340; GRom, p. 200 (version of Ben21: Postquam surrexit dominus a cenam misit aquam in pelvem, coepit lavare pedes discipulorum; hoc exemplum reliquit eis). Also compare antiphon CAO 4889; GRom, p. 202 (Si ego Dominus et Magister vester lavi vobis pedes, quanto magis vos debetis alter alterius lavare pedes)

Alleluia. ℣ Posuisti in capite eius coronam de
lapi / / / [de pretioso?]

Alleluia: Ben35/202v (Stephen); Ben40/112v (Lawrence, cued sn)

Text: Ps. 20:4. The text is widely used in many liturgies for feasts of saints, using both "in capite eius" and "super caput eius"

MIL: Alleluia (in capite eius), Oxf. 151v; *Manuale*, 11, 382; AMed, p. 352. Psalmellus (super caput eius), Oxf. 122; *Manuale*, 11, 286; AMed, p. 463. Antiphon (in capite eius), Oxf. 245; LVesp, p. 457

GREG: texts all begin "Posuisti domine." Gradual (MSS have both "in capite" and "super caput"), *Sextuplex*, pp. 36–7 (see also index p. 237). Offertory (in capite eius), *Sextuplex*, pp. 157–9; GRom, p. 48. Communion (in capite eius), *Sextuplex*, see index, p. 250; GRom, p. [10]. Antiphon (super caput eius) CAO 4344. Responsory (super caput eius), see CAO 7412–14. The text is used as a Gregorian Alleluia-verse only in ninth–tenth century MSS: see Hesbert, "L'antiphonale" (2), p. 151

ROM: texts all begin "Posuisti domine." Gradual (super caput eius), F22/93v; 5319/126v; MMMA, p. 83. Alleluia, Bodmer/517. Communion (in capite eius), Bodmer/455; F22/94v; 5319/26; MMMA, p. 471. Antiphon (super caput eius), B 79/180v; 29988/148. ℟ (super caput eius), 29988/147

Precursor domini venit de quo ipse testatur
nullus maior inter natos mulierum iohanne baptista.
℣ Qui autem minor est in regno celorum maior est. Ioh[anne. . .].

John the Baptist responsory: Solesmes/3

Text: compare Luke 7:28 (maior inter natos mulierum propheta Iohanne Baptista nemo est qui autem minor est in regno Dei maior est illo)

MIL: ℟ (℣ De ventre), Oxf. 138v; *Manuale*, 11, 302; LVesp, p. 648

GREG: ℟, CAO 7420 (℣ Ipse praeibit or ℣ Hic est enim)

ROM: ℟ (℣ Hic est enim): B 79/130; 29988/101

Prima predicationis voce compunctus
beatus andreas agnum dei videre meruit
et pretiosam pro eo non dubitavit ponere animam.

Andrew ingressa: Ben38/140; Ben40/142; Rome, Vall. c 9/172v (palimpsest)

Proskynumen ton stauron su
ke ton tipon tu stauru su
ke ton stauronthentos tin dinamin.

[Προσκυνοῦμεν τὸν σταυρόν σου,
καὶ τὸν τύπον τοῦ σταυροῦ σου,
καὶ τοῦ σταυρωθέντος τὴν δύναμιν.]

Good Friday antiphon: Ben40/10v; Vat. lat. 10673/28v
2 tus: Vat. 10673
3 staurothentos: Vat. 10673

Text: Greek version of "Adoramus crucem tuam," see pp. 209–14

GREG: for a version of this text from Ravenna, see table 5.6

Psallite domino qui ascendit super celos celorum
alleluia alleluia.

Ascension communion: Ben38/93v; Ben40/71v

Text: see Ps. 67:33–4 (Rom)

MIL: compare Ascension ingressa, Oxf. 53; *Manuale*, 11, 243; AMed, p. 241 (Psallite domino qui ascendit super celos celorum ad orientem, alleluia)

GREG: compare Ascension communion, *Sextuplex*, pp. 122–3; GRom, p. 287 (text as in MIL ingressa). ℟, CAO 7445 (text as in MIL ingressa, ℣ Ecce dabit)

ROM: compare Ascension communion, Bodmer/507; F22/61v; 5319/106; MMMA, p. 431 (text as in MIL ingressa with 2 alleluias; 5319 adds ℣. Ecce dabit). See ℟, B 79/121; 29988/92bis (text as in MIL ingressa with 2 alleluias; ℣ Ecce dabit)

> Que est ista que progreditur quasi aurora consurgens
> pulcra ut luna electa ut sol
> terribilis ut castrorum acies ordinata.

Assumption offertory: Ben38/128; Ben40/118v

Text: Song of Songs 6:9 (some sources omit "castrorum")

GREG: Assumption antiphon, CAO 4425
1 ascendit sicut (progreditur quasi)

> Quid ad nos egea tu numquid solvere me venisti
> aut forte penitentia ductus credere desideras.

Andrew communion: Ben38/140v; Ben40/143
1 solverem: Ben40

Text: see Mombritius, I, 107, ll. 13–16

MIL: antiphon, F.2.2/6; *Manuale*, II, 14
1 Egeatha (egea tu); penitentiam; me desideris: F.2.2

GREG: compare antiphon, CAO 4531 (Ben21 only): Quid tu ad nos, Aegea, venisti? Si vis credere. . .

> Qui manducaverit corpus meum
> et biberit sanguinem meum
> ipse in me manet et ego in eum
> Alleluia alleluia alleluia.
> ℣ Gloria et honor deo patri et filio et spiritui sancto.
> Alleluia.
> Et nunc et semper et in secula seculorum amen.
> Alleluia.

Easter communion: Ben38/53; Ben40/28; Rome, Vall. C 9/167 (palimpsest)
2 meam: Ben40
3 eo: Ben40
4 *only one* alleluia: Ben40

Text: see John 6:57 (Qui manducat meam carnem et bibit meum sanguinem in me manet et ego in illo)

MIL: Transitorium, common of Sundays: Oxf. 328; *Manuale*, II, 410; AMed, p. 318
4 *om; add* dicit dominus
5–8 *om*

GREG: compare communion, Thursday of Lent I: *Sextuplex*, 66–7; GRom, p. 344 (Qui manducat carnem meam et bibit sanguinem meum in me manet et in eo dicit dominus)

ROM: compare communion, Thursday of Lent II: Bodmer/473; F22/28; 5319/52v; MMMA, p. 464 (text as in Greg comm. except: carne (5319); bibit; in eum)

> Quis te supplantavit iudas
> ut adversus dominus meditareris traditionem
> fuisti discipulus sed malignus
> secundum malitiam tuam recepisti.

Communion; Palm Sunday: Ben38/38; Maundy Thurs: Ben40/5 (cued. sn), Vat. lat. 10657/2

Respice cuncta quia tua sunt domine
et da faciem roris super terram.

Rogation antiphon: Ben34/160v; Ben35/91v; Ben38/73; Ben39/62v; Ben40/49; Vat. Reg. lat. 334/74; Naples XVI A 19/8v

Respice cuncta quia tua sunt domine
et da faciem solis super terram
abstolle pluviam deus noster.

Rogation antiphon: Ben35/92; Vat. Reg. lat. 334/76v
2　roris: Reg. lat. 334

Alleluia. ℣ Resurrexit tamquam dormiens dominus
quasi potens crapulatus a vino.
℣ Laudate pueri dominum laudate nomen domini
sit nomen domini benedictum.

Easter vigil Alleluia: Ben30/75v (Easter day); Ben33/79; Ben34/126 (Easter day); Ben35/68; Ben38/46v; Ben39/27v; Ben40/19v; MC Comp. v (Easter vespers); Farfa/Bv (fragmentary: no text visible); Baltimore Walters 6/124v; Vat. lat. 10657/A (palimpsest)
1　tamquam: Ben34; after Alleluia, Ben38 and Ben39 add the prosa
　　"Laudes ordo in excelsis decantant agmina sacra"
2　potans: Ben35
1–2　Farfa *om* Resurrexit. . . vino
3–4　*om* Ben30, Ben33, Walters, MC Comp.; second verse marked "non" in later hand, Ben34, marked "prosa" in Ben38
Text: ℣, 1 Ps. 77:65 (excitatus [one source has "Resurrexit"]; potans *or* potens); ℣, 2 Ps. 112:1–2A
MIL: the text of verse 1 widely used, with the text "quasi potans": Alleluia (Holy Saturday), Oxf. 4; *Manuale*, II, 211; AMed, p. 202. Alleluia (martyrs in paschal time): Oxf. 252, AMed, p. 297. Offerenda, Easter Friday (+alleluia), Oxf. 25; *Manuale*, II, 224; AMed, p. 225. Responsory (+alleluia alleluia alleluia), Oxf. 12; *Manuale*, II, 215 (2 alleluias). Psallenda, Easter Monday (+pascere iacob populum suum . . .), Oxf. 14; *Manuale*, II, 217
GREG: ℣ 1 set to GREG melody *Justus ut palma* in Ben38/47; compare Alleluia ℣ Laudate pueri domini laudate nomen domini: *Sextuplex*, see index, p. 242 (Saturday *in albis* and other feasts); GRom, pp. 42, 260
ROM: compare Alleluia ℣ Laudate pueri dominum laudate nomen domini. ℣ Sit nomen domini benedictum ex hoc nunc et usque in seculum (Saturday after Pentecost): Bodmer/496; F22/58; 5319/95v; MMMA, p. 180; also in Bodmer/510 for Monday after Pentecost. Note: Cutter, *Musical Sources*, lists Alleluia ℣ Resurrexit in Bodmer/492 for Easter

Salve crux que in corpore xpisti dedicata es
suscipe me et redde magistro meo.

Andrew offertory: Ben40/142v
Text: see Mombritius, I, 106, ll. 51–2; 107, l. 1
MIL: antiphon, F.2.2/6v; *Manuale*, II, 15; LVesp, p. 529
1　corpori (in corpore): LVesp; *om* in: F.2.2, *Manuale*
2　redde me magistro meo
GREG: compare antiphon, CAO 4694; and ℟, CAO 7563

Sancta maria exora semper pro xpistianis omnibus
ut per te liberentur ab hostium insidiis
quorum patrona pia es et domina.

Assumption offertory: Ben38/128v (cued); Ben40/118v; antiphon: Vat. Ottob. lat. 145/124; Berkeley 1000:6
2　liberemur: Ottob. 145; ostium: Ottob. 145
3　patronána pia esse domina: Ottob. 145

Sancte vir dei libera nos per deum qui te salvavit.

Nazarius and Celsus antiphon: Ben20/236 [Ben21/213: MIL melody (CAO 4722)]

Text: Mombritius, II, 332, ll. 17–18

MIL: antiphon, Mugg. p. 249; Oxf. 167; *Manuale*, II, 319; Ben21/213
1   creavit (salvavit): *Manuale*
GREG: Alleluia ℣, Ben35/134v; see Schlager, *Thematischer Katalog*, no. 285

Sancti enim ducti ad dioclitianus dice-/
. . .cola sumus tuam iussam maxime complere nequimus.
. . .superatum se ap vero dioclitianus videns indignatus
. . .cap[   ]talem suvire sententiam sanctus
. . .gloriam accepit.

Antiphon, for an unidentified feast immediately preceding St Eustasius (20 May): Venice, Archivio di Stato, Atti div.
MSS B. 159 n. 28

Sanctissimus arontius dixit valeriano
quemcumque nostrum presseris immolari
potius in xpisto mori eliget quam in idolis vivere.

Twelve Brothers antiphon: Ben20/279; Ben21/235v (CAO 4755); Melk 1027/Z; MC Comp. v
2   quecumque: Melk
3   iydolis: MC Comp. v; viveret: Ben21

Text: see AA SS, Sept. I, 141, n. 10

Sanctissimus dei cultor barbatus
ex obsessis corporibus minis aliquando vel fusis
precibus inmundo spiritu eiciebat
invocato nomine xpisti varios curabat languores.

Barbatus antiphon: Ben21/87v (CAO 4756); Ben22/146v; Vat. lat. 14446/38
2   obscessis: Vat. 14446; mitis: Ben21; mini: Vat. 14446; fusi: Ben22
3   inmundos spiritus: Ben22
4   invovocato: Ben21; langores: Ben21

Text: see AA SS, Feb. III, 141, n. 4

Sancti vero uno ore dixerunt valeriano
scimus quia non credis sed ut cognoscas potentiam xpisti
cesset indignatio maris.

Twelve Brothers antiphon: Ben20/278; Ben21/236 (CAO 4742); Melk 1027/Z
2   potentia: Ben21, Melk

Text: see AA SS, Sept. I, 140, n. 10

Sancti videntes angelum fulgentem sicut solem
Gaudio gavisi sunt laudantes creatorem
Vincula dirrupta territi sunt custodes
Ilico vox insonuit vox digni estis nomen
alleluia.
Predicare eum gentibus ut credant salvatorem
Qui vitam mundi tribuit per sanguinis cruorem
alleluia. Alle[luia.]

Twelve Brothers ingressa: Ben40/121v

Sanctus. Sanctus. Sanctus dominus deus sabaoth.
Pleni sunt celi et terra gloria tua
osanna in excelsis
benedictus qui venit in nomine domini.
Osanna in excelsis.

Ben35/202, Christmas

Scribite die[m] hunc in libris paternis ves[tris]
et in testamento patrum vestrorum notate
quoniam lapides isti in testimonium vobis erunt ante dominum.
℣ Conv[er]timini unusquisque a via sua mala
et ab iniquitate que est in manibus vestris. Not[ate.]

Stephen gradual: Ben35/202v

Text: respond inspired from Joshua 24:26-27; for ℣ see Jonah 3:8: and also Jer. 18:11; 25:5; 35:15; Ps. 7:4; Ps. 25:10; Is. 59:6.
See Hesbert, "L'antiphonale" (2), pp. 146-51

Sicut cervus desiderat ad fontes aquarum
Ita desiderat anima mea ad te deus
Sitivit anima mea ad deum vivum
Quando veniam et apparebo ante faciem dei.

Holy Saturday tract: Ben38/46v (palimpsest); Ben40/18; Bari benedictional; Vat. lat. 10673/34v; Vat. lat. 10657/A (palimpsest)
1 cerbus: Vat. 10673
3 sitibit; vibum: Vat. 10673

Text: Ps. 41:2-3 (Rom)

MIL: compare Holy Saturday cantus, BL, p. 259; *Manuale*, II, 204; AMed, p. 198. Text as in BEN lines 1-2

GREG: compare Holy Saturday tract, *Sextuplex*, pp. 98-9; GRom, p. 232. Text as in BEN plus Ps. 41:4

[ROM: GREG tract in F22/53; 5319/82; MMMA, p. 241]

Si quis catechuminus est procedat
Si quis iudeus est procedat
Si quis hereticus est procedat
Si quis paganus est procedat
Si quis arrianus est procedat
Cuius cura non est procedat.

Holy Saturday dismissal: Ben33/78 sn; Ben35/67v; Ben38/46v (mostly palimpsest); Ben39/27v (cathecuminus); Ben40/19
(cathecuminus); Farfa/Bv (incomplete); Vat. Barb. lat. 631/75 (line 1 only, sn); Vat. Ottob. lat. 576/211; Vat. Urb. lat.
602/99v (later hand); Bari benedictional; Rome, Vall. C 32/31
The order of lines 1-5 varies:
  cathecuminus-hereticus-iudeus-paganus-arrianus: Ben33; Ottob. 576 (ereticus; huius curam); Vall. C 32; Vat. Urb. lat. 602;
  Farfa (lacks lines 1-2)
  cathecuminus-arrianus-hereticus-iudeus-paganus: Bari
  cathecuminus (*om* est)-arrianus-hereticus-pangamus (sic)-iudeus: Ben35

MIL: Sabbato in traditione symboli: BL, p. 219; *Manuale*, II, 168:
  Si quis catechuminus procedat
  Si quis iudeus procedat
  Si quis paganus procedat
  Si quis hereticus procedat
  Cuius cura non est procedat.

Alleluia. ℣ Specie tua et pulcritudine tua.

Assumption Alleluia: Ben38/128; Ben40/118

Text: Ps. 44:5A (Ga and some Rom sources: others have "Speciem tuam et pulcritudinem tuam")

GREG: compare antiphon, CAO 4987; ℞, CAO 7679, 7680. For use as Alleluia-verse see Schlager, *Thematischer Katalog*, no. 271. All use full text of verse 5 (BEN text+"intende, prospere procede et regna")

ROM: compare Alleluia, Bodmer/442; 5319/3; MMMA, p. 214. Second ℣ of Alleluia ℣ Diffusa; text as in BEN+"intende et prospere procede et regna." ℣ "Specie" sometimes alone; see MMMA, 707–8

Alleluia. ℣ Spiritus domini replevit orbem terrarum.

Pentecost Alleluia: Ben40/80 sn

Text: Wisdom 1:7

MIL: compare Pentecost Alleluia, Oxf. 100; *Manuale*, II, 273; AMed, p. 255 (text as in BEN+et hoc quod continet omnia scientiam habet vocis)

GREG: compare Pentecost Alleluia (*Sextuplex*, pp. 124–5); Pentecost introit (*Sextuplex*, pp. 124–5; GRom, p. 292; text as in BEN+alleluia et hoc quod continet omnia scientiam habet vocis); antiphon, CAO 4998 (text as in BEN+alleluia); ℞, CAO 7689, 7690 (text as in MIL Alleluia)

ROM: compare Pentecost Alleluia, F22/13; 5319/107v; MMMA, p. 177 (text as in MIL Alleluia except: "scientia"); and Pentecost introit, F22/62v; 5319/107; MMMA, p. 177 (text as in GREG introit with three final alleluias)

> Stephanus autem dum lapidaretur a Iudeis
> deprecabatur dominum dicens
> domine ego pa[ti]or ego lapidor
> in me seviunt in me fremunt
> sed ne statuas illis hoc ad peccatum
> quia nesciunt quid faciunt
> quia ego patior in carne non isti pereant in mente.

Stephen ingressa: Ben35/202

Text: inspired from Acts 7:50–60, but with much freedom; "nesciunt quid faciunt" is derived from Luke 23:34. The two invocations ("ne statuas" and "nesciunt") are combined also in the text *Lapidaverunt* used as a responsory in MIL (BL, p. 65; *Manuale*, II, 63), GREG (℞, Video, CAO 7865)

> Stolam iocunditatis induit eum dominus
> et coronam pulcritudinis posui[t] super caput eius.

Martin ingressa: Ben40/138v

Text: Ecclesiasticus 6:32, not Vulgate version

GREG: antiphon (CAO 5034), common of confessors; ℞ (CAO 7710, with various verses), common of a martyr

ROM: ℞ (apostles), B 79/176v; 29988/144. ℣ Quoniam prevenisti

> Surge propera columba mea formosa mea et veni
> Iam hiems transiit imber abiit et recessit
> Flores apparuerunt in terra
> Tempus putationis advenit
> Vox turturis audita est in terra nostra.

Assumption ingressa: Ben38/128; Ben40/118

Text: Song of Songs 2:10–12; for variants of line 1 see *Vulgata*

> Tenebre facte sunt super universam terram
> dum crucifixerunt hiesum iudei
> et circa horam nonam exclamavit hiesus voce magna
> Deus deus quid me dereliquisti
> et inclinato capite emisit spiritum.
> Tunc unus ex militibus lancea latus eius aperuit
> et continuo exivit sanguis et aqua.
> ℣ Ecce terremotus factus est magnus
> nam velum templi scissum est
> et omnis terra tremuit. Tunc.

Good Friday responsory: Ben33/71v cued, verse noted; Ben40/14; Vat. lat. 10673/31; Benevento fragment B (fragment);
2 iudeis: Ben40

Text: arranged from Matt. 27:45–46, 50–51; John 19:34, 30. See Hesbert, "Le répons Tenebrae"

MIL: Good Friday responsory: BL, p. 247; *Manuale*, II, 187; AMed, p. 180
- 4 line 6 precedes line 5
- 6 perforavit (aperuit): *Manuale*, AMed
- 7 *om*
- 10 Et inclinato (Tunc)

GREG: Good Friday responsory (CAO 7760)
- 1 *om* super universam terram
- 2 crucifixissent
- 4 ut quid
- 5–7 MS C omits l. 7, inverts 5 and 6
- 6 perforavit (1 MS: aperuit)
- 8–10 ℣ Et velum templi scissum est a summo usque deorsum, et omnis terra tremuit (9 MSS); ℣ Cum ergo acepisset acetum, dixit: Consummatum est (2 MSS)

ROM: Good Friday responsory: B 79/99v; 29988/69v
- 2 crucifixissent
- 4 Deus deus meus ut quid
- 7 *om*
- 8–10 ℣ [Et (B 79)] Cum gustasset acetum (29988: aceto tum) dixit consummatum est

> Alleluia. ℣ Territus andreas orat miserere magister.

Andrew Alleluia: Ben38/140v; Ben40/142v

> Testificata est turba que erat cum hiesu
> quando lazarum vocavit de monumento
> et suscitavit eum a mortuis
> pro eo cum ramis palmarum occurrerunt clamantes et dicentes
> osanna rex israhel
> benedictus qui venit in nomine domini
> osanna in excelsis.

Palm Sunday ingressa: Ben38/37v; Rome, Vall. c 9/19v? (palimpsest)

Text: arranged from John 12:12–18; but "osanna in excelsis" is from Mark 11:10

MIL: Palm Sunday psallenda, BL, p. 223; *Manuale*, II, 173; AMed, p. 153
- 2 quia dominus (quando)
- 4 propter hoc (pro eo); obviavit ei (occurerunt); clamans et dicens

5 regis (rex): BL; regi: *Manuale*, AMed

> Ton stauron su proskynumen kyrie
> ke tin agian su anastasin doxazome
> deute pantes proskynisumen
> tin tu xpistu anastasin.

> [Τὸν σταυρόν σου προσκυνοῦμεν Κύριε
> καὶ τὴν ἁγίαν σου ἀνάστασιν δοξάζομεν
> δεῦτε πάντες προσκυνῶμεν
> τὴν τοῦ Χριστοῦ ἀνάστασιν.]

Good Friday antiphon: Ben40/10v; Vat. lat. 10673/28v

3 proskynumen: 10673

Text: Greek transliteration; for Latin version see "Crucem tuam adoramus"

> Tristis est anima mea usque ad mortem
> sustinete hic et vigilate mecum.

Good Friday antiphon, L606/155

Text: Matt. 26:38

MIL: compare Maundy Thursday Transitorium, BL, p. 241; *Manuale*, II, 183; AMed 173

GREG: compare responsory, CAO 7780

ROM: compare Good Friday responsory: B 79/95v; 29988/65

> Tu es pastor. . .

Peter offertory: Ben38/116, cued

Text: probably the non-biblical text (Tu es pastor ovium princeps apostolorum; tibi tradidit dominus [or tradite sunt] claves. . .) widely used for antiphons and responsories

MIL: compare antiphon (Oxf. 146v; *Manuale*, II, 307; LVesp, p. 557); and R (Oxf. 149; *Manuale*, II, 308; LVesp, p. 556)

GREG: compare antiphon (CAO 5207); and R (CAO 7787)

ROM: compare antiphon (B 79/134v; 29988/105v); and R (B 79/133; 29988/104)

> Alleluia. V Tu es petrus et super petram hanc
> ecclesiam hedificabo.

Peter Alleluia: Ben40/99

Text: Matt. 16:18 (. . . tu es Petrus et super hanc petram aedificabo ecclesiam meam); the Beneventan version appears nowhere else. The biblical text cited here is the version widely used elsewhere, as in all the examples cited below

MIL: compare Alleluia V (Oxf. 152; *Manuale*, II, 309; AMed, p. 430); offerenda (Oxf. 152; *Manuale*, II, 309; AMed, p. 431); and psallenda "Ut cognosceris" (Oxf. 150v; *Manuale*, II, 309)

GREG: compare Alleluia V (*Sextuplex*, p. 138; GRom, pp. 409, 534); communion (*Sextuplex*, pp. 136–7; GRom, pp. 412, 534); antiphon (CAO 5208; AMon, pp. 935, 990); and R (CAO 7788)

ROM: compare Alleluia V (F22/81v; 5319/117; MMMA, p. 173); communion (F22/81v; 5319/115; MMMA, p. 464); antiphon (B 79/136; 29988/106v); and R (B 79/132v; 29988/104v)

> Tunc hi tres quasi ex uno ore laudabant et glorificabant et
> benedicebant deum in fornace dicentes
> Benedictus es domine deus patrum nostrorum
> Et laudabilis et superexaltatus in secula. amen.
> 5 Benedicite omnia opera domini dominum.
> Ymnum dicite et superexaltate eum in secula. amen.
> Benedicite celi domini dominum: ym[num].
> Benedicite angeli domini dominum: ym[num].
> Benedicite maria et flumina domini dominum: ym[num].
> 10 Benedicite fontes domini dominum: ym[num].
> Benedicite sacerdotes domini dominum: ym[num].
> Benedicite spiritus et anime iustorum dominum: ym[num].
> Benedicite anania azaria misahel dominum: ym[num].
> Benedicimus patrem et filium cum sancto spiritu.
> 15 Ymnum dicimus et superexaltamus eum in secula. amen.
> Quoniam eripuit nos ab inferis et de manu mortis liberavit nos.
> Confitemini domino quoniam bonus
> quoniam in seculum misericordia eius.

Good Friday canticle: Ben33/71; Ben39/23 (lines 1–2 only); Ben40/12v; Vat. lat. 10673/30v (lacuna after line 5); Macerata 378/127v (Holy Saturday: line 3 cued with BEN melody)

3   test (es): Ben33
4   superexaltate *altered to* -tus: Ben33
7–9   *om*: Ben33
11–12   *om*: Ben33
15   ymnum *only*: Ben33

Text: Daniel 3:51–

MIL: Good Friday (BL, p. 248; *Manuale*, II, 189; AMed, p. 183)
1   Tunc hi tres quasi ex uno ore hymnum dicentes glorificabant; Dominum (deum)
4   gloriosus (superexaltatus); *add* Et benedictum nomen gloriae tuae, quod est sanctum et laudabile et gloriosum in saecula. Amen. Benedictus es super sedem regni tui, et laudabilis et gloriosus in saecula. Amen.
5   domino (dominum)
7   domino (domini dominum)
8   domino (dominum)
9–10   *om; add* Benedicite omnes virtutes domini domino: hymnum (etc.)
11   domino (dominum); *add* Benedicite servi domini domino; hymnum (etc.)
12   domino (dominum); *add* Benedicite sancti et humiles cordi domino; hymnum (etc.)
13   domino (dominum)
14   Benedicamus; et sanctum spiritum
15   dicamus; superexaltemus
16   *add* et eripuit nos de media fornace ignis ardentis
18   secula (*Manuale*)

> Tunc imperator eraclius offerens hierusolimis multa donaria
> ecclesias reparari iussit ex ipsius sumptibus
> et constantinopolim rediit divina fretus potentia.

Holy Cross II communion: Ben40/125

Text: see Mombritius, I, 381, ll. 22–5

> Turbati sunt nautae vehementer
> videntes nazarium per mare ambulantem
> et crediderunt in deo eius.

Nazarius antiphon: Ben20/236 (BEN melody?); [Ben21/213, with MIL melody (CAO 5257)]

Text: compare Mombritius, II, 332, ll. 4–25

MIL: antiphon, Mugg. p. 253; Oxf. 170v; *Manuale*, II, 321

3   deum (deo)

> Usque in senectam et summam senectutem
> ne derelinquas me domine deus meus.

Xistus antiphon: Ben20/249; Ben21/216 (CAO 5283)

Text: compare Ps. 70:18 (usque in senectam et senium Deus ne derelinquas me)

MIL: Xistus antiphon, Oxf. 179v; *Manuale*, II, 327

> Ut audivi vocem salutaris tue in auribus meis
> exultavit infans in utero meo. ℣. Beata

John the Baptist antiphon: Solesmes/2

Text: adapted from Luke 1:41

MIL: antiphon, Oxf. 137v; *Manuale*, II, 301; LVesp, p. 647

1   tui
2   no ℣

> Ut cognosceret me
> spiritus patris mei manifestavit tibi dicit dominus
> et ego dico tibi tu es petrus
> tibi enim tradidit claves regni celorum
> paulus vero vas electionis est michi
> alleluia alleluia alleluia.

Peter communion: Ben40/99v; Vat. lat. 10657/101 (palimpsest); MC 361, p. 150 (palimpsest)

Text: compare Acts 9:15; Matt. 16:18–19

MIL: psallenda, Oxf. 149v; *Manuale*, II, 309

1   cognosceres
3   dicam
4   trado
6   1 alleluia

> Vadit propitiator ad immolandum pro omnibus
> non ei occurrit petrus qui dicebat pro te morior.
> Reliquid eum thomas qui clamabat dicens
> omnes cum eo moriamur
> et nullus de ipsis sed ipse solus ducitur
> qui nos omnes redemit dominus et deus noster.
>   ℣ Venite et videte omnes populi
> deum et hominem extensum in cruce. Qui nos.

Maundy Thursday gradual: Ben40/5; Vat. lat. 10657/2 (palimpsest)

Text: translation of a Greek composition of Romanos (see PM v, pp. 6–9, 25–7)

MIL: Good Friday ℟: BL, p. 243; *Manuale*, II, 184. See PM XIV, p. 279

1   vadis
2   tibi (ei); moriar
3   reliquit te
5   et nullus de illis sed tu solus duceris

6 qui immaculatam me conservasti filius et deus meus.

7–8 ℣ Venite et videte deum et hominem pendentem in cruce. Et nullus (BL: Sed nullus)

GREG: Good Friday ℟, occasionally elsewhere: essentially the Milanese text (see CAO 7816). In addition to the manuscripts listed in PM XIV, p. 278, the following include this responsory: Bergamo MSS Γ III 18, f. 75 and Ψ III 8, f. 132v (text edited in Drumbl, "Gli improperi," p. 80); Vat. Rossi 231, f. 72 (cue *Vadis propiciator*, sn); Monza C 13/76, f. 95v (according to Drumbl, "Die Improperien," pp. 81–2)

ROM: Good Friday ℟, B 79/99; 29988/69

1 Vadis (B 79); propitiatus
2 tibi (ei); mori tecum (pro te morior)
3 Reliquid te (B 79:me); agebat (dicebat), 29988; aiebat: B 79; *om* dicens: B 79
5 et ne unus de (B 79: ex) illis sed tu solus duceris
6 qui castam me conservasti (B 79: confortasti) filius et deus meus.

7–8 B 79: ℣ Promittentes tecum in carcerem et in mortem ire relicto te fugierunt. Et ne. Vadis propi. 29988: ℣ Mulier. ℣ O vos omnes qui transitis per viam aspicite et videte deum et hominem in ligno pendentem. Qui.

> Velum templi scissum est et omnis terra tremuit
> sanctorum dormientium resurrexerunt corpora.
> ℣ Postquam crucifixerunt iudei dominum nostrum hiesum xpistum:
> tremente terra concussu ilico a summo usque deorsum.

Good Friday antiphon: Ben21/132 (CAO 5315); Ben38/43v; Ben39/25v; Ben40/15; L606/156; Subiaco XVIII/77v sn; Vat. Ottob. 576/166v cued sn

3 postquam autem: Ben21
4 trementem: Ben21, Subiaco; concussum: Ben21, Ben40, L606, Subiaco

Text: adapted from Matt. 27:51–52

MIL: Holy Saturday antiphon, BL, p. 256; *Manuale*, II, 197: antiphon only, no verse

> Venit angelus domini ad martires dicens
> misit me dominus solvere vincula vestra.

Twelve Brothers antiphon: Ben20/278; Ben21/236 (CAO 5341); Melk 1027/z; MC Comp. v

1 martyres: Ben20, MC Comp. v

Text: AA SS, Sept. I, 138, n. 2

GREG: used as verse of gradual *Existentibus in penis* in the (twelfth-century?) mass for the Holy Twelve Brothers in Naples XVI A 19, f. 45v

> Venite omnes veneremur lignum sancte crucis
> per quos nos xpistus sacro redemit sanguine suo.
> ℣ Defuncto chosroe eraclius suscepit gloriosissimum lignum
> sancte et vivifice crucis
> quod cum ingenti honore hierusolimam detulit.
> ℣ Gaudentes itaque omnes populi
> cum ymnis et canticis victorie regi
> obviam exierunt cernere desiderantes.

Holy Cross II ingressa: Ben40/124v

Text: see Mombritius, I, 38–47

> Vere cognoscent omnes
> quia sanctus apollinaris est gloriosus martyr
> in civitate ravenna
> prestans beneficia in xpisto credentibus
> alleluia.

Apollinaris antiphon: Ben20/226; Ben21/211v (C A O 5365); Vat. lat. 14733/11v illegible

> Vir dei silvester libera nos
> vel uno anno a nece draconis
> ut credamus xpistum tuum divinitatis habere virtutem.

Silvester antiphon: Ben19/12; Ben21/36 (C A O 5432); Ben22/78v; MC 542/p. 31; MC Comp. v (incomplete)

Text: see Mombritius, II, 529, l. 36

> Vir domini barbatus actionibus celebs et coruscus miraculis
> sectam internicionis pellendo beneventi effulsit.

Barbatus antiphon: Ben21/87 (C A O 5433); Ben22/146; Vat. lat. 14446/38

1 celeps: Ben21; corruscus: Vat. lat. 14446
2 pellendum: Ben21, Ben22

Text: compare AA SS, Feb. III, 139, n. 2; 140, n. 5

> Ymnum canite agni mundi
> lavacro fontis renati
> satiati corpore xpisti
> alleluia alleluia alleluia.

Holy Saturday communion: Ben33/79v; Ben35/68; Ben38/47; Ben38/52v (cued in Easter G R E G mass); Ben40/20; Vat. lat. 4770/114 (sn; marked as antiphon)

1 cantate: Vat. lat. 4770
2 labacro; *om* renati: Vat. lat. 4770
3 xpistis: Ben35
4 2 alleluias; *add* Una autem sabbati diluculo venerunt ad monumentum portantes que paraverant aramota [sic] alleluia: Vat. lat. 4770 (a second antiphon, unlabeled?)

M I L: Easter Thursday transitorium, Oxf. 26; *Manuale*, II, 222; AMed, p. 225: 2 alleluias

> Zacharias pater eius prophetavit dicens
> benedictus dominus deus israhel
> quia visitavit et fecit redemptionem plebis sue.

John the Baptist communion: Ben40/89v; antiphon: Solesmes/3

Text: adapted from Luke 1:68

MANUSCRIPT SOURCES OF
BENEVENTAN CHANT

The manuscripts containing Beneventan chant are listed here in the alphabetical order of the cities in which they are located. Their contents of Beneventan chant, where not supplied here, can be determined from the repertory table in Appendix 1. All manuscripts are in Beneventan script except where noted. With each source is a brief bibliography in which further references may be found. Two forthcoming works should provide significant further information on the manuscripts of Benevento: the second volume of Mallet and Thibaut, *Les Manuscrits* (I follow their usage of omitting the preceding Roman numerals from the shelf-marks of manuscripts of Benevento), and John Boe and Alejandro Planchart, editors, *Beneventanum troporum corpus*.

Avezzano, Curia vescovile, Exultet roll
  Description: Exultet roll
  Provenance: Montecassino (?)
  Date: Middle eleventh century
  Literature: TBS, 11, 13; Avery, *Exultet Rolls*, p. 11, plates 1–3; Gamber, CLLA, no. 495e; Grégoire, "Repertorium," p. 475
  An Exultet roll containing the Vulgate text and the Beneventan melody.

Baltimore, Walters Art Gallery, MS w 6
  Desc: Missal, 232 folios, 190×120 mm (145×89), 17 text lines
  Prov: Canosa
  Date: eleventh century (after 1054)
  Lit: TBS, 11, 13–14; Gamber, CLLA, no. 445; Grégoire, "Repertorium," p. 476; PM xv, no. 109 (p. 76); Faye, *Supplement*, p. 196, no. 112; Rehle, *Missale beneventanum von Canosa* (edition); *Les Sources*, p. 29
  A noted missal in "Bari-type" Beneventan script and rather archaic notation without lines or clefs (but with custos), containing votive masses and those for principal feast days. Beneventan contents are limited to the Alleluia *Resurrexit tamquam dormiens* and an adaptation of it (*Hodie natus est*) for Christmas.

Bari, Archivio del Duomo, benedictional roll
  Desc: rotulus, 4 pieces, 3,122×415 mm
  Prov: Bari
  Date: first half eleventh century
  Lit: TBS, 11, 15; Grégoire, "Repertorium," p. 476; PM xiv, see table, p. 469; PM xv, no. 3 (p. 52); Avery, *Exultet Rolls*, p. 14 and plates 12–16; Cavallo, *Rotoli*, pp. 81–3 and plates 12–17; see index, p. 253; Babudri, *L'Exultet*

A decorated rotulus in four pieces, including benedictions of fire and water for use on Holy Saturday. Beneventan script, "Bari-type," and Beneventan notation without lines or clefs. Included are the related Beneventan antiphon *Omnes sitientes* and the tract *Sicut cervus*.

Bari, Archivio del Duomo, Exultet Roll 1
Desc: Exultet roll
Prov: Bari
Date: first half eleventh century (before 1056)
Lit: TBS, II, 15; Avery, *Exultet Rolls*, pp. 11–13, plates 4–11; Cavallo, *Rotoli*, pp. 47–55 and plates I–II; Babudri, *L'Exultet*; Gamber, CLLA, no. 485; Grégoire, "Repertorium," p. 476; PM XV, no. 1 (p. 51); Lowe, *Scriptura beneventana*, plate LXV
An Exultet roll with Beneventan text and melody.

Bari, Archivio del Duomo, Exultet Roll 2
Desc: Exultet roll, palimpsest
Prov: Bari
Date: eleventh century (lower script); thirteenth century (upper script)
Lit: TBS, II, 16; Avery, *Exultet Rolls*, pp. 14–15 and plates 17–23; Cavallo, *Rotoli*, pp. 99–102 and plates 18–27; Babudri, *L'Exultet*; Grégoire, "Repertorium," p. 476; PM XV, no. 2 (p. 51)
The original Beneventan text and notation of this roll have been erased and overwritten with the Vulgate text of the Exultet and the Roman melody in square notation of the thirteenth century. Almost nothing remains of the original writing.

Bari, Archivio del Duomo, Exultet Roll 3
Desc: Exultet roll, palimpsest
Prov: Bari
Date: late twelfth century
Lit: TBS, II, 16; Avery, *Exultet Rolls*, pp. 15–16 and plate 24; Grégoire, "Repertorium," p. 476
An earlier Greek text has been erased and overwritten with the Vulgate text of the Exultet and an elaborated version of the Beneventan melody.

Benevento, Biblioteca capitolare, MS 19
Desc: mixed missal and breviary, *pars hiemalis*, 279 ff., 382×276 mm, writing area 310×225, 30 lines in 2 columns
Prov: Benevento
Date: twelfth century
Lit: TBS, II, 19; Gamber, CLLA, no. 460; Grégoire, "Repertorium," pp. 478–9; PM XIV, see table, p. 469; PM XV, no. 5 (p. 52); *Les Sources*, p. 32
A mixed breviary-missal for non-monastic use, *pars hiemalis*, temporal and sanctoral mixed, from St Nicholas to Wednesday of Lent IV. Written in two columns in Beneventan script and notation, fully diastematic though without lines or clefs. A companion volume is Benevento 20.

Benevento, Biblioteca capitolare, MS 20
Desc: mixed missal and breviary, *pars aestiva*, 300 ff., 364×253 mm, writing area 300×205, 2 columns of 30 lines
Prov: Benevento
Date: twelfth century
Lit: TBS, II, 19; Gamber, CLLA, no. 460; Grégoire, "Repertorium," p. 479; PM XIV, see table, p. 469; PM XV, no. 5 (p. 52); *Les Sources*, p. 32
A mixed breviary-missal for non-monastic use, *pars aestiva*, temporal and sanctoral mixed, from Easter Tuesday to Saints Cosmas and Damian. Written in two columns in Beneventan script and notation similar to that of Benevento 19, which is a companion volume.

Benevento, Biblioteca capitolare, MS 21
> Desc: antiphoner, 304 ff., 350×225 mm, writing area 295×175, 12 (occasionally 11) lines
> Prov: Benevento
> Date: twelfth–thirteenth century
> Lit: TBS, II, 20; Grégoire, "Repertorium," p. 479; PM XV, no. 6 (p. 52); CAO, II, pp. XX–XXIV
>   and plate XII; the volume contains a complete inventory; volumes III–IV edit the texts with
>   those of other manuscripts of the office

An almost-complete monastic antiphoner, beginning with the Tuesday before Advent II. Beneventan script and notation with lines and custos. There is no evidence that the manuscript was made for the abbey of San Lupo in Benevento.

Benevento, Biblioteca capitolare, MS 22
> Desc: noted monastic breviary, 216 ff., 320×218 mm, writing area 255×155, 30 ruled lines in 2 columns
> Prov: Benevento (cathedral?)
> Date: twelfth century
> Lit: TBS, II, 20; Grégoire, "Repertorium," p. 479; PM XV, no. 110 (p. 76)

A monastic breviary, *pars hiemalis*, from Advent to Maundy Thursday. In two columns, Beneventan script and notation with one (sometimes two) colored lines and clefs. The feast of the dedication (*Ded. eccle. s. marie*) between Saints Lucy and Thomas is probably 18 December, the dedication date of the cathedral of Benevento (dedicated to the virgin).

Benevento, Biblioteca capitolare, MS 30
> Desc: missal, 213 ff., 238×165 mm, writing area 203×124, 20 or 21 lines
> Prov: Benevento?
> Date: thirteenth century
> Lit: TBS, II, 20; PM XV, no. 9 (p. 53); *Les Sources*, p. 32

Only partially notated, the missal, in Beneventan script and notation, is almost complete, beginning with the sixth Sunday after Epiphany. Beneventan music is limited to the Good Friday ℞ *Lavi pedes* (f. 71) and the Alleluia *Resurrexit* in the Easter mass (f. 75v).

Benevento, Biblioteca capitolare, MS 33
> Desc: missal, 139 ff., 330×235 mm, writing area 265×200, 2 columns of 29 or 30 lines
> Prov: unknown, probably not Benevento (Salerno?)
> Date: tenth–eleventh century
> Lit: TBS, II, 21; Grégoire, "Repertorium," p. 480; Gamber, CLLA, no. 430; *Les Sources*, p. 32;
>   PM XIII, 96–9 and fig. 12; PM XIV, 216, see table, p. 469, plates I–VII (ff. 45–46v, 130–131);
>   PM XV, no. 10 (p. 53); PM XX, complete facsimile, with introduction and tables; Rehle,
>   "Missale beneventanum", edition

A plenary missal, in Beneventan script and notation. Incomplete at beginning and end (extends from the vigil of Christmas to the common of one apostle). One of the oldest witnesses of Gregorian chant in southern Italy, and of Beneventan notation. The absence of any materials for the Holy Twelve Brothers or for the Translation of St Bartholomew suggests a non-Beneventan origin; on connections with Salerno, see Mallet, *Les manuscrits*, p. 90. For Beneventan contents, see table 2.1.

Benevento, Biblioteca capitolare, MS 34
> Desc: gradual, 288 ff., 310×190 mm, writing area 255×142, 10 lines
> Prov: Benevento
> Date: first half twelfth century
> Lit: TBS, II, 21; Gamber, CLLA, no. 475; Grégoire, "Repertorium," p. 480; PM XIV, see table,
>   p. 469; PM XV, complete facsimile: description and tables, pp. 162–92; *Les Sources*, p. 32

A nearly complete gradual, with tropes and sequences, and Kyriale. Beneventan notation on dry-point lines, two of them colored. Probably the latest of the five surviving graduals from Benevento, this manuscript contains the Good Friday bilingual antiphon *Panta/Omnes gentes* (f. 119) and the Alleluia *Resurrexit* in the Easter mass (f. 126; marked *non* in a later hand), as well as two rogation antiphons in Beneventan style. Monastic saints have been added to the Holy Saturday litany in the margin of f. 121v; the musical variant labeled "in s. sophia" on f. 94 suggests that the original destination is not Santa Sofia.

Benevento, Biblioteca capitolare, MS 35, ff. 202–202v
Desc: gradual fragment (1 folio), 350×172 mm, writing area 258×110, 14 lines
Prov: Benevento?
Date: eleventh century
Lit: TBS, 11, 21; Gamber, CLLA, no. 478; Grégoire, "Repertorium," p. 480; PM xiv, plate xxv
(ff. 65v–66), see table, p. 469; PM xv, no. 12 (p. 53); *Les Sources*, p. 32
The final, mutilated flyleaf attached to a twelfth-century gradual of Benevento preserves a single page from an older gradual of the Beneventan rite. It includes the end of a mass for Christmas and the beginning of one for Saint Stephen, with no intervening Gregorian music. For contents see Appendix 1.

Benevento, Biblioteca capitolare, MS 35
Desc: gradual, 201 ff., 350×172 mm, writing area 270×150, 12 lines
Prov: Benevento
Date: early twelfth century
Lit: TBS, 11, 21; Gamber, CLLA, no. 478; Grégoire, "Repertorium," p. 480; PM xiv, plate xxv
(ff. 65v–66), see table, p. 469; PM xv, no. 12 (p. 53); *Les Sources*, p. 32
Gradual with tropes and sequences, Kyriale. Incomplete at the beginning (begins 1 January). Beneventan notation on dry-point lines, two colored. The final flyleaf (see entry above) is from a gradual in Beneventan chant. In addition to much Beneventan music for Holy Week (see table 2.1), the manuscript includes two Beneventan antiphons for the Purification, four Rogation antiphons, and a Sanctus with Beneventan melodic characteristics (see Appendix 2).

Benevento, Biblioteca capitolare, MS 37
Desc: monastic chapter-book, various contents, 158 ff., 260×154, in various formats
Prov: based on materials of Santa Sofia, Benevento; used at St Peter's *intra muros*, Benevento
Date: late eleventh century
Lit: TBS, 11, 22; Grégoire, "Repertorium," p. 480; PM xv, no. 14 (p. 53); Mallet, *Les Manuscrits*,
pp. 78–80
A book containing a collection of responsories, hymns, litanies, martyrology-necrology, Rule of St Benedict, etc. The presence of a responsory (f. 8v) beginning "Sepultus extat beatus Mercurius in hoc optimo loco" (which has a Beneventan verse-melody), and the many references to Santa Sofia in the calendar of the martyrology, suggest a close connection with that church, as does the fact that in the litanies some saints of Santa Sofia (Donatus, first of the Holy Twelve Brothers, Mercurius, but also Petrus) are heightened with color, while other Beneventan saints, who are not buried in Santa Sofia (Bartholomew and Barbatus) are distinguished only with capital letters. On the use of the book at St Peter's, Benevento, see Mallet, *Les Manuscrits*, pp. 78–80.

In the collection of responsories that opens the book is *Magnus es domine*, whose melody is a Beneventan one that has been adapted to Gregorian usage by the alteration of the Beneventan cadences.

Benevento, Biblioteca capitolare, MS 38
Desc: gradual, 176 ff., 280×180 mm, writing area 240×125 mm, 12 lines
Prov: Benevento

Date: first half of eleventh century (ff. 1–167)

Lit: TBS, II, 22; Grégoire, "Repertorium," pp. 480–1; Gamber, CLLA, no. 474; PM XIV, plate
       XXIV (ff. 44v–45), see table, p. 469; PM XV, no. 15 (p. 53); *Les Sources*, p. 32

Gradual, with tropes, sequences, and Kyriale. Temporal and sanctoral mixed. Begins incomplete with Septuagesima. Lacunae, notably in Holy Week. Diastematic Beneventan notation; lines and clefs occasionally added in a later hand.

Like so many manuscripts of Benevento, to provenance of Ben38 is uncertain. Liturgical divergences make it clear that it is not intended for the same church as Benevento 40. Rubrics for the Easter *Quem queritis*, in which a single deacon represents the three Marys, recall the rubrics of Ben39 and suggest use in a convent, perhaps one of those dedicated to St Peter in Benevento. References to a bishop, however (f. 42v), are puzzling in a monastic book. The thirteenth-century liturgical materials appended to the end of the manuscript (ff. 168–76) including litanies with the names of monastic saints, and a prayer for "abbatissa nostra" (f. 169v), probably originated at the monastery of Goleto (see Mallet, *Les Manuscrits*, pp. 77–8). The addition of local stations to some Lenten masses in the thirteenth and fourteenth centuries suggests that the gradual may then have been in use at the cathedral of Benevento.

This manuscript is one (the other is Ben40) of two principal sources for the Beneventan repertory, preserving it in three ways: (1) eight Beneventan masses are included as "doublets" following their Gregorian counterparts; (2) the manuscript also contains substantial survivals of Beneventan music for Palm Sunday, and for mixed Gregorian-Beneventan rites of Good Friday and Holy Saturday (Maundy Thursday is lacking owing to a lacuna); (3) it includes as well four Beneventan rogation antiphons within a basically Gregorian series. These pieces are detailed in Appendix 1.

The manuscript is palimpsest in several places. On f. 46, recto and verso, the Beneventan tract *Attende celum*, and the dismissal *Si quis catechumenus est, procedat* have been overwritten with a litany. The bottom of f. 97v (sequence of Pentecost), all of f. 98, and the first three and a half lines of f. 98v, are palimpsest, or at least in another hand. It is impossible to see what, if anything, is written beneath. Ff. 99–99v are palimpsest; they contained the Beneventan mass for Pentecost, whose opening initial F (for the ingressa *Factus est repente*) is still visible. Here the sequence of the Gregorian mass (ff. 97v–99) and the Beneventan mass have been erased and covered over with the sequence *Sanctus spiritus adsit*, which skips from f. 98v to 99 with a cross (+) sign. The last three lines of f. 165v, and both sides of ff. 166 and 167, are palimpsest; it is not possible to tell what lies beneath.

Benevento, Biblioteca capitolare, MS 39

Desc: gradual, 195 ff., 282×180 mm, writing area 243×135, 11 lines

Prov: Benevento, convent of St Peter [*intra muros?*]

Date: late eleventh century

Lit: TBS, II, 22; Gamber, CLLA, no. 476; Grégoire, "Repertorium," p. 481; PM XIV, plate XXIII
       (ff. 22v–23), see table, p. 469; PM XV, no. 16 (p. 53); Mallet, *Les Manuscrits*, p. 79, n. 1;
       Les Sources, p. 33

Gradual with tropes and sequences. Lacunae, incomplete at beginning (begins with Monday of Passion Week). The extraordinary richness of material (tropes, sequences) for the feast of St Peter is the basis of the assignment to one of the nunneries of St Peter in Benevento. In addition to materials for Holy Week (see table 2.1) the manuscript contains two Beneventan processional antiphons (*In tribulationibus*, f. 3; *Respice*, f. 62v) and adaptations of the Beneventan Alleluia *Resurrexit tamquam dormiens*, for St Peter (*Hodie migravit*, f. 121) and the Transfiguration (*Hodie transfiguratus*, f. 140v).

Benevento, Biblioteca capitolare, MS 40

Desc: gradual, 165 folios, 255×150 mm, writing area 225×105 mm, 12 lines

Prov: Benevento (Santa Sofia?)

Date: first half of eleventh century

Lit: TBS, II, 22; Grégoire, "Repertorium," p. 481; Gamber, CLLA, no. 471; PM XIV, plates
       XII–XXII (ff. 9v–20); PM XV, no. 17 (p. 54); *Les Sources*, p. 33

Gradual, with sequences and tropes. Incomplete at the beginning, the manuscript now begins with Monday in Holy Week. Partially diastematic notation without lines or clefs. Several lacunae: after ff. 11, 26 (f. 159, misbound, should follow f. 26, but does not complete the lacuna), 64, 82, 88, 100, 116, 122. That the manuscript may have originated at Santa Sofia is suggested by the presence of the Beneventan mass of the Holy Twelve Brothers, and by paleographical similarities to Vatican, Ottob. lat. 145, which is connected with that monastery.

With Ben38 this is one of two principal sources of Beneventan music. It includes thirteen "doublet" masses, and mixed Beneventan-Gregorian rites for Holy Week. It does not, however, include any Beneventan rogation antiphons (details in Appendix 2). Numerous differences of liturgy and calendar make it clear that this manuscript was designed for use in a different church from Ben38.

Benevento, Biblioteca capitolare, fragments B
  Desc: three small fragments from a single leaf of a mixed Gregorian-Beneventan gradual (43×32 mm,
      40×37, 42×12)
  Prov: Benevento
  Date: eleventh century
  Lit:
Recovered from the binding of Benevento MS 26 and kept in an envelope, these three fragments are from a leaf containing music for the end of Good Friday and the beginning of Holy Saturday in Beneventan script and notation without lines. In addition to portions of the Gregorian canticles *Cantemus*, *Vinea*, and *Attende*, there are portions of the Beneventan Good Friday responsory *Tenebre* and the Holy Saturday antiphon *Ad vesperum*.

Berkeley (California), University of California, Bancroft Library MS ff. 2MS A2M2 1000:6
  Desc: fragmentary folio of an antiphoner (?), *c.* 240×100 mm, 14 lines visible
  Prov: unknown
  Date: eleventh century
  Lit: TBS, 11, 23
This fragmentary leaf, in very poor condition, is evidently from a Gregorian antiphoner, judging from the few pieces which can be identified (ant. *Exaltata es*, Inv. *Sancta Maria*). At the bottom of what appears to be the verso, apparently functioning as an antiphon, is the Beneventan communion *Sancta Maria*, to which is added a psalmodic ending.

Bologna, Biblioteca del Civico Museo Bibliografico Musicale G.B. Martini, Cod. 144 (Q10), framm. 3
  Desc: antiphoner (fragment), 1 folio, 210×148 mm, writing area 205×105, 9 lines visible
  Prov: unknown
  Date: second half of eleventh century
  Lit: TBS, 11, 26; Grégoire, "Repertorium," p. 483
A fragmentary leaf from an antiphoner in Beneventan script and notation using colored clef-lines. The fragment contains the end of the office for Maundy Thursday and the beginning of that for Good Friday. On the recto, as the last piece for Maundy Thursday, can be seen fragments of the Beneventan responsory *Lavi pedes*.

Bologna, Biblioteca universitaria, MS 2551
  Desc: gradual (fragment), 1 folio, 245×160 mm, writing area 235×145, 12 lines visible
  Prov: unknown
  Date: eleventh century
  Lit: TBS, 11, 26; PM xv, no. III (p. 76); Gamber, CLLA, no. 484i; *Les Sources*, p. 36
A single final flyleaf (f. 34) attached to a thirteenth-century processional-cantatorium from Brescia in ordinary minuscule. The leaf, from an eleventh-century gradual in Beneventan script and notation, includes the end of the mass for St Vincent, and a series of processional antiphons for the Purification, one of which (*Lumen ad revelationem*) is Beneventan.

Capua, Biblioteca Arcivescovile, Exultet roll
   Desc: Exultet roll, fragment, in five pieces
   Prov: Capua
   Date: eleventh century
   Lit: TBS, II, 29–30; Avery, *Exultet Rolls*, p. 16, plates 25–9; Gamber, CLLA, no. 495c; Grégoire,
         "Repertorium," p. 490–1; PM XV, no. 19 (p. 54)
   This roll presents an incomplete Vulgate Exultet with the Beneventan melody.

Farfa, Biblioteca dell'Abbazia, MS A F. 338 Musica XI (formerly A B.F. Musica XI)
   Desc: gradual (?), mutilated bifolium, 275×173 mm, writing area 260+ ×150, 13 lines
   Prov: Veroli?
   Date: eleventh century
   Lit: TBS, II, 41; Gamber, CLLA, no. 484a; Gregoire, "Repertorium," p. 496; PM II, plate 20;
         PM XIV, plates XXVI–XXVII (in the original printing labeled "Cava"), see table, p. 470;
         PM XV, no. 24 (p. 54); *Les Sources*, p. 50
   A mutilated bifolium, next to innermost in its gathering, in Beneventan script and notation without
   lines or clefs, containing part of the ceremonies of Holy Saturday; it includes parts of two versions of
   the Exultet and concludes with the neumes of Alleluia V̸ *Laudate pueri*. The innermost bifolium in the
   gathering is now Trento, Museo Provinciale d'Arte, s.n. (formerly Lawrence Feininger collection);
   it contains the end of the Vulgate Exultet and most of the Beneventan version. The two bifolia were
   still together when their Beneventan Exultet was edited in PM XIV, pp. 385–6 (1931). The Veroli
   provenance of these fragments has been suggested by Virginia Brown on paleographical grounds.

Gaeta, Archivio del Duomo, Exultet roll 1
   Desc: Exultet roll, in seven pieces
   Prov: Gaeta
   Date: first half of eleventh century
   Lit: TBS, II, 45; Avery, *Exultet Rolls*, p. 17, plates 30–3; Gregoire, "Repertorium," p. 509; PM XV,
         no. 27 (p. 55)
   The original Beneventan text of this Exultet is palimpsest, and has been replaced with the Vulgate text
   and fourteenth-century staff notation; of the original notation nothing remains, but the Beneventan
   melody was surely part of the original document.

Gaeta, Archivio del Duomo, Exultet roll 2
   Desc: Exultet roll, fragment, in four pieces
   Prov: Gaeta
   Date: eleventh century
   Lit: TBS, II, 46; Avery, *Exultet Rolls*, pp. 17–18, plates 34–47; Grégoire, "Repertorium," p. 509;
         PM XV, no. 27 (p. 55)
   This roll contained the Vulgate text of the Exultet with the Beneventan melody.

Gaeta, Archivio del Duomo, Exultet roll 3
   Desc: Exultet roll
   Prov: Gaeta
   Date: eleventh-twelfth century
   Lit: TBS, II, 46; Avery, *Exultet Rolls*, pp. 18–19, plates 38–42; Grégoire, "Repertorium," p. 509;
         PM XV, no. 28 (p. 55)
   Modeled on Gaeta 2, this Exultet likewise uses the Vulgate text and the Beneventan melody.

Leningrad, Sobranie inostrannykh Rukopisei Otdela Rukopisnoi i Redkoi Knigi Biblioteki Akademii
Nauk SSSR, MS F. no. 200

Desc: lectionary (78 ff.) and pontifical (83 ff.), 290×185 mm, writing area 195×120. "Bari-type" Beneventan script with occasional musical notation
Prov: southern Italy, used at Kotor
Date: twelfth century
Lit: TBS, II, 153; Gyug, "An Edition"
Two manuscripts, early joined together and used at Kotor on the Dalmatian coast. One bifolium (ff. 78 and 83) is palimpsest, apparently from a missal. Very little is now readable, but the lower margin of f. 83r shows in the reversed lower script the conclusion of a piece of Beneventan chant, whose text ending with *alleluia alleluia* has the melody used in the Beneventan Easter communion and elsewhere; the preceding music does not match that of any known piece. A psalm-tone ending is appended. On the other leaf of the bifolium can be read a prayer (*Omnipotens sempiterne Deus qui me peccatorem*) found in early sacramentaries (Fulda, Monza, Bergamo) for a priest's private mass. No other texts or music can at present be deciphered.

London, British Library, Additional manuscript 30337
Desc: Exultet roll
Prov: Montecassino
Date: late eleventh century
Lit: TBS, II, 52; Avery, *Exultet Rolls*, pp. 19–20, plates 43–51; PM XV, no. 30 (p. 55)
A Vulgate Exultet with Beneventan melody.

London, British Library, MS Egerton 3511 (formerly Benevento 29)
Desc: missal, 290 ff., 315×210 mm, writing area 270×170, 2 columns of 25–6 lines
Prov: St Peter's *intra muros*, Benevento
Date: twelfth century
Lit: TBS, p. 53; Gamber, CLLA, no. 452; Grégoire, "Repertorium," p. 480; PM XIV, see table, p. 469 (under Benevento VI 29); PM XV, no. 8 (p. 52); *The British Library. Catalogue of Additions 1946–1950*, pp. 330–3
The missal, in Beneventan script with occasional notation, contains the Exultet with Vulgate text and Beneventan melody, as well as notated lection-tones for the canticles of Jonah and Azarias.

Lucca, Biblioteca Capitolare Feliniana, MS 606
Desc: missal, 193 ff. plus 1 parchment flyleaf (f. I, twelfth century), 620×450 mm, writing area 480×310, 2 columns of 40 to 41 text lines
Prov: Lucca?
Date: early eleventh century
Lit: Gamber, CLLA, no. 1417; PM XIV, see table, p. 470; plates XXXIV–XLIII (ff. 150v–153, 154v–156); PM XV, no. 31 (p. 55); *Les Sources*, p. 65
A plenary missal in ordinary minuscule with central Italian musical notation (with the exception of Alleluia *Adorabo*, f. 137, noted in Beneventan). An integral part of the original manuscript is an appendix (ff. 150v–156v), in ordinary minuscule with partially-diastematic Beneventan notation, containing music for special Holy Week rites: Palm Sunday, Maundy Thursday, Good Friday, Holy Saturday (see table 2.1). There are no masses for any of these feasts in the appendix, and the rites of Maundy Thursday through Easter Tuesday are missing from the missal owing to a lacuna after f. 71v. This appendix is a compilation of additional materials for special functions, with rubrics appropriate for a monastic church. There are references to other books ("sicut in sacramentario continentur"), and many musical pieces are cued; the pieces noted in full seem to be those not commonly known (or found in other books, or in the main manuscript). Much of the music is Beneventan.

The tenth-century Montecassino MS 175 (pp. 587–8) contains an "ordo qualiter agatur in parasceben" (edited in *Bibliotheca casinensis*, IV, 33–4) whose language and ritual match that of Lucca almost exactly, except that all vespers psalms are sung under a single antiphon.

Macerata, Biblioteca comunale "Mozzi-Borgetti", MS 378
   Desc: pontifical, 216 ff., 283×190 mm, writing area 213×130, 17–19 lines
   Prov: Benevento
   Date: early twelfth century
   Lit: TBS, II, 55; Grégoire, "Repertorium," p. 516; Garbelotto, "Catalogo," pp. 110–14; Paci, *Inventario*, pp. 142–3; Adversi, *Inventari*, I, 92
   This pontifical, containing very little notation, nevertheless cues the Beneventan version of the canticle *Benedictus es, Domine* for Holy Saturday.

Macerata, Biblioteca comunale, MS 1457.XII
   Desc: antiphoner (fragment), 1 f., 148×215 mm, writing area 115 + ×155, 6 lines visible, spaced approx.
      21 mm apart
   Prov: unknown
   Date: eleventh century
   Lit:
   A much mutilated folio of a Gregorian antiphoner in Beneventan script and notation; only the recto is legible; the blank verso was glued to a copy of *Antichità di Roma* (Rome, Antonio Blado, 1575). On the recto is a series of antiphons of lauds for the second Sunday of Lent. Following the antiphon *Assumpsit ihesus* is the rubric "al [alia? aliae?] sec[undum] ambro[sianum]," indicating the beginning of a section of Beneventan music.

Manchester, John Rylands University Library, MS 2
   Desc: Exultet, fragmentary, in three strips
   Prov: southern Italy
   Date: early eleventh century
   Lit: TBS, II, 56; Avery, *Exultet Rolls*, p. 21, plates 52–5; James, *A Descriptive Catalogue*, I, 4–6, 11, plates 2–7; Gamber, CLLA, no. 495d; PM XV, no. 32 (p. 56)
   Beneventan text and music of the Exultet, incomplete.

Melk, Stiftsbibliothek, MS 1012, ff. A–B; MS 1027, f. Z
   Desc: antiphoner, 3 flyleaves, approx. 215×155 mm, writing area approx. 210(?)×115, 13(?) lines. Much mutilated
   Prov: unknown; Benevento?
   Date: eleventh century
   Lit: Angerer, "Unbekannte Fragmente," with facsimiles
   Three leaves from an antiphoner in Beneventan script and notation without clefs or lines: MS 1012, f. Av (only the verso is visible, the leaf being pasted to the inside of the binding) contains the end of the office of the Beheading of St John the Baptist, and the beginning of the office of the Holy Twelve Brothers; MS 1027, f. Zr followed immediately in the original antiphoner, and continues the office which is incomplete on the recto (the verso is pasted to binding boards).

Mirabella Eclano, Archivio della Chiesa Collegiata, Exultet roll 1 (on deposit in the Biblioteca Nazionale, Naples)
   Desc: Exultet roll, fragment in four pieces
   Prov: Mirabella Eclano?
   Date: eleventh century
   Lit: TBS, II, 57; Avery, *Exultet Rolls*, p. 21, plates 56–9; Grégoire, "Repertorium," p. 526
   An Exultet with Beneventan text and music, incomplete.

Mirabella Eclano, Archivio della Chiesa Collegiata, Exultet roll 2 (on deposit in the Biblioteca Nazionale, Naples)

Desc: Exultet roll, in 3 pieces
Prov: Mirabella Eclano?
Date: second half of eleventh century
Lit: TBS, II, 57–8; Avery, *Exultet Rolls*, p. 21, plate 60; Grégoire, "Repertorium," p. 527; PM XV, no. 33 (p. 56)
This incomplete roll uses the Vulgate text of the Exultet, notated with the Beneventan melody.

Montecassino, Archivio della Badia, MS 361
   Desc: palimpsest fragments of a Beneventan gradual, re-used in the present manuscript (222 pages, 243×165 mm)
   Prov: Montecassino
   Date: lower script, eleventh century; upper script, twelfth century
   Lit: Inguanez, *Codicum Casinensium*, II, pars 2, pp. 208–12; TBS, II, 84; Grégoire, "Repertorium," p. 535; PM XV, no. 128 (p. 78); Kelly, "Montecassino," pp. 64–9; Bloch, "Der Autor," pp. 105–27; Meyvaert, "The Autographs," plate I (facs. of p. 143)
The present manuscript, in the minuscule hand of Peter the Deacon, who was appointed librarian of Montecassino in 1131 or 1132 (see Meyvaert, "The Autographs"), contains works of classical authors and of Peter the Deacon himself.

   Twelve single folios from an earlier manuscript of Beneventan chant, folded to receive new text (Beneventan palimpsest pages, originally in two columns, had a writing space approx. 280×190 mm), can be identified as bifolia in MC 361 (pp. 103–6; 125–6/135–6; 143–4/149–50; 157–8/167–8; 159–60/165–6; 161–4; 175–6/189–90; 177–8/187–8; 179–80/185–6; 197–8/207–8; 199–200/205–6; 201–4); all of them contained Beneventan chant, of which sometimes only fragments can be read. Two other palimpsest leaves also contain fragmentary remains of Beneventan chant (pp. 139–40, 193–4). Thirteen further leaves from the original manuscript have nothing left but touches of ink and the general layout of the original music manuscript. These are pp. 115–6, 119–20, 123–4, 129–32 (a bifolium), 137–8, 141–2, 145–8 (a bifolium), 151–2, 153–4/169–70 (a bifolium), 174–5. Touches of gold (for example, on pp. 156, 200), the quality of the initials, the generous spacing and margins, and the general care in writing, suggest that the original manuscript was intended to be elegant and important.

   The pieces that can be identified in the lower script are listed below:

Palimpsest Beneventan music in Montecassino 361

Page	Incipit	Feast	Function in other MSS
126	*Credo* (fragment)		
143	*Factus est repente*	Pentecost	Ingressa
144	The following rubrics are faintly visible (continuation of Pentecost mass?):		
	V [Gradual verse?]		
	Initial *A*[lleluia] followed by *V*		
	of [Offertory]		
150	*Ut cognosceret*	Peter and Paul	Communion
150	. . .*te paul*[ ] *ap*. . .	Paul?	?
162	*Ad honorem*	All Saints	Communion (Ben40, f. 134)
			Offertory (Ben40, f. 134v)
166	*Circuierunt*	XII Fratrum	Offertory
166	*Hos duodecim*	XII Fratrum	Communion

Montecassino, Archivio della Badia, MS 542
  Desc: antiphoner, monastic, Advent IV to Maundy Thursday; 194 pp., approx. 280×170, writing area
      235×125, 13 lines; somewhat damaged at top center; Beneventan script and notation with clefs
      and lines (one colored red)
  Prov: Montecassino?
  Date: second half twelfth century
  Lit: Inguanez, *Codicum Casinensium*, III, 203; TBS, II, 89–90; PM xv, no. 42, p. 57; Grégoire,
      "Repertorium," p. 538
  Like other antiphoners of the region, this manuscript contains antiphons for St Silvester, St Vincent,
  and St Benedict which have a number of Beneventan features.

Montecassino, Archivio della Badia, Exultet Roll 1
  Desc: Exultet roll, fragment
  Prov: southeastern Italy (?)
  Date: eleventh century
  Lit: TBS, II, 93; Avery, *Exultet Rolls*, pp. 21–2, plate 61; Grégoire, "Repertorium," p. 540; PM xv,
      no. 54 (p. 58)
  A fragment of the Beneventan Exultet with notation.

Montecassino, Archivio della Badia, Exultet Roll 2
  Desc: Exultet roll
  Prov: Sorrento
  Date: 1106–20
  Lit: TBS, II, 94; Avery, *Exultet Rolls*, p. 22, plates 62–71; Grégoire, "Repertorium," p. 540; PM xv,
      no. 53 (p. 58)
  This roll contains the Vulgate text of the Exultet, with additions from the Beneventan text, and the
  Beneventan melody.

Montecassino, Archivio della Badia, Compactiones v
  Desc: breviary, 113 leaves, approx. 500×350 mm, writing area approx. 430×240, 2 columns of
      50 text-lines
  Prov: Montecassino?
  Date: late eleventh century?
  Lit: TBS, II, 92
  Fragments from various manuscripts at Montecassino are kept in large folders labeled *Compactiones*.
  Folder v contains, among other things, a group of 113 folios from a large late eleventh-century noted
  monastic breviary, written in two columns in Beneventan script and notation without lines or clefs.
  Beneventan antiphons are found in the offices of the Holy Twelve Brothers, Saints John and Paul, and
  St Vincent, and the Alleluia V̵ *Resurrexit* appears as a Responsory in Easter vespers.

Montecassino, Archivio della Badia, Compactiones xxii
  Desc: gradual fragment, approx. 365×245 mm, writing area approx. 330×180, 11 lines
  Prov: Montecassino
  Date: eleventh century
  Lit: Boe, "Old Beneventan"
  Folder xxii in the Compactiones contains four leaves from a Gregorian gradual in Beneventan script
  and notation typical of Montecassino; the last leaf contains most of the pseudo-Gregorian mass *Vir dei
  Benedictus* for St Benedict. Following the Gregorian communion *Hodie dilectus* is the rubric *ali. co̅.
  ambro.* followed by the Beneventan communion *Gloriosus confessor domini* (incomplete).

Naples, Biblioteca nazionale, MS vi g 34
  Desc: processional, 139 ff., 200×135 mm, writing area 165×90

Prov: Troia (?)

Date: late twelfth century

Lit: TBS, II, 102; Arnese, *I codici notati*, pp. 146–9 and plate 10; PM XV, no. 59 (p. 59); Husmann,
    Tropen, pp. 175–6; Grégoire, "Repertorium," p. 545

A processional, including tropes for Kyrie and Gloria, farced epistles, hymns, in Beneventan script and
notation with lines and clefs, includes a single Beneventan antiphon (*Peccavimus*, f. 6), and the responsory *Magnus es Deus*, a Beneventan melody adapted to Gregorian style.

Naples, Biblioteca nazionale, MS XVI A 19

Desc: processional (ff. 1–15), 300×180 mm, writing area 270×120, 12 lines

Prov: Benevento (Santa Sofia?)

Date: twelfth century (ff. 1–15), twelfth–thirteenth century (ff. 16–48)

Lit: TBS, II, 105; Gamber, CLLA, no. 482; Grégoire, "Repertorium," p. 546; Arnese, *I codici notati*,
    pp. 172–5, plate XI; PM XV, no. 142 (p. 79)

Composed of two manuscripts: ff. 1–15, in Beneventan script and notation with lines and clefs, com-
prise an incomplete processional, including three Beneventan antiphons (see Appendix 1); ff. 16–48
include litanies, responsories, and liturgical material for Saint Mercurius and for the Holy Twelve
Brothers, and hence might be designed for Santa Sofia.

New York, Pierpont Morgan Library, MS M. 379

Desc: missal, 273 ff., 387×255 mm, writing area 280×165, 2 columns of 31 lines; central Italian script

Prov: Subiaco (?) for use at a monastery in or near Spoleto

Date: eleventh–twelfth century

Lit: De Ricci, *Census*, II, 1437

An almost complete missal; the sparse musical notation is derived from the Beneventan. The Vulgate
text of the Exultet (ff. 108v–110v) is preceded by an elaborate *Lumen Christi* similar to those of Rome,
Vall. B 23 and Subiaco XVIII. The Beneventan melody, slightly elaborated, is used up to *Vere dignum*;
the Roman preface-tone is used thereafter, but it is interrupted twice, for the blessing of incense and
the lighting of the candle.

Oxford, Bodleian Library, MS Canonici Bibl. lat. 61

Desc: gospel lectionary, 197 ff., 286×195 mm, writing area 198×112, 19 lines

Prov: Zadar

Date: late eleventh century

Lit: TBS, pp. 109–10; Gamber, CLLA, no. 1170; Lowe, *Scriptura beneventana*, plate LXXIV; PM XV,
    no. 166 (p. 177); Nicholson, *Early Bodleian Music*, pp. xiii, lxxiii–lxxiv, and plates 37 (f. 115v–116)
    and 38 (ff. 122v–123); Novak, "Vecénegin," including facsimiles of ff. 121, 122v, 115v (color),
    117 (color): the text of the Exultet is edited on pp. 38–44

A decorated gospel-lectionary containing the Exultet (ff. 116v–123) with Vulgate text and Beneventan
melody.

Oxford, Bodleian Library, MS Canonici liturg. 277

Desc: hours, 154 ff., 135×100 mm, writing area 90×52, 13 lines

Prov: Zadar, Benedictine convent of St Mary

Date: late eleventh century

Lit: TBS, II, 110; van Dijk, "Handlist," IV, 2–3; Nicholson, *Early Bodleian*, pp. lxxiv–lxxv, and
    plate 39 (ff. 72v–73) and 40 (f. 150v)

An unlabeled votive office contains the texts (without notation) of two Beneventan antiphons used
elsewhere for rogations: *Peccavimus* (f. 125) and *Gemitus noster* (f. 125v).

Oxford, Bodleian Library, MS Canonici liturg. 342

Desc: missal, 122 ff., approx. 250×165 mm, writing area approx. 180×100, 23 lines; the manuscript has been mutilated and rearranged.

Prov: Dubrovnik (Santa Maria de Rabiata?)

Date: thirteenth century

Lit: TBS, 11, 111; PM XIV, see table, p. 471; PM XV, no 60 (p. 59); *Les Sources*, p. 88

This noted missal includes an Exultet (Vulgate text) with a highly-elaborated melody that may be a version of the Beneventan melody (see PM XIV, 399–416); and the Good Friday antiphon *Crucem tuam* (f. 51).

Paris, Bibliotheque nationale, MS nouv. acq. lat. 710

Desc: Exultet roll

Prov: Fondi, St Peter

Date: *c.* 1100

Lit: TBS, 11, 116; Avery, *Exultet Rolls*, pp. 23–4, plates 72–80; PM XV, no. 62 (p. 60)

Clearly related to Montecassino by its texts and its miniatures, this Exultet contains the Vulgate text with the Beneventan melody.

Pisa, Museo Nazionale di San Matteo, Exultet roll

Desc: Exultet roll, separated into 12 pieces

Prov: southern Italy

Date: eleventh century

Lit: TBS, 11, 119; Avery, *Exultet Rolls*, pp. 24–6, plates 82–97; Grégoire, "Repertorium," p. 556; PM XV, no. 65 (p. 60)

This roll contains the Vulgate text of the Exultet with additions from the Beneventan version; the melody is Beneventan.

Rome, Biblioteca Casanatense, MS 724

Desc: Exultet roll, separated into 10 pieces

Prov: Benevento

Date: twelfth century

Lit: TBS, 11, 123; Avery, *Exultet Rolls*, pp. 29–30, plates 118–129; Avitabile, Censimento I, pp. 1137–8; Gamber, CLLA, no. 499; PM XV, no. 67 (p. 61)

This roll, containing the full Beneventan text and melody, has been cut up and bound with two earlier rotuli from Benevento, a pontifical (written 957–69) and a benedictional of Archbishop Landolf I (written 969–82): see Belting, *Malerei*, pp. 144–66.

Rome, Biblioteca Vallicelliana, MS C 9

Desc: palimpsest fragments of a Beneventan gradual in a composite manuscript (411 ff., 293×205 mm)

Prov: unknown; Benevento?

Date: lower script, eleventh century; upper script, early twelfth century (ff. 1–137), late twelfth century (ff. 138–173)

Lit: TBS, 11, 127–8; PM XV, no. 70 (p. 61); Avitabile, Censimento II, pp. 1037–8; Kelly, "Palimpsest evidence"; de Nonno, "Contributo"; Vettori, "Inventarium," ff. 1202–1202v

The first part of the present manuscript (ff. 1–173 bis), in Beneventan script, contains Dialogues of Gregory the Great; pseudo-Jerome on the Nativity of the Virgin Mary; sermon and miracles on the conception of the Virgin Mary; poems to St Mary Magdalen; Johannes Osareus, commentary on Matthew; the Sequence *Stans a longe*; and an anonymous letter on the marriage of priests.

The palimpsest Beneventan pages (writing area 299×140 mm, 13 lines) are in two groups: (1) two single leaves and three bifolia used individually in fascicles 2 through 5 of the present MS (ff. 11/14, 19, 20, 24/29, 32/37); (2) a complete fascicle used in its original order (ff. 167–73 bis). Though many musical and textual fragments remain to be deciphered, the following pieces from the Benevent repertory have been identified:

Palimpsest Beneventan music in Vallicelliana c 9

Folio	Incipit	Feast	Function in other MSS
f. 14v	*Credo* (fragment)	?	
f. 19r	*Postquam surrexit*	M. Thurs.	Ingressa
f. 19r	*Domine audivi*	M. Thurs.	Tract
f. 19v	*Testificata* (?)	Palm Sun.	Ingressa
f. 20	. . .*iordanis stupuit*	Epiphany?	?
	[*co*]*lumba prote*[*statur*]		
	. . .*filius* [*meus hic est?*]		
f. 24v	. . .*et libera nos*	[Lent?]	Tract?
	(followed by rubric *of*)		
f. 29r	Rubric . . .*esima Ing*[*res*]*sa*		
f. 32v	*Domine audivi*	Holy Sat.	Tract
f. 32v	*Cantabo*	Holy Sat.	Tract
f. 167r	*Credo* (fragment)	Easter	
f. 167r	*Angelus domini*	Easter	Offertory
f. 167r	*Qui manducaverit*	Easter	Communion
f. 168v	*Michi autem absit*	InvHCross	Ingressa
f. 168v	*Dum sacra misteria*	Michael	Ingressa
f. 169r	*Ecce sedet in medio*	Ascension	Ingressa
f. 169r	*Factus est repente*	Pentecost	Ingressa
f. 169v	*Lumen quod animus*	John Bapt.	Ingressa
f. 169v	*Petrus dormiebat* (?)	Peter and Paul	Ingressa
f. 170v	*Gloria in excelsis* (end)	?	?
f. 170v	*Kyrie*	?	?
f. 172v	*Prima predicationis*	Andrew	Ingressa
f. 173	*Michi autem nimis*	Apostles?	Ingressa
f. 173	[*In omnem*] *terram exivit*	Apostles?	?

Rome, Biblioteca Vallicelliana, MS B 23

Desc: missal, 287 ff., 331×222 mm, writing area 260×168, in two columns of 26 lines; ordinary minuscule writing, with rare peripheral Beneventan notation

Prov: S. Gioveni di Monte Lupo (prov. Macerata), according to R. Amiet as reported in the library's bibliographical *schedario*

Date: first half of twelfth century

Lit: Avitabile, Censimento II, p. 1024

An almost complete missal, essentially without notation. On ff. 124v–126v, the Exultet (preceded by a very elaborate *Lumen Christi*) has the Beneventan melody at the beginning (up to *Vere dignum*), the Roman preface-tone thereafter. An elaborate praise of the bees (from *Apis ceteris*), without notation, is marked "hic mutat sensum quasi legens," notation resuming with "O vere beata nox que expoliavit."

Rome, Biblioteca Vallicelliana, MS B 43

Desc: sacramentary, 131 ff., 291×192 mm, writing area 190×95, 26 lines; ordinary minuscule writing with sparse Beneventan notation

Prov: central Italy; perhaps Rome

Date: late twelfth century

Lit: Avitabile, Censimento II, pp. 1028–9

A complete sacramentary, with calendar and *ordo missae*. On folios 49–53v the Vulgate text of the Exultet is provided with the Beneventan melody.

Rome, Biblioteca Vallicelliana, MS C 32
    Desc: ritual, 105 ff., 252×175 mm, writing area 205×130, 21 lines
    Prov: unknown; Montecassino?
    Date: eleventh century (ff. 1–96); 2 opening flyleaves (apocalypse), late eleventh century; ff. 97–105
        (palimpsest, lower script *c.* eleventh century), twelfth–thirteenth century
    Lit: TBS, II, 128; Gamber, CLLA, no. 1593; PM XIV, see table, p. 471; PM XV, no. 71 (p. 62);
        Avitabile, Censimento II, 1040–1; Odermatt, *Ein Rituale* (edition)
A ritual in Beneventan script and notation. The Holy Saturday rite contains the antiphon *Omnes sitientes*, and the Exultet with essentially a Vulgate text: edited in Odermatt, pp. 136, 274–6.

[Salerno, Archivio capitolare: according to Latil, "Un 'Exultet' inedito," a missal of 1431 contains an Exultet with Beneventan text and elaborated Beneventan melody.]

"Solesmes flyleaves": Private collection, facsimiles at abbey of St Pierre, Solesmes
    Desc: antiphoner (fragment), 4 ff., 250–75×180 mm, writing area approx. 280×145, sixteen lines
    Prov: unknown; Benevento?
    Date: eleventh century
    Lit: Kelly, "Une nouvelle source"
Four leaves, trimmed at top and bottom, in Beneventan script and notation without lines or clefs; the pages are now numbered i–viii. The four folios contain the end of the Gregorian office of Saints Gervasius and Protasius, the office of Saint John the Baptist, and the beginning of the office of Saints John and Paul. Inserted before the Gregorian office of St John the Baptist is a Beneventan vespers of St John the Baptist (ff. ii–iii), preceded by the rubric "viiij [ante] k[a]l[endas] iul[ii] vig[ilia]. s[ancti]. ioh[ann]is bap[tistae]. a[ntiphonae] ambro[sianae]. ad vesp[eras]."

Subiaco, Biblioteca del Protocenobio di Santa Scolastica, MS XVIII (19)
    Desc: missal, 171 ff., 790×400 mm, writing area approx. 620×310 in 2 columns of 32 lines
    Prov: Subiaco
    Date: thirteenth century
    Lit: Allodi, *Inventario*, p. 9 (no. 19); *Les Sources*, p. 141
A missal in northern script, only partially notated, with Beneventan notation using colored lines. The entire Beneventan vespers of Good Friday appears without notation, and the Exultet (Vulgate text) has the Beneventan melody for part of its length.

Trento, Museo Provinciale d'Arte s.n. (formerly Lawrence Feininger collection)
    Desc: gradual, 1 mutilated bifolium, approx. 306×210 mm, writing area 306+ ×150, 13 lines
    Prov: Veroli?
    Date: eleventh century
    Lit: TBS, II, 139
The central bifolium of a quire containing portions of two versions (Vulgate and Beneventan) of the Exultet, with notation. The next outer bifolium of the same manuscript is Farfa, Biblioteca dell'Abbazia MS AF. 338 Musica XI. The two bifolia were still together *c.* 1930. For information on provenance and for further literature see above under Farfa.

Troia, Archivio del Duomo, Exultet 1
    Desc: Exultet roll
    Prov: Troia
    Date: second half of eleventh century
    Lit: TBS, II, 141; Avery, *Exultet Rolls*, p. 37, plates 164–7; Cavallo, *Rotoli*, pp. 135–8 and plates 28–35;
        Gamber, CLLA, no. 488; Grégoire, "Repertorium," p. 563; PM XV, no. 100 (p. 69)
This roll contains the Exultet with Beneventan text and melody.

Troia, Archivio del Duomo, Exultet 2
  Desc: Exultet roll, fragmentary
  Prov: Troia
  Date: early twelfth century
  Lit: TBS, II, 141; Avery, *Exultet Rolls*, pp. 37–8, plates 168–70; Cavallo, *Rotoli*, pp. 157–9 and plates
       36–41; Grégoire, "Repertorium," p. 563
An incomplete version of the Beneventan Exultet.

Troia, Archivio del Duomo, Exultet 3
  Desc: Exultet roll, partially palimpsest
  Prov: Troia
  Date: twelfth century (for the original hand)
  Lit: TBS, II, 141; Avery, *Exultet Rolls*, pp. 38–40, plates 171–85; Cavallo, *Rotoli*, pp. 175–85 and plates
       42–61
An Exultet of the twelfth century containing the complete Vulgate text; the original contemporaneous Beneventan melody has been erased and written over with the "Roman" melody in Beneventan notation with lines and clefs.

Vatican City, Biblioteca Apostolica Vaticana, MS Barberinianus latinus 560
  Desc: missal, Lent – St Paul, 106 ff., 320×262 mm, writing area 247×212, in two columns. Ordinary
       minuscule script, no musical notation in original hand. One line in Beneventan writing and
       notation (twelfth century) is added in upper margin of folio 16v ("Dominus vobiscum; Et cum
       spiritu tuo; Lectio sancti evangelii secundum iohannem; Gloria tibi domine")
  Prov: central Italy
  Date: tenth–eleventh century
  Lit: TBS, II, 161; Gamber, CLLA, no. 1414; Frénaud, "Les témoins," pp. 67–8; Salmon, *Les
       Manuscrits*, II, no. 250; Bannister, *Monumenti*, no. 311 (p. 118), no. 361 (p. 125); PM XV, no. 155
       (p. 81); *Les Sources*, p. 123
Related to Vat. lat. 4770 by its script and its liturgy, the rites of Holy Week have been altered in this missal by the erasure of almost all the rubrics indicating chants, ceremonies, and the like. A rubric for Good Friday in a second hand over an erasure (f. 51) indicates the Beneventan adoration antiphons: "et ant Adoramus. Crucem tuam. Laudamus." Original rubrics indicate the chanting of the canticles of Jonah and of the Three Children on Holy Saturday (see Chapter 4).

Vatican City, Biblioteca Apostolica Vaticana, MS Barberinianus latinus 592
  Desc: Exultet roll, five fragments
  Prov: Montecassino
  Date: late eleventh century
  Lit: TBS, II, 161–2; Avery, *Exultet Rolls*, pp. 34–5, plates 147–53; Bannister, *Monumenti*, no. 366
       (p. 128) and plate 74; Salmon, *Les Manuscrits*, II, no. 158; PM XV, no. 84 (pp. 65–6)
Closely related to the Montecassino Exultet roll in the British Library (Add. 30337); Vulgate text, with lacunae. A now-lost fragment of this roll (without notation) was published in Martinus Gerbert, *De Cantu* (St Blasien, 1774), and is reprinted in Avery, *Exultet Rolls*, plate 147.

Vatican City, Biblioteca Apostolica Vaticana, MS Barberinianus latinus 603
  Desc: missal, 90 ff., 377×267 mm, writing area 305×192, 2 columns
  Prov: Caiazzo (near Caserta)
  Date: twelfth–thirteenth century
  Lit: TBS, II, 162; Salmon, *Les Manuscrits*, II, no. 256; III, no. 158; Gamber, CLLA, no. 458;
       Bannister, *Monumenti*, no. 371 (p. 130), no. 889 (p. 192); *Les Sources*, p. 123; PM XIV, see index,
       p. 471; PM XV, no. 85 (p. 66)

A noted missal, extending from the Ember Days of Advent to the fourth Sunday after Pentecost, with lacunae. Beneventan script and notation using the dry-point text-line, without clefs. The only Beneventan element is the Exultet (ff. 57–8) in a somewhat later hand, whose Vulgate text uses the Beneventan melody at its beginning and end, but the now-standard preface tone for most of its length.

Vatican City, Biblioteca Apostolica Vaticana, MS Barberinianus latinus 697
Desc: pontifical, f. I plus 109 ff., 305×207 mm, writing area 172×125, 22 lines
Prov: Capua
Date: fourteenth century. Flyleaves: f. I, early thirteenth century; f. 109, late thirteenth century
Lit: TBS, II, 162; Salmon, *Les Manuscrits*, I, nos. 501, 617; III, no. 162; V, no. III
Bound with two flyleaves from a Gregorian antiphoner and a notated breviary in Beneventan script and notation, the fourteenth-century ritual of Capua, in ordinary script, contains an *Ordo ad catachuminus faciendum* which includes the text of the Beneventan antiphon *Dum sanctificatus fuero* twice (ff. 17 and 20 – marked xiij and xvj), without notation.

Vatican City, Biblioteca Apostolica Vaticana, MS Borgianus latinus 339
Desc: evangelistary, 59 ff., approx. 560×390 mm, writing area 400×250, 19 lines; "Bari-type" script
Prov: San Nicola, Osor (Dalmatia)
Date: 1082
Lit: TBS, II, 163–4; Salmon, *Les Manuscrits*, II, no. 73; Bannister, *Monumenti*, no. 365 (pp. 127–8) and
      plate 73b (Exultet, f. 58); PM XIV, 382, 383; PM XV, no. 90 (p. 67)
The Exultet (ff. 53–58v) contains the Vulgate text with an extended praise of the bees (this latter edited in PM XIV, 383, col. I), using the Beneventan melody.

Vatican City, Biblioteca Apostolica Vaticana, MS Ottobonianus latinus 145
Desc: monastic manual, 162 ff., 220×140–160 mm
Prov: Santa Sofia, Benevento (?), based on Montecassino materials
Date: first half of eleventh century
Lit: TBS, II, 165; PM XV, no. 92 (p. 67); Gamber, CLLA, no. 465a; Gamber, *Manuale* (edition);
      Bannister, *Monumenti*, no. 348 (p. 122) and plate 70b (f. 7), no. 350 (pp. 123–4) and table 71b
      (f. 134); Boe, "A new source" (includes facsimiles); Salmon, *Les Manuscrits*, I, no. 150; III,
      no. 180; V, nos. 229, 423
A monastic manual in various formats containing a variety of antiphons, hymns, canticles, *ordo ad monachum faciendum*, *mandatum*, and collects. In the course of the *mandatum* ceremony are presented (ff. 124–124v) six Beneventan antiphons (used elsewhere as communions or offertories), which are described as being "Ambrosian."

The manuscript appears to be based on a Montecassino original (f. 121r: "in hoc monasterio ubi sacratissimum corpus eius [Benedict] humatum est"), but it was perhaps designed for Santa Sofia in Benevento: the Holy Twelve Brothers are named individually in a litany, f. 111v, and Saints Graficus and Quineclus, *martyrum in S. Sophia*, are named on f. 112: see Chapter 1, p. 14.

Vatican City, Biblioteca Apostolica Vaticana, MS Ottobonianus latinus 576
Desc: missal, in two volumes, 377 ff., 270×175 mm, writing area 250×115, 24–8 text-lines
Prov: unknown, monastic; Montecassino?
Date: twelfth century (ff. 2–220), thirteenth century (ff. 1, 221–337)
Lit: TBS, II, 166; Gamber, CLLA, no. 454; Salmon, *Les Manuscrits*, II, no. 305; Bannister, *Monumenti*,
      no. 368 (pp. 128–9) and plate 75a (f. 171); PM XIV, see table, p. 471; PM XV, no. 94 (p. 68);
      Les Sources, p. 127
A plenary missal, mixed temporal and sanctoral. Beneventan script and notation on lines (ff. 123–95 are in "Bari-type" script); notation is not continued after the second Sunday after the Octave of Easter.

Parts of two missals are the lower script of palimpsest folios (ff. 1, 341–77; see Gamber, CLLA, no. 437; Dold, "Ein Palimpsestblatt"); contains no rite for Maundy Thursday. In addition to the Holy Saturday antiphon *Omnes sitientes* and the dismissal *Si quis catechuminus est*, the manuscript contains the Exultet with Vulgate text but Beneventan melody, and notated Beneventan lection-tones for Holy Saturday.

Vatican City, Biblioteca Apostolica Vaticana, MS Reginensis latinus 334
Desc: processional, 100 ff., 250×130 mm
Prov: St Dominic, Sora
Date: twelfth century (ff. 1–56); eleventh–twelfth century (ff. 57–100)
Lit: TBS, II, 168; Wilmart, *Bibliothecae*, pp. 246–50; Salmon, *Les Manuscrits*, IV, no. 612; PM XV, no. 96 (p. 68); Bannister, *Monumenti*, no. 365 (pp. 126–7), plate 73b (f. 58)
Composed of two manuscripts: ff. 1–56, in ordinary minuscule, contain prayers, litanies, etc.; ff. 57–100 (writing area 200×95 mm, 10 lines) are an incomplete processional, in Beneventan script and notation, and include a Beneventan responsory (*Ante sex dies*, f. 58v) and antiphons for processions (*Congregamini*, f. 57; *In tribulationibus*, f. 71v; *Peccavimus*, f. 72; *Respice*, f. 74, 76v) as well as an antiphon in Gregorian style (*Maria vidit*: see Appendix 2), related to the text of the Beneventan Easter ingressa.

Vatican City, Biblioteca Apostolica Vaticana, MS Urbinas latinus 602
Desc: troper, 108 ff., 158×94 mm, writing area 103×55, 6 or 7 lines
Prov: Montecassino
Date: eleventh–twelfth century palimpsest portions (ff. IV–23v, 99v–100v) rewritten thirteenth century
Lit: TBS, II, 170; Stornajolo, *Codices urbinates*, pp. 126–9; Salmon, *Les Manuscrits*, II, no. 194, V, no. 411; Bannister, *Monumenti*, no. 349 (pp. 122–3) and plate 71a (ff. 41v–42); no. 370 (p. 130); Husmann, *Tropen*, p. 198; PM XIV, pp. 430, 431, n. 1; PM XV, no. 97 (p. 68); Boe, "The 'lost' palimpsest Kyries"
A troper, arranged by liturgical category, designed for Montecassino use; much of it has been erased and written over, probably in the thirteenth century. On ff. 99v–100, over an earlier erased text, appears the Beneventan series of monitions *Si quis catechuminus est procedat*, etc.

Vatican City, Biblioteca Apostolica Vaticana, MS Vaticanus latinus 3784
Desc: Exultet roll, in four pieces
Prov: Montecassino
Date: Second half of eleventh century (Desiderian)
Lit: TBS, II, 148; Avery, *Exultet Rolls*, pp. 30–1, plates 130–4; Gamber, CLLA, no. 495b; Bannister, *Monumenti*, no. 346 (pp. 119–20) and plate 69; Salmon, *Les Manuscrits*, II, no. 195; PM XIII, p. 95, fig. 11; PM XV, no. 75 (p. 62)
The manuscript contains only the introduction up to the preface *Vere dignum*, using the Beneventan melody; script and music to a large extent have been retraced by a later hand. To this introduction (which presumably once continued with Beneventan text and melody) has been attached a fourteenth-century Neapolitan Vulgate continuation.

Vatican City, Biblioteca Apostolica Vaticana, MS Vaticanus latinus 4770
Desc: plenary missal, 254 ff., 345×270 mm, writing area 270×200, 29–35 lines (music and text use one line only)
Prov: monastery of St Bartholomew, Musiano, near Bologna (Salmon); Abruzzi (Gamber); Subiaco (PM XIV, 243, n. 5)
Date: tenth–eleventh century

Lit: TBS, II, 149; Gamber, CLLA, no. 1413; Salmon, *Les Manuscrits*, II, no. 401; Bannister, *Monumenti*,
       no. 162 (pp. 47–9) and plate 21 (f. 13v); PM XIV, see table, p. 471; *Les Sources*, p. 124
A monastic missal-gradual, temporal and sanctoral mixed, beginning incomplete in the second mass of
Christmas. Written in ordinary minuscule, middle Italian notation. A connection with southern Italy
is seen in the use of Beneventan script to continue the main text on ff. 216–216v. Beneventan musical
contents are slight: pieces for the Good Friday adoration and chants for the Easter vigil mass, without
notation (see table 2.1).

Vatican City, Biblioteca Apostolica Vaticana, MS Vaticanus latinus 6082
   Desc: notated missal, 319 ff., 294×200 mm, writing area 210×115, 31 lines
   Prov: Montecassino or San Vincenzo al Volturno
   Date: twelfth century
   Lit: TBS, II, 152; Salmon, *Les Manuscrits*, II, no. 413, III, nos. 103, 278; Gamber, CLLA, no. 455;
           PM XIV, see table, p. 471; PM XV, no. 77 (p. 63); Bannister, *Monumenti*, no. 369 (pp. 129–30)
           and plate 75b (f. 251); *Les Sources*, p. 125; Dold, "Die vom Missale"; Fiala, "Der Ordo missae"
This missal, in addition to the Vulgate Exultet with Beneventan melody (ff. 120v–122v), contains
notated lessons from Jonah and Daniel for Holy Saturday using Beneventan recitation tones.

Vatican City, Biblioteca Apostolica Vaticana, MS Vaticanus latinus 9820
   Desc: Exultet roll, in twenty pieces
   Prov: Benevento, St Peter's *extra muros*
   Date: late tenth century (lower script)
   Lit: TBS, II, 153; Avery, *Exultet Rolls*, pp. 31–4, 46–9, plates 135–46; *Exultet*: complete facsimile;
           Gamber, CLLA, no. 495a; Salmon, *Les Manuscrits*, II, no. 199; Bannister, *Monumenti*, no. 345
           (pp. 118–19) and plate 68; Belting, *Malerei*, pp. 167–83; Lowe, *Scriptura beneventana*, plate LIV;
           PM XV, no. 79 (pp. 63–4)
This Exultet roll, now in twenty pieces, is almost entirely palimpsest; the earlier script (late tenth cen-
tury) and notation can be seen at the end of the roll (Avery, plate CXLVI; Lowe, *Scriptura*, plate LIV).
In the twelfth century the original (Beneventan) text was replaced by the Vulgate text, now written
reversed with respect to the miniatures, with the Beneventan melody.

Vatican City, Biblioteca Apostolica Vaticana, MS Vaticanus latinus 10645, ff. 3–6
   Desc: two bifolia from a handsome noted missal, 285×215 mm, writing area 245×166, in two columns
           of 24 lines. "Bari-type" script, Beneventan notation without lines or clefs
   Prov: unknown; southeast Italy
   Date: eleventh century
   Lit: TBS, II, 154–5; Gamber, CLLA, no. 432; Vatasso, *Codices*, p. 572; Salmon, *Les Manuscrits*, I,
           no. 593; PM XIV, p. 231 and plate 8 (f. 6v); PM XV, no. 81 (pp. 64–5); Bannister, *Monumenti*,
           no. 344 (p. 118) and plate 67b (f. 5v); Hesbert, "Les dimanches," pp. 198–222 and plate (f. 6v)
           facing p. 200; Suñol, *Introduction*, plates 19, 20 (f. 5v) on p. 162
Two separate bifolia from the same handsome noted missal; ff. 3–4 contain portions of Sts Nereus and
Achilleus, the Sunday after the Ascension, St Urban, and the vigil of Pentecost. This last includes the
Beneventan antiphon *Ipse super maria*. Ff. 5–6 include prayers for the assumption of Elijah.

Vatican City, Biblioteca Apostolica Vaticana, MS Vaticanus latinus 10646
   Desc: two bifolia (ff. 48–51) from a noted breviary; each bifolium measures approx. 395×210 mm;
           writing area of one page is 296+ ×165, in 2 columns
   Prov: unknown
   Date: eleventh–twelfth century
   Lit: TBS, II, 155; Gamber, CLLA, no. 465b; Vatasso, *Codices*, p. 593; Salmon, *Les Manuscrits*, I,
           no. 409; *Les Sources*, p. 125

The present manuscript is composed of fragments. Ff. 48–51 are two bifolia from a noted breviary, in Beneventan script and notation with lines and clefs. A portion of the office of St Benedict includes the Beneventan antiphon *Dum famis inopia* (f. 51).

Vatican City, Biblioteca Apostolica Vaticana, MS Vaticanus latinus 10657
Desc: palimpsest fragments of a Beneventan gradual, 121 ff., 325×215 mm. Beneventan palimpsest pages 324×205 mm, writing space approx. 278×140, 14 lines
Prov: Santa Maria de Tremiti (upper script)
Date: lower script, eleventh century; upper script, thirteenth century
Lit: TBS, 11, 155; Vatasso, *Codices*, pp. 614–629; Gamber, CLLA, no. 484b; Bannister, *Monumenti*, no. 353 (p. 124); PM XV, no. 83 (p. 65); Kelly, "Montecassino," pp. 61–5; Petrucci, *Codice diplomatico*; edition of upper script; *Les Sources*, p. 126

The present manuscript contains the cartulary of the abbey of Santa Maria in the Tremiti Islands, written in several Beneventan hands of the thirteenth century. Four bifolia, arranged in two fascicles, are re-used leaves of a Beneventan gradual: ff. A (preceding f. 1) through 3; and ff. 98–103 (a fascicle), excluding the non-palimpsest single leaves of ff. 99 and 102. Much of the music and text has not as yet been deciphered successfully. The pieces and fragments that can be recognized are listed below:

Palimpsest Beneventan music in MS Vatican lat. 10657

Folio	Incipit	Feast	Function in other MSS
f. Ar	*Sicut cervus*	Holy Sat.	Tract
f. Ar	*Omnes sitientes*	Holy Sat.	Antiphon
f. Ar	*Doxa en ips./Gloria*	Holy Sat.	Antiphon
f. Ar	*Alleluia*	Holy Sat.	Alleluia
	V̛ *Resurrexit*		
	V̛ *Laudate pueri*		
f. Ar	*Omnes qui in Christo*	Holy Sat.	Offertory
f. 2r	*Vadit propitiator*	M. Thurs.	Gradual
f. 2r	*Quis te supplantavit* (cued	M. Thurs.	Communion (Ben40)
	without notation)	Palm Sun.	Communion (Ben38)
f. 2r	*Accipiens. . .* (Communion?)		
f. 2v	*Ad vesperum*	Holy Sat.	Antiphon
f. 2v	*Domine audivi*	Holy Sat.	Tract
f. 100	*Petrus dormiebat*	Peter and Paul	Ingressa
f. 100v	[*Petrus dormiebat*, continued]		
f. 100v	R̛ [a rubric indicating the start of a Gradual?]		
f. 101	[*of*] *Ut cognosceret*	Peter and Paul	Communion
f. 103	The following rubrics are faintly visible successively in the right margin:		
	V [Alleluia-verse?]		
	of [Offertory]		
	co [Communion]		
f. 103	*Lumen quod animus*	John Bapt.	Ingressa
f. 103v	R̛ [a rubric indicating the start of a Gradual?]		

Vatican City, Biblioteca Apostolica Vaticana, MS Vaticanus latinus 10673
Desc: gradual, 35 ff., 260×175 mm, writing area approx. 200×124, 15–17 lines
Prov: Benevento? Puglia?
Date: early eleventh century

Lit: TBS, II, 155; Gamber, CLLA, no. 470; Vatasso, *Codices*, pp. 641–2; PM XIII, 99–106 and fig. 13; PM XIV: complete facsimile, plates 1–71, table, pp. 474–6, see index, p. 471; PM XV, no. 83 (p. 65); Salmon, *Les Manuscrits*, II, no. 202; Suñol, *Introduction*, pp. 160–3; Bannister, *Monumenti*, no. 347 (pp. 120–2) and plate 70a (f. 10v); *Les Sources*, p. 126

An incomplete gradual, from Septuagesima to Holy Saturday *Exultet*. Beneventan script and notation without lines or clefs. There are substantial Beneventan Holy Week contents (see table 2.1), which are the subject of an extensive study in PM XIV.

Vatican City, Biblioteca Apostolica Vaticana, MS Vaticanus latinus 14446
  Desc: notated breviary (secular), incomplete (Septuagesima – Lent I, incomplete sanctoral), 63 ff., 350×240 mm, writing area 285×165, 2 columns of 28 lines (usually; varies from 26 to 29)
  Prov: Caiazzo
  Date: thirteenth century
  Lit: TBS, II, 156; Salmon, *Les Manuscrits*, I, no. 487; *Nuove testimonianze*, 879–81 and plate XIII

An incomplete noted breviary; the sanctoral includes the office of St Barbatus (f. 38–40v) and an incomplete office of St Benedict (ff. 61–63v), each of which contains antiphons with Beneventan melodies (identified in Appendix 1).

Vatican City, Biblioteca Apostolica Vaticana, MS Vaticanus latinus 14733
  Desc: ff. 11–12, mutilated bifolium from an antiphoner, approx. 305×255 mm. Folio 11 measures approx. 245×160, 14 lines visible
  Prov: unknown, Caiazzo?
  Date: eleventh century?
  Lit: TBS, II, 158

This manuscript, a collection of fragments, includes two badly damaged leaves from an antiphoner. Portions of two Beneventan antiphons of St Apollinaris can be deciphered.

Velletri, Museo capitolare, Exultet roll
  Desc: Exultet roll, fragmentary, in four pieces
  Prov: Montecassino
  Date: late eleventh century
  Lit: TBS, II, 170; Avery, *Exultet Rolls*, p. 40, plates 186–9; Grégoire, "Repertorium," p. 568; PM XV, no. 101 (p. 69)

This fragmentary roll, whose miniatures were repainted in the fourteenth century, contains portions of the Beneventan text and melody of the Exultet.

Venice, Archivio di Stato, Atti diversi manoscritti B. 159 n. 28
  Desc: eleven fragmentary folios from a Gregorian antiphoner in Beneventan script and notation
  Prov: unknown
  Date: eleventh century
  Lit:

Eleven unnumbered folios from a single antiphoner are now kept together in the Archive. They include music for Ascension, the Invention of the Holy Cross, the Invention of St Michael, St Eustasius, and responsories from the Book of Kings for July. One of the leaves, now mutilated and incomplete on one side, concludes the office preceding that of St Eustasius (10 May) with an antiphon in Beneventan style whose entire text cannot be read, but which begins "Sancti enim ducti ad Diocletianus (sic) dice. . ."

Wolfenbüttel, Herzog-August-Bibliothek, MS Gudianus graecus 112
  Desc: palimpsest fragment; present manuscript 149 ff., approx. 155–115 mm
  Prov: unknown
  Date: tenth–eleventh century lowest script.

Lit: TBS, II, 173; Gamber, CLLA, no. 434; Dold, "Untersuchungsergebnisse"; PM XV, no. 173
       (p. 178)

A triple palimpsest whose two upper scripts are in Greek, the topmost being of the thirteenth century. Ff. 128–136, 139–40, 143, 145, and 148 contain liturgical lections and notated chant pieces in Beneventan script. Very faintly on ff. 136–136v can be seen traces of the Beneventan tract *Domine audivi*.

Zadar, Ordinarijat Zadar, MS 38 (15/b)
   Desc: Bifolium from a Gregorian antiphoner, 330×186 mm (bif), 1 f. 179+ ×186, writing area
         179+ ×120
   Prov: Zadar?
   Date: eleventh–twelfth century
   Lit:

This is one of five bifolia (the others are numbered 10 (17/1), 28 (9/a), 33 (13/a), 36 (15/a) from an antiphoner in Beneventan script and notation, formerly nailed to the back of the choir stalls of the cathedral and covered on one side with green paint and stylized black flowers. Some of the leaves are evidently incomplete, lacking their initial letters and rubrics. On the legible side of this leaf the right hand folio contains music for Maundy Thursday, that on the left for Palm Sunday. In the latter appears the Beneventan responsory *Ante sex dies pasche* with its verse *Magister dicit*, and a second verse *Gloria patri*. This is evidently the last responsory of the feast, as it is followed by the antiphon *Faciem meam*, regularly the first antiphon for Tuesday in Holy Week. I am grateful to Dr. Richard Gyug for information on these fragments.

BIBLIOGRAPHY

AA SS   *Acta sanctorum quotquot toto orbe coluntur, vel à Catholicis Scriptoribus celebrantur, Quae ex Latinis & Graecis, aliarumque gentium antiquis monumentis collegit, digessit, Notis illustravit Ioannes Bollandus.* 67 vols. to date. Amsterdam and elsewhere, 1643–1925

Acocella, Nicola, ed. *La longobardia meridionale (570–1077). Il ducato di Benevento. Il principato di Salerno.* Politica e storia, 19. Rome, 1968 [contains reprint of Hirsch, *Il ducato,* and Schipa, "Storia del principato"]

Adversi, Aldo. *Inventari dei manoscritti delle biblioteche d'Italia.* Vol. 100: *Macerata. Biblioteca Comunale 'Mozzi-Borgetti'.* 2 vols. Florence, 1981

Aggiornamento   *L'Art dans l'Italie méridionale. Aggiornamento dell'opera di Emile Bertaux,* ed. Adriano Prandi. 4 vols. (numbered IV–VI, plus *Indici*). Rome, 1978

Albers, Bruno. *Consuetudines monasticae* III, Montecassino, 1907

Allodi, Leone. *Inventario dei manoscritti della Biblioteca dell'Abbazia di Subiaco.* Forlì, 1891

Amatus, *Storia*   *Storia de' Normanni di Amato di Montecassino volgarizzata in antico francese,* ed. Vincenzo de Bartholomaeis. Fonti per la storia d'Italia, 76. Rome, 1935

Ambrosii Autperti opera, ed. Robert Weber. 3 vols., Corpus christianorum, Continuatio Mediaevalis, 27, 27A, 27B. Turnhout, 1975–9

AMed   *Antiphonale missarum juxta ritum Sanctae Ecclesiae Mediolanensis.* Rome, 1935. Desclee no. 816

Amelli, Ambrogio M. "L'epigramma di Paolo Diacono intorno al canto Gregoriano e Ambrosiano," *Memorie Storiche Forogiuliesi,* 9 (1913), 153–75, plus plate

AMon   *Antiphonale monasticum pro diurnis horis.* Tournai, 1934. Desclee no. 818

Analecta hymnica medii aevi, eds. Guido Maria Dreves and Clemens Blume. 55 vols. Leipzig, 1886–1922

Andoyer, Raphaël. "L'ancienne liturgie de Bénévent," *Revue du chant grégorien,* 20 (1911–12), 176–183; 21 (1912–13), 14–20, 44–51, 81–5, 112–5, 144–8, 169–74; 22 (1913–14), 8–11, 41–4, 80–3, 106–11, 141–5, 170–2; 23 (1919–20), 42–4, 116–8, 151–3, 182–3; 24 (1920–1), 48–50, 87–9, 146–8, 182–5

Andrieu, Michel. *Les Ordines romani du haut moyen âge.* 5 vols. Spicilegium sacrum lovaniense, études et documents, 11, 23, 24, 28, 29. Louvain, 1931–61.

Angerer, Joachim F. "Unbekannte Fragmente beneventanischer Provenienz aus der Stiftbibliothek Melk." In Johannes Berchmans Göschl, ed., *Ut mens concordet voci: Festschrift Eugène Cardine zum 75. Geburtstag.* St Ottilien, 1980, pp. 377–403

Arnese, Raffaele. *I codici notati della Biblioteca Nazionale di Napoli.* Biblioteca di bibliografia italiana, 47. Florence, 1967

Atkinson, Charles M. "The earliest Agnus Dei melody and its tropes." JAMS, 30 (1977), 1–19

Avagliano, Faustino. "I codici liturgici dell'Archivio di Montecassino." *Benedictina,* 17 (1970), 300–25

"Monumenti del culto a San Pietro in Montecassino." *Benedictina,* 14 (1967), 57–76

Avagliano, Faustino, ed. *Una grande abbazia altomedioevale nel Molise: San Vincenzo al Volturno. Atti del 1º convegno di studi sul medioevo meridionale (Venafro–S. Vincenzo al Volturno, 19–22 maggio 1982).* Miscellanea cassinese, 51. Montecassino, 1985

Avery, Myrtilla. *The Exultet Rolls of South Italy.* Only volume 2 published. Princeton, 1936

"The Beneventan lections for the Vigil of Easter and the Ambrosian chant banned by Pope Stephen IX at Montecassino." *Studi gregoriani,* 1 (1947), 433–58, with table after p. 456

Avitabile, Censimento I Lidia Avitabile, Maria Clara Di Franco, Viviana Jemolo, and Armando Petrucci. "Censimento dei codici dei secoli X–XII." *Studi medievali,* series III, 9/2 (1968), 1115–94

Avitabile, Censimento II Lidia Avitabile, Franca De Marco, Maria Clara Di Franco, and Viviana Jemolo. "Censimento dei codici dei secoli X–XII." *Studi medievali,* series III, 11/2 (1970), 1013–1133

Babudri, Francesco. *L'Exultet di Bari del sec. XI.* Quaderni dell'archivio storico pugliese, 10. Bari, 1959

Bailey, Terence. *The Ambrosian Alleluias.* Egham, 1983

"Ambrosian chant in southern Italy." *Journal of the Plainsong and Mediaeval Music Society,* 6 (1983), 1–7

Bannister, Henry Marriott. *Monumenti vaticani di paleografia musicale latina.* 2 vols. Leipzig, 1913

"Ordine 'Ambrosiano' per la settimana santa." *Miscellanea Ceriana.* Milan, 1910, pp. 127–41

"The *Vetus Itala* text of the Exultet." *The Journal of Theological Studies,* 11 (1910), 43–54

Bardy, G. "Formules liturgiques grecques à Rome au IVe siècle." *Recherches de science réligieuse,* 30 (1940), 109–12

Baroffio, Bonifazio. "Liturgie in beneventanischen Raum." *Geschichte der katholischen Kirchenmusik,* ed. Karl Gustav Fellerer. 2 vols. Kassel, 1972–6, I, 204–8

"Benevent." *Die Musik in Geschichte und Gegenwart.* Vol. 15 (supplement). Kassel, 1973, cols. 653–6

"Le origini del canto liturgico nella chiesa latina e la formazione dei repertori italici." *Renovatio,* 13 (1978), 26–52

Barré, Henri. "La fête mariale du 18 Décembre à Bénévent au VIIIe siècle." *Ephemerides mariologicae,* 6 (1956), 451–61

Bartoloni, Franco. "Note di diplomatica vescovile beneventana." *Atti della Accademia nazionale dei Lincei: Rendiconti. Classe de Scienze morali, storiche e filologiche.* Eighth series, 5 (1950), pp. 425–49

Battelli, Giulio. "Il lezionario di S. Sofia di Benevento." *Miscellanea Giovanni Mercati.* Studi e testi, 126, Vatican City, 1946, VI, 282–91

Baumstark, Anton. "Byzantinisches in den Weihnachtstexten des Römische Antiphonarius officii." *Oriens christianus,* third series, 11 (1936), 163–87

"Ein frühchristliches Theotokion in mehrsphrachiger Überlieferung und verwandte Texte des ambrosianischen Ritus." *Oriens christianus,* neue serie, 9 (1920), 36–61

"Die Hodie-antiphonen." *Die Kirchenmusik,* 10 (1910), 153–60

"Der Orient und die Gesänge der Adoratio Crucis." *Jahrbuch für Liturgiewissenschaft,* 2 (1922), 1–17

Baumstark, Anton and Theodor Kluge. "Quadragesima und Karwoche Jerusalems im siebten Jahrhundert." *Oriens christianus,* neue serie, 5 (1915), 201–33

Becker, Gustavus Heinrich. *Catalogi bibliothecarum antique,* Bonn, 1885

Belting, Hans. "Studien zum beneventanischen Hof im 8. Jahrhundert." *Dumbarton Oaks Papers,* 16 (1962), 141–93, plus 6 plates

Belting, *Malerei* Hans Belting, *Studien zur beneventanischen Malerei.* Wiesbaden, 1968

Benoit-Castelli, Georges. "Le 'Praeconium paschale'." EL, 67 (1953), 309–34

Bertaux, Emile. *L'Art dans l'Italie méridionale.* Published as volume 1. Paris, 1904

Bertolini, Ottorino. "Gli *Annales Beneventani.*" *Bullettino dell'Istituto Storico Italiano,* 42 (1923), 1–163

"Carlomagno e Benevento." In *Karl der Grosse: Lebenswerk und Nachleben,* ed. Wolfgang Braunfels; vol. I: *Persönlichkeit und Geschichte,* ed. Helmut Beumann. Düsseldorf, 1965, pp. 609–71

"Le chiese longobarde dopo la conversione al cattolicesimo e i loro rapporti con il papato." *Settimane di studio,* 7 (1960), 455–92

"I documenti trascritti nel 'Liber preceptorum beneventani monasterii S. Sophiae' ('chronicon S. Sophiae')." *Studi di storia napoletana in onore di Michelangelo Schipa* (Naples, 1926), pp. 11–47

"Longobardi e byzantini nell'Italia meridionale." *Centro italiano di studi sull'alto medioevo. Atti del 3⁰ congresso internazionale di studi sull'alto medioevo* (Spoleto, 1959), pp. 103–24

"I vescovi del 'regnum Langobardorum' al tempo dei Carolingi." In *Vescovi e diocesi*, pp. 1–26

Bertolini, Paolo. "Arechi I." *Dizionario biografico degli italiani*, 4 (Rome, 1962), 68–71

"Arechi II." *Dizionario biografico degli italiani*, 4 (Rome, 1962), 71–8

"I duchi di Benevento e San Vincenzo al Volturno – le origini," in Avagliano, *Una grande abbazia*, pp. 85–177

"Studi per la cronologia dei Principi Langobardi di Benevento: da Grimoaldo I a Sicardo (787–839)." *Bullettino dell'Istituto Storico Italiano*, 80 (1968), 25–135

BHL *Bibliotheca hagiographica latina antiquae et mediae aetatis ediderunt Socii Bollandiani*. 2 vols. with supplement. Brussels, 1898–9, 1900–1, 1911

Biblioteca casinensis seu codicum manuscriptorum qui in tabulario casinensi asservantur series. 5 vols. (I–IV, plus V, 1). Montecassino, 1873–94

Bignami Odier, Jeanne. *La Bibliothèque Vaticane de Sixte IV à Pie XI*. Studi e testi, 272. Vatican City, 1973

Binon, Stéphane. *Essai sur le cycle de Saint Mercure*. Bibliotheque de l'École des Hautes Etudes; Sciences réligieuses, 53. Paris, 1937

Bischoff, Bernhard. *Paläographie des römischen Altertums und des abendländischen Mittelalters*. Grundlage der Germanistik, 24. Berlin, 1979

Bloch, Herbert. "Der Autor der 'Graphia aureae urbis Romae'." *Deutsches Archiv für Erforschung des Mittelalters*, 40 (1984), 55–175, plus plates 1–4

"Monte Cassino, Byzantium, and the West in the earlier Middle Ages." *Dumbarton Oaks Papers*, 3 (1946), 163–224, plates 217–58

"Montecassino's teachers and library in the High Middle Ages." *Settimane di Studio*, 19 (Spoleto, 1972), II, 563–605

"The schism of Anacletus II and the Glanfeuil forgeries of Peter the Deacon of Monte Cassino." *Traditio*, 8 (1952), 159–264, plus 1 plate

Bloch, MMA Herbert Bloch, *Monte Cassino in the Middle Ages*. 3 vols. Rome, 1986

Boe, John. "The Beneventan apostrophus in south Italian notation A.D. 1000–1100." *Early Music History*, 4 (1983), 43–66

"Gloria A and the Roman Easter Vigil Ordinary." *Musica Disciplina*, 36 (1982), 5–37

"The 'lost' palimpsest Kyries in the Vatican manuscript Urbinas latinus 602." *Journal of the Plainsong and Mediaeval Music Society*, 8 (1985), 1–24

"A new source for Old Beneventan chant: the Santa Sophia Maundy in MS Ottoboni lat. 145." *Acta Musicologica*, 52 (1980), 122–33

"Old Beneventan chant at Monte Cassino: Gloriosus Confessor Domini Benedictus." *Acta Musicologica*, 55 (1983), 69–73

Boe, John and Alejandro Planchart. *Beneventanum troporum corpus*. Forthcoming

Böhmer, Regesta II/5 Johann Friedrich Böhmer. *Regesta imperii, II: Sächsische Zeit, 5. Abteilung: Papstregesten 911–1024*, ed. Harald Zimmermann. Vienna, 1969

Bognetti, Gian Piero. "La continuità delle sedi episcopali e l'azione di Roma nel regno longobardo." *Settimane di studio*, 7 (1960), 415–54

L'età longobarda. 4 vols. Milan, 1966–1968

Bonnard, F. "Bénévent," in *Dictionnaire d'histoire et de géographie écclesiastique*, 7 (Paris, 1934), cols. 1280–9

Borders, James M. "The northern Italian antiphons *ante evangelium*." Communication to the fifty-second annual meeting of the American Musicological Society, November, 1986

Borella, Pietro. "Il capitulum delle Lodi Ambrosiane e il Versus ad repetendum romano." *Ambrosius*, 9 (1933), 241–52

"La *missa o dimissio catechumenorum* nelle liturgie occidentali." EL, 53 (1939), 60–110

Borgia, Stefano. *Memorie istoriche della pontificia città di Benevento.* 3 vols. Rome, 1763–9

Borsari, Silvano. "Monasteri bizantini nell'Italia meridionale longobarda (Sec. X e XI)." *Archivio storico per le province napoletane*, 71 (nuova serie, 32, 1950–1), 1–16

The British Library. Catalogue of Additions to the Manuscripts 1946–1950. Part 1: Descriptions. London, 1975

Brou, Louis. "Les chants en langue grecque dans les liturgies latines." *Sacris erudiri*, 1 (1948), 165–80

    "Les chants en langue grecque dans les liturgies latines: premier supplément." *Sacris erudiri*, 4 (1952), 226–38

Brown, Virginia. Hand List of Beneventan MSS. Volume 2 of TBS

Brunner, Lance W. "A perspective on the southern Italian sequence: the second tonary of the manuscript Monte Cassino 318." *Early Music History*, 1 (1981), 117–64

Cagin, Paul. *Codex sacramentorum bergomensis.* Auctuarium solesmense, series liturgica, 1, Solesmes, 1900

Callewaert, Camillus Aloysius. "S. Grégoire, les scrutins et quelques messes quadragésimales." EL, 53 (1939), 191–203

CAO René-Jean Hesbert. *Corpus antiphonalium officii.* 6 vols. Rerum ecclesiasticarum documenta, series maior, fontes 7–12. Rome, 1963–79

Capelle, Bernard. "Alcuin et l'histoire du symbole de la messe." *Recherches de Théologie ancienne et médiévale*, 6 (1934), 249–60

    "L'introduction du symbole à la messe," *Mélanges Joseph de Ghellinck, S. J.* (2 vols., Museum lessianum – section historique, nos. 13–14. Gembloux, 1951), II, pp. 1003–27

    "L'origine antiadoptianiste de notre texte du symbole de la messe." *Recherches de Théologie ancienne et médiévale*, 1 (1929), 7–20

    "La procession du *Lumen Christi* au Samedi-saint." *Revue bénédictine*, 44 (1932), 105–19

Caravita, Andrea. *I codici e le arti a Monte Cassino.* 3 vols. Montecassino, 1869–70

Carusi, Enrico. "Intorno al *Commemoratorium* dell'abate Teobaldo (*a.* 1019–22)." *Bullettino dell'Istituto Storico Italiano*, 47 (1932), 173–90, plus plate

Casinensia: miscellanea di studi cassinesi pubblicati in occasione del XIV centenario della fondazione della badia di Montecassino. Montecassino, 1929

Caspar, Erich. "Echte und gefälschte Karolingerurkunden für Monte Cassino." *Neues Archiv der Gesellschaft für ältere deutsche Geschichtskunde*, 33 (1907–8), 53–73

    Petrus Diaconus und die Monte Cassineser Fälschungen. Berlin, 1909

Cattaneo, Enrico. "L'adorazione della Croce nell'antico Rito ambrosiano." *Ambrosius*, 9 (1933), 175–86

    "Croce VII. La Croce nella liturgia." *Enciclopedia cattolica*, vol. 4, cols. 960–4

    Note storiche sul canto ambrosiano. Archivio ambrosiano, 3. Milan. 1950

Cavallo, Gugliemo. "Manoscritti italo-greci e cultura benedettina (secoli X–XIII)," in *L'esperienza monastica*, 1: 169–95, plus plates I–XXIV

    Rotoli di Exultet dell'Italia meridionale. Bari, 1973

    "Struttura e articolazione della minuscola beneventana libraria tra i secoli X–XII." *Studi medievali*, third series, 11/1 (1970), 343–68

    "La trasmissione dei testi nell'area beneventano-cassinese." *Settimane di studio*, 22 (1975), 357–424

Cecchelli, Carlo. "L'Arianesimo e le chiese ariane d'Italia." *Settimane di studio*, 7 (1960), 743–74

Chalandon, F. "L'état politique de l'Italie méridionale à l'arrivée des Normands." *Mélanges d'archéologie et d'histoire*, 21 (1901), 411–52

Chavasse, Antoine. "Les fêtes de saint Pierre (29 juin) et de saint Paul (30 juin), au VIIe-VIIIe siècle." EL, 74 (1960), 166–7

    "Les fragments palimpsestes du Casinensis 271 (Sigle z 6)." *Archiv für Liturgiewissenschaft*, 25 (1983), 9–33

    "L'oraison 'Super sindonem' dans la liturgie romaine." *Revue bénédictine*, 70 (1960), 313–23

Chevalier, Ulysse. *Repertorium hymnologicum. Catalogue des chants, hymnes, proses, séquences, tropes en usage dans l'église latine depuis les origines jusqu'à nos jours.* 6 vols. Louvain and Brussels, 1892–1920

Chron. mon. cas. *Chronica monasterii Casinensis [Die Chronik von Montecassino]*, ed. Hartmut Hoffmann. MGH Scriptores, x x x i v. Hannover, 1980

Chron. salern. *Chronicon Salernitanum. A Critical Edition with Studies on Literary and Historical Sources and on Language*, ed. Ulla Westerbergh. Studia Latina Stockholmiensia, 3. Lund, 1956

Chron. vult. *Chronicon vulturnese del monaco Giovanni*, ed. Vincenzo Federici. 3 vols., Fonti per la storia d'Italia, 58–60. Rome, 1925–38 [Preface published in Rome, 1940 as part of volume I]

Cilento, Nicola. *Le origini della signoria capuana nella longobardia minore.* Istituto storico italiano per il medio evo, Studi storici, 69–70. Rome, 1966

"La storiografia nell'Italia meridionale." *Settimane di studio*, 17 (1970), 521–56

Citarella, Armando D. and Henry M. Willard. *The Ninth-Century Treasure of Monte Cassino in the Context of Political and Economic Developments in South Italy.* Miscellanea cassinese, 50. Montecassino, 1983

Claire, Jean. "L'évolution modale dans les répertoires liturgiques occidentaux." *Revue grégorienne*, 40 (1962), 196–211, 229–245, plus examples

"La psalmodie responsoriale antique." *Revue grégorienne*, 41 (1963), 8–29, 49–62, 77–102, 127–151, plus examples

Cod. dipl. cav. *Codex diplomaticus cavensis*, eds. Michaele Morcaldi, Mauro Schiani, Sylvano de Stephano. 8 vols. Naples, Milan, Pisa, 1873–93

Connolly, Thomas H. "Introits and archetypes: some archaisms of the Old Roman chant." JAMS, 25 (1972), 157–74

Cowdrey, H. E. J. *The Age of Abbot Desiderius. Montecassino, the Papacy, and the Normans in the Eleventh and Early Twelfth Centuries.* Oxford, 1983

Cutter, Paul F. *Musical Sources of the Old-Roman Mass.* American Institute of Musicology, Musicological Studies and Documents, 36. Neuhausen-Stuttgart, 1979

DACL *Dictionnaire d'archéologie chrétienne et de liturgie*, eds. Fernand Cabrol, Henri Leclercq, Henri Marrou. 15 vols. in 30. Paris, 1903–53

Deér, Josef. "Zur Praxis der Verleihung des auswärtigen Patriziats durch den byzantinischen Kaiser." *Archivum historiae pontificiae*, 8 (1970), 7–25

Delahaye, Hipployte. "La translatio S. Mercurii Beneventum." *Melanges Godefroid Kurth.* 2 vols., Bibliothèque de la Faculté de Philosophie et Lettres de l'Université de Liège, Serie Grand in-8o (Jésus), 1–2. Liège and Paris, 1908, 1:16–24

de Leo, Pietro, ed. *Il Mezzogiorno medievale nella storiografia del secondo dopoguerra: risultati e prospettive.* Atti del IV Convegno Nazionale. Associazione dei Medievalisti Italiani, Convegni, 4. Soveria Mannelli, 1985

Del Treppo, Mario. "Longobardi Franchi e papato in due secoli di storia vulturnese." *Archivio storico per le province napoletane*, 73, nuova serie, 34 (1953–4), 37–59

De Luca, Attilio, Caterina Tristano, Fabio Troncarelli, Mario Roncetti, Maria Pecugi Fop. "Nuove testimonianze di scrittura beneventana." *Studi medievali*, series 3, 18/1 (1977), 353–400, plus 16 plates

De Nicastro, Giovanni. *Benevento sacro.* Edited with introduction and notes by Gaetana Intorcia. Collana di studi e documenti di storia del Sannio, 3. Benevento, 1976

De Nonno, Mario. "Contributo alla tradizione di Prisciano in area beneventano-cassinese: il 'Vallicell. C. 9'." *Revue d'histoire des textes*, 9 (1979), 123–39

De Ricci, Seymour and W. J. Wilson. *Census of Medieval and Renaissance Manuscripts in the United States and Canada.* 2 vols. New York, 1935, 1937

Desiderius, Abbot of Montecassino. "Dialogi de miraculi sancti Benedicti," ed. Gerhard Schwarz and Adolf Hofmeister, in MGH Scriptores, 30/2, 1111–51

De Vita, Johannes [Giovanni]. *Thesaurus antiquitatum beneventanarum.* 2 vols. (the second entitled *Thesaurus alter antiquitatum beneventanarum medii aevi*). Rome, 1754, 1764

de Vogüé, Adalbert and Jean Neufville. *La Règle de saint Benoît.* 7 vols. Sources chrétiennes, 181–6 bis. Paris, 1972–7

Devreesse, Robert. *Les Manuscrits grecs de l'Italie méridionale (histoire, classement, paléographie).* Studi e Testi, 183. Vatican City, 1955

Dix, Gregory. *The Shape of the Liturgy.* Second ed., London, 1945

Dold, Alban. "Eine alte Bussliturgie aus Codex Vaticanus latinus 1339." *Jahrbuch für Liturgiewissenschaft,* 11 (1931), 94–130

"Fragmente eines um die Jahrtausendwende in beneventanischer Schrift geschriebenen Vollmissales aus Codex Vatic. lat. 10645." *Jahrbuch für Liturgiewissenschaft,* 10 (1930), 40–55

"Die vom Missale Romanum abweichenden Lesetexte für die Messfeiern nach den Notierung des aus Monte Cassino stammenden Codex Vat. lat. 6082." Sonderdruck aus der Benediktus-Festschrift der Beuroner Kongregation 547–1947. Münster in Westfalen, n.d

"Ein Palimpsestblatt mit zwei verschiedenen Messliturgien (Fol. I im Sammelcodex Ottob. lat. 576 P I)." EL, 52 (1938), 187–8

Vom Sacramentar Comes und Capitulare zum Missale. Texte und Arbeiten, 34. Beuron, 1943

"Umfangreiche Reste zweier Plenarmissalien des 11. und 12. Jhs. aus Monte Cassino." EL, 53 (1939), 111–67

"Untersuchungsergebnisse einer doppelt reskribierten Wolfenbütteler Handschrift." *Zentralblatt für Bibliothekswesen,* 34 (1917), 233–50

Die Zürcher und Peterlinger Messbuch-Fragmente. Texte und Arbeiten, 1 Abt., Heft 25. Beuron, 1934

Dragoumis, Markos Ph. "The survival of Byzantine chant in the monophonic music of the modern Greek church," in *Studies in Eastern Chant,* eds. Egon Wellesz and Miloš Velimirović, 1 (London, 1966), 9–36

Drumbl, Johann. "Gli improperi del venerdì santo nei manoscritti liturgici italiani." *Bergomum,* 65 (1971), fasc. IV, pp. 77–96

"Die Improperien in der lateinische Liturgie." *Archiv für Liturgiewissenschaft,* 15 (1973), 68–100

"Zweisprachige Antiphonen zur Kreuzverehrung." *Italia medioevale e umanistica,* 19 (1976), 41–55

Du Cange, Carolus Du Fresne. *Glossarium mediae et infimae latinitatis.* 8 vols. (1883–7), repr. Graz, 1954

Duchesne, Louis Marie Olivier. *Le Liber pontificalis. Texte, introduction et commentaire.* Rev. by Cyrille Vogel. 3 vols. Paris, 1955–7

"Les évêchés d'Italie et l'invasion lombarde." *Mélanges d'archéologie et d'histoire,* 23 (1903), 83–116; 25 (1905), 365–99

Duval-Arnould, Louis. "Les manuscrits de San Vincenzo al Volturno," in Avagliano, *Una grande abbazia,* pp. 353–78

Dyer, Joseph. "Latin psalters, Old Roman and Gregorian chants." *Kirchenmusikalisches Jahrbuch,* 68 (1984), 11–30

"The offertory chant of the Roman liturgy and its musical form." *Studi musicali,* 11 (1982), 3–30

EL *Ephemerides liturgicae*

Enciclopedia cattolica. 12 vols. Vatican City (printed Florence), 1948–54

Erchempert "Erchemperti historia langobardorum beneventanorum," ed. G. Waitz. In MGH SS Lang., pp. 231–64

Ewald, P. "Die Papstbriefe der Brittischen Sammlung." *Neues Archiv der Gesellschaft für deutsche Geschichtskunde,* 5 (1879–80), 275–414, 503–96

Exultet. Codex Vaticanus lat. 9820. Vollständige Facsimile-Ausgabe in Originalformat des Codex Vaticanus lat. 9820 der Biblioteca Apostolica Vaticana. Graz, 1974

Falco, Giorgio. "Lineamenti di storia cassinese nei secoli VIII e IX," in *Casinensia,* 457–548

Faye, *Supplement* *Supplement to the Census of Medieval and Renaissance Manuscripts in the United States and Canada,* originated by C. U. Faye, continued and edited by W. H. Bond. New York, 1962

Feine, Hans Erich. "Studien zum langobardisch-italischen Eigenkirchenrecht. II. Teil." *Zeitschrift der Savigny-Stiftung für Rechtsgeschichte. Kanonistische Abteilung,* 31 (1942), 1–105

Ferrante, Mario. "Chiesa e chiostro di S. Sofia in Benevento." *Samnium*, 25 (1952), 73–91, plus 5 pages of plates

Ferretti, Paolo M. *Esthétique grégorienne*. Rome, 1934. Unique volume published as vol. 1

Fiala, Virgil. "Der Ordo missae im Vollmissale des Cod. Vat. lat. 6082 aus dem Ende des 11. Jahrhunderts." In *Zeugnis des Geistes: Gabe zum Benedictus-Jubilaeum 547–1947*. Beiheft zum XXIII. Jahrgang der Benediktinischen Monatschrift (Beuron, 1947), pp. 180–224

Follieri, Henrica [Enrica]. *Initia hymnorum ecclesiae graecae*. 6 vols., numbered I–V bis. Studi e testi, 211–15 bis. Vatican City, 1960–6

Follieri, Henrica [Enrica] and Oliver Strunk, eds. *Triodium athoum*. Monumenta musicae byzantinae, 9. Copenhagen, 1975

Frénaud, Georges. "Les témoins indirects du chant liturgique en usage à Rome aux IXe et Xe siècles." *Études grégoriennes*, 3 (1959), 41–74

Frere, Walter Howard. *Antiphonale sarisburiense. A Reproduction in Facsimile of a Manuscript of the Thirteenth Century with a Dissertation and Analytical Index*. 2 vols. [n. p., n.d.]

Frere, Studies II   Walter Howard Frere. *Studies in Early Roman Liturgy. Vol. II: The Roman Gospel-Lectionary*. Alcuin Club collections, no. 30. Oxford, 1934

Frere, Studies III   Walter Howard Frere. *Studies in Early Roman Liturgy. Vol. III: The Roman Epistle-Lectionary*. Alcuin Club collections, no. 32. Oxford, 1935

Galasso, Elio. "Caratteri paleografici e diplomatici dell'atto privato a Capua e a Benevento prima del secolo XI." In *Il contributo*, pp. 291–317, plus plates 1–10

Gamber, Klaus. "Das basler Fragment. Eine weitere Studie zum altkampanischen Sakramentar und zu dessen Präfationen." *Revue bénédictine*, 81 (1971), 14–29

"Fragment eines mittelitalienischen Plenarmissale aus dem 8. Jahrhundert." EL, 76 (1962), 335–41

"Fragmenta Liturgica V." *Sacris erudiri*, 21 (1972–3), 241–66

"Fragmente eines Missale beneventanum als Palimpsestblätter des Cod. Ottob. lat. 576." *Revue bénédictine*, 84 (1974), 367–72

"Heimat und Ausbildung der Gelasiana saec. VIII (Junggelasiana)." *Sacris erudiri*, 14 (1963), 99–129

"Die kampanische Lektionsordnung." *Sacris erudiri*, 13 (1962), 326–52

"Das kampanische Messbuch als Vorläufer des Gelasianum. Ist der hl. Paulinus von Nola der Verfasser?" *Sacris erudiri*, 12 (1961), 5–111

"La liturgia delle diocesi dell'Italia centro-meridionale dal IX all' XI secolo." In *Vescovi e diocesi*, pp. 145–56

Missa romensis. Beiträge zur frühen römischen Liturgie und zu den Anfängen des Missale Romanum. Studia patristica et liturgica, 3. Regensburg, 1970

"Die mittelitalienisch-beneventanischen Plenarmissalien. Der Messbuchtypus des Metropolitangebiets von Rom im 9./10. Jahrhundert." *Sacris erudiri*, 9 (1957), 265–85

"Il sacramentario di Paolo Diacono." *Rivista di storia della chiesa in Italia*, 16 (1962), 412–38. A translation of "Heimat und Ausbildung"

"Die Sonntagsmessen nach Pfingsten im Cod. VI 33 von Benevent." EL, 74 (1960), 428–31

"Väterlesungen innerhalb der Messe an Heiligenfesten in Beneventanischen Messbüchern." EL, 74 (1960), 163–5

Gamber, CLLA   Klaus Gamber. *Codices liturgici latini antiquiores*. Spicilegii Friburgensis subsidia, 1. Second ed., 1 vol. in 2 parts. Freiburg/Schweiz, 1968

Gamber, *Manuale*   Klaus Gamber and Sieghild Rehle. *Manuale casinense (Cod. Ottob. lat. 145)*. Textus patristici et liturgici, 13. Regensburg, 1977

Garbelotto, Antonio. "Catalogo del fondo musicale fino all'anno 1800 della Biblioteca comunale di Macerata." In Aldo Adversi, ed., *Studi sulla Biblioteca Comunale e sui tipografi di Macerata*. Macerata, 1966

Garms-Cornides, Elisabeth. "Die langobardischen Fürstentitel (774–1077)." *Mitteilungen des Instituts für Österreichische Geschichtsforschung. Erganzungsband*, 24: 341–452

Gasparri, Stefano. *I duchi longobardi*. Istituto storico italiano per il medio evo, Studi storici, 109. Rome, 1978

Gattola, Erasmo. *Ad historiam abbatiae Cassinensis accessiones*. 2 vols. Venice, 1734
    Historia abbatiae Cassinensis per saeculorum seriem distributa. 2 vols. Venice, 1733

Gay, Jules. *L'Italie méridionale et l'empire byzantin depuis l'avènement de Basile Ier jusqu'à la prise de Bari par les Normands (867–1071)*. Bibliothèque des Écoles françaises d'Athènes et de Rome, 90. Paris, 1904
    "Le monastère de Trémiti au XIe siècle d'après un cartulaire inédit." *Mélanges d'archéologie et d'histoire*, 17 (1897), 387–405

Gevaert, François Auguste. *La Melopée antique dans le chant de l'église latine*. Gand, 1895

Giorgetti Vichi, Anna Maria and Sergio Mottironi. *Catalogo dei manoscritti della Biblioteca Vallicelliana*, I. Ministero della Pubblica Istruzione, Indici e Cataloghi, nuova serie, 7. Rome, 1961

Giovardi, Victorio. *Acta passionis, & translationis sanctorum martyrum Mercurii, ac XII. fratrum. Necnon lectiones pro solemni Basilice Sanctae Sophiae Beneventi dedicatione*. Rome, 1730

Gottlieb, Theodor. "Alte Bücherverzeichnisse aus Italien." *Centralblatt für Bibliothekswesen*, 5 (1888), 481–97

Grégoire, Reginald. *Les Homéliaires du moyen âge. Inventaire et analyse des manuscrits*. Rerum ecclesiasticarum documenta, series maior, fontes, 6. Rome, 1966
    "Repertorium Liturgicum Italicum." *Studi medievali*, serie 3, IX (1968), 465–592

Gregorii magni dialogi libri IV, ed. Umberto Moricca. Fonti per la storia d'Italia, 57. Rome, 1924

GRom   *Graduale Sacrosanctae Romanae Ecclesiae*. Tournai, 1948. Desclée no. 696

Gyug, Richard. "An Edition of Leningrad, B. A. N., F. no. 200: The Lectionary and Pontifical of Kotor." Unpublished doctoral dissertation, University of Toronto, 1983

Hallinger, Kassius. *Corpus consuetudinum monasticarum*. Vol. I: *Initia consuetudinis benedictinae*. Siegburg, 1963

Hammerstein, Reinhold. "Tuba intonet salutaris: die Musik auf den süditalienischen Exultet-Rollen." *Acta musicologica*, 31 (1959), 109–29

Hanssens, Jean Michel. *Amalarii episcopi opera liturgica omnia*. 3 vols., Studi e Testi, 138–140. Vatican City, 1948–50

Hartmann, Ludo Moritz. *Geschichte Italiens im Mittelalter*. 3 vols. Gotha, 1897–1911

Hesbert, René-Jean. Articles on Beneventan liturgy under the general title "L''antiphonale missarum' de l'ancien rit bénéventain":
    (1) EL, 52 (1938), 28–66
    (2) "Messe de saint Étienne." EL, 52 (1938), 141–58
    (3) "Le dimanche des Rameaux." EL, 53 (1939), 168–90
    (4) "Le Jeudi-Saint (Bénévent VI 40)." EL, 54 (1945), 69–95
    (5) "Le Vendredi-Saint." EL, 60 (1946), 103–41
    (6) "Le Samedi-Saint." EL, 61 (1947), 153–210
    "Un antique offertoire de la Pentecôte: 'Factus est repente'." In *Organicae voces: Festschrift Joseph Smits van Waesberghe* (Amsterdam, 1963), pp. 59–69
    "Les dimanches de carême dans les manuscrits romano-bénéventains." EL, 48 (1934), 198–222
    "La messe 'Omnes gentes' du VIIe dimanche après la Pentecôte et l''Antiphonale Missarum' Romain." *Revue grégorienne*, 17 (1932), 81–9, 170–9; 18 (1933), 1–14
    "L'évangéliaire de Zara (1114)." *Scriptorium*, 8 (1954), 177–204, plus plates 20–1
    "Le répons 'Tenebrae' dans les liturgies Romaine, Milanaise et Bénéventaine. Contribution à l'histoire d'une interpolation évangélique." *Revue grégorienne*, 19 (1934), 4–24, 57–65, 84–9; 20 (1935), 1–14, 201–13; 21 (1936), 44–62, 201–13; 22 (1937), 121–36; 23 (1938), 20–5, 41–54, 81–98, 140–3, 161–70; 24 (1939), 44–63, 121–39, 161–72
    see also CAO, *Sextuplex*

Hirsch, Ferdinand[o]. *Il ducato di Benevento sino alla caduta del regno longobardo*, trans. by Michelangelo Schipa. Naples, 1890. Reprinted in Acocella, *La longobardia*

"Papst Hadrian I. und das Fürstenthum Benevent." *Forschungen zur Deutschen Geschichte*, 13 (1873), 33–68

Hirsch, Siegfried. *Jahrbücher des deutschen Reichs unter Heinrich II.* 3 vols. Leipzig, 1862–75, repr. Berlin, 1975

Hodgkin, Thomas. *Italy and Her Invaders.* 8 volumes in 9. Oxford, 1885–99

Hoffmann, Hartmut. "Chronik und Urkunde in Montecassino." *Quellen und Forschungen aus italienischen Archiven und Bibliotheken*, 51 (1971), 93–206

"Zur Geschichte Montecassinos im 11. und 12. Jahrhundert." In Heinrich Dormeier, *Montecassino und die Laien im 11. und 12. Jahrhundert.* Schriften der Monumenta Germaniae Historica, vol. 27. Stuttgart, 1979, pp. 1–20

See Chron. mon. cas.

Houben, Hubert. "Benevent und Reichenau: süditalienisch-alemannische Kontakte in der Karolingerzeit." *Quellen und Forschungen aus italienischen Archiven und Bibliotheken*, 63 (1983), 1–19

Hucke, Helmut. "Gregorian and Old Roman chant." *The New Grove*, 7:693–7

"Toward a new historical view of Gregorian chant." JAMS, 33 (1980), 437–67

Huglo, Michel. "L'ancien chant bénéventain." *Ecclesia orans*, 2 (1985), 265–93

"L'annuncio pasquale della liturgia ambrosiana." *Ambrosius*, 33 (1957), 88–91

"Le chant 'vieux-romain'. Liste des manuscrits et témoins indirects." SE, 6 (1954), 96–124

"Fragments de Jérémie selon la vetus latina." *Vigiliae christianae*, 8 (1954), 83–6

"The Old Beneventan chant." *Studia musicologica*, 27 (1985), 83–95

"Relations musicales entre Byzance et l'Occident." *Proceedings of the XIIIth International Congress of Byzantine Studies. Oxford, 5–10 September 1966.* London, New York, Toronto, 1967, repr. 1978, pp. 267–80

"Vestigia di un antico repertorio musicale dell'alta Italia apparentato col canto ambrosiano." *Ambrosius*, 31 (1955), 34–9

Huglo, Michel, Luigi Agustoni, Eugène Cardine, and Ernesto Moneta Caglio, eds. *Fonti e paleografia del canto ambrosiano.* Archivio ambrosiano, 7. Milan, 1956

Husmann, Heinrich. *Tropen- und Sequenzenhandschriften.* Répertoire international des sources musicales B . V . I. Munich, 1964

Il contributo   *Il contributo dell'archidiocesi di Capua alla vita religiosa e culturale del Meridione: Atti del Convegno Nazionale di Studi Storici promosso dalla Società di Storia Patria di Terra di Lavoro, 26–31 ottobre 1966.* Rome, 1967

Inguanez, Mauro. *Codicum Casinensium manuscriptorum catalogus.* 3 vols. Montecassino, 1915–41

"Due frammenti del *Liber miraculorum monachorum Casinensium* di Pietro Diacono." *Studi medievali*, nuova serie 2 (1929), 191–3

IP VIII   Paul Fridolin Kehr. *Regesta pontificum romanorum. Italia pontificia.* Vol. 8. Berlin, 1935

IP IX   Paul Fridolin Kehr. *Regesta pontificum romanorum. Italia pontificia*, ed. Walther Holtzmann. Vol. 9. Berlin, 1962

James, Montague Rhodes. *A Descriptive Catalogue of the Latin Manuscripts in the John Rylands Library at Manchester.* 2 vols. Manchester, 1921

JAMS   *Journal of the American Musicological Society*

Jungmann, Josef Andreas. *Missarum sollemnia.* Second ed., 2 vols. Vienna, 1949

Kaminsky, Hans H. "Zum Sinngehalt des Princeps-Titels Arichis' II. von Benevent." *Frühmittelalterliche Studien*, 8 (1974), 81–92

Kelly, Thomas Forrest. "Beneventan fragments at Altamura." *Mediaeval Studies*, 49 (1987), 466–79

"Beneventan and Milanese chant." *Journal of the Royal Musical Association*, 112 (1987), 173–95

"Montecassino and the Old Beneventan chant." *Early Music History*, 5 (1985), 53–83

"Non-Gregorian music in an antiphoner of Benevento." *The Journal of Musicology*, 5 (1987), 478–97

"Une nouvelle source pour l'office vieux-beneventain." *Études grégoriennes*, 22 (1988), 5–23

"Palimpsest evidence of an Old-Beneventan gradual." *Kirchenmusicalisches Jahrbuch*, 67 (1983), 5–23

Klauser, Theodor. "Der Übergang der römischen Kirche von der griechischen zur lateinischen Litur-
giesprache." *Miscellanea Giovanni Mercati*, 2 vols. (Studi e testi, 121–2; Vatican City, 1946), 1: 467–82

Klewitz, Hans-Walter. "Studien über die Wiederherstellung der römischen Kirche in Süditalien durch
das Reformpapsttum." *Quellen und Forschungen aus italienischen Archiven und Bibliotheken*, 25 (1933-4),
105–57

"Zur Geschichte der Bistumsorganisation Campaniens und Apuliens im 10. und 11. Jahrhundert."
Quellen und Forschungen aus italienischen Archiven und Bibliotheken, 24 (1932-3), 1–61

La chiesa greca in Italia. Atti del convegno storico interecclesiale (Bari, 30 apr. – 4 magg. 1969). 3 vols. (Italia
sacra, 20–2). Padua, 1973

Latil, Agostino. "Un 'Exultet' inedito." *Rassegna gregoriana*, 7 (1908), cols. 125–34

Leccisotti, Tommaso. *Abbazia di Montecassino. I regesti dell'archivio*. 11 vols. to date (Ministero dell'interno,
Pubblicazioni degli archivi di stato, 54, 56, 58, 60, 64, 74, 78–79, 81, 86, 95). Rome, 1964–75. From
vol. 9 edited with Faustino Avagliano

Le Colonie cassinesi in Capitanata. III: Ascoli Satriano. Miscellanea Cassinese, 19. Montecassino, 1940

Montecassino. 10th edition, Montecassino, 1983

"Le relazioni fra Montecassino e Tremiti e i possedimenti cassinesi a Foggia e Lucera." *Benedictina*,
3 (1949), 203–15

Leclercq, Henri. "Croix (invention et exaltation de la vraie)." DACL, III, cols. 3131–9

"Pentecôte." DACL, XIV, cols. 260–74

"Toussaint et trépassés." DACL, XV, cols. 2677–82

Leclercq, J. "Tables pour l'inventaire des homiliaires manuscrits." *Scriptorium*, 2 (1948), 195–214

Lehmann-Brockhaus, Otto. *Schriftquellen zur Kunstgeschichte des 11. und 12. Jahrhunderts für Deutschland
Lothringen und Italien*. 2 vols. Berlin, 1938

Lenormant, Francois. *La Grande-Grèce, paysages et histoire*. 3 vols. Paris, 1881–4

Lentini, Anselmo. "La grammatica d'Ilderico documento dell'attività letteraria di Paolo Diacono." *Centro
Italiano di studi sull'alto medioevo. Atti del 2° congresso internazionale di studi sull'alto medioevo* (Spoleto,
1953), pp. 217–40

Lentini, Anselmo and F. Avagliano, eds. *I carmi di Alfano I, arcivescovo di Salerno*. Miscellanea Cassinese,
38. Montecassino, 1974

*L'esperienza monastica L'esperienza monastica benedettina e la Puglia. Atti del convegno di studio organizzato
in occasione del XV centenario della nascita di San Benedetto (Bari – Noci – Lece – Picciano, 6–10 ottobre 1980)*, ed. Cosimo Damiano Fonseca. 2 vols. Galatina, 1983, 1984

Leuterman, Teodoro. *Ordo casinensis hebdomadae maioris (saec. XII)*. Miscellanea Cassinese, 20. Montecassino, 1941

Levy, Kenneth. "Charlemagne's archetype of Gregorian chant." JAMS, 40 (1987), 1–30

"*Lux de Luce*: the origin of an Italian sequence." *The Musical Quarterly*, 57 (1971), 40–61

"The Byzantine Sanctus and its modal tradition in East and West." *Annales musicologiques*, 6 (1958–63),
7–67

"The Italian neophytes' chants." JAMS, 23 (1970), 181–227

Loew, Elias Avery. *Die ältesten Kalendarien aus Monte Cassino*. Quellen und Untersuchungen zur
lateinischen Philologie des Mittelalters, III, part 3. Munich, 1908

The Beneventan Script. See TBS2

Lowe [Loew], Elias Avery. *Scriptura beneventana*. 2 vols. Oxford, 1929

LVesp *Liber vesperalis juxta ritum Sanctae Ecclesiae Mediolanensis*. Rome, 1939. Desclee no. 811

Magistretti, Marco. *Beroldus sive ecclesiae ambrosianae mediolanensis kalendarium et ordines saec. XII*. Milan,
1894, repr. 1968

Manuale ambrosianum ex codice saec. XI olim in usum canonicae vallis travaliae. 2 vols. Monumenta veteris
liturgiae ambrosianae, 2–3. Milan, 1904–5

Maio, Lauro. "Davide Beneventano: un vescovo della Longobardia meridionale (782–796)." *Samnium*, 56 (1983), 1–50

Mallardo, Domenico. "La Pasqua e la settimana maggiore a Napoli dal secolo V al XIV." EL, 66 (1952), 3–36

"S. Gennaro e compagni nei più antichi testi e monumenti." *Società Reale di Napoli. Rendiconti della R[eale] accademia di archeologia lettere e belle arti.* Nuova serie, 20 (1939–40), 161–267, plus four plates

Mallet, Jean and André Thibaut. *Les Manuscrits en écriture bénéventaine de la Bibliothèque capitulaire de Bénévent. Tome I: manuscrits 1–18.* Paris, 1984

Martelli, A. Massimo. "Un fenomeno della liturgia gallicana e del Gelasiano: le messe con più orazioni prima della segreta." *Studia Patavina*, 20 (1973), 546–69

"I formulari della messa con due o tre orazioni prima della segreta nei sacramentari romani." *Studia Patavina*, 19 (1972), 539–79

Martène, Edmond and Ursin Durand. *Veterum scriptorum et monumentorum historicorum, dogmaticorum, moralium, amplissima collectio.* 9 vols. Paris, 1724–33

Ménager, L. R. "La 'Byzantinisation' réligieuse de l'Italie méridionale (IXe–XIIe siecles) et la politique monastique des normands d'Italie." *Revue d'histoire ecclésiastique*, 53 (1958), 747–74; 54 (1959), 5–40

Μηναῖα τοῦ ὅλοῦ ἐνιαυτοῦ. 6 vols. Rome, 1888–1901

Meomartini, Almerico. *I monumenti e le opere d'arte della città di Benevento.* Benevento, 1889; repr. (Collana di studi e documenti di storia del Sannio, 5) Benevento, 1979

Meyvaert, Paul. "The autographs of Peter the Deacon." *Bulletin of the John Rylands Library*, 38 (Manchester, 1955–6), 114–38, plus 4 plates

Mezei, János. "Das Responsorium 'Vadis propitiator' in den ungarischen Handschriften." *Studia musicologica*, 27 (1985), 97–107

MGH   *Monumenta germaniae historica*

MGH Dipl. Kar., I   *MGH Diplomatum Karolinorum Tomus I.* Hannover, 1906; 2nd ed. Berlin, 1956

MGH Diplomata, I   *MGH Diplomatum regum et imperatorum Germaniae Tomus I.* Hannover, 1879–84

MGH Diplomata, II   *MGH Diplomatum regum et imperatorum Germaniae Tomus II.* Hannover, 1888–93

MGH Diplomata, III   *MGH Diplomatum regum et imperatorum Germaniae Tomus III.* Hannover, 1900–3; 2nd ed. Berlin, 1957

MGH Diplomata, IV   *MGH Diplomatum regum et imperatorum Germaniae Tomus IV.* Hannover and Leipzig, 1909

MGH Diplomata, V   *MGH Diplomatum regum et imperatorum Germaniae Tomus V.* Berlin, 1931

MGH Epistolae, I   *MGH Epistolarum Tomus I: Gregorii I papae registrum epistolarum Tomus I*, eds. Paul Ewald and Ludwig M. Hartmann. Berlin, 1887–91

MGH Epistolae, II   *MGH Epistolarum Tomus II: Gregorii papae registrum epistolarum Tomus II*, ed. Ludwig Hartmann. Berlin, 1893–9

MGH Epistolae, III   *MGH Epistolarum Tomus III: Epistolae merowingici et karolini aevi I.* Berlin, 1892

MGH Epistolae, VII   *MGH Epistolarum Tomus VII. Epistolae karolini aevi Tomus V.* Berlin, 1892

MGH Leges, III   *MGH Legum Tomus III.* Hannover, 1868

MGH Leges, IV   *MGH Legum Tomus IV*, ed. Georg Heinrich Pertz. Hannover, 1868

MGH Poetae, I   *MGH Poetarum latinorum medii aevi Tomus I (Poetae latini aevi carolini Tomus I)*, ed. Ernst Dümmler. Berlin, 1881

MGH Poetae, II   *MGH Poetarum latinorum medii aevi Tomus II (Poetae latini aevi carolini Tomus II)*, ed. Ernst Dümmler. Berlin, 1884

MGH Scriptores, I   *MGH Scriptorum Tomus I*, ed. Georg Heinrich Pertz. Hannover, 1826

MGH Scriptores, III   *MGH Scriptorum Tomus III*, ed. Georg Heinrich Pertz. Hannover, 1839

MGH Scriptores, XXX   *MGH Scriptorum Tomus XXX.* Hannover, 1896 (pars I), 1926–1934 (pars II)

MGH SS Lang.   *MGH Scriptores rerum langobardicarum et italicarum saec. VI–IX.* Hannover, 1878, repr. 1964

MMMA *Monumenta monodica medii aevi. Band II: Die Gesänge des altrömischen Graduale Vat. lat. 5319.* Introduction by Bruno Stäblein; transcriptions, critical report, and indexes by Margareta Landwehr-Melnicki. Kassel and elsewhere, 1970

Moeller, Edmond (Eugène). *Corpus praefationum.* 5 vols. (Corpus christianorum. Series latina, vols. 161, 161A–161D), Turnhout, 1980–1

Mohlberg, Leo Cunibert. "Note su alcuni sacramentarii." *Atti della Pontificia Accademia Romana di Archeologia (Serie III). Rendiconti,* 16 (1940), 131–79

Mohlberg, Leo Cunibert, Leo Eizenhöfer, and Petrus Siffrin. *Missale Gallicanum Vetus (Vat. Palat. lat. 493).* Rerum ecclesiasticarum documenta, series maior, fontes 3. Rome, 1958

Mombritius Boninus Mombritius [Bonino Mombrizio], *Sanctuarium seu vitae sanctorum. Novam hanc editionem curaverunt duo monachi solesmenses.* 2 vols. Paris, 1910

Monachus [Monaco], Michaele. *Recognitio sanctuarii capuani.* Naples, 1637

 Sanctuarium Capuanum, opus in quo sacrae res Capuae, et per occasionem plura, tam ad diversas civitates regni pertinentia, quam per se curiosa continentur. Naples, 1630

Moran, Neil K. *The Ordinary Chants of the Byzantine Mass.* 2 vols. Hamburger Beiträge zur Musikwissenschaft, 12. Hamburg, 1975

Morelli, Camillo. "I trattati di grammatica e retorica del cod. casanatense 1086." *Rendiconti della Reale Accademia dei Lincei. Classe de scienze morali, storiche et filologiche.* Series v, 19 (1910), 287–328

Morin, Germain. "Capitula Evangeliorum Neapolitana." *Analecta Maredsolana,* 1 (1893), 426–35

 "Formules liturgiques orientales en occident aux IVe–Ve siècles." *Revue bénédictine,* 40 (1928), 134–7

 "Liturgie et basiliques de Rome au milieu du VIIe siècle d'après les listes d'évangiles de Würzburg." *Revue bénédictine,* 28 (1911), 296–330

 "Le plus ancien *comes* ou lectionnaire de l'église romaine." *Revue bénédictine,* 27 (1910), 41–74

 "Pour la topographie ancienne du Mont-Cassin." *Revue bénédictine,* 25 (1908), 277–303, 468–86

 "Les quatre plus anciens calendriers du Mont-Cassin (VIIIe et IXe siècles)." *Revue bénédictine,* 25 (1908), 486–97

Musca, Giosuè. *L'emirato di Bari 847–871.* Università degli Studi di Bari, Istituto di Storia Medievale e Moderno, Saggi, 4. Bari, 1967

Neff, Karl. *Die Gedichte des Paulus Diaconus.* Quellen und Untersuchungen zur lateinischen Philologie des Mittelalters, III, part 4. Munich, 1908

The New Grove *The New Grove Dictionary of Music and Musicians,* ed. Stanley Sadie. 20 vols. London, 1980

Newton, Francis. "The Desiderian scriptorium at Monte Cassino: the Chronicle and some surviving manuscripts." *Dumbarton Oaks Papers,* 30 (1976), 35–54

 "Leo Marsicanus and the dedicatory text and drawing in Monte Cassino 99." *Scriptorium,* 33 (1979), 181–205, and plate 20

Nicholson, Edward Williams Byron. *Early Bodleian Music. Introduction to the Study of Some of The Oldest Latin Musical Manuscripts in the Bodleian Library, Oxford.* London, 1913

Nitti di Vito, Francesco. "Il tesoro di San Nicola di Bari" *Napoli nobilissima,* 12 (1903), 21–7, 59–63, 74–8, 105–9, 157–9, 171–5. Published separately, Trani, 1903

Novak, Viktor. "La paleografia latina e i rapporti dell'Italia meridionale con la Dalmazia." *Archivio storico pugliese,* 14 (1961), 145–58

 "Većenegin evanđelistar." *Jugoslavenska Akademija Znanosti I Umjetnosti. Starine,* 51 (1962), 5–48, plus 28 plates

Nuove testimonianze Maria Clara Di Franco, Viviana Jemolo, and Rino Avesani, "Nuove testimonianze di scrittura beneventana in biblioteche romane," *Studi medievali,* third series, 8 (1967), 857–81

Oddy, W. A. "Analysis of the gold coinage of Beneventum." *The Numismatic Chronicle. Seventh Series,* 14 (1974), 78–109, and plates 5–10

Odermatt, Ambros. *Ein Rituale in beneventanischer Schrift: Roma, Biblioteca Vallicelliana, Cod. C 32, Ende des 11. Jahrhunderts.* Spicilegium Friburgense, 26. Freiburg/Schweiz, 1980

Officia propria festorum salernitanae ecclesiae. Naples, 1594

Officia propria festorum salernitanae ecclesiae. Naples, 1696

Omlin, Ephrem. "Ein Messbuchfragment im Stiftarchiv Luzern." *Innerschweizerisches Jahrbuch für Heimat-kunde,* 8/10 (1944/46), 39–60, plus plate

Ὡρολόγιον τὸ μέγα. Rome, 1876

Oury, Guy. "Formulaires anciens pour la messe de saint Martin." *Études grégoriennes,* 7 (1967), 21–40

Paci, Libero. *Inventario dei manoscritti musicali della Biblioteca comunale 'Mozzi-Borgetti'.* Macerata, 1972

Pantoni, Angelo. "L'identificazione della basilica di S. Martino a Montecassino." *Benedictina,* 7 (1953), 347–56

Papadopoulos-Kerameus, A. Ἀνάλεκτα Ἱεροσολυμιτικῆς σταχυολογίας. 5 vols. St Petersburg, 1891–8

Paredi, Angelo. *Sacramentarium bergomense.* Monumenta bergomensia, 6. Bergamo, 1962

Paul, HL "Pauli historia langobardorum," eds. L. Bethmann and G. Waitz. In *MGH SS Lang.,* pp. 12–187

Πεντηκοστάριον. Rome, 1883

Petrucci, Armando. *Codice diplomatico del monastero benedettino di S. Maria de Tremiti (1005–1237),* 3 vols. Fonti per la storia d'Italia, 98*–98***. Rome, 1960

PG *Patrologiae cursus completus. Series graeca,* ed. Jacques-Paul Migne. 161 vols. Paris, 1857–1866

Picasso, Giorgio. "Montecassino e la Puglia." In *L'esperienza monastica,* 1, 37–53

Pietschmann, Petrus. "Die nicht dem Psalter entnommenen Messgesangstücke auf ihre Textgestalt unter-sucht." *Jahrbuch für Liturgiewissenschaft,* 12 (1932), 87–144

Pinell, Jordi M. "La benedicció del ciri pasqual i els seus textos." *Scripta et documenta 10: Liturgia 2* (Montserrat, 1958), pp. 1–119

PL *Patrologiae cursus completus. Series latina,* ed. Jacques-Paul Migne. 221 vols. Paris, 1878–90

Planchart, Alejandro. "Antiphonae ante evangelium." Communication to the fifty-second annual meeting of the American Musicological Society, November, 1986

    "New wine in old bottles." Communication to the International Medieval Conference, Kalamazoo, 1983

Planchart, Alejandro and John Boe. *Beneventanum troporum corpus.* Forthcoming

PM *Paléographie musicale. Les principaux manuscrits de chant grégorien, ambrosien, mozarabe, gallican, publiés en facsimilés phototypiques par les moines de Solesmes.* Successively edited by André Mocquereau, Joseph Gajard, and Jean Claire. Solesmes and elsewhere, 1899–

PM II   Vol. 2: *Le Répons-graduel Iustus ut palma reproduit en fac-similé d'après plus de deux cents antiphonaires manuscrits d'origines diverses du IXe au XVIIe siècle.* Solesmes, 1891

PM IV   Vol. 4: *Le Codex 121 de la Bibliothèque d'Einsiedeln.* Solesmes, 1894

PM V   Vol. 5: *Antiphonarium ambrosianum du Musée Britannique (XIIIe siecle): Codex additional 34 209* (Introduction and facsimile). Solesmes, 1896

PM VI   Vol. 6: *Antiphonarium ambrosianum . . .* Transcriptions. Solesmes, 1900

PM XIII   Vol. 13: *Le Codex 903 de la Bibliothèque nationale de Paris (XIe siecle). Graduel de Saint-Yrieix.* Tournai, 1925

PM XIV   Vol. 14: *Le Codex 10 673 de la Bibliothèque Vaticane.* Tournai, 1931, repr. Berne, 1971

PM XV   Vol. 15: *Le Codex VI. 34 de la Bibliothèque Capitulaire de Bénévent.* Tournai, 1937

PM XX   Vol. 20: *Le Missel de Bénévent VI–33.* Introduction by Jacques Hourlier, tables by Jacques Froger. Bern and Frankfurt, 1983

PM XXI   Vol. 21: *Le Chant Bénéventain.* Introduction by Thomas Forrest Kelly. Forthcoming

Pochettino, Giuseppe. *I Langobardi nell'Italia meridionale (570–1080).* Caserta, 1930

Poupardin, René. "Étude sur la diplomatique des princes lombards de Bénévent, de Capoue et de Salerne." *Mélanges d'archéologie et d'histoire*, 21 (1901), 117–180

"Études sur l'histoire des principautés lombardes de l'Italie méridionale et de leurs rapports avec l'Empire franc." *Le Moyen âge*, 19 [second series, 10] (1906), 1–26, 245–74; 20 [second series, 11] (1907), 1–25

Les Institutions politiques et administratives des principautés lombardes de l'Italie méridionale (IXe–XIe siècles). Paris, 1907

Pratesi, Alessandro. "Influenze della scrittura greca nella formazione della beneventana del tipo di Bari," in *La chiesa greca in Italia*, 1095–1109

Presenza musicale *Presenza musicale nella casa di S. Benedetto: mostra di Codici e Stampati con il Patrocinio del Ministero BBCC.* Montecassino, 1985

Procopius. *History of the Wars. With an English Translation by H. E. Dewing.* The Loeb Classical Library, 3 vols. Cambridge, Mass., 1914–19

Rehle, Sieghild. "Missale beneventanum (Codex VI 33 des Erzbischöflichen Archivs von Benevent)." SE, 21 (1972–3), 323–405

Missale beneventanum von Canosa (Baltimore, Walters Art Gallery, MS W6). Textus patristici et liturgici, 9. Regensburg, 1972

Rodgers, Robert H. *Petri Diaconi Ortus et vita iustorum cenobii casinensis.* Berkeley, 1972

Rom *Le Psautier romain et les autres anciens psautiers latins,* ed. Robert Weber. Collectanea biblica latina, 10. Rome, 1953.

Rotili, Marcello. *Benevento romana e longobarda. L'immagine urbana.* Benevento, 1986

Rotili, Mario. L'"Exultet' della Cattedrale di Capua e la miniatura 'beneventana'," In *Il contributo*, pp. 197–210, and plates XXVI–XXXVII

Rousseau, Olivier. "La visite de Nil de Rossano au Mont-Cassin," in *La chiesa greca in Italia*, 1111–37

Ruggiero, Bruno. *Principi, nobiltà e Chiesa nel Mezzogiorno longobarda. L'esempio di s. Massimo di Salerno.* Naples, 1973

Salmon, Pierre. *Les Manuscrits liturgiques latins de la Bibliothèque Vaticane.* 5 vols., Studi e testi, 251, 253, 260, 267, 270. Vatican City, 1968, 1969, 1970, 1971, 1972

L'Office divin au moyen âge. Histoire de la formation du bréviaire du IXe au XVIe siècle. Lex orandi, 43. Paris, 1967

Sarnelli, Pompeo. *Memorie cronologiche de' vescovi, ed arcivescovi Della S. Chiesa di Benevento Colla serie de' Duchi, e Principi Longobardi della stessa Città.* Naples, 1691

Schipa, Michelangelo. "Storia del principato Longobardo di Salerno." Reprinted in Acocella, *La longobardia*, pp. 87–278, from *Archivio storico per le province napoletane*, 12 (1887), 79–137, 209–64, 513–88, 740–77

Schlager, Karl-Heinz. "Anmerkungen zu den zweiten Alleluia-Versen." *Archiv für Musikwissenschaft*, 24 (1967), 199–219

"Beneventan rite, music of the." *The New Grove*, 2:482–4

"Ein beneventanisches Alleluia und seine Prosula." *Festschrift Bruno Stäblein zum 70. Geburtstag*, ed. Martin Ruhnke. Kassel, etc., 1967, pp. 217–25

Thematischer Katalog der ältesten Alleluia-Melodien. Erlanger Arbeiten zur Musikwissenschaft, 2. Munich, 1965

Schmidt, Hermanus A. P. *Hebdomata sancta.* 2 vols. Rome, 1956–7

Schuster, Ildefonso. "A proposito d'una nota di topografia cassinese in un codice del secolo undecimo," in *Casinensia*, pp. 65–87

SE *Sacris erudiri*

Sestan, Ernesto. "La storiografia dell'Italia longobarda: Paolo Diacono." *Settimane di studio*, 17 (1970), 357–86

Settimane di studio   *Settimane di studio del Centro Italiano di Studi sull'Alto Medioevo*. Spoleto, various dates

Sextuplex   *Antiphonale missarum sextuplex*, ed. René-Jean Hesbert. Brussels, 1935; repr. Rome, 1985

Smidt, Wilhelm. *Das Chronicon Beneventani monasterii S. Sophiae. Eine quellenkritische Untersuchung.* Berlin, 1910

Les Sources   *Le Graduel romain. Édition critique par les moines de Solesmes*. Vol. 2: *Les Sources*. Solesmes [1957]

Stäblein, Bruno. "Alt- und neurömischer Choral." *Kongressbericht: Gesellschaft für Musikforschung Lüneburg 1950*, ed. Hans Albrecht, Helmut Osthoff, and Walther Wiora. Kassel and Basle, n.d., pp. 53–6

Stornajolo, *Codices urbinates*   Cosimus Stornajolo, *Bibliothecae Apostolicae Vaticanae codices manu scripti recensiti . . . Codices urbinates latini. Vol. II: Codices 501–1000*. Rome, 1912

Strunk, Oliver. *Specimina notationum antiquiorum*. Monumenta musicae byzantinae, 7. Copenhagen, 1966

Suñol, Grégoire Marie [Gregorio Maria]. *Introduction à la paléographie musicale grégorienne*. Paris, 1935. Translation of *Introduccio a la paleografia musical gregoriana*, Montserrat, 1925

Swete, Henry Barclay. *The Old Testament in Greek According to the Septuagint*. Second edition, 3 vols. Cambridge, 1896–1901

TBS   Elias Avery Loew. *The Beneventan Script; A History of the South Italian Minuscule. Second Edition prepared and enlarged by Virginia Brown.* 2 vols. (Sussidi eruditi, 33–4). Rome, 1980; an expanded version of the first edition, Oxford, 1914

Thannanbaur, Peter Josef. *Das einstimmige Sanctus der römischen Messe in der handschriftlichen Überlieferung des 11. bis 16. Jahrhunderts.* Erlanger Arbeiten zur Musikwissenschaft, 1. Munich, 1962

Thibaut, Jean-Baptiste. *Ordre des offices de la Semaine Sainte à Jérusalem du IVe au Xe siècle.* Paris, 1926

Tosti, Luigi. *Storia della badia di Monte-Cassino.* 3 vols., Naples, 1842–3; second edition, 4 vols. Rome, 1888–90

Toubert, Hélène. "Le bréviaire d'Oderisius (Paris, Bibliothèque Mazarine, MS 364) et les influences byzantines au Mont-Cassin." *Mélanges de l'École Française de Rome. Moyen Âge–Temps Moderne,* 83 (1971), 187–261

Treitler, Leo. "Homer and Gregory: the Transmission of Epic Poetry and Plainchant." *The Musical Quarterly,* 60 (1974), 333–72

Trinchera, Francisco [Francesco]. *Syllabus graecarum membranarum.* Naples, 1865

Τριῴδιον. Rome, 1879

Troya, Carlo. *Codice diplomatico longobardo dal DLXVIII al DCCLXXIV.* Vol. 4, in 5 vols. (1852–5), of Troya's *Storia d'Italia del medio-evo.* Naples, 1839–59

Ughelli, Ferdinando. *Italia sacra sive de episcopis Italiae, et insularum adjacentium.* Second edition, 10 vols., ed. Nicolo Coletti. Venice, 1717–22

van Dijk, S. J. P. "Handlist of the Latin Liturgical Manuscripts in the Bodleian Library, Oxford." Typescript (7 vols.), 1957–60, on deposit in the library

"The Urban and Papal Rites in Seventh- and Eighth-Century Rome." SE, 12 (1961), 411–82

Vasiliev, Aleksandr Aleksandrovich. *Histoire de l'empire byzantin.* Translated from Russian by P. Brodin and A. Bourgouina. 2 vols. Paris, 1932

Vatasso, *Codices*   Marco Vatasso and H. [Enrico] Carusi. *Bibliothecae Apostolicae Vaticanae codices manu scripti recensiti. Codices Vaticani latini, Codices 10301–10700.* Rome, 1920

Vecchi, Ioseph, ed. *Troparium sequentiarium nonantulanum. Cod. Casanat. 1741. Pars prior.* Monumenta lyrica medii aevi italica 1, Latina 1. Bologna, 1955

Vehse, Otto. "Benevento als Territorium des Kirchenstaates bis zum Beginn der Avignonesischen Epoche." *Quellen und Forschungen aus italienischen Archiven und Bibliotheken,* 22 (1930–1), 87–160; 23 (1931–2), 80–119

Verbeke, Gérard, "S. Grégoire et la messe de S. Agathe." EL, 52 (1938), 67–76

Vescovi e diocesi in Italia nel medioevo (sec. IX–XIII). Atti del II convegno di storia della chiesa in Italia

(Roma, 5–9 sett., 1961). Italia sacra, 5. Padua, 1964

Vettori, Inventarium   [Vincenzo Vettori]. "Inventarium omnium codicum manuscriptorum Graecorum et Latinorum Bibliothecae Vallicellianae digestum anno domini MDCCXLIV." Three volume hand-written catalogue in the Biblioteca Vallicelliana, Rome

Viscardi, Antonio. *Storia letteraria d'Italia. Le origini*. Fourth edition. Milan, 1966

Vogel, Cyrille. "Les échanges liturgiques entre Rome et les pays francs jusqu'à l'époque de Charlemagne." *Settimane di studio*, 7 (1960), 185–295

   La Réforme cultuelle sous Pépin le Bref et sous Charlemagne, preceded by Erna Patzelt, *Die Karolingische Renaissance*. Graz, 1965

   "La réforme liturgique sous Charlemagne," in *Karl der Grosse. Lebenswerk und Nachleben*, ed. Wolfgang Braunfels. Vol. 2: *Das geistige Leben*, ed. Bernhard Bischoff (Düsseldorf, 1965), pp. 217–32

von Falkenhausen, Vera. *La dominazione bizantina nell'Italia meridionale dal IX all'XI secolo*. Bari, 1978; translation of *Untersuchungen über die byzantinische Herrschaft in Süditalien vom 9. bis 11. Jahrhundert* (Wiesbaden, 1967)

   "I longobardi meridionali," in André Guillou, Filippo Burgarella, Vera von Falkenhausen, Umberto Rizzitano, Valeria Fiorani Piacentini, and Salvatore Tramontana, *Il mezzogiorno dai Bizantini a Federico II. Storia d'Italia*, directed by Giuseppe Galasso, vol. 3 (Turin, 1983), pp. 249–364, plus 4 pp. of plates

   "Il monachesimo italo-greco e i suoi rapporti con il monachesimo benedettino." In *L'esperienza monastica*, 1: 119–35

von Rintelen, Wolfgang. *Kultgeographische Studien in der Italia byzantina. Untersuchungen über die Kulte des Erzengels Michael und der Madonna di Constantinopoli in Süditalien*. Archiv für vergleichende Kultur-wissenschaft, 3. Meisenheim am Glan, 1968

Vulgata   Biblia sacra iuxta Vulgatam versionem, ed. Robert Weber. 2 vols. Stuttgart, 1975

Wagner, Peter. *Einführung in die gregorianischen Melodien*. Third edition, 3 vols. Leipzig, 1911–21

Wellesz, Egon. *Eastern Elements in Western Chant. Studies in the Early History of Ecclesiastical Music*. Monumenta musicae byzantinae. Subsidia, 11, no. 1, American Series. Oxford, 1947

   "Über die Zusammenhänge zwischen dem Gesang der Ost- und Westkirche." In Hugo Rahner and Emmanuel von Severus, eds., *Perennitas: Beiträge zur christlichen Archäologie und Kunst, zur Geschichte der Literatur, der Liturgie und des Mönchtums sowie zur Philosophie des Rechts und zur politischen Philosophie: P. Thomas Michels OSB zum 70. Geburtstag*. Münster, 1963, pp. 155–9

Westerbergh, Ulla. *Beneventan Ninth Century Poetry*. Studia Latina Stockholmiensia, 4. Stockholm, 1957

Wickham, Chris. *Early Medieval Italy. Central Power and Local Society 400– 1000*. Totowa, N.J., 1981

Wilmart, André. *Bibliothecae Apostolicae Vaticanae codices manu scripti recensiti: Codices Reginenses latini. Tomus II: Codices 251–500*. Vatican City, 1945

   "Le *comes* de Murbach." *Revue bénédictine*, 30 (1913), 25–69

   "Nouvelles remarques sur le feuillet de Besançon. Description du manuscrit 184." *Revue bénédictine*, 30 (1913), 124–32

Wordsworth-White   John Wordsworth and Henry Julian White. *Novum testamentum Domini Nostri Iesu Christi latine*. 3 vols. Oxford, 1889–1954

Zazo, Alfred. "Benevento che fu: la basilica di S. Bartolomeo." *Samnium*, 31 (1958), 226–31

   Curiosità storiche beneventane. Collana di studi e documenti di Storia del Sannio, 4. Benevento, 1976

   "Un vescovo beneventano del IX secolo: 'Petrus Sagacissimus'." *Samnium*, 23 (1950), 179–86

INDEX OF MANUSCRIPTS

INDEX OF LITURGICAL TEXTS

All the surviving musical pieces of Beneventan chant are listed here alphabetically, whether or not they are mentioned in the text; they are printed here in italics, and are edited, with references to similar texts in other liturgies, in Appendix 2. This index also lists other liturgical texts mentioned in chapters 1–5, and musical pieces reproduced in the plates. Many of these texts serve more than one function; the liturgical usage of the texts used in Beneventan chant can be found by consulting Appendix 2. References marked with an asterisk (*) indicate musical transcriptions, whole or partial. Spellings have been partially regularized here.

GENERAL INDEX

Adam, abbot of Tremiti: 38n2
Adelais, duke of Benevento: 9
Adelchis, duke of Benevento: 26
Adelperga: 22
Agapitus II, pope: 35
Agilulf, king of the Lombards: 7, 8n18
Alboin, king of the Lombards: 8n16
Alexander, Byzantine emperor: 27n143
Alexander II, pope: 38n2
Aligern, abbot of Montecassino: 205
Amalarius of Metz: 19, 135
Ambrose Autpert: 16n71, 24
Ambrose of Milan: 197
Ambrosian, liturgy and chant: *see* Milan
Amelli, Ambrogio: 24
Anastasius, bishop of Naples: 205
Andoyer, Raphaël: xi
Antipertus, provost of Santa Sofia: 34n1
Apollinaris, bishop of Ravenna: 70
Arabs: 26-7
Arianism: 8, 93
Arichis I, duke of Benevento: 7
Arichis II, duke of Benevento: 7, 9-13, 16, 22,
    26, 33, 187, 203, 218 (Pl. 1)
Arioald, king of the Lombards: 8n18
Atenolf, abbot of Montecassino: 36
Atenolf, count of Capua: 27
Atenolf, duke of Benevento-Capua: 27n143, 36
Atenolf II, duke of Benevento-Capua: 27n143
Atenolf III, duke of Benevento: 34
Authar, king of the Lombards: 8 and n18
Azzo, abbot of Santa Sofia: 35n2

Bailey, Terence: xii
Balduin, abbot of Montecassino: 34, 36

Barbatus, bishop of Benevento: 8, 9, 11n40, 28-9
Bari: 2, 17, 26, 59, 206n1
Baroffio, Bonifazio: xii
Bartholomew, translation: 73
Basil, Saint: 204
Bassacius, abbot of Montecassino: 34
Belting, Hans: 12
Benedict, Saint: 204
Benedict VIII, pope: 9n22, 36
Benedict XIII, pope: xi
Beneventan chant
    called "Ambrosian": 3, 6, 24, 30, 39, 43, 181-3
    history: early history: 6-9; origins: 161;
        geography: xvi, 17-18; use of: 24-5, 30;
        eradication: 30-40, 55-9; late survival: 40
        and n230
    lectio cum cantico: 127, 156-60
    manuscripts: xii, xvi, 31-2, 41-52, 153-4
    musical notation: 4-5, 21, 115n7, 153-4
    musical pieces by type: antiphon: 60-1, 83,
        138-44; alleluia: 76-7, 124; communion:
        78-9; Exultet: 46-8, 59-60; gradual: 75,
        118-19; ingressa: 74, 111-18; offertory: 77-8,
        124-6; ordinary chants: 90-4, 130-1; respon-
        sory: 119, 135-8; tract: 54, 76, 90, 127,
        185-6; versus ad repetendum: 74, 143, 145-6
    musical style
        general: 3-4, 97-110
        melisma: 119-22, 129, 140
        melodic formulae: 96-160, esp. 97-108,
        154-5; opening: 100-4; medial: 104-8;
        closing: 97-100
        melodies for several texts: 139-44
        modality: 147-8, 153-7
        pitch: 153-7